World Yearbook of Education 2013

The *World Yearbook of Education 2013* offers ways of understanding how and with what consequences national systems of education and the work of education professionals are being re-regulated in the context of contemporary global transitions. National education systems are being transformed into more complex education spaces within nation-states, as well as creating transnational organizations, relations and practices that impinge on the work of education and learning globally, nationally and locally.

It approaches this agenda by focusing firmly on the way that educators themselves encounter and renegotiate ideas and practices that travel globally as they seek to enact their established professional projects. This framing recognizes that educators' professional projects are historically anchored in national institutional trajectories, but that these are currently disturbed as globally mobile ideas and practices 'touch down' within national systems of education.

The theme of this volume, the effect on national systems of education in global transition, brings together a new approach to perspectives on curriculum today and a new collection of insights into the changes from different parts of the world which discuss:

- What re-regulatory trajectories are evident in national education spaces and how do they impact on educators?
- What processes of renegotiation are used by educators as they mediate between globally mobile ideas, practices and national institutional trajectories?
- What are the implications of these mediations and renegotiations for education professionals and their professional projects?

This volume will be of great interest to education researchers, graduate students, teacher educators and education policy-makers.

Terri Seddon is Professor of Education at Monash University, Australia.

John S. Levin is Bank of America Professor of Education Leadership and Director, California Community College Collaborative, University of California, USA.

World Yearbook of Education Series

Series editors: Terri Seddon, Jenny Ozga, Gita Steiner-Khamsi and Agnès Van Zanten

World Yearbook of Education 2013

Educators, Professionalism and Politics:
Global Transitions, National Spaces and
Professional Projects

Edited by Terri Seddon and John S. Levin

Routledge
Taylor & Francis Group

LONDON AND NEW YORK

First published 2013
by Routledge
2 Park Square, Milton Park, Abingdon, Oxon OX14 4RN

Simultaneously published in the USA and Canada
by Routledge
711 Third Avenue, New York, NY 10017

Routledge is an imprint of the Taylor & Francis Group, an informa business

British Library Cataloguing in Publication Data
A catalogue record for this book is available from the British Library

Library of Congress Cataloging in Publication Data
A catalog record for this book has been requested

ISBN: 978-0-415-52914-3 (hbk)
ISBN: 978-0-203-07394-0 (ebk)

Typeset in Minion
by Bookcraft Ltd, Stroud, Gloucestershire

Printed and bound by CPI Group (UK) Ltd, Croydon, CR0 4YY

Contents

Illustrations

Figure

Tables

Contributors

María Luisa Zorrilla Abascal is an Assistant Professor at the Instituto de Ciencias de la Educación at the Universidad Autonoma del Estado de Morelos, Mexico. She is Director of the Multimodal Educational Space at UAEM which is aimed to strengthen the use of ICT and virtual learning environments within the university community. She gained her Ph.D. in Education at the University of East Anglia, UK. Her main research interests include non-conventional modalities in education, with especial focus on e-learning and b-learning. Her recent work focuses on the introduction of virtual learning environments in higher education, its relationship with public policies, and influence on academic practices in public state universities in Mexico. She has also designed faculty training programmes for non-conventional modalities and online tutoring.

Stephanie Matseleng Allais leads research into education and the labour market at the Education Policy Unit (EPU) of the University of the Witwatersrand. Her current focus is professional and occupational knowledge. Her research interests are in the sociology of education, policy, education and development, curriculum, sociology of knowledge and political economy of education. She was previously a postdoctoral fellow at the Centre for Educational Sociology at the University of Edinburgh. She has managed and conducted comparative research qualifications frameworks in 16 countries, for the International Labour Organization. Before this, she was the director of the Research and Development unit of Umalusi, the statutory body responsible for the quality assurance of primary, secondary and vocational education and training in South Africa. She has worked across the South African education system, including distance education through a non-governmental organization, running the education department of a trade union, teaching in a high school, and in adult basic education and training, and leading a student organization. Her Ph.D. is in education policy from the School of Public and Development Management at Wits University in South Africa.

Sarah Amsler is Senior Lecturer in Education in the Centre for Educational Research and Development at the University of Lincoln, UK. She is author of *The Politics of Knowledge in Central Asia: Science between Marx and the market* (2007) and various essays on the politics of knowledge, education and culture. Her current research focuses on affective politics of critical pedagogical work, and the role of education and knowledge in movements to facilitate radical democracy.

William C. Brehm is currently pursuing his Ph.D. at the University of Hong Kong. His research focuses on private tutoring in Cambodia. Before moving to Hong Kong, he lived in Siem Reap, Cambodia for two years developing a research department for This Life Cambodia, an Australian non-governmental organization. During this time, he was the co-primary investigator (with Iveta Silova) for an Open Society Foundation-funded research project on the equity implications of private tutoring in Cambodian public education. Brehm is also the associate editor of the journal *European Education: Issues and Studies*, and a member of the Tagore-SenGupta Foundation board of directors. His research interests include international educational development, the privatization of public education, and educational history/biography. His publications have explored topics such as global citizenship education, education and the social contract, and William Brickman.

Andy Hargreaves is the Thomas More Brennan Chair in Education at Boston College, USA. Before this he taught in several English universities and was Professor in Education at the Ontario Institution of Education in Canada where he co-founded the International Center for Educational Change. His books on teaching and professionalism include *Changing Teachers, Changing Times* (1994), which received the Outstanding Book Award from the American Association of Colleges for Teacher Education, and *Teachers' Professional Lives* (with Ivor Goodson, 1996). He has written many articles on his research on the emotions of teaching, and his most recent book, with Michael Fullan, on *Professional Capital: Transforming teaching in every school* (Routledge) is currently in press. Andy holds an Honorary Degree from the University of Uppsala in Sweden.

Le Thuy Linh has been a lecturer at the faculty of English, Hanoi National University of Education (HNUE) in Vietnam since 1999, and is currently a Ph.D. student at Monash University, Australia. She is co-director of the Centre for Development Studies and Education, under the Institutes of Social Sciences, HNUE. She completed her MA in TESOL in 2004 at Vietnam National University, Hanoi. She has been actively involved in English language training and English language teacher education through her work at HNUE and with various teacher development projects in Vietnam. Her research interests cover the fields of English language education and English language teacher education, the professionalization of English language teaching, teacher identity and the internationalization of higher education.

John S. Levin is the Bank of America Professor of Education Leadership and the Director and Principal Investigator of the California Community College Collaborative (C4), Graduate School of Education, University of California, Riverside. His books include *Globalizing the Community College* (2001), *Community College Faculty: At work in the new economy* (2006, 2010),

Non-Traditional Students and Community Colleges: The conflict of justice and neo-liberalism (with Susan Kater and Richard Wagoner, 2007) and *Community Colleges and their Students: Co-construction and institutional identity* (with Virginia Montero Hernández, 2009). His forthcoming book, *Understanding Community Colleges* (with Susan Kater, Routledge) is for use in graduate programmes in the field of higher education. His most recent research addresses faculty work, including non-tenure track faculty in universities, faculty and institutional practices in Mexican state universities, faculty identity in colleges and universities, and graduate students' career paths to faculty roles.

Mei Li is an Associate Professor at the Institute of Higher Education, School of Education Science in East China Normal University, Shanghai. She earned her Ph.D. from the University of Hong Kong in 2006. Her research interests focus on the globalization and internationalization of Chinese higher education, higher education policy and the academic profession in China. Her latest book is *The International Markets for Higher Education: The global flow of Chinese students* (2008).

Virginia Montero Hernández is an Assistant Professor at the Instituto de Ciencias de la Educación at the Universidad Autonoma del Estado de Morelos, Mexico. She obtained her Ph.D. in Curriculum and Instruction at the Graduate School of Education at the University of California, Riverside. She has co-authored a book and several book chapters that address community college students in the United States. She participates in a US–Mexico collaborative research network that aims to study the development of academic identity and practices in public universities. Her research interests involve the use of qualitative methodology to study academic identity, student development and organizational identity in the higher education system in both the US and Mexican context.

Romuald Normand is Associate Professor of Sociology of Education at the Ecole Normale Supérieure, Lyon, France. He works on education policies and politics, Europeanization and the transformations of the State. He is co-editor of the Routledge book series *Sociologies of European Education* with Martin Lawn and Kerstin Martens.

Jenny Ozga is Professor of the Sociology of Education and Senior Research fellow, Green Templeton College, Oxford. Her recent Research Council-funded research is on data and education governance, resulting in the book, *Fabricating Quality in Europe: Data and education governance* (co-edited with Peter Dahler-Larsen, Christina Segerholm and Hannu Simola, Routledge, 2011), and she is currently working on a project on Inspection and Education Governance.

Phan Le Ha is a Senior Lecturer in Culture and Pedagogy in the Faculty of Education, Monash University, Australia. She also holds honorary positions at universities in Vietnam and holds a Visiting Professorship at the University of Reading, UK. She specializes in English language education, identity studies, international education and academic writing. Her publications are in all these areas. She is the author of *Teaching English as an International Language: Identity, resistance and negotiation* (2008) and has co-edited two volumes on English academic writing issues and TESOL pedagogy.

Omar García Ponce de León is an Associate Professor and Director of Innovation through knowledge transfer at the Universidad Autonoma del Estado de Morelos (UAEM), Mexico. He obtained his Ph.D. in Sociology at the University of Barcelona in Spain. He is the leader of a US–Mexico collaborative research project funded by the National Council of Science and Technology in Mexico aimed at the study of the construction of academic practices in state public universities in Mexico. His research interests include higher education policy and organizational analysis.

Qiongqiong Chen is a Ph.D. candidate in the Department of Educational Leadership and Policy at the State University of New York at Buffalo. Her current research interests include transnational academic mobility, higher education internationalization and cultural globalization.

Risto Rinne is Professor of Education and Director of the Department of Education at the University of Turku, Finland. He is also director of the Centre for Research on Lifelong Learning and Education (CELE) and of the national graduate school (GROW). Key areas of his research are the sociology of education, international comparative education research, education policy and education history, and he has published more than 400 scientific works in these areas.

Susan L. Robertson is Professor of Sociology of Education, Graduate School of Education, Bristol, UK. Susan has a long-standing research interest in the transformation of the state, global and regional processes that materialize and mediate education projects, and teachers' work. She is founding co-editor of the journal, *Globalisation, Societies and Education*. She is also the Director of the Centre for Globalisation, Education and Societies, which she established in 2003. Susan has published widely on the political sociology of education.

Saskia Sassen is the Robert S. Lynd Professor of Sociology at Columbia University, New York. Her research focuses on globalization, immigration, global cities, the new technologies, and changes within the liberal state that result from current transnational conditions. Her publications include *The Mobility of Labor and Capital* (1988), *The Global City* (1991, 2001), *Territory, Authority, Rights: From medieval to global assemblages* (2006) and the fourth edition of *Cities in a World Economy* (2012).

Michele Schweisfurth is Reader in Comparative and International Education and Director of the Centre for International Education and Research at the University of Birmingham, UK. Her research interests include democracy and learner-centred education, and the pedagogical and intercultural experiences of mobile students. She brings to these themes a concern for how global and local forces interact in contemporary education, and the experiences of individuals in reconciling these.

Terri Seddon is Professor of Education at Monash University, Australia. Her current funded research has examined the teaching occupation in learning societies using case studies to investigate intersecting processes of globalization, lifelong learning travelling reforms, and educational work. Her most recent book is *Learning and Work and the Politics of Working Life: Global transformations and collective identities in teaching, nursing and social work* (with Lea Henriksson and Beatrix Niemeyer, 2010).

Iveta Silova, Ph.D., is an Associate Professor of Comparative and International Education in the College of Education, Lehigh University, Pennsylvania, USA. Her research and publications cover a range of issues critical to understanding post-socialist education transformation processes, including the professional development of teachers and teacher educators, gender equity trends in Eastern/Central Europe and Central Asia, minority/multicultural education policies in the former Soviet Union, and the scope, nature and implications of private tutoring in a cross-national perspective. She serves as the co-editor (with Noah W. Sobe) of the journal *European Education: Issues and Studies*.

Noah W. Sobe is Associate Professor of Cultural and Educational Policy Studies and Director of the Center for Comparative Education at Loyola University Chicago, USA. His research examines the transnational circulation of educational policies and practices. He is the author of *Provincializing the Worldly Citizen: Slavic cosmopolitanism and Yugoslav student and teacher travel in the interwar era* (2009) and *American Post-conflict Education Reform: From the Spanish-American War to Iraq* (2009). Active in the fields of comparative education and the history of education, he currently co-edits (with Iveta Silova) the journal *European Education: Issues and Studies*.

Manuel Francisco Aguilar Tamayo is an Associate Professor at the Universidad Autonoma del Estado de Morelos, Mexico. He obtained his Ph.D. in Education in Mexico. His research interests include cultural artefacts, knowledge representation, and their role in the learning process of scientific concepts. Other related interests are the use of concept mapping and other knowledge representation techniques applied to qualitative data analysis.

David Watson is Principal of Green Templeton College and Professor of Higher Education at the University of Oxford. He was previously Professor of Higher Education Management at the Institute of Education, London, and Vice-Chancellor of the University of Brighton (1990–2005). His most recent books are *Managing Civic and Community Engagement* (2007), *The Dearing Report: Ten years on* (2007), *The Question of Morale: Managing happiness and unhappiness in university life* (2009) and *The Engaged University* (2011). His substantial contributions to UK higher education include membership of the Higher Education Funding Council (1992–6) and the Dearing Inquiry into Higher Education (1996–7). He chaired the national Inquiry into the Future for

Lifelong Learning, and co-authored its report *Learning Through Life* (2009). He was knighted in 1998 for services to higher education and, in 2009, received the *Times Higher Education* Lifetime Achievement Award.

Anthony Welch is Professor of Education at the University of Sydney. A policy specialist, with extensive publications in numerous languages, he has consulted to state, national and international governments and agencies, and US institutions and foundations, particularly in higher education. Substantial project experience includes East and Southeast Asia. A Fulbright New Century Scholar on higher education (2007–8), he has also been Visiting Professor in the USA, UK, Germany, France, Japan and Hong Kong (China). His most recent books are *The Professoriate: Profile of a profession* (2005), *Education, Change and Society* (2007, 2010), *ASEAN Industries and the Challenge from China* (2011) and *Higher Education in Southeast Asia* (2011). Professor Welch also directs the national research project, *The Chinese Knowledge Diaspora*.

Malak Zaalouk is Director of the Middle East Institute for Higher Education (MEIHE) and Professor of Practice at the American University in Cairo Graduate School of Education, Egypt. Prior to this she was the UNICEF Regional Senior Advisor for Education in the Middle East and North Africa based in Amman. She joined UNICEF in April 1992 as the Education Section Chief in Egypt. She was engaged in the founding of community schools/education and promoted girls' education and quality education reform. Dr Zaalouk holds a Diploma in Educational Planning from the International Institute of Educational Planning (IIEP) in Paris and a Ph.D. in Social Anthropology (Hull, UK). She held an Expert position in the National Research Center for several years and sits on the board of international organizations and global publications, including the Global Monitoring Report (GMR) for the Education For All (EFA) movement. Her most recent book is *The Pedagogy of Empowerment* (2004, 2006).

Acknowledgements

We would like to thank Xuhong Wang for her assistance in producing this manuscript and Sally Newman for her contributions in editing key chapters in this collection.

The preparation of this volume was supported as part of a research project that examined *The Teaching Occupation in Learning Societies: A global ethnography of occupational boundary work* under the Australian Research Council's Discovery Project funding scheme (Project Number: DP0986413).

Series Editors' Introduction

Given the international composition of its authors and readers, the *World Yearbook of Education Series* is ideally situated to identify new developments that educational researchers across the globe find fascinating. As editors of the series, we came to realize that the search for common interests is easier than one would suspect. It is noticeable that similar educational reforms – often only in name but sometimes also in design – surface in different parts of the world despite vast cultural differences, particular political legacies and varied economic contexts. Arguably, the preoccupation with 'travelling reforms' requires a very specific method of inquiry: it requires a cross-national comparative perspective. By virtue of tracing the trajectories, understanding the rationales and determining the agencies of such global education policies, one becomes a comparative researcher.

Comparative educational research is predestined to dig deeper into understanding phenomena that occur globally. However, detecting travelling reforms is relatively easy when compared to understanding them. For understanding the phenomenon of globalization requires more than simply applying a 'bird's-eye view' on developments in various national educational systems. It is not sufficient to state that a reform in one country resembles that of another, but it is important to understand at what level, with what means and, last but not least, for whose benefit and at whose expense convergence occurs. Clearly, more sophisticated methods of comparison are needed to capture the complexity of globalization. Rather than asking what globalization does to education systems, authors in this volume examine how professionals make use of globalization at critical moments, for particular purposes and with varied outcomes. For this particular method of comparison, local contexts and actors matter a great deal. Contextual comparison refutes the bird's-eye view on national educational developments and replaces it with a lens that simultaneously focuses on forces within as well outside the system and interactions between the system and its environment. Globalization is such an external force or, more accurately, a quasi-external force. Globalization is real but actors in the system constantly negotiate the meaning they attach to it. They imagine or reconfigure globalization to meet national and local agendas. Thus, globalization is both a concept and a reality. As a result, some actors more than others resort to international standards, 'best practices' and other reference systems that are closely associated with globalization. Similarly, policy makers, professionals and practitioners in education vary in their degree of association with OECD, the World Bank, the United Nations system or other regulatory regimes and typically invoke them at critical stages as a quasi-external stamp of approval for their own actions. More often than not, it is a network of actors that, for a variety of reasons, resort to 'globalization' as the smallest common denominator to constitute themselves as a coalition in favour of change.

Studies that use contextual comparison as the preferred method of inquiry typically emphasize agency and power in order to understand change. In this volume, the dual orientation is manifest in the interpretive frameworks and the selection of cases. The contributors in this book are mindful of a methodological fallacy common in studies on globalization. The greatest challenge is to avoid falling into the trap of first establishing national boundaries, only to demonstrate afterwards that these boundaries have indeed been transcended. Ideas, policies or practices do not necessarily have a home base, a territory or a nationality, and therefore do not 'belong' to a particular education system. Thus, policy borrowing and lending – the theme of the last volume of the Routledge *World Yearbook of Education* – is nowadays framed much more broadly and increasingly goes beyond national actors to include global players that actively disseminate reforms across space and time at particular stages of the lifespan of a reform. Global education policies ebb and flow. Over the past two decades or so, neoliberal thought, in particular the uncritical belief in markets, non-state actors and supranational agencies, has swept away all other types of reform endeavours that targeted incremental or gradual change. As a result, globalization and neoliberalism have been intertwined. It is too early to judge, but the world economic crisis may very well be the end of wholesale de-regulation in the economy as well as in other subsystems of society. The emergence of new types of re-regulation may be seen as the contours of a new era of global transitions.

Besides the shared understanding of contextual comparison and the focus on agency and power, the contributors to this book have several interests in common that are briefly presented in the following.

First, the studies compiled here deal with global transitions. The site for analysing this fascinating phenomenon is not a particular country or a number of countries, as is frequently done in studies on globalization, but rather a *field*: teacher professionalism. Authors of this book analyse how the two concepts – globalization and teacher professionalism – interrelate and, at particular moments and for particular purposes, draw on each other to absorb, resist or modify change. Different from the debates in transitology that emanated in the 1990s after the collapse of communism, there is no directionality implied by the term 'transition'. That is, international convergence does not mark the end of the transition. Rather, the term signals that globalization functions like a project that generates pressure to constantly 'do boundary work' or transition from one education space to another and from one frame of reference to another.

Second, globalization in education is not only an interpretive framework or a perspective for understanding developments in a particular country, region, or – as is the case here – in a particular field, but globalization is often presented as a *project* that calls for a dramatic economic, political and educational alignment of national systems and structures. How have education and training systems dealt with the coercive power of globalization? Moreover, the very purpose of education and the daily work of educators are not exempt from the pressure to change. Precisely because 'professionalism' allows for different interpretations, the direction of change is unpredictable. The local politics proves to be as important for understanding changes in the conceptions of teacher professionalism as global discourses and quasi-external pressures.

Third, several chapters in this book apply a sociological lens with a focus on the politics of professionalization. Unsurprisingly, *boundary work* is a central notion to understand how educators constantly have to move between various education spaces, work places and identities in an attempt to negotiate between local actions and global agendas.

Finally, this volume presents a distinctive methodological approach for case selection that, so to speak, resembles a critical events analysis gone multidimensional. The term '*hotspots of change*' best captures the multidimensionality of the case selection in this book. Several authors of the book apply a three-step approach to pinpoint hotspots of change that are visibly affected by globalization. They first examine globalization within national territories in order to understand how educators are implicated in contemporary global transitions. They then investigate how global policy agendas constantly force educators to engage in boundary work, that is, to negotiate their own professional work and identity in a space or environment that inhabits both local as well as global realities. Finally, they consider ways in which educators are actively engaging in the politics of teacher professionalism to resolve protracted policy negotiations.

We are pleased that we were able to attract so many interesting and original contributions to the volume, from scholars based in different parts of the world, to write about these new developments in education.

Gita Steiner-Khamsi, New York
Jenny Ozga, Oxford
Terri Seddon, Melbourne

Introduction

1 Global Transitions and Teacher Professionalism

Terri Seddon with Jenny Ozga and John S. Levin

Global transitions are transforming national education and training systems around the world as nation-states drive re-regulatory education reform agendas. Since 2005, the Routledge *World Yearbook of Education* has engaged directly with globalization, compiling research and evidence, and also developing theory that helps to explain the character of our globalizing times and their implications for education and societies – learners and educators. Over nine annual volumes, the *Yearbook* has unravelled the dynamics of globalization in terms of shifting relations between nation-states and their education systems, and with global agencies and global flows of ideas, people and goods. In doing this, the *Yearbook* has developed an audit of globalization within national territories, and the re-spatialization of education, and of the ways in which this domain of social practice is represented in everyday life.

This volume of the *World Yearbook of Education* focuses on the work of education professionals, who support learners' learning as teachers and decision makers across different sectors of provision. The *World Yearbook of Education* considers ways of understanding how and with what consequences national systems of education and education professionals are being remade through contemporary global transitions. This agenda is captured in three key questions:

1 What re-regulatory trajectories are evident in national education spaces and how do they affect educators?
2 What processes of renegotiation do educators mobilize in their workplaces and working lives as they mediate between globally mobile ideas and practices, and national institutional trajectories and professionalising projects?
3 What are the implications of these mediations and renegotiations for education professionals and their professionalising projects?

These questions invite reflections about the historical trajectory of 'teacher professionalism' and the underpinning social and political processes of negotiating professionalization within the broad field of Education. They also problematize universalized narratives about teacher professionalism that are, in practice, often anchored in specific countries, education sectors and disciplinary traditions.

We approach this agenda by focusing firmly on the ways in which educators themselves encounter and renegotiate ideas and practices that travel globally, and the kinds of 'boundary work' that enable, and disable, their professionalizing projects. This framing recognizes that educators' professionalizing projects are historically anchored in educators' occupational agency, which is framed by national institutional trajectories. Yet, currently, these national practices of educational work are disturbed by travelling reforms: globally mobile ideas, policies, people and goods. These travelling reforms 'touch down' within national territories and their systems of education, which requires educators to navigate and negotiate these shifting terms and conditions of work.

With contributors drawn from around the world, we examine the ways in which educators engage with globalization within nation-states. The chapters in the volume document the ways in which educators confront and experience global imperatives within nationally located workplaces, which are now networked with a wider global education workspace, to create globally distributed education. Each chapter provides a window on hotspots of change where national and global imperatives intersect, creating dilemma-driven educational workplaces. We find that in these workplaces educators actively engage in boundary work that attempts to both secure and rebuild professional knowledge and expertise in ways that can challenge and also confirm older patterns of professional praxis and ethics. Through this boundary work, they contribute to the remaking of national education systems and to the re-ordering of the familiar contours that distinguish national education spaces, which developed through the twentieth century.

There are two core insights that inform the conceptual framework that we set out in this introduction: first, that globalization is a complex form of boundary work that disturbs the spatial, temporal, relational and knowledge boundaries that once secured specific national forms of teacher professionalism; second, that the trajectory of teacher professionalism depends, in turn, on the ways educators engage in spatial, temporal, relational and knowledge boundary work in order to create a platform for their professionalizing projects and the necessary symbolic politics of claiming professionalism and, therefore, space for educational work. We expand on these points below.

Troubling Teacher Professionalism

Understanding globalizing developments and their potential futures opens up questions about the historical trajectory of 'teacher professionalism' and its underpinning social and political processes of negotiating professionalization within the broad field of education. We suggest that globalization is a specific form of geopolitical interaction and relational remaking that plays out between nation-states and the international system of states, and also within national territories and sub-national spaces. These multi-scale processes of globalization disturb the spatial, temporal, relational and knowledge boundaries that once secured specific national education systems, their nation-building social logics, and their forms of teacher professionalism.

These global transformations that challenge territorial assumptions and nation-building projects have informed a variety of imaginaries about learning societies since the 1960s. Initially framed as calls for reflexive, open and accessible education (e.g. Hutchins, 1970; Schön, 1971; Delors, 1996), governments and global policy agencies translated these social imaginaries into economic narratives that informed logics for twenty-first-century education reform. The discourse of 'knowledge economy' took up the imaginaries of 'learning society' as a means of addressing the increasingly competitive relations between nation-states within the interstate system (Kenway *et al.*, 2006; Seddon, 2010). These new society models privileged 'learning' as a foundational competence required by citizens, communities and societies on a global scale. It was a dominant discourse that had significant effects within national territories (Kuhn, 2007).

This trajectory of social change appeared as a liquefaction of everyday life as entities that once seemed solid shifted and slid. This 'liquid modernity' (Bauman, 2000) had clear continuities with the capitalist social order that Karl Marx described in the nineteenth-century: industrialization, class and gender formations, and new forms of social conflict that drove change. But now those processes of change acquired new meanings, melting not just social relations and cultural understandings but also nineteenth- and twentieth-century social institutions, systems and the idea of order within them.

> The solids whose turn has come to be thrown into the melting pot and that are in the process of being melted at the present time … are the bonds that interlock individual choices in collective projects and actions – the patterns of communication and coordination between individually conducted life policies on the one hand and political actions of human collectivities on the other.
> (Bauman, 2000: 6).

Anglo-American, Australian and European education research, on which this analysis of teacher professionalism mainly rests, suggests that there was a pervasive nation-building educational project through the twentieth century. It produced forms of education and professionalism that were embedded in public service, commitments to people-rights, and the formation of publics, which were made through structures, practices and deliberative agency that guided public life (Apple, 2009). Democracy and a sociality based on trust and achievement were seen to require spaces of public deliberation where educational purposes and practices were 'constituted to include difference, enable participation, voice and dissent, through to collective judgment and decision, that is in turn accountable to the public' (Ranson, 2003: 476). Yet the social forces that shaped twentieth-century education, which in England were characterized as the old humanists, the public educators and industrial trainers, were increasingly out of balance (Williams, 1961; Jones, 2002). The direction of education reform endorsed market mechanisms and instrumental and technical rational learning but without affirming moral and political principles that orient learning towards citizenship (Ranson, 1992: 72).

This emerging 'neo-liberal' educational project was a travelling reform, centred by the social logic of human capital formation within learning societies. It was justified as an individual's private investment in their future employability and earning capacity, and also as a means to national competitive advantage in a global knowledge economy and to manage residual and resistant populations through social inclusion. Its discursive themes, increasingly familiar across countries and all education sectors, included prioritizing useful skills for work, individual betterment and innovation through collaboration and mobility. In universities these agendas were described as 'academic capitalism' (Marginson, 1997; Slaughter and Leslie, 1997). They endorsed knowledge building as a service industry and a way of servicing the employability agenda negotiated between government and employers. In secondary and post-compulsory schooling the vocationalizing orientation reflected concerns with human resource development and building skills for work and employability (Levin, 2001). In primary and pre-primary schooling, the emphasis was on basic skills, literacy and numeracy, all to provide a foundation for subsequent schooling and work (Apple, 1986). Across all sectors there were trends towards learner-centred education framed by knowledge-based technologies. This individualization of learning placed responsibility on learners to find their way through a process of choice-based, continuous self-improvement. Meanwhile the re-technologization of education inverted the social logic of twentieth-century education and its emphasis on socialization as a means of nation building (Kuhn, 2007). Older technologies, such as teachers and teacher education, were themselves technologized via knowledge-based regulation tools that created new classificatory schema and standardizing processes, which anchored accountability regimes and international comparisons (e.g. the OECD Programme for International Student Assessment (PISA) and formed audit cultures and audit-sensitive identities (Ozga *et al.*, 2011).

These education reforms reconfigured the work and working lives of educators across all educational sectors (schools, colleges, universities, further and vocational education, and pre-schools) and across countries. Historically, and particularly through the twentieth century, educators had been significant actors in advancing non-governmental civil society agendas in ways that shaped national policy and political rationales. Educators were a key social technology working on behalf of governments in nation-building projects. They also contributed in significant ways to social movements in civil society because they encouraged ways of knowing and acting that advanced particular social and cultural movements at local levels. These local movements ranged across the political spectrum. Educators were important in struggles for and against fascism, involved in nationalist and postcolonial movements, and activist in relation to faith, feminism and social justice. Yet these historical contributions to social formations and struggles for deliberative democracy counted for little in projected knowledge economies, where citizenship was understood in terms of being a stakeholder who benefited from economic development (Seddon, 1990, 2007).

These neo-liberal policy trajectories shifted over time in response to their intended and unintended economic and social consequences, but their underpinning social logic was consolidated through processes of permanent change. Persistent reform and reform fatigue further disturbed and diffracted the national organization and ordering of education, including its professionals and their claims to professionalism. Exhaustion as much as policy changes derailed their professionalizing projects, through which they had negotiated and secured their twentieth-century contributions and value in nation-building projects. And this troubling of teacher professionalism played out in debates about the meaning, significance, potential trajectory and even existence of teacher professionalism.

Researching Teacher Professionalism

These processes of globalization have disturbed both practical and theoretical boundaries that once anchored understandings of teacher professionalism. Reconfiguring boundaries encouraged interdisciplinary research initially at the national scale and, more recently, through cross-national and globally scaled studies. We track this research history through three major debates. These indicate the way in which 'teacher professionalism' has been problematized, creating ambiguities and debates that are difficult to reconcile without explicit specification of the spatial, temporal, relational and knowledge boundaries that inform knowledge building. We suggest that the growth of globally scaled education research is beginning to re-theorize teacher professionalism as a form of boundary work that rests on a particular global politics of knowledge. We use the term 'educational work' to capture this distinctive practical and theoretical educational boundary work that is reframing 'teacher professionalism'.

The earliest analyses of what would come to be identified as neo-liberal education reforms and professionalism drew on sociological studies of teaching. They showed that travelling reforms, which endorsed learner-centred learning societies, had direct effects on the terms and conditions of teachers' work. These policy effects were reconfiguring the 'labour process' of teaching, which was understood through the sociology of work as '(1) a purposeful activity, that is work itself, (2) the object on which that work is performed, and (3) the instruments of that work' (Marx, 1976: 284; Braverman, 1974). Travelling education reforms were shifting each of these elements that constituted the job of teaching. The changes included deskilling teachers, intensifying their work and de-professionalizing them as an occupational group (Apple, 1986; Smyth *et al.*, 2001).

The counter argument drew on social psychology, organizational studies and cultural studies, suggesting educators took on a 'new professionalism' as education modernized. Learner-centred education required educators to take up more facilitative roles and encouraged interest in critical pedagogies, applied learning and learning in diverse contexts: workplaces and communities as well as schools and colleges. Research also showed a growing emphasis on educators as active learners who endorsed their processes of professional learning and development. Critical social research on teacher identity formation was applied in designs for professional learning that would enable educators to take 'guide on the side' positions when working with learners, colleagues and stakeholders, and in complex interprofessional and intercultural settings. The educator was still a 'sage', but less 'on the stage' and, instead, involved in translation, intercultural relationship building and partnership work in communities of practice (McWilliam, 2008).

A second debate reoriented studies of teachers' work in ways that focused on detailed studies of policy that also shifted the locus of agency in educational change. The role of the state and teachers' agency in negotiating regulatory frames through industrial relations and public policy making were always one dimension of research on teachers' work (Connell, 1985; Ozga and Lawn, 1988; Dale, 1989; Lawn, 1996; Seddon, 1997), but the growth of policy sociology problematized this view of teachers as political actors. For example, Ball's (1990) analyses of policy as discourse emphasized the knowledge that was mobilized in the re-regulation and re-culturing of teaching. It also encouraged research that read discourse users in ways that, often unwittingly, strengthened the assumptions of dominant actors in their deployment of policy discourse as they drive market reforms in education. Subaltern groups were identified as subject to policy discourse and who therefore perform policy effects. This includes contingent labour, teacher professionals who do not have security of employment (Levin and Shaker, 2011; Levin *et al.*, 2011). The binary construction of powerful–powerless lined up with the binary of policy use–policy effect to suggest a story about the power of the powerful in travelling education reform. In the process, teacher agency and the space for challenge within policy discourses were not always unpacked (Bacchi, 2000). Neo-liberal governmentality disturbed the work practices of teaching and also constituted self-governing neo-liberal teacher identities and a performative culture, which 'terrorized' and disciplined teachers, encouraging compliant, professional practice (Ball, 2003).

Yet, regulatory reforms never guarantee governable subjects and ungovernable professionals were well documented in studies of 'de-professionalization' and 're-professionalization' (Hoyle, 1995; Ozga, 1995; Seddon, 1997; Levin, 2007). From this perspective, educators not only contested reforms but also navigated around these governing practices, which were usually far too simple to address the complexities of educational workplaces. In any case, educational workplaces continued to diversify: they were re-imagined as temporary stopping points in processes of transition that were organized through learning pathways and self-motivated learning careers; they accommodated culturally diverse students and they became more open to ideas and cultural traditions that travelled via students, teachers, the web, materials and other flows in and out of the old familiar education spaces.

The third debate rereads teacher professionalism as a symbolic politics in processes of globalization that occur within the national territories. This debate has developed as education research on globalization has focused on the effects of travelling education reforms in local policy settings (Alexiadou and Jones, 2001; Steiner-Khamsi, 2012) and then examined the emerging learning spaces, that are also workplaces, where education professionals work and produce knowledge claims about teacher professionalism (Gewirtz *et al.*, 2009). Such research reconfirms established insights about the work that educators do. For example, educational workplaces are not simple places but complex social and cultural boundary zones where educators work, learn and also negotiate space for educating (Connell, 1985; Ozga and Lawn, 1988; Lawn, 1996; Felstead *et al.*, 2009; Montero-Hernandez and Levin, 2011). These workplaces are now diversifying as public sector reform and privatization processes re-spatialize educational workplaces, which are globally networked through a distributed workspace (Farrell, 2006). Yet the educators who inhabit these educational workplaces continue to be disciplined by national traditions and by some form of employment contract, which are organized through the labour process. Their 'professionalism' entails a social and symbolic politics that accompanies these everyday politics in working life. It becomes evident as educators engage through 'activist' as well as 'terrorized' professionalism (Sachs, 2000). Their 'educational work' is a particular form of occupational boundary work that sustains educational labour with its distinctive moral and ethical commitments to learners' development as a means of building civilized societies. This occupational boundary work is deeply contextualized; it is focused and framed by prevailing spatialized social relations, knowledge frames, rules and resources, temporal rhythms and scales (Colley *et al.*, 2012; Newman *et al.*, 2012). These politics of working life rest on mobilizations of educators' practical and theoretical knowledges (expertise) and organizational arrangements, which define collective occupational capabilities and actors' capacity to say 'we' (Seddon *et al.*, 2010).

'Educational work' is a distinct form of occupational boundary work. It is the labour that constructs, orients and enacts educational spaces, which yields learning. The character and consequences of this particular form of labour rests on the negotiation of specific spatial, temporal, relational and knowledge boundaries at three distinct scales. First, there is the familiar labour process of teaching, which is about doing the job of pedagogy that enables learners' learning. This job occurs as educators negotiate the terms and conditions of work in workplaces (schools, colleges, universities, and also workplaces embedded in other industries and communities) and, through those practices, engage with compartmentalizations advocated by other agencies. These negotiations construct and limit educational spaces and the way they support learners' learning (Connell, 1985; Levin, 2001). This contestation of the way educational spaces are governed segues into more externally oriented politics, which are focused on the intersections between teaching occupations, states and civil societies (Ozga and Lawn, 1988). This second dimension of educational work constructs the social space in which industrial relations and interfaces with service users and sub-national networks in civil society are mobilized to make claims for educational space and resources. It is also where the political action of educators in mobilizing their occupational expertise and resources is delimited through boundary constructions, which define and also police disciplinary discourses, such as the 'good teacher' and educational 'quality' (Ozga and Lawn, 1988; Lawn, 1996). Finally, there are also more interior-oriented work practices that centre on individual and occupational 'self-work' (Chappell, 2003), through which educators come to embody particular forms of occupational expertise: the deeply contextualized knowledge, skills and dispositions that are enacted as educators exercise their capacities for educating and do the job of teaching (or coaching, mentoring, training and other similar activities) that yields learning (Felstead *et al.*, 2009).

Rereading teacher professionalism research this way problematizes the spatial configuration of teacher 'professionalisms' as well as their historical specificities. It challenges the taken-for-granted reference points for much education research that naturalizes national frames and particular educational settings (e.g. schools) as the obvious or only locales for educational professionalism. Such methodological nationalist and methodological educationist assumptions, unless explicitly acknowledged, fail to capture the particular relationalities, spatialities and temporalities that both locate and frame, and therefore structure and culture, teacher professionalism (Dale, 1989). Maguire (2010) makes this point reflecting on the idea of a 'global teacher'. She notes that travelling reforms create globalized expectations and a 'version of teacher' who is compliant not critical, and who does rather than thinks. This is a social construction of 'the teacher' that is disciplined by data and selective transparency provided through league tables, which has controlling and regulating effects in England. This 'global teacher' is made through direct state rule mediated by explicit performance expectations and framed by the rhetoric of choice. Yet, she asks, is this casting of the global teacher as an 'entrepreneurial manager rather than an organic intellectual ... everywhere the case?' (Maguire, 2010: 62).

This question begins to capture the methodological complexities in reframing research on teacher professionalism in ways that grasp the 'global'. It also shows that the assumption of methodological globalism is more than a rhetorical device, using 'the world' as a motif. Instead, it refocuses attention on the spatialization of power that orders educators' working lives and the politics of the educational knowledges that flow between national education systems as well as within national spaces. These educational knowledge flows, developed through policy, practice and research, are differentially sticky in terms of their mobility and they are always structured, as Maguire suggests, by the geopolitics of knowledge and the legacies of colonialism (Connell, 2007; Chen, 2010). Yet the ways in which educational knowledge is made and used, by whom and for what purpose, and under what terms and conditions, are central to understanding both teacher professionalism and how educators are engaging in professionalizing projects and remaking education.

Professions, Professionalism and Professionalization

These methodological complexities mean that it is difficult to gain purchase on the theory and practice of teacher professionalism without explicit specification of knowledge frames and intellectual traditions that inform particular analysis and understandings of 'professions', 'professionalism' and 'professionalization'. Here we draw on US, UK, Canadian, Australian and European sociological research on professions to elaborate our reconceptualization of professions and professionalism. This knowledge tradition sees 'professionalism' as a particular symbolic politics that is central to boundary work, which establishes the form, function, capability and sustainability of professions.

Boundaries and boundary work are central to professions and professionalism. For professions are categories of occupational classification, whose professionals claim knowledge and virtue on the basis of 'categorizations of technical and ethical standards' (Gewirtz *et al.*, 2009). In the first half of the twentieth century, Anglo-American research on professions focused on social groups, particularly the old professions of self-employed doctors and lawyers, and assumed firm boundaries. This methodological assumption centred attention on professions as a distinct social category within the societal division of labour. Assuming a social group with firm boundaries, researchers documented the traits that distinguished these professionals and made a case for their significance in society as an altruistic third party, a 'middle class', between capital and labour. But revisionist critiques quickly developed.

In the US the early Chicago school looked behind the social category of 'profession' and the claims made about their 'professionalism' to document the way people really did their jobs. While Everett Hughes (1958) wrote about *Men and Their Work*, Willard Waller (1961) formulated a *Sociology of Teaching*. He argued that the interactions and interrelationships that are centred by a job, the job of teaching, construct the social world of schooling and the work and identities of those who inhabit that social space as a relational ecology. Such research documented the social boundaries that divided professions as social groups and the cultural boundaries that distinguished them from other occupations and from amateurs. These cultural boundaries rested on:

> conceptual distinctions made by social actors to categorize objects, people, practices, and even time and space. They are tools by which individuals and groups struggle over and come to agree upon definitions of reality. [They reveal] the dynamic dimensions of social relations, as groups compete in the production, diffusion, and institutionalization of alternative systems and principles of classification.
>
> (Lamont and Molnar, 2002: 168)

This debate between categorical and relational perspectives on professions revealed the way professionals were implicated in the social and cultural making of professions. These 'two sociologies' – one viewing 'action as a derivative of the system' and the other viewing a 'system as the derivative of action' – were resolved through historical analysis, which documented the formation of social entities and their boundaries (Dawe, 1970: 214). Rather than treating professions as a system or emphasizing the continually disputed interactions over knowledge claims associated with professionalism, sociological research was expected to examine social action over time. The sociology of professions examined the social and cultural practices that formed 'professions' and 'professionalism' through the interplay of structure and agency, its temporal sequencing and rhythms, and the way these social processes were mediated by power and politics. Professionals were identified as social actors who became part of the structure of privilege in capitalist societies (Wilensky, 1964). Professionals engaged in 'professionalizing projects', which mobilized scarce resources of expertise in exchange for recognition and reward (Larson, 1990). Their boundary work created gatekeeping mechanisms, which secured their livelihoods and also their exclusive knowledge claims that underpinned their status, wealth and power in an unequal society (Gieryn, 1983).

Understanding 'professions' as products of social action also opened up spatial questions about processes of 'professionalization' that claimed and occupied social space. As Waller had suggested, professionals make space for their work. Professionalization occurs as particular occupational social actors coalesce to do a job that occupies a space. This occupation is constructed as professionals do their work and also negotiate with other external actors and subgroups within the occupation to secure agreements about the organization of the job and the way it is ordered through particular work practices and occupational identities. This occupational space, the space defined by the job, becomes evident both as a 'workplace', subject to social and economic rationales, and as a 'jurisdiction', where political agreements about licence (permission) to practice and mandate, or elbow room to do the job, are debated and determined (Abbott, 1988, 2005).

The character of professional practice is therefore a consequence of the terms and conditions of work and shows national and cross-national variations. As European researchers argued, Anglo-American theorizations of professions universalized normative assumptions on the basis of specific practices of professionalization that were embedded in Anglo-American liberal welfare state regimes and in research that saw men as actors but not women. In rather different European welfare state regimes, professionalization commonly took the form of state professionalism that encouraged the collectivization of labour in nation building (Henriksson *et al.*, 2006). In practice, this state-based support for professionalization was evident in many countries, particularly in human service work that supported socially reproductive labour in largely feminized fields of work (e.g. teaching, nursing and social work). These state-focused professionalizing projects enabled workers, particularly women and minorities, to build up occupational organization and profile to claim professional status (Ozga and Lawn, 1981; Preston, 1996).

It was these state-focused professionalizing projects that became embedded in twentieth-century national education systems. They developed because educators coalesced, by choice, idealism and the disciplinary imperatives of employment around a nation-building educational project (Lawn, 1996). These institutional forms and the specialist workforce that was designed to enact public education were in turn framed by the social logics of particular national state regimes, which rested on specific territorial assumptions. It is these national frames that are being remade through globalization and travelling neo-liberal reforms, which are disembedding educators and their educational work from those earlier state-focused professionalizing projects (Robertson, 1996).

It is this unfinished trajectory towards remaking national education systems as a lifelong learning educational order (Field, 2006) that challenges educators in the present. Addressing this challenge means looking beyond the symbolic politics that sets different rhetorics of 'professionalism' against one another and the research that universalizes assumptions about educators' powerlessness in bleak discursive struggles about who can speak and who will be heard. Instead, we suggest it is necessary to examine cases of educators' agency to understand the emerging terms and conditions of 'liquid learning' in which travelling reforms, perpetual learning and the de-anchoring of knowledge traditions engage educators in processes of professional renewal that are remaking education through educational work (Seddon, forthcoming).

Globalization and Boundary Work

Twentieth century patterns of education melted alongside shifting assumptions, practices and boundary conditions that governed national sovereignty and territorial integrity. This 'globalization' challenges the territorial boundaries and border regimes that were made by states as they became nation-states – a process that began in Europe in the 1600s but continues with the formation of new nation-states to the present time (Hunter, 1994). Yet the existence of territorializing nation-states is not the only form of boundary work that orders and organizes social space. As already noted, occupational boundary work that is motivated and oriented by particular professionalizing projects also contributes to the 'boundarying' of social spaces, which organizes knowledge and power at the national, sub-national and supra-national scales. The remaking of education and teacher professionalism is tensioned between these two forms of boundary work: territorialization and other forms of social and cultural boundarying.

The concept of 'territorialization' refers to the particular forms of boundary work that establish a 'territory': the land that supplies a given population with basic resources and names an area of the earth's surface, which is claimed by or associated with a particular group or political entity (Dahlman, 2009). Territorial practices at the national scale construct the boundaries and contents of nation-states as partly mythical and partly pragmatic entities.

Patterns of territorialization create a distinctly national social ecology, which is negotiated by sub-national actors through other processes of 'boundarying'. As globalizing processes interrupt nation-states' territorial regimes it becomes obvious that the borders that define and order national spaces 'extend far beyond the geographic line of internationally recognized treaties and its directly linked institutions such as consulates and airport immigration controls: borders are constituted through many more institutions and have more locations than standard representations suggest' (Sassen, 2007: 215).

In this way, twentieth-century education and its specialist teaching workforce can be seen as a territorializing practice. Education was a way of socializing the inhabitants of the nation in line with national priorities and public conventions that aligned territory, authority and rights, such as citizenship, liberal freedoms and commitments to community (Sassen, 2006). Education helped to make the nation by forming national identities with capacities for work, living together and using power responsibly (Connell, 1995). In turn, these inhabitants came to embody these territorial practices, political orders, rights and responsibilities as members of this 'imagined community' (Anderson, 1991). Occupation, as a national community, therefore meant that inhabitants enacted territorial claims simply by doing what they always do in that place (Paasi, 2003).

Yet education was also made through the boundarying activities of educators as they negotiated their educational space, work and identities, and enacted their professional communities. While globalization is now disturbing the established twentieth-century social logics and ecologies of education, it is not just a consequence of state de- and re-territorialization (Robertson *et al.*, 2002). Rather, it is the intersecting boundary work enacted by states, professions and other social actors in civil societies that is remaking education.

As the sociology of professions and occupations suggests, the labour of 'boundarying' continues to enclose social spaces as distinct social ecologies and jurisdictions. This boundary work involves civil society actors, including educators, in everyday practical politics. Their agency is framed by state power and the territorializing practices negotiated between states and the interstate system, as well as oriented and motivated by actors' own normative-pragmatic social logics. Their labour in occupying and organizing social space makes social ecologies that are enacted within, against and sometimes without regard to states' territorial regimes that pattern authority and rights at the national scale. This boundarying produces and, within specific spatial and temporal limits, secures social and political arrangements that endorse and authorize particular capabilities. These capabilities are designed to address imperatives, which are generated and justified in terms of the social ecology and its interrelations with other ecologies at different scales. The terms and conditions of boundary work defined by these internal and external relations and processes produce these capabilities as 'collective productions whose development entails time, making, competition, and conflicts, and whose utilities are, in principle, multivalent because they are conditioned on the character of the relational systems within which they can function' (Sassen, 2006: 18).

The intersecting effects of territorializing and boundarying practices cannot be assumed on the basis of generic commentaries about globalization, accounts of travelling education reforms or commentaries on teacher professionalism. Rather, understanding these globalizing effects requires analysis of particular spaces to reveal how the disaggregated effects of travelling reform, historical context and patterns of boundarying play out in specific places (Sassen, 2006). We identify these particular places where territorialization and boundarying are renegotiated as 'hotspots of change': points where national institutional trajectories confront globalizing transitions that materialize in specific but uneven ways across national territories (Gieryn, 2000). Using this methodological principle, we examine the ways educators are actively remaking educational places that now reach well beyond the formally organized schools, universities and vocational colleges of twentieth-century national schooling. It is a strategy that offers a way of understanding the contemporary global reconfiguration of education along with insights into the kind of educational work that might claim the label of professionalism.

Rethinking Teacher Professionalism

In this single volume of the *World Yearbook of Education*, we do not claim to resolve contemporary debates about teacher professionalism. However, we add to the intellectual debates that are beginning to grasp the problems confronting teacher professionalization by disaggregating the problem of globalizing teacher professionalism research. We use 'boundary work' as a lens for rethinking teacher professionalism as a globalizing professionalizing project. This framework recognizes that globalization and professionalization are both negotiated and formed at the interfaces between linked ecologies. It treats the way phenomena and entities are made through boundary politics as the primary question for investigation. It problematizes the boundaries of these phenomena and entities that seem quasi-permanent, such as 'the teaching profession', as an open-ended formation whose features and characteristics are secondary questions analytically (Abbott, 2005; Dürrschmidt *et al.*, 2007).

This focus on globalization and professionalization highlights the way boundary politics are centred by politics of knowledge that are both theoretical and practical. As the discussion of 'educational work' suggests, this analytical frame refocuses attention on everyday workplace politics where contested knowledge claims are negotiated to secure meanings and agreements between educators, employers and other state and civil society actors. This knowledge politics is governed by the wider politics that negotiates the availability of knowledge resources. This wider politics uses knowledge-about-the-world and discourse, or ways of using words, to establish concepts and assumptions, which are ordered on the basis of their theoretical standing through research, policy and education (Abbott, 1995).

The selection, production, mobilization and dissemination of these knowledges and orders of discourse are critical to governance (Somers, 1994; Bonnell and Hunt, 1999). They are, therefore, a key resource in professionalization. Professions are 'occupational groupings that exercise [a] relatively high degree of control over the conditions and conduct of their work and this kind of arrangement provides a mechanism for organizing some aspects of social life in a way that properly deploys professional knowledge' (Gewirtz *et al.*, 2009: 4). However, the way they engage these wider knowledge politics, which define powerful knowledge, has profound implications for their capacity to negotiate their preferred social logics as educational projects.

The chapters that make up this volume have been written following invitations to authors who are actively researching globalization and professionalization from around the world. Each author wrote out of a particular hotspot of change in response to a preliminary book proposal. The process of drafting and editing confirmed the significance of boundary work in determining the boundaries and contents that delineate social spaces and the contradictory boundary work by states and educators that is remaking education and reclaiming professionalism. These chapters are organized in three parts. Part I includes chapters that elaborate the broad argument that globalization occurs within national territories. Part II documents the way educational formations are being remade as states and educators engage with intersecting processes of boundary work. The final part offers perspectives on engaging professionalism.

Part I: Globalization Within the National Space

The three chapters that open this volume provide theoretical arguments about the nature of globalization and globalizing processes that contribute to the re-spatialization and re-culturing of national territories and sub-national spaces, including education.

Saskia Sassen (Chapter 2) begins by distinguishing forms of globalization at the global scale, and within nation-states. She identifies three trajectories of globalization within the national space by drawing on her studies of global cities. These global cities develop within national territories but differ from prior national cities because they anchor networks between cities at national and transnational scales, and also locate and expel circuits of people, goods and ideas through those city spaces. Making reference to parallel processes that are evident in relation to the organization and ordering of national education systems, Sassen shows that global transformation entails particular localizations of reforms that travel globally: they generate emergent global formations, such as global cities, public-private initiatives and discourses of professionalism, within national territories; and they unleash unpredictable social innovations, movements and demands that step outside familiar national codes and conventions. Similar to the 'urban street', these reforms occupy social space as a space of disputation between fundamentalisms and patterns of democratic participation. Sassen calls for conceptual frameworks that offer ways of understanding the effects of global transformations within nation-states by mobilizing and reframing existing empirical research and evidence conducted within prior national frames.

Noah W. Sobe (Chapter 3) suggests that ideas and practices of teacher professionalism take on particular notions of 'best practice' that are premised on imaginaries of 'one-worldness' or 'the global' through processes of comparison and competition. He examines the construction of particular concepts of best practice in teacher professionalism through 'scopic systems' that both project and reflect certain kinds of one-world best practice. Sobe illustrates these contentions by tracking the idea of best practice in teaching historically in the US, by examining the adoption of particular nineteenth-century teaching ideologies, namely Pestalozzianism and Herbartianism. He then shows how the Great Exhibitions acted as scopic systems to concentrate multiple images of this best practice professionalism in ways that embraced teachers' idealism and motivated their practice. The OECD's international comparisons, through schemes such as PISA and the *Teaching and Learning International Survey* (TALIS), are now serving a similar function to the nineteenth-century Great Exhibitions.

Finally in this section, Iveta Silova and William C. Brehm (Chapter 4) outline the way education experts carry neo-liberal policies into specific national spaces through their work. International policy agencies, funding bodies and comparative education researchers contribute to the construction of market-based education service provision, such as private tutoring, which the authors discuss in two contexts: Central and Southeast Asia. They argue that these privatizing travelling reforms de-professionalize teachers and established teaching arrangements but, in turn, teachers use this 'private' space to evade and sometimes defy the multiple regulations permeating their work in public schools. By occupying this private space in ways that are oriented towards sustaining local visions of 'quality' education and 'good' life, teachers work towards innovative student-centred learning and curricula. As teachers redraw the boundaries between the global and the local (as well as the public and the private), they reclaim professionalism and, equally important, redefine the global neo-liberal agenda itself.

Part II: Remaking Educational Formations and the National Education Space

The varied chapters in this section accurately reflect the mixed state of play in the remaking of educational formations and 're-boundarying' of professional work. Across countries and sectors, professional and professionalizing workforces are engaged in different forms of interaction with global transitions and their localizations, which make specific places and spaces of educational work. They locate 'hotspots' where change is endemic because national institutional trajectories confront globalizing processes within national territories. These chapters illustrate how change is promoted by global agencies, such as the OECD and the World Bank, as well as by consultants, experts, students and academic travellers who 'touch down' in education spaces that are already inhabited, organized and ordered as uneven national education territories. Some spaces are more receptive to 'touchdown' (Sassen, Chapter 2) than others. They may contain both incomplete translations of globalizing processes and places that seem to solidify global practices and make them visible. For example, urban centres with their coffee shops and corporate headquarters develop alongside geographically patterned suburbs, which house those who are either more, or less, integrated into this urban culture. The urban centres are geographically and culturally distanced from the hinterland that reaches out to rural and remote regions. Such socio-spatial patterning creates distinctive landscapes, cultures and work and workforce concentrations, which influence education and educators' professionalizing projects.

Across these differentiated educational places, educators reach out to mobile ideas and practices as resources that prompt and inform boundary work at three scales. First, travelling reforms represent processes of de- and re-territorialization that are reconfiguring national education systems through boundary work that is tensioned between imperatives to service global flows of capital, people and knowledge, and also sustain the nation. Susan L. Robertson (Chapter 5) considers the sudden sharp rise in interest in teachers from these global agencies, and examines how the national and sub-national are being enrolled as important sites for globalization through a specific focus on the OECD's TALIS and the World Bank's SABER-Teachers. Continuing this theme, Risto Rinne and Jenny Ozga (Chapter 6) examine the global re-regulation of teachers' work through a focus on OECD's TALIS as a knowledge-based regulation tool and consider the ways in which the construction of such instruments as evidence-based, objective and policy-informing enables them to travel and for their 'translation' to be attempted in contrasting contexts. Anthony Welch (Chapter 7) examines the effects of a wider range of travelling reforms in Asia, focusing particularly on their implications for the professoriate – those educators who work in Asian universities. He argues that the professoriate stand at an uncertain crossroads. They are confronted by challenges of global university reform as well as ageing demographics, but established and emerging transnational diasporas cut across these effects within national spaces and fuel forms of regionalism.

Second, educators continue to engage in boundarying through their 'educational work': this specific form of occupational boundary work makes, orients and enacts spaces for learning. However, this occupational boundarying is tensioned between state re-territorializing imperatives and the diffraction of responses and choices that accompanies 'perpetual learning' in times of social and educational change (Wyn, 2009). Stephanie Matseleng Allais (Chapter 8) moves the focus to South Africa to explore the possibilities for autonomous professionalism for educators in South African Further Education and Training colleges. College lecturers' work in South Africa, she argues, has been shaped by economic inequalities, shifting curriculum and qualification policy, and insecure work conditions aggravated by neo-liberal models of educational delivery. It has created an educational space weakened by internal divisions, not least among educators and their organizations. Omar García Ponce de León and his colleagues (Chapter 9) draw on a large-scale US–Mexican comparative study to focus on professionalizing programmes for higher education workers in Mexico, looking at the movement of global measures of performance and excellence into that space, which demand that academics affirm the research function alongside their existing teaching and service functions. Their closely observed study reveals that academics engage with these changes in their work with reluctant acceptance, and develop a range of strategies for managing the conflicting demands of external professionalizing processes and their sense of their own professional identity. In Chapter 10, Michele Schweisfurth returns to the South African setting, but illuminates re-territorialization through learner-centred education considered as a travelling policy with a mainly 'Western' provenance and with support at the supranational, international and national levels, that is, nevertheless, extremely dependent on teachers for its implementation in classrooms. She draws on a convincing body of research to show how problematic such implementation is given the character of teacher professionalism in developing countries. In Chapter 11, Romuald Normand illustrates the power of particular kinds of knowledge claims and historically embedded resources that are available to educators in France. Normand demonstrates that, historically, the French comprehensive school has been strongly linked with the foundation of republican principles and has been at the core of French society attached to equality of opportunities. This gives educators considerable power, but, at the same time, the failure of schools to provide greater social equality makes them vulnerable to some attempts at reform that have created doubts and uncertainty among educators, who are caught up in issues of boundary work and their relationship with the state.

Finally, there are places of innovation and imagination where professionals direct their efforts towards securing spaces for learning at the hotspots where territorialization and perpetual learning intersect. Where territorialization drives forms of boundary work that secure national socialization as an educational project, in both nation-building and neo-liberal forms, perpetual learning generates new forms of practice as citizens and professionals depart from conventions and reach out to social and cultural resources available through social webs at sub-national, national and global scales. Sassen (Chapter 2) theorizes these spaces, which exist as contested boundary zones, in terms of the 'urban street': a raw public space 'where new forms of the social and the political can be made, rather than a space for enacting ritualized routines'. These are emergent places of professional praxis whose outcomes inevitably vary as they are negotiated in the moment-by-moment movements of history. Malak Zaalouk (Chapter 12) highlights the networks of professionals and international agencies that have made and remade particular forms of teacher professionalism in Egypt. Documenting the shifting patterns of teacher professional development, she tracks the persistence of empowerment approaches to teaching across three periods of educational reform: framed by the Dakar and Jomtien Education for All frameworks for action and the frame emerging alongside the Arab Spring, which is encouraging growth of regional networks that reassert empowerment approaches in teacher professionalism. Phan Le Ha and Le Thuy Linh (Chapter 13) describe contested professionalisms being negotiated in the field of English Language Teaching as Vietnamese teachers of English confront demands for Global English and policies endorsing a particular teaching approach, Communicative Language Teaching. They show both how this particular discursive practice of teaching English rubs up against the established Vietnamese norms that frame a teacher as a moral guide and how teachers mediate these dilemmas in their professional identities and practices. Qiongqiong Chen and Mei Li (Chapter 14) also highlight contradictory spaces, which Chinese academics occupy when they return to China after studying or working internationally. These are places of frustration as well as innovation because returnee academics' integration into the Chinese academy is not always linear and beneficial but is constrained by existing power relations and circumstances. The authors draw out the implications of these processes of movement, displacement and resettlement for the returnees' academic identities, and how their practices affect university culture and higher education policies in China.

Part III: Re-Engaging Professionalism

This *World Yearbook of Education* prompts questions about the terms and conditions that enable and disable educators' claims about professionalism and the three final chapters speak to these concerns. Sarah Amsler (Chapter 15) opens the final section of this volume by asking how we can navigate neo-liberalism and its limits as a globalized travelling discourse. She answers this question by considering the ways professionals embody this discourse in nationally located approaches but also work towards platforms that anchor critical knowledge building, which can inform societies and professionals about ways of maintaining and remaking themselves. She reflects on contradictions between debates in England, which critique the privatization of universities, and Central Asia, where a history of state-controlled knowledge building makes privatization attractive as a means of building critical capacities and knowledge about the world. This analysis reveals some of the limits of neo-liberalism as a one-world discourse. It shows how debates about university reforms are framed by cross-cutting political projects, which justify different strategies for holding open a space for building knowledge that can be disseminated through teaching as resources for remaking education and societies. Amsler argues that we need a language for speaking this political agenda that is about knowledge building in which education and the design of education professionals are a critical means to an end: the end of securing a sustainable life that is of social interest to citizens and countries.

David Watson (Chapter 16) extends this line of argument by examining what it means to be an academic that entails a version of teacher professionalism. He suggests there is an anachronistic discourse of nostalgia, which looks back to the way universities were understood historically but without recognising that the days of publicly funded universities were historically specific. This ahistoricism fails to see and critique the categorical mistakes that are currently being projected as core principles of the contemporary university. He challenges the idea of the university as an entity and, instead, suggests that it is a membership organization which is formed through the actors that participate in and collaborate through it. The task for academics is not to achieve work–life balance but to engage in self-care of the identities – individual, collective and organizational – that constitute, sustain and secure those knowledge-building networks. In changing times, this means working towards a new reconfiguration of universities that understands and adapts these persistent principles, which grasp the value of membership organizations where network-based knowledge traditions are co-located and debated, and serve as both a knowledge repository and locus of dissemination.

Finally, Andy Hargreaves (Chapter 17) reflects on the idea of 'capital' and the different kinds of capital that are identified as having worth in the contemporary debate about teacher professionalism. He highlights the importance of human capital in national economic and social development and also the way the processes of building human capital are mediated by educators. This allows Hargreaves to develop the concept of 'professional capital', which is mobilized individually and collectively in workplaces that yield learning and is developed continuously as a national, as well as individual, resource. On this basis, he makes a strong case for the value of professional capital as an integrated form of human capital, social capital and decisional capital that can only flourish by professionalizing educators and their work.

Re-Boundarying Teacher Professionalism

Together, these chapters in the *Yearbook* remind us that 'professionalism' is a claim to be knowledgeable and, therefore, trusted to do a job. Such claims are secured through social and cultural boundary work. In the case of professionals who teach or enable others' learning in less formalized ways, these politics of professionalization entail forms of boundarying that are premised on the distinctive intellectual-practical labour of educational work: anchored by the job of educating and the way educators identify, occupy and secure mandates across social spaces.

A take-away message from this *Yearbook* is that this educational labour is not entirely governable through state-centric regulatory technologies. The re-territorialization of national education systems is complemented by the educational boundary work that engages educators across all education sectors, and in emerging private and civil society spaces beyond state-centric education provision. These processes of occupational boundarying distinguish and also constitute the spaces that educators occupy, the work they do and the identities that motivate and orient their practices.

These politics of professionalization intersect with globalizing processes that are remaking and re-spatializing education; how it is done is significant for the future. With neo-liberal input–output logics offering only limited recognition of educators' professional capacities, it is not surprising that they are divided about the future of teacher professionalism. Yet educators can still claim their capacity to profess, communicate and translate; it is a capacity that is becoming more significant as global flows and mobility accelerate. Educators' specialist knowledge is mobilized through educational projects that make and remake educational spaces and yield learning – that, in turn, is embodied by learners, citizens, communities and societies. This is a capacity that is increasingly deployed beyond, as well as within, the regulatory frames of state-centric educational projects: in public, private and civil society settings that are subject to de-nationalizing imperatives at every scale. Across these changing spatial frames, the distinctive character of educational work and its politics of professionalization become important – because educational work is not just about securing individual learning outcomes or skills for work; it's about forming citizens' capacities for living together and using power responsibly to build societies that are, more or less, civilized and sustainable.

References

Abbott, A. (1988) *The System of Professions: An essay on the division of expert labor*, Chicago, IL: University of Chicago Press.

Abbott, A. (1995) Things of boundaries, *Social Research*, 62: 857–82.

Abbott, A. (2005) Linked ecologies: states and universities as environments for professions, *Sociological Theory*, 23(3): 245–72.

Alexiadou, N. and Jones, K. (2001) *Travelling Policy/Local Spaces*, paper presented at the Congrès Marx International III, Paris.

Anderson, B. (1991) *Imagined Communities: Reflections on the origin and spread of nationalism*, London: Verso.

Apple, M.W. (1986) *Teachers and Texts: A political economy of class and gender relations in education*, New York: Routledge and Kegan Paul.

Apple, M.W. (2009) Foreword, in S. Gewirtz, P. Mahony, I. Hextall and A. Cribb (eds) *Changing Teacher Professionalism: International trends, challenges and ways forward*, London: Routledge, pp. xiv–xviii.

Bacchi, C. (2000) Policy as discourse: What does it mean? Where does it get us? *Discourse*, 21(1): 45–57.

Ball, S. (1990) *Politics and Policy Making in Education*, London: Routledge.

Ball, S.J. (2003) The teacher's soul and the terrors of performativity, *Journal of Education Policy*, 18(2): 215–28.

Bauman, Z. (2000) *Liquid Modernity*, Cambridge: Polity.

Bonnell, V.E. and Hunt, L. (eds) (1999) *Beyond the Cultural Turn: New directions in the*

study of society and culture, Berkeley, CA: University of California Press.

Braverman, H. (1974) *Labor and Monopoly Capital: The degradation of work in the twentieth century*, New York: Monthly Review Press.

Chappell, C. (2003) *Reconstructing the Lifelong Learner: Pedagogy and identity in individual, organisational and social change*, London and New York: RoutledgeFalmer.

Chen, K.H. (2010) *Asia as Method: Toward deimperialization*, Durham, NC: Duke University Press.

Connell, R.W. (1985) *Teachers' Work*, Sydney: Allen and Unwin.

Connell, R.W. (1995) Education as transformative work, in M. Ginsburg (ed.) *The Politics and Culture of Educators' Work*, New York: Garland.

Connell, R.W. (2007) *Southern Theory: The global dynamics of knowledge in social science*, Sydney: Allen and Unwin.

Colley, H., Henriksson, L., Niemeyer, B. and Seddon, T. (2012) Competing time orders in human service work: towards a politics of time, *Time and Society*, in press.

Dahlman, C.T. (2009) Territory, in C. Gallaher, C.T. Dahlman, M. Gilmartin, A. Mountz and P. Shirlow (eds) *Key Concepts in Political Geography*, Los Angeles, CA: Sage, pp. 77–86.

Dale, R. (1989) *Education and the State*, Milton Keynes: Open University Press.

Dawe, A. (1970) The two sociologies, *British Journal of Sociology*, 21(2): 207–218.

Delors, J. (1996) *Learning, the Treasure Within: Report to UNESCO of the International Commission on Education for the Twenty-first Century*, Paris: UNESCO.

Dürrschmidt, J. and Taylor, G. (2007) *Globalization, Modernity and Social Change: Hotspots of transition*, Basingstoke: Palgrave Macmillan.

Farrell, L. (2006) *Making Knowledge Common: Literacy and knowledge at work*, New York: Peter Lang.

Felstead, A., Fuller, A., Jewson, N. and Unwin, L. (2009) *Improving Working as Learning*, London: Routledge.

Field, J. (2006) *Lifelong Learning and the New Educational Order*, Stoke on Trent: Trentham Books.

Gewirtz, S., Mahony, P., Hextall, I. and Cribb, I. (2009) *Changing Teacher Professionalism: International trends, challenges and ways forward*, London: Routledge.

Gieryn, T.F. (1983) Boundary-work and the demarcation of science from non-science: strains and interests in professional ideologies of scientists, *American Sociological Review*, 48: 781–95.

Gieryn, T.F. (2000) A space for place in socology, *Annual Review of Sociology*, 26: 463–96.

Henriksson, L., Wrede, S. and Burau, V. (2006) Understanding professional projects in welfare service work: revival of old professionalism? *Gender, Work and Organization*, 13(2): 174–92.

Hoyle, E. (1995) Changing conceptions of a profession, in R.S.H. Busher (ed.) *Managing Teachers as Professionals in Schools*, London: Kogan Page, pp. 59–70.

Hughes, E.C. (1958) *Men and their Work*, Glencoe, IL: The Free Press.

Hunter, I. (1994) *Rethinking the School: Subjectivity, bureaucracy, criticism*, St Leonards, NSW: Allen and Unwin.

Hutchins, R.M. (1970) *The Learning Society*, Harmondsworth: Penguin.

Jones, K. (2002) *Education in Britain: 1944 to the present*, London: Wiley.

Kenway, J., Bullen, E., Fahey, J. and Robb, S. (2006) *Haunting the Knowledge Economy*, London: Routledge.

Kuhn, M. (2007) *New Society Models for a New Millenium: The learning society in Europe and beyond*, New York: Peter Lang.

Lamont, M. and Molnar, V. (2002) The study of boundaries in the social sciences, *Annual*

Review of Sociology, 28: 167–95.

Larson, M.S. (1990) In the matter of experts and professionals, or how impossible it is to leave nothing unsaid, in R. Torstendahl (ed.) *The Formation of Professions: Knowledge, state and strategy*, London: Sage, pp. 24–50.

Lawn, M. (1996) *Modern Times? Work, professionalism and citizenship in teaching*, London: Falmer.

Levin, J.S. (2001) *Globalizing the Community College: Strategies for change in the twenty-first century*, New York: Palgrave.

Levin, J.S. (2007) Globalizing higher education: neo-liberal policies and faculty work, in J. Smart and W. Tierney (eds) *Handbook of Higher Education, Volume 22*, Norwell, MA: Kluwer Academic Publishers, pp. 451–96.

Levin, J.S. and Shaker, G. (2011) Arrested development, undervalued teaching, and personal satisfaction: the hybrid identity of full-time nontenure-track faculty in U.S. universities, *American Behavioral Scientist*, 55(11): 1461–84.

Levin, J.S., Shaker, G. and Wagoner, R. (2011) Post neoliberalism: the professional identity of faculty off the tenure-track, in B. Pusser, K. Kempner, S. Marginson and I. Ordorika (eds) *Universities and the Public Sphere: Knowledge creation and state building in the era of globalization*, New York: Routledge, pp. 197–217.

McWilliam, E. (2008) *The Creative Workforce: How to launch young people into high flying futures*, Sydney: UNSW Press.

Maguire, M. (2010) Towards a sociology of the global teacher, in M.W. Apple, S.J. Ball and L.A. Gandin (eds) *The Routledge International Handbook on the Sociology of Eduction*, London: Routledge, pp. 58–68.

Marginson, S. (1997) *Educating Australia: Government, economy and citizen since 1960*, Sydney: Allen and Unwin.

Marx, K. (1976) *Capital, Volume 1* (B. Fowkes, trans.), Harmondsworth: Penguin.

Montero-Hernandez, V. and Levin, J. (2011) *The Pursuit of Academic Productivity: The construction of strategies of achievement among full time faculty members in contemporary public state universities in Mexico and the United States*, research paper presentation for the annual meeting of the Association for the Study of Higher Education, Charlotte, NC, November.

Newman, S., Niemeyer, B., Seddon, T., Devos, A., Joseph, C. and Henriksson, L. (2012) Global transformations and educational work: remaking the idea of a teaching occupation, *Globalization, Societies and Education*, 12(2) (special issue).

Ozga, J. (1995) Deskilling a profession: professionalism, deprofessionalism and the new managerialism, in H.B.R. Saran (ed.) *Managing Teachers as Professionals in Schools*, London: Kogan Page, pp. 21–37.

Ozga, J. and Lawn, M. (1981) *Teachers, Professionalism, and Class: A study of organized teachers*, London: Falmer.

Ozga, J. and Lawn, M. (1988) Schoolwork: interpreting the labour process of teaching, *British Journal of Sociology of Education*, 9(3): 323–36.

Ozga, J., Dahler-Larsen, P., Segerholm, C. and Simola, H. (2011) *Fabricating Quality in Education: Data and governance in Europe*, London: Routledge.

Paasi, A. (2003) Territory, in J. Agnew, K. Mitchell and G. Toal (eds) *A Companion to Political Geography*, Malden, MA: Blackwell, pp. 109–22.

Preston, B. (1996) Award restructuring: a catalyst in the evolution of teacher professionalism, in T. Seddon (ed.) *Pay, Professionalism and Politics: Changing teachers, changing education*, Camberwell, VIC: Australian Council for Educational Research.

Ranson, S. (1992) Towards the learning society, *Educational Management Administration Leadership*, 20(2): 68–79.

Ranson, S. (2003) Public accountability in the age of neo-liberal governance, *Journal of Education Policy*, 18: 459–80.

Robertson, S. (1996) Markets and teacher professionalism: a political economy analysis, *Melbourne Studies in Education*, 37(2): 23–39.

Robertson, S., Bonal, X. and Dale, R. (2002) GATS and the education service industry: the politics of scale and global reterritorialization, *Comparative Education Review*, 46(4): 472–95.

Sachs, J. (2000) The activist profession, *International Journal of Educational Change*, 1(1): 77–95.

Sassen, S. (2006) *Territory, Authority, Rights: From medieval to global assemblages*, Princeton, NJ: Princeton University Press.

Sassen, S. (2007) *A Sociology of Globalization*, New York: W.W. Norton.

Schön, D.A. (1971) *Beyond the Stable State: Public and private learning in a changing society*, London: Maurice Temple Smith.

Seddon, T. (1990) Teachers' work and political action, in T. Husen and N. Postlethwaite (eds) *International Encyclopedia of Educational Research*, Oxford: Pergamon.

Seddon, T. (1997) Education: deprofessionalised? Or reregulated, reorganised and reauthorised? *Australian Journal of Education*, 41(3): 228–46.

Seddon, T. (2007) The European in transnational times: a case for the learning citizen, in M. Kuhn (ed.) *Who Is the European? A new global player?*, New York: Peter Lang, pp. 29–52.

Seddon, T. (2010) Knowledge economy: policy discourse and cultural resources, in M. Simons, M. Olssen and M. Peters (eds) *Re-reading Education Policies: Studying the policy agenda of the 21st century*, Rotterdam: Sense, pp. 257–76.

Seddon, T., Henriksson, L. and Niemeyer, B. (2010) *Learning and Work and the Politics of Working Life: Global transformations and collective identities in teaching, nursing and social work*, London: Routledge.

Seddon, T. (forthcoming) *Re-boundarying Education: Globalization, liquid learning and the politics of educational work*, London: Routledge.

Slaughter, S. and Leslie, L. (1997) *Academic Capitalism, Politics, Policies, and the Entrepreneurial University*, Baltimore, MD: The Johns Hopkins University Press.

Smyth, J., Dow, A., Hattam, R., Reid, A. and Shacklock, G. (2001) Teachers' work in a globalizing economy, *British Journal of Educational Studies*, 49(1): 103–5.

Somers, M.R. (1994) The narrative constitution of identity: a relational and network approach, *Theory and Society*, 23: 605–49.

Steiner-Khamsi, G. (2012) Understanding policy borrowing and lending: building comparative policy studies, in G. Stein-Khamsi and F. Waldow (eds) *Policy Borrowing and Lending in Education: World yearbook of education, 2012*, London: Routledge, pp. 3–17.

Waller, W. (1961) *The Sociology of Teaching*, New York: Wiley.

Wilensky, H.L. (1964) The professionalization of everyone? *American Journal of Sociology*, 70: 137–58.

Williams, R. (1961) *The Long Revolution*, London: Chatto and Windus.

Wyn, J. (2009) *Touching the Future: Building skills for life and work*, Australian Education Review 55, Camberwell, VIC: ACER.

Part I

Globalization Within the National Space

2   When the Global Arises from Inside the National

Saskia Sassen

What is it we are trying to name with the term 'globalization'? In my reading of the evidence it is actually two distinct sets of dynamics. One of these involves the formation of explicitly global institutions and processes, such as the World Trade Organization, global financial markets, the new cosmopolitanism and the War Crimes Tribunals. The practices and organizational forms through which these dynamics operate are constitutive of what is typically thought of as global scales.

But there is a second set of processes that does not necessarily scale at the global level as such, yet, I argue, is part of globalization. These processes take place deep inside territories and institutional domains that have largely been constructed in national terms in much, though by no means all, of the world. What makes these processes part of globalization even though they are localized in national, indeed sub-national settings, is that they involve transboundary networks and formations, which connect or articulate multiple local or sub-national processes and actors.

In my work I have particularly wanted to focus on these latter types of processes and have insisted in conceptualizing them as also constitutive of globalization, even though we do not usually recognize them as such. When the social sciences focus on globalization – which is still rare deep in the academy – it is typically not on these types of nationally and sub-nationally scaled practices and dynamics but rather on the self-evidently global scale.

This expanded way of understanding the current global era gives us a far larger lens on social transformations than approaches that assume that the global only happens at the global scale. It also means that educators and researchers can begin to engage the global from types of knowledge and literatures that they have long worked with and feel strong in. The challenge lies in the work of making conceptual architectures that allow scholars to situate their familiar terminologies and understandings in global-sensitive framings. In this way, one can detect 'globalization' in a familiar situation – stumble on the global when you least expect it.

Such an approach also carries implications for those people in national societies who are less advantaged, the immobile and the segregated. The fact that these people may lack the means to travel to foreign countries does not preclude their being part of the global. Rather, it means that they are familiar with particular instances of the global, right there in their neighbourhoods and in their schools.

My aim in this chapter is to expand the meaning of globalization by including the sub-national scale as one set of sites for globalizing processes. I also discuss some of the multiple research agendas that come out of this analytic move, which opens up the field of globalization studies.

I approach these tasks by selecting some key institutions and processes as lenses for understanding the theoretical, methodological and empirical contributions of diverse social science studies to the study of globalization. I refer both to studies that do this global reframing explicitly and knowingly, and to studies that are not focused on the global at all, even though they contribute to its understanding. The field of education research is one example where globalization is shifting the established spatial configuration of education. These effects are evident as travelling reforms, like lifelong learning, which circulate across the world, reappearing in distinct but recognizably similar form in different countries (Steiner-Khamsi, 2012). Therefore studies focused on understanding the effects of this global touchdown in national educational systems provide pertinent findings of 'social thickness' in the local; this contributes to understandings of the global. I conclude with a brief examination of what I conceptualize as 'The Global Street', a perhaps extreme version that illustrates how very local practices and dynamics can be part of the global.

But first allow me a brief biographical detour to clarify these methodological claims. It might be helpful given the theme of this chapter, which is about recovering the global inside the national that may become evident as a locality, a movement or the state itself. This detour allows me to elaborate my insistence that the local and the immobile can be part of the global; that mobility is not a prerequisite for studies of globalisation. I base this claim on my experience, which reveals the significance of mobility and immobility in research and building knowledge.

A Methodological Reframing

As an immigrant student, I have experienced how strategically educators are positioned vis-à-vis the growing number of foreign and immigrant students in our educational systems. Yet assuming that these students have an automatic interest in the global is unwarranted in my view. Having this international background is of great value in understanding today's globalizing world but it does not define what they want to focus on in university. In what follows I very briefly explore in autobiographical terms what it is that being an immigrant or a foreign student brings to the table in the educational setting.

One way that educators influence students is through their choice of subjects and careers. In the case of foreign and immigrant students in our educational systems, this influence may be even stronger than with native students. A form of this influence that I have encountered is a tendency to assume that such internationally mobile students are automatically interested in globalization because they have a foreign origin. I think this assumption is unwarranted, as is its obverse, that native students are less interested in the global than those students who are internationally mobile. While an international background can influence educators' advice and students' choice of subjects and careers, it is not critical to the way students become knowledgeable and produce knowledge.

Being out of place, slightly but also permanently, led me to see conditions and to seize on actions that were not *of* the place. One possible response, which is the way I moved, is to use theory to compensate imperfect knowledge of language and being slightly out of place. These resulting theoretical concerns and work may have little to do with the global; what is significant is that it inflects and informs a way of thinking and seeing the world. It is this indirect connection between mobility, which means one is out of place, rather than the fact of growing up in more than one country, which captures the influence of my internationally mobile life on my scholarship. It frames my way of thinking. It shaped my perhaps peculiar way of theorizing in which theory gets constituted through the text itself, rather than through a model that stands outside the specifics of the subject under consideration. It is a way of working with words through the process of research and building knowledge that has shaped my need to develop new categories for analysis, such as that of the global city and, more recently, the denationalized state.

This falling back on, or jumping ahead to, theory because of one's imperfect knowledge of a language (and feeling slightly out of place) may also feature in the minds and imaginations of many of our foreign-origin students. As educators, we may read their work as confused or resisting the dominant modes of scholarly work in a given time and place. Yet, in fact, they may be opening up new analytic ground – for analysis, for examination and for interpretation.

The difficulty for us educators is to recognize this distinction between intellectual confusion and scholarly innovation. It is something that I have experienced from the receiving end. For instance, 12 publishers rejected the dissertation-based manuscript that became my first book. The thirteenth took it but it was not a US press. It was Cambridge University Press in the UK and it became an acclaimed book, which continues to be reprinted. I never gave up on that manuscript because I believed it was good. But not all foreign doctoral students have the confidence to persist with their belief in their own academic work. Many give up long before that. As my academic life proceeded, it showed that even 12 rejections from the gate-keeping system does not necessarily mean that you are out. You can still cross that border that defines knowers and those that do not know, even if you come with some wounds (see Sica and Turner, 2005).

As these biographical reflections suggest, globalization has multiple effects. Globalizing processes create social changes in the international interstate system and within the territorial boundaries of nation-states. The local and the immobile can be part of the global, and mobility is not a prerequisite for studies of globalization. They also destabilize the seemingly secure knowledge frames that have developed through nationally framed research cultures and reveal the interstitial spaces that exist between words and the worlds they portray, which is the medium of knowledge building.

Expanding the Analytic Terrain for Studying the Global

One way of opening up the subject of globalization to disciplines that have resisted the category of globalization is to posit that the global – whether an institution, a process, a discursive practice or an imaginary – both transcends the exclusive framing of national states and partly emerges and operates within that framing.

Seen this way, globalization is more than its common representation as growing interdependence across the world and the formation of self-evidently global institutions. It includes sub-national spaces, processes, actors, and more. Among these processes I include cross-border networks of activists engaged in specific localized struggles with an explicit or implicit global agenda. These emerging cross-border networks are clearly evident in human rights and environmental organizations, and also professional networks. In education research national research associations are aligning in cross-border agencies, such as the European Conference on Education Research (ECER) and the World Education Research Association (WERA). Cross-border policy networks underpin the work of states, creating policy discourses that travel around the world and drive reform agenda. An example in the economy is the use of certain monetary and fiscal policies critical to the constitution of global markets. An example in the world of education is the growth of standardizing technologies that govern by numbers and signoffs, which drive 'lifelong learning', endorse performance pay for teachers, and govern education 'quality' (Ozga *et al.*, 2011). Parallel developments are evident in the use of international human rights instruments in national courts. Non-cosmopolitan forms of global politics and imaginaries, which remain deeply attached or focused on localized issues and struggles, can become part of global lateral networks that connect and contain other similar localized efforts.

Identifying these different types of cross-border processes and actors as part of globalization prompts the question, what remains 'national'? The particular challenge in this intellectual move lies in the work of decoding at least some of what continues to be experienced and represented as national. If the global gets partly structured inside the national, then state-centric social sciences confront methodological and theoretical challenges, which are different from those posed by the common binary of the global versus the national. It means that the work of decoding structurations of the global inside the national can build on methodological and conceptual tools that are already available through research and writing not concerned with globalization per se.

In my work I have particularly wanted to focus on sub-national practices and dynamics and have insisted in conceptualizing them as also constitutive of globalization, even if they are not usually recognized as such. When the social sciences focus on globalization it is typically not on these types of sub-national practices and dynamics but rather on developments at the global scale. Although the social sciences have made important contributions to this study of the global scale by establishing the fact of multiple globalizations – only some of which correspond to neoliberal corporate economic globalization – there is much work left to be done. At least some of this work entails distinguishing (a) the various scales that global processes constitute, ranging from supranational and global to sub-national; and (b) the specific contents and institutional locations of this multi-scalar globalization. Geography more than any other of the social sciences today has contributed to a critical stance towards scale.

Research that takes the analysis of scale seriously recognizes the historicity of scales and resists the reification of the national scale that is so prevalent in most of social science. This methodological framing suggests, first, that globalization is not only an extension of certain forms of practice and dynamics to the globe (i.e. the global scale) but also a repositioning of what we have historically constructed and experienced as the local and the national. Second, this happens in many different and specific ways and in a growing number of domains – economic, political, cultural and ideational. It does mean for me that we need new conceptual architectures for social science research. But it does not mean that we have to throw all existing research techniques and data sets out of the window.

I use the term 'conceptual architecture' with care. It is a term that refers to an organizing logic that can accommodate multiple diverse components operating at different scales (e.g. data about various localized practices and dynamics and also self-evidently global ones) without losing analytic closure, or at least retaining a modicum of such closure. Studying the global, then, does not only entail a focus on that which is explicitly global in scale. It also demands a focus on: locally scaled practices and conditions that are articulated with global dynamics; and the multiplication of cross-border connections among various localities. Further, this reframing reveals that many of the globally scaled practices and dynamics, such as the global capital market, actually are partly embedded in sub-national sites, and they also move between these differently scaled practices and organizational forms. Thus the global capital market is constituted both through electronic markets with global span, and through locally embedded conditions, i.e. financial centres in global cities. Similarly, the global education market is partly constituted through the OECD's PISA data and its translation through benchmarking exercises into policy frameworks with global span; but it is also constituted through the reconfiguration of qualifications, funding and accountability regimes that have specific local and embedded effects in the education sectors, universities and schools of countries and on the identities of those who inhabit them.

A focus on such sub-nationally based processes and dynamics of globalization requires methodologies and theorizations that engage not only global scalings but also sub-national scalings as components of global processes. This framing, in turn, destabilizes older hierarchies of scale (e.g. top-down, bottom-up) and conceptions of nested scalings (e.g. the analogy of Matryoshka dolls with the global enclosing the national, enclosing the sub-national). Studying both the global and the sub-national has some advantages over only focusing on globally scaled conditions because it provides a key to understanding some of the critical transformations afoot. It also makes it possible to use long-standing research techniques (quantitative and qualitative) in the study of globalization. This reframing gives us a bridge for using the wealth of national and sub-national data sets, and specialized scholarships such as area studies and interdisciplinary education research, as part of studying the global – in short we do not need to start from scratch, documenting and researching everything.

But this methodological reframing that rereads existing quantitative and qualitative research also poses specific challenges. Existing studies and data sets need to be situated in conceptual architectures that are not quite those held by the researchers who generated these research techniques and data sets, as their efforts mostly had little to do with globalization. One central task is to decode particular aspects of the 'national', which may in fact have shifted away from what had historically been considered or constituted as national. This is in many ways a research and theorization logic that is present in global city studies: today we have come to recognize and code a variety of components in these cities as part of the global (Sassen, 2001/1991). But there is a broader range of conditions and dynamics of other parts of national societies and economies that are still coded and represented as local and national even though they are in fact already part of the global. In my current research project I focus on how this all works out in the realm of politics (Sassen, 2008, 2012a, 2012b).

Work to be Done: What There Is and What We Need to Add

The most widely accepted definition of globalization emphasizes the growing interdependence of the world and the formation of global institutions. Elements of this are present in scholarship that took off in the 1980s (e.g. Portes and Walton, 1981; Chase-Dunn, 1984; Beck, 1986; Giddens, 1986; Thomas *et al.*, 1987; Sassen, 1988; Castells, 1989; Potts, 1990; Ricca, 1990; Ward, 1991; Robertson, 1992; but see also earlier texts, such as, e.g. Palloix, 1975; Amin, 1980; Sassen, 1982). In the 1990s, this scholarship grew rapidly (e.g. Arroyo *et al.*, 1993; King, 1995; Sklair, 1995; Hirst and Thompson, 1996; Evans, 1997; Pijl, 1998; Abu-Lughod, 1999; Sayad, 1999). But the subject remained somewhat marginal to the core social science disciplines and their canons.

One key, often implicit, assumption in many of these more familiar definitions of globalization is that the global and the national are two mutually exclusive domains. Such an assumption easily leads to the notion that what the global gains, the national loses, and vice versa. This, in turn, implies a correspondence of national territory with the national: that is to say, if a process or condition is located in a national institution or in national territory, it must be national. For example, national education systems are seen to be national even though, historically, international flows of ideas and people have affected their form (see Sobe, and Silova and Brehm, this volume). Even when national universities establish branch campuses and teaching programmes in other countries, they are still claimed to be national institutions in their source countries. Social science approaches inevitably tend to focus on something that is inside the national, and in so doing they can tell us something about structurations of the global inside the national. But these global structurations are not always recognized or understood. Typically they are claimed to be national or are seen as what the global does to a national condition. It is not taken further.

Conceiving of globalization as emerging from inside the national opens up a vast agenda for research and politics. It means that research on globalization need not just focus on interdependence and global institutions, but must also include detailed studies, notably ethnographies, of the multiple national conditions and dynamics that are likely to be engaged by the global and often are the global as it functions inside the national.

What complicates matters and requires decoding is that such conditions and dynamics are often still experienced and represented as national. Examples are global cities, immobile or localized activists who are part of transnational networks, and even particular state institutions, such as ministries of finance, central banks and even education systems and organizations; these have all played a role in implementing the new economic logics of the global corporate economy and the emerging notions of a global commons. This does not mean that everything about these cities, localized activists or state institutions is global. It might be simply that they house or enable particular global dynamics and conditions. As for politics, such a broader understanding of globalization opens up the possibility of national actors (legislators, courts, citizens, local NGOs) doing global politics from inside the national; it also means that the immobile, those who do not or cannot cross borders, may nonetheless participate in global politics.

Mapping an analytic terrain for the study of globalization that captures this more complex understanding takes work. Elsewhere (Sassen, 2007), I have examined a range of social science studies that, although not concerned with the global, make significant methodological, data and theoretical contributions to the study of globalization. In the 2000s we saw rapid growth of a type of social science work that expressly addresses the global in ways that include, but also move beyond understandings of globalization as growing interdependence and global institutions (Appadurai, 2000; Sennett, 2003; Albrow, 2004; Alderson and Beckfield, 2004; Dasgupta, 2004; Madigan, 2004; McMichael, 2004; Latham and Sassen, 2005; Smith and Favell, 2006; Touraine, 2006; Datz, 2007; Pries, 2008; Sassen, 2008, 2011; Body-Gendrot *et al.*, 2009). Part of the research work we see in these and other texts entails detecting the presence of such globalizing dynamics in thick social environments that mix national and non-national elements.

One critical proposition from my perspective (Sassen, 2007, 2008) is that to study the global we *can* use existing research techniques and data sets developed with the national in mind. But it requires addressing the fact that such studies often depend on analytic closure at the level of the nation-state. This is quite common in most of the social sciences, though far less in disciplines such as Anthropology and Geography than in Sociology and Political Science, for instance. Some of the most influential data sets in the social sciences are at the national level, and some of the most advanced methods require closure of the unit of analysis, which then happens typically at the level of the nation-state.

All of this means that, if we use the results of older empirical studies, we need to analyse them through new conceptual and interpretive frameworks – frameworks that recognize that the national and the sub-national can be sites for the global. Surveys of factories that are part of global commodity chains; in-depth interviews that decipher individual imaginaries about globality; and ethnographies of national financial centres: all expand the analytic terrain for understanding global processes. We need both a focus on interdependence at a global scale and also a focus on how the global gets constituted inside the national, often in thick micro-settings.

The tendency to examine and to interpret issues from the perspective of the nation-state has been extensively critiqued and debated over the decades, though more so in recent times given the rise and evidence of globalization. Scholars such as Beck (2006) and Taylor (2000), name this way of framing analysis 'methodological nationalism', in that it excludes transnational processes. I add a twist to the discussion about methodological nationalism by insisting that the sub-national can become partly denationalized insofar as the global can get constituted inside the national (Sassen, 2008: chs 1, 8–9). My criticism of methodological nationalism focuses on reasons other than the fact of transnationalism. In many ways, my critique focuses on the other end of the transnationalism dynamic: I look for the global inside the national, which allows me to use, albeit through a new conceptual architecture, many of the data sets, methods and concepts of social science scholarship not explicitly concerned with the global. Further, I posit that, because the national is thick and highly institutionalized, it is not always easy to detect the often partial or highly specialized denationalizations that are taking place. Mine is, then, a critique of methodological nationalism with a starting point not exclusively predicated on the existence of transnationalism as the source of the critique, but rather on the possibility of a partial denationalizing of conditions and processes historically constituted as national.

Once we accept that the global is partly structured inside the national, we open up analytic terrain for diverse traditional disciplines to study globalization even when they have never had a global subject of study. A key proposition for me is that existing social science studies, which may not have been concerned with globalization at all, can in fact contribute to the study of globalization. This helps to override a key assumption in the social sciences: the implied correspondence between national territory and national institutions. In other words, this methodological reframing challenges the assumption that, if a process or condition is located in a national institution or in national territory, it must be national. This may have been the case, though never fully, for much of the history of the modern state, especially since the First World War, and to some extent still holds a bit. What is different today is that these conditions are partly but actively being unbundled. Different also is the scope of this unbundling.

Developing the theoretical and empirical specifications that allow us to accommodate such conditions is a difficult and collective effort. It requires methodological strategies that destabilize older hierarchies of scale. Here I flag three approaches: the endogenization of global dynamics into the national; formations that emerge as particular actors negotiating a global and local scale; and the work of decoding denationalizations of what were historically national conditions and actors.

The Destabilizing of Older Hierarchies of Scale

Global dynamics can destabilize older hierarchies of scale that were constituted through the practices and power projects of past eras, and through which the national scale eventually predominated. Today we see what resembles a return to older imperial spatialities for the economic operations of the most powerful actors: the formation of a global market for capital, a global trade regime, and the internationalization of manufacturing production. These developments are, of course, not simply a return to older forms; it is crucial to recognize the specificity of today's practices and the capabilities enabling these practices. This specificity partly consists of the fact that today's transboundary spatialities had to be produced in a context where most terrritory is encased in a thick and highly formalized national framework marked by the exclusive authority of the national state. This is, in my reading (Sassen, 2008: chs 1, 4 and 5), one of the key features that distinguish the current from older phases of globalization.

The intersections between these emerging transboundary spatialities and thick, nationally encased territories constitute strategic scales of social action that are not simply the national or the global scale. They become evident in the global project of powerful firms, the new technical capabilities associated with information and communication technologies, and some components of the work of states that together constitute strategic scales other than the national scale (Castells, 1996; Pijl, 1998; Brenner, 2004; Robinson, 2004; Appelbaum and Robinson, 2005; Gereffi *et al.*, 2005; Sassen, 2008; Chant and Richey, 2010; Ernst, 2010; Graham, 2010; Lash, 2010). These strategically scaled practices and dynamics also emerge at sub-national scales, such as the global city, and supranational scales, for example as global markets (Fainstein, 2010; Chen, 2005; Badie and Vidal, 2009; *Urban Geography*, 2008; Aalbers, 2012; Burdett and Sudjic, 2011; Krippner, 2011). And there are also multiplying horizontal civic global networks and projects, which scale social and political action sub- and supranationally (Naples and Desai, 2002; Moghadam, 2005; Benayoun and Schnapper, 2006; Jacobson and Ruffer, 2006; Hagedorn, 2007; Amin and Roberts, 2008; Brotherton and Kretsedemas, 2008). These processes and practices that are economic, political and civic destabilize the familiar scale hierarchies that expressed the power relations and political economy of earlier periods (Bonilla *et al.*, 1998; Calhoun *et al.*, 2002; Silver, 2003; Dubet and Lustiger-Thaler, 2004; Aneesh, 2006; Fraser, 2009; Mansell *et al.*, 2009; Marcuse, 2009; Sonnenfeld and Mol, 2011).

Recognizing these strategic multi-scalar practices and dynamics reveals the significance of the local in many of the circuits that constitute economic and political globalization. A focus on places allows us to disaggregate globalization in terms of multiple specialized cross-border circuits on which different types of places are located, or patterns of strategically scaled social action. Global cities are some of the most complex emerging spaces that localize strategically scaled processes and practices. They are sub-national places where multiple global circuits of strategic action intersect; this positions such cities on diverse structured cross-border geographies. Each of these global cities exists as a place with distinct scopes that are constituted through particular practices and actors. For instance, at least some of the circuits connecting Sao Paulo to global dynamics are different from those of Frankfurt, Johannesburg or Bombay. These distinct sets of overlapping circuits also contribute to the constitution of differentially structured cross-border geographies that network these global cities. Such a multiplication of cities and circuits can intensify older hegemonic geographies even as it introduces new elements: for instance, the increase in transactions between New York, Miami, Mexico City and Sao Paulo. This type of analysis gives us a different picture of globalization from that of overarching global markets and global trade.

The role of the new interactive technologies in repositioning the local scale invites us to examine critically how we conceptualize the local. Through these new technologies a financial services firm can become a micro-environment with continuous global span. But so can resource-poor organizations or households that are part of global activist networks. These micro-environments can be oriented to other such micro-environments located far away. Such multi-scalar effects begin to destabilize both the notion of context, one typically understood as part of the local, and the notion that physical proximity is one of the attributes of the local (Sassen, 2007: ch. 6). A critical reconceptualization of the local along these lines entails an at least partial rejection of the notion that local scales are inevitably part of nested hierarchies of scale running from the local to the regional, the national and the international. Rather, new rescalings emerge alongside the old ones, and the new ones can often trump the latter. Existing theory, largely centred on the national, is not enough to map today's multiplication of practices and actors that are constituting such new rescalings. Let me illustrate this argument with a short examination of one case.

'The Global Street': When Powerlessness Becomes Complex

The 2011 uprisings in the Arab world, the daily neighbourhood protests in China's major cities, Latin America's *piqueteros* and poor people's demonstrations with pots and pans, the *Indignados* in Spain – all are vehicles for making social and political claims. So were the over 100,000 people marching in Tel Aviv, a first for this city. They marched not to bring down the government, but to ask for access to housing and jobs; part of the demonstration was Tel Aviv's temporary tent city, housing mostly impoverished middle-class citizens. These are also the claims of the 600,000 who went to the streets in late August in several cities in Chile. And they were the claims that got the Occupy movement started in the US in September 2011.

Together, these diverse instances of strategic political action lead me to a concept that takes us beyond the empirics of each case and connects each site with a multi-sited global movement. This concept is 'The Global Street' (Sassen, 2011). In each of these cases, I would argue, 'the street' – the urban street as public space – is differentiated from the classic European notion of more ritualized spaces for public activity, with the piazza and the boulevard the emblematic European instances. I think of the space of 'the street', which of course includes squares and any available open space, as a raw and less ritualized space. The street can, thus, be conceived as a space where new forms of the social and the political can be *made*, rather than a space for enacting ritualized routines. With some conceptual stretching, we might say that politically, the 'street and square' are marked differently from 'boulevard and piazza': the first signals action and the second, rituals.

Seen this way, there is an epochal quality to the current wave of street protests, no matter their enormous differences. They range from the extraordinary courage and determination of protesters in Syria to the flash crowds convoked via social media to invade a commercial street block for ten minutes in cities in the US, the UK and Chile. These diverse politics have at least one strategic moment in the space that is 'the street' – the urban street, not the rural or suburban street. The city is the larger space that enables some of this action and also the lens that allows us to capture the history-making qualities of these protests. The background is a sharp slide into inequalities, expulsions from familiar places and livelihoods, corrupt political classes, unfettered greed, and in the most significant of these struggles, extreme oppression (*Globalizations*, 2010).

The city is a space where the powerless can make history. That is not to say it is the only space, but it is certainly a critical one. Becoming present, visible, to each other can alter the character of powerlessness. I make a distinction (Sassen, 2008: chs 6 and 8) between different types of powerlessness because powerlessness is not simply an absolute condition that can be flattened into the absence of power. Under certain conditions powerlessness can become complex, by which I mean that it contains the possibility of making the political, or making the civic, or making history. There is a difference between powerlessness and invisibility or impotence. Many of the protest movements we have seen in the Middle East and North Africa (MENA) are a case in point: these protesters may not have gained power, they are still powerless, but they are making a history and a politics. This then leads me to a second distinction, which contains a critique of the common notion that if something good happens to the powerless it signals empowerment. By contrast, the notion that powerlessness can become complex characterizes a condition that is not quite empowerment. Powerlessness can be complex even if there is no empowerment.

The current uprisings in the cities of the MENA region are quite different from what they might have been in the medieval city as portrayed in Max Weber's book *The City* (1921/1986). Weber identifies a set of practices that allowed the burghers to set up systems for owning and protecting property against more powerful actors, such as the king and the church, and to implement various immunities against despots of all sorts. Today's political practices, I would argue, have to do with the production of 'presence' by those without power, and with a politics that claims rights to the city and to the country rather than protection of property. What the two situations share is the notion that through these practices new forms of the political (for Weber, citizenship) are being constituted and that the city is a key site for this type of political work. The city is, in turn, partly constituted through these dynamics. Far more so than a peaceful and harmonious suburb, the contested city is where the civic is made.

We see this potential of urban space in the making of the civic across the centuries. Historically, the processes of overcoming urban conflicts have often been the source for an expanded civicness. The cases that have become iconic in western historiography are Augsburg and Moorish Spain. In both places, a genuinely enlightened leadership and citizenry worked at constituting a shared civicness. But there are many other cases, both old and new. Old Jerusalem was a space of commercial and religious coexistence for long periods of time. Modern Baghdad, under the brutal leadership of Saddam Hussein, was a city where religious minorities (though not necessarily the majority, which was always a threat), such as Christians and Jews, lived in more relative peace than they do today. Outsiders in Europe's cities, notably immigrants, have experienced persecution for centuries; yet in many a case their successful claims for inclusion had the effect of expanding and strengthening the rights of citizens as well.

Conclusion

This chapter challenged the idea of globalization as a self-evidently global process and, instead, focused on how the global can become structured inside the national. This type of perspective revises older, often taken-for-granted, hierarchies of scale to identify the strategic rescalings that are diversifying and remaking formats for social and political action. This conceptual and methodological reframing expands the analytic terrain within which to understand emerging global practices and dynamics in ways that allow us to use methods, concepts and data, even when these were not designed to address global trajectories.

I identified at least three ways in which we can design objects of study that make national territories one of the terrains for the emergence of globally scaled strategic action. Each of these methodological strategies is illustrated in the chapters that make up this 2013 volume of the *World Yearbook of Education*, which each focus on the way global practices and dynamics contribute to the remaking of education. One strategy consists of the endogenizing or the localizing of global dynamics in national space. A second consists of emerging actors, cultures or projects whose study requires negotiating a global and a local scale. The third strategy involves recognizing that much of what has historically been constructed as national and may still continue to be experienced, represented and coded as such is actually being denationalized. This problematizes objects of study that are contained within national frames; often these need to be decoded in order to understand whether they are still national. Examples are national education systems that are key generators of types of human capital needed by global firms. These three methodological strategies help us make visible types of globalizing instances that can easily escape notice.

A focus on such sub-nationally based processes and dynamics of globalization requires methodologies and theorizations that engage global scalings but also sub-national scalings as components of global processes. Studying global conditions that get constituted sub-nationally has some advantages over studies focused only on globally scaled dynamics; but it also poses specific challenges. It allows us to use long-standing quantitative and qualitative research techniques aimed at national level research, in the study of globalization. It also provides a bridge that enables us to use the wealth of national and sub-national data sets as well as specialized scholarships such as area studies. Both types of nationally framed studies, however, need to be resituated in conceptual architectures that grasp the distinctiveness of contemporary globalization.

References

Aalbers, M.B. (ed.) (2012) *Subprime Cities*, Boston, MA: Blackwell.

Abu-Lughod, J.L. (1999) *New York, Chicago, Los Angeles: America's Global Cities*, Minneapolis, MN: University of Minnesota Press.

Albrow, M. (2004) The global shift and its consequences for sociology, in N. Genov (ed.) *Advances in Sociological Knowledge*, Wiesbaden: VS Verlag.

Alderson, A.S. and Beckfield, J. (2004) Power and position in the world city system, *American Journal of Sociology*, 109: 811–51.

Amin, A. and Roberts, J. (eds) (2008) *Community, Economic Creativity and Organization*, Oxford: Oxford University Press.

Amin, S. (1980) *L'Accumulation a l'échelle mondiale*, Paris: Anthropos.

Aneesh, A. (2006) *Virtual Migration: The programming of globalization*, Durham, NC: Duke University Press.

Appadurai, A. (2000) *Globalization*, Raleigh, NC: Duke University Press.

Appelbaum, R.P. and Robinson, W.I. (eds) (2005) *Critical Globalization Studies*, Oxford: Routledge.

Arroyo, M., Milton Santos, M.A., De Souze, A. and Scarlato, F.C. (eds) (1993) *Fim de seculo e globalizacao*, São Paulo: Hucitet.

Badie, B. and Vidal, D. (eds) (2009) *L'Etat du monde 2010*, Paris: La Découverte.

Beck, U. (1986) *Risikogesellschaft auf dem Weg in eine andere Moderne*, Frankfurt: Suhrkamp.

Beck, U. (2006) *Cosmopolitan Visions*, Cambridge: Polity Press.

Benayoun, C. and Schnapper, D. (2006) *Diasporas et nations*, Paris: Odile Jacob.

Body-Gendrot, S., Garcia, M. and Mingione, E. (2009) Comparative social transformations in urban regimes, in A. A. Sales (ed.) *Sociology Today: Social transformations in a globalizing world*, Thousand Oaks, CA: Sage.

Bonilla, F., Melendez, E., Morales, R. and de los Angeles Torres, M. (eds) (1998) *Borderless Borders*, Philadelphia, PA: Temple University Press.

Brenner, N. (2004) *New State Spaces: Urban governance and the rescaling of statehood*, Oxford: Oxford University Press.

Brotherton, D. and Kretsedemas, P. (eds) (2008) *Keeping Out the Other*, New York: Columbia University Press.

Burdett, R. and Sudjic, D. (eds) (2011) *Living in the Endless City*, London: Phaidon Press.

Calhoun, C.J., Price, P. and Timmer, A.S. (2002) *Understanding September 11*, New York: New Press.

Castells, M. (1989) *The Informational City: Information technology, economic restructuring and the urban regional process*, Oxford and Cambridge: Blackwell.

Castells, M. (1996) *The Rise of the Network Society*, Cambridge, MA: Blackwell.

Chant, S. and Richey, L.A. (2010) *The International Handbook of Gender and Poverty: Concepts, research, policy*, Northampton, MA: Edward Elgar.

Chase-Dunn, C. (1984) Urbanization in the world system: new directions for research, in M.P. Smith (ed.) *Cities in Transformation*, Beverly Hills, CA: Sage.

Chen, X. (2005) *As Borders Bend: Transnational spaces on the Pacific rim*, Oxford: Rowman and Little.

Dasgupta, S. (2004) *The Changing Force of Globalization*, New Delhi: Sage.

Datz, G. (2007) Global-national interactions and sovereign debt restructuring outcomes, in S. Sassen (ed.) *Deciphering the Global: Its spaces, scales and subjects*, New York and London: Routledge.

Dubet, F. and Lustiger-Thaler, H. (2004) The sociology of collective action reconsidered, *Current Sociology* (special issue), 52(4): 557–73.

Ernst, D. (2010) A smart response to China's 'indigenous innovation' policies, *EWC News*. Available at www.eastwestcenter.org/news-center/east-west-wire/a-smart-response-to-chinas-indigenous-innovation-policies (accessed 11 July 2011).

Evans, P. (1997) The eclipse of the state? Reflections on stateness in an era of globalization, *World Politics*, 50: 62–87.

Fainstein, S.S. (2010) *The Just City*, Ithaca, NY: Cornell University Press.

Fraser, N. (2009) *Scales of Justice: Reimagining political space in a globalizing world*, New York: Columbia University Press.

Gereffi, G., Humphrey, J. and Sturgeon, T. (2005) The governance of global value chains, *Review of International Political Economy*, 12: 78–104.

Giddens, A. (1986) *The Constitution of Society: Outline of the theory of structuration*, Berkeley, CA: University of California Press.

Globalizations (2010) Globalization and the financial crisis, *Globalizations* (special issue), 1 and 2.

Graham, S. (2010) *Cities Under Siege: The new military urbanism*, London: Verso.

Hagedorn, J. (ed.) (2007) *Gangs in the Global City: Exploring alternatives to traditional criminology*, Chicago, IL: University of Illinois Press.

Hirst, P. and Thompson, G. (1996) *Globalization in Question*, Cambridge: Polity Press.

Jacobson, D. and Ruffer, G.B. (2006) Social relations on a global scale, in M. Giugni, and F. Passy (eds) *Dialogues on Migration Policy*, Lanham, MD: Lexington Books.

King, Anthony D. (1995) *The Bungalow: Production of a global culture*, Oxford: Oxford University Press

Krippner, G.R. (2011) *Capitalizing on Crisis: The political origins of the rise of finance*, Cambridge, MA: Harvard University Press.

Lash, S. (2010) *Intensive Culture: Religion and social theory in contemporary culture*, London: Sage.

Latham, R. and Sassen, S. (eds) (2005) *Digital Formations: IT and new architectures in the global realm*, Princeton, NJ: Princeton University Press.

McMichael, P. (2004) *Development and Social Change: A global perspective*, 3rd edn, Thousand Oaks, CA: Pine Forge Press.

Madigan, C. (ed.) (2004) *Global Chicago*, Chicago, IL: University of Illinois Press.

Mansell, R., Avgerou, C., Quah, D. and Silverstone, R. (eds) (2009) *The Oxford Handbook of Information and Communication Technologies*, Oxford: Oxford University Press.

Marcuse, P. (2009) Comments at the Conference on Cities and the New Wars, Columbia University, 28 September. Available at http://cgt.columbia.edu/events/cities_and_new_wars/ (accessed 18 October 2012).

Moghadam, V.M. (2005) *Globalizing Women: Transnational feminist networks*, Baltimore, MD: Johns Hopkins University Press.

Naples, N.A. and Desai, M. (eds) (2002) *Women's Activism and Globalization: Linking local struggles and transnational politics*, New York: Routledge.

Ozga, J., Dahler-Larsen, P., Segerholm, C. and Simola, H. (2011) *Fabricating Quality in Europe: Data and education governance*, London: Routledge.

Palloix, C. (1975) *L'Internationalisation du capital: éléments critiques*, Paris: F. Maspero.

Pijl, K.V.D. (1998) *Transnational Classes and International Relations*, London: Routledge.

Portes, A. and Walton, J. (1981) *Labor, Class and the Internationational System*, New York: Academic Press.

Potts, L. (1990) *The World Labor Market: A history of migration*, London: Zed Books.

Pries, L. (2008) *Dies Transnationalisierung der sozialen Welt*, Frankfurt: Suhrkamp.

Ricca, S. (1990) *Migrations internationales en Afrique*, Paris: L'Hamattan.

Robertson, R. (1992) *Globalization: Social theory and global culture*, Thousand Oaks, CA: Sage.

Robinson, W. (2004) *A Theory of Global Capitalism: Transnational production, trans-national capitalists, and the transnational state*, Baltimore, MD: Johns Hopkins University Press.

Sassen, S. (1982) Recomposition and peripheralization at the core, in M. Dixon and S. Jonas (eds) *The New Nomads: Immigration and changes in the international division of labor*, San Francisco, CA: Synthesis.

Sassen, S. (1988) *The Mobility of Labor and Capital: A study in international investment and labor flow*, New York: Cambridge University Press.

Sassen, S. (2001/1991) *The Global City: New York, London, Tokyo*, Princeton, NJ: Princeton University Press.

Sassen, S. (2007) *A Sociology of Globalization*, New York: W.W. Norton.

Sassen, S. (2008) *Territory, Authority, Rights: From medieval to global assemblages*, Princeton, NJ: Princeton University Press.

Sassen, S. (2011) The global street: making the political, *Globalizations*, 8: 565–71.

Sassen, S. (2012a) *Cities in a World Economy*, 4th edn, Thousand Oaks, CA: Sage/Pine Forge.

Sassen, S. (2012b) Interactions of the technical and the social: digital formations of the powerful and the powerless, *Information, Communication & Society*, 15: 455–78.

Sayad, A. (1999) *La Double absence. Des illusions de l'émigré aux souffrances de l'immigré*, Paris: Seuil.

Sennett, R. (2003) *Respect in an Age of Inequality*, New York: Norton.

Sica, A. and Turner, S. (2005) *The Disobedient Generation: 68ers and the transformation of social theory*, Chicago, IL: University of Chicago Press.

Silver, B.J. (2003) *Forces of Labor: Workers' movements and globalization since 1870*, Cambridge: Cambridge University Press.

Sklair, L. (1995) *Sociology of the Global System,* Baltimore, MD: Johns Hopkins University Press.

Smith, M.P. and Favell, A. (eds) (2006) *The Human Face of Global Mobility: International highly skilled migration in Europe, North America and the Asian Pacific*, New Brunswick, NJ: Transaction Press.

Sonnenfeld, D.A. and Mol, A.P.J. (2011) Social theory and the environment in the new world (dis)order, *Global Environmental Change* (special issue), 21(3): 771–5.

Steiner-Khamsi, G. (2012) Understanding policy borrowing and lending: building comparative policy studies, in G. Steiner-Khamsi and F. Waldow (eds) *Policy Borrowing and Lending in Education: World yearbook of education 2012*, London: Routledge.

Taylor, P.J. (2000) World cities and territorial states under conditions of contemporary globalization, *Political Geography*, 19: 5–32.

Thomas, M.G., Meyer, J.W., Ramirez, F.O. and Boli, J. (1987) *Institutional Structure: Constituting state, society and the individual*, Newbury Park: Sage.

Touraine, A. (2006) *Un Nouveau paradigme: pour comprendre le monde d'aujourd'hui*, Paris: LGF.

Urban Geography (2008) Chicago and Los Angeles: paradigms, schools, archetypes, and the urban process, *Urban Geography* (special issue), 29(2).

Ward, K. (1991) *Women Workers and Global Restructuring*, Ithaca, NY: Cornell University Press.

Weber, M. (1921/1986) *The City*, Glencoe, IL: Free Press.

3   Teacher Professionalization and the Globalization of Schooling

Noah W. Sobe

This chapter takes up the question of how we might theorize teacher professionalism in relation to global processes and phenomena. I take the position that it is important not solely to conceptualize 'the global' as something 'outside' or as an external force or set of pressures that enter into a given cultural context or 'local' arena. Instead, we need to understand exactly how it is that certain ideas, practices and actors take on the aura of 'being global'. Attention needs to be paid to the alliances that need to be built, the relations that need to be established, and the work that needs to be done so that a particular set of professional practices and discourses comes to be understood as having extra-local features that are potentially globe-spanning. We also need to think about how, in a recursive process, these become actualized in particular individual interactions and come to shape human lives.

The question of how we understand teacher professionalization in relation to matters global is of great importance to how education researchers analyse and make sense of the worldwide expansion of mass schooling and the role(s) that formal institutions of schooling play in different societies. International development initiatives such as Education For All (EFA) underscore a point that nowadays is so commonplace it can be easily overlooked: the very fact that today one can find schools all around the globe. On one level this seems an uncontestable and banal observation. Nonetheless, it is important to be cognizant of the fact that educational researchers still grapple with the question of how best to characterize analytically what appear as the universal features of educational practices and educational institutions. Though there is generally ready acknowledgement that the specificities of any and all educational contexts mean that such 'universal' features play out differently (and indeed sometimes quite divergently (Anderson-Levitt, 2003)), there is not complete agreement on what these universal features are, nor is there agreement on how to conceptualize and name these 'features'. For example, some historians of education have proposed that there is a 'grammar of schooling' (David Tyack, Larry Cuban); others speak of a '*forme scolaire*' and '*culture scolaire*' (Guy Vincent, Dominique Julia); in the field of comparative and international education much has been written on 'world culture models' of education (John Meyer, Francisco Ramirez). This chapter engages with the question of how we might understand the potentially universalizing, global implications of teacher professionalization.

Methodologically, this chapter is designed as a theorizing/conceptualizing piece and is not reporting the results of an empirical study. I discuss a range of scholarship on globalization and apply this to thinking through the problem of how we should consider the relation of globalization processes and phenomena to the claims that teachers can and do make about being members of an occupational group that enacts and protects expert knowledge. Though not a comprehensive historical study, I do use some specific historical examples from the United States to illustrate the global and local dimensions of the boundarying and re-boundarying work that occurs as teachers make occupational claims and access (or dispute) systems of expert knowledge. The focus of the first part of the chapter is on how professional discourses are accessed for strategic advantage and how certain elements can become imbued with the aura of being 'global' best practices. According to some (e.g. Meyer and Ramirez), with increased discursive/semantic convergence on a particular set of professional practices we should expect an eventual, inevitable global-spanning homogenization of pedagogy and schooling. I don't believe this to be the case. If we want to interrogate the connections between teacher professionalism and the globalization of schooling we need to consider both 'global reaching' and the ways in which notions of global one-worldness are produced in the first place, which is the topic I take up in the second part of the chapter. In eschewing the notion of globalization as force-from-without and in focusing instead on teacher professionalization as a political arena where 'globality' and 'global one-worldness' may be produced, this chapter proposes that we see globalization as a process that is internal to educational spaces and indeed to educators' own bodies.

Reaching Up, Down, Out and In

In the politics of teacher professionalization, as expert knowledge claims are advanced in relation to occupational statuses, prerogatives and responsibilities, it is not uncommon to find 'non-local' examples being leveraged to strategic advantage. Currently in the US, one sometimes finds references to Finnish schools and to Finland's policies of providing strong professional development and preparation time for teachers being used in policy debates and political activity around teachers' occupational statuses (e.g. CReATE, 2012). Anchored by Finland's successful performances on international assessments, these strategic references often point to the minimal presence of standardized testing within Finnish education generally, thus bringing a 'successful international example' into a local (US) discussion for purposes of skewing a policy discussion in a particular direction. There are multiple instances – contemporary and historical – of teacher professionalization being entangled with 'global reaching' and so to better sort this out analytically it will be useful to give some attention to what we might mean by the 'global' and the 'local' in these conversations.

As the editors note in the introduction to this volume, Saskia Sassen's (2001) work on 'global cities' provides a powerful reminder that many of the specific practices and operations that take place within national institutional settings are no longer geared to national agendas but rather frequently are more cued

into transnational or global 'interests'. Pauline Lipman (2003) has carefully exca-
vated how this can be the case with regard to schooling in her studies of education in Chicago, which suggest that some of the inequalities in this particular
urban school system derive from an interest in creating both a technology-savvy
managerial elite and a service sector-destined workforce; the idea is that both
of these in combination are necessary for Chicago to maintain a competitive
edge as a 'global city'. Scholars studying the European Union note the sometimes
uncanny dissolution of the old Russian 'matryoshka doll' model of conceptualizing scale as a series of larger/smaller concentric circles (e.g. in the notion of
district-level, provincial-level, national-level). New complexities and possibilities
are introduced when Basque politicians or Sami indigenous activists can side-
step national 'containers' and articulate political demands in Brussels or New
York City (or even, one is tempted to add, in the virtual spaces of Twitter and
Facebook). As Debora Reed-Danahay's (2003) ethnographic work on education
in France's Auvergne region has shown, we now witness considerably increased
possibilities for individual schools/teachers/classrooms to make 'lateral' local-to-
local connections with other schools in the EU. This is all worthy of note because
when objects, discourses and actors are put into relation with one another, the
regulative processes and normative ideals that shape educational practices can
potentially be affected.

Destabilizing concentric-circle notions of scale (Sassen, 2008) and attempting
to centre our analyses on the contingent and somewhat elusive assembling
together of heterogeneous but interrelating elements also helps to move away
both from theorizing the global and the local as a 'dialectic' (see Burbules and
Torres, 2000) and from needlessly fixating on a supposed 'global–local nexus'.
While the dialectic conceptualization can usefully illuminate the processual,
unfolding nature of social and cultural configurations, as deployed it too often
runs the risk of taking the 'local' and the 'global' as pre-arrayed or pre-arranged
configurations out of whose contested and politicized interaction a third or
hybrid form arises. If shifting from the concept of the 'dialectic' to that of a
'nexus' allows researchers to pay more attention to the ways that locality and
globality are generated, the nexus approach has the drawback of postulating an
automatic, necessary faultline. Particularly if we are interested in the notion that
the 'global is a series of locals' (Sassen, this volume), it becomes increasingly difficult to assume a priori that we can in fact decisively distinguish between the
global and the local. Technology, hypermodernity and neoliberalism may make
it seem that in the contemporary world knowing what is 'global' and what is
'local' is an increasingly fraught proposition (Riles, 2000). Yet, if we take empires,
imperialism, capitalism and the various other catholicons of the last several
millennia of human history as projects ruled by contingency and put into place
through intense labours (of an ANT/Actor-Network Theory variety), it becomes
clearer that the distinction between universals and particulars has long been a
matter of building alliances and binding various elements into certain relations,
always with uncertain outcomes.

As a historical illustration of the proposition that, rather than assume that
an external 'global' intrudes into local spaces, we should consider the particular

dynamics and specifics of any and all assemblages, I offer the example of a very minor episode in the history of the teaching and teacher professionalization in the United States. In the 1860s the Pestalozzian object lesson became entrenched in American teacher preparation largely through the work of Edward A. Sheldon (1823–97) at the Oswego Normal School in New York State. This was hardly the first time that Pestalozzi had been trumpeted by American educators. Pestalozzian ideas were advanced by William Maclure and Robert Owen at New Harmony in the 1820s and also advanced by Henry Barnard in the late 1830s (Ogren, 2005); however, Sheldon is frequently credited with implanting object teaching as the educational 'best practice' of the time, particularly as his network of students quickly spread out to occupy important positions at normal schools around the country (Hollis, 1898; Dearborn, 1925; Rogers, 1961). Pestalozzianism is a superb example of a 'global best practice' of the nineteenth century. In fact one can even say that it played a starring role in the purported founding of the field/discipline of comparative education in that one of the field's 'founding fathers', Marc-Antoine Jullien, had spent time with Johann Heinrich Pestalozzi (1746–1827) at Yverdon (Gautherin, 1993). Jullien's (1816/17) Linneas-like proposal for a scientific survey of education systems of the world included questions about the extent to which Pestallozian object teaching was present in different school systems (Sobe, 2002). Needless to say, as with other 'international' educational reform trends, Pestalozzianism took on very different forms in different settings. It was not a global model whose distinct features automatically or inevitably 'colonized' unique national contexts. For example, within Pestalozzian object teaching as it was propagated in America in the 1860s and 1870s, children's interest and their discipline (mental and otherwise) were key concerns – and they were concerns that were supposed to structure the craft techniques employed by teachers. These very same keywords 'interest' and 'discipline' recur in American Herbartianism, the educational movement that by the 1880s and 1890s had by certain measures succeeded the Oswego juggernaut. Yet in Herbartianism they were put into a very different relation to the aims and objectives of education and in fact became considerably altered in relation to the methods that teachers were to use. (And of course, just as Oswego Pestalozzianism represented a specific assemblage of 'Pestalozzianism', it is abundantly evident that 'American Herbartianism' – particularly as articulated and propagated by Charles McMurry, Frank McMurry and Charles De Garmo – also represented a specific and uniquely contoured reworking of the ideas of Johann Friedrich Herbart (1776–1841).)

It will be profitable to further pursue this example of the flourishing of Pestalozzianism in the US in the 1860s and 1870s. In the field of comparative and international education researchers are developing increasingly sophisticated tools for studying what is sometimes referred to as educational borrowing and lending (e.g. the 2012 *World Yearbook of Education* edited by Gita Steiner-Khamsi and Florian Waldow). However, rather than seeking to further explain or refine that body of scholarship, I would like to explore the assemblage of Pestallozzianism in the US by delving further and connecting Pestalozzianism with another important contemporaneous phenomenon in the history of teaching and teacher professionalization in the US: African-American schooling in the

American South after the end of slavery. As an extensive quantity of scholarship has explored (see, inter alia, Anderson, 1988; Butchart, 2010), with the reconstruction of the American South after the Civil War, African-American education rose to the fore as a pressing education policy issue. Who was to teach freed slaves and how and what they were to be taught became a pressing question, one that was both philosophical and practical. Nor, it should be added, was this question simply one debated by actors 'outside' Southern African-American communities seeking to determine what should be done for and to freed Blacks. As Adam Fairclough (2007) shows in his carefully researched study of Black teachers in the South from 1865 to 1954, these were questions that African-American communities also tackled with intensity and alacrity. Present here was the question of the educator's pedagogical expertise and what professional preparation and professional status were necessary for the effective education of African-Americans. And, Pestalozzian object teaching became one of the elements to enter the picture. A considerable number of schools were established by ex-slaves right as the Civil War was ending and in the immediate years after the war Freedmens' Bureau agents worked to establish which of these 'native' institutions most needed the assistance of professionally trained educators. White missionary – and some Black missionary – teachers from the North arrived in southern towns to employ their professional pedagogical best practices for the purpose of the advancement of Black southerners. In the ensuing decades, as efforts shifted to the training of Black southerners as teachers in institutions such as Virginia's Hampton Normal and Agricultural Institute (established 1868), the Pestalozzian object lesson similarly became one of the best practices propagated, for example, in the *Southern Workman*, a monthly newspaper distributed to all Hampton graduates.

I offer this detour as an illustration of professional teacher expertise being actualized in one particular concrete situation. In this assemblage (Deleuze and Guattari, 1987; Ong and Collier, 2005; Marcus and Saka, 2006), the 'global' and 'modern' best practice of Pestalozzian object teaching crossed with a wide-ranging set of heterogeneous elements, including the unique historical trajectory of Black education in the American South; institutionalized racism and race knowledge; the activist social, political and economic agendas of Black reformers and advocates; the technique of using the educator's professional pedagogic craft expertise to include and to exclude; and the material conditions of African-American schools in the South. It is an ancillary question whether this was or was not a significant chapter in the global dissemination of Pestalozzianism. However, this minor episode does show how, in a specific set of cultural and social circumstances, locality and globality can be produced in the ways that the teacher's professional pedagogic practices are deployed and intervened upon. In this instance the reaching out to a body of professional expertise (that had its origins in a cosmopolitan European social reform setting and that was later scientificized, again within a certain cosmopolitan idiom) was incorporated into a complicated and racialized algorithm of qualification and disqualification. This reaching out can also be seen as a reaching in, as a way of penetrating into the Black, Hampton-graduated teacher to discipline and govern his or her actions.

Nineteenth-century Pestalozzianism as well as Lancastrianism (Caruso and Roldán Vera, 2007), not to mention John Dewey and the global and/or American dimensions of the early twentieth-century progressive education movement (Popkewitz, 2005), all drive home the point that teaching has long been located within a transnational framing. Teacher professionalization needs to be located within this long historical trajectory. The comparative education borrowing and transfer of scholarship alluded to above often evidences an interest in the social science modelling and typologizing of different sorts of 'external' imports and references (Phillips and Ochs, 2004; Rappleye *et al.*, 2011). A good example of the ways this can provide education researchers with a valuable lens and tool is Steiner-Khamsi's (2004) discussion of the practice of using the foreign example to 'stigmatize' within a domestic education policy conversation. (The leveraging of lessons from Finland alluded to above might well fall under this designation.) While this scholarly literature can be useful when it pays proper attention to the political and rhetorical purposes that 'lessons from elsewhere' can serve, it sometimes brushes up against its own limitations when forced into the binary decision on whether a transfer occurred just in rhetoric or also in practice (Beech, 2006). In contrast, more post-structuralist approaches would tend to see discourse and practice as not entirely separable. In the case of the history of teacher professionalization, I think it is overwhelmingly the case that the heterogeneity, conflicts, ephemerality and indeterminacy within any given assemblage require that we recognize incommensurability, multiplicity and the irreducibility of social and cultural projects to a single prevailing logic or outcome (Sobe, 2009). In this vein, then, saying that teacher professionalization is not simply a matter that unfolds within the political, economic and social contours of a particular (national) system-world but rather has long taken place within a global frame is not in any way to comment on standardization or any isomorphic tendencies that might (or might not) undergird the worldwide schooling revolution that we have witnessed over the past several hundred years. For thinking about how teachers' professional pedagogical practices intersect with globalization processes (as opposed to just with global phenomena), it can be useful to turn to other tools.

Scopic Systems and Global Reality/Reflexivity

Much of what I have been discussing in the preceding section could be grouped under the heading 'networks', and indeed network analyses have proven to be of great value in educational research. In particular, as I alluded to above, studies that draw on aspects of Bruno Latour's Actor-Network Theory have provided us with valuable insights into how particular educational ideas and practices are 'made mobile' and/or 'blackboxed' (e.g. Resnik, 2006). However, alongside examinations of the educational networks and the ways that the knowledge bases that support teachers' professional pedagogical practices also move in networked ways, it is valuable to investigate the ways that these knowledge bases might move in non-networked ways and what consequences this might have (Sobe and Ortegón, 2009).

In the standard understanding of a network, various nodes are linked together as if by pipes. And through these pipes resources (e.g. various mobile forms of capital) as well as information and sets of knowledge can pass. Networks are most commonly visualized through the metaphor of a net or a web, which means that individual nodes can be linked to a varying number of other nodes and can be joined to multiple other collectives. As an alternative to this, however, the anthropologist Karen Knorr Cetina (2003, 2008; Knorr Cetina and Bruegger, 2002) has discerned a radically different organizational schema in the currency markets that she investigates in her research. While most financial markets are organized as centralized markets where transactions – even if electronic – are actually executed in a particular central location, foreign currency exchange is an over-the-counter market that inheres in inter-dealer transactions that are housed within various global banking institutions. Knorr Cetina reports that currency traders have up to six computer screens in front of them, fully capturing their gaze, with 'the market [composing] itself in these produced-and-analysed displays to which traders are attached'. These terminals 'deliver the reality of financial markets, the referential whole to which "being in the market" refers' (2008: 71). She proposes that the relational idiom of 'network' or 'being networked' does not capture the totality and reflexive comprehensiveness of the projection and reality being composed in this instance. Instead, she proposes the concept of a 'scopic system' to describe this structure:

> Like an array of crystals acting as lenses that collect light, focusing it on one point, such mechanisms collect and focus activities, interests and events on one surface … When such a mechanism is in place, coordination and activities respond to the projected reality to which participants become oriented … When such an ordinary observer constructs a textual or visual rendering of the observed and televises it to an audience, the audience may start to react to the features of the reflected, represented reality rather than to the embodied, pre-reflexive occurrences.
>
> (Knorr Cetina, 2008: 8)

Information that moves through a scopic system thus has considerably different effects than information that moves through networks, and below I will further explicate what implications this has for reflexivity and cultural/institutional formations. Against an embedding of circulation in social relations, Knorr Cetina's work suggests a way of seeing a global system that actually tends towards a single collective (as opposed to multiple collectives or 'pluri-centered' clusters). Based on her ethnographic study of currency trading floors in Zurich and New York, she proposes that the configuration of screens, content and options that traders confront compose a 'global reflex system'. Within this system, coordination is flat and non-hierarchical, yet nonetheless based on a view of things that appears to be – or, perhaps more to the point understands itself as being – comprehensive and summative. This is a view of the world that is at once a reflection and a projection.

Even though the ethnographic work just described took place in a rather unusual and somewhat unique setting, we can draw from it insights into how it is possible to generate 'one-worldness' notions in the domain of education. By this, I mean the idea that human beings belong to a single collective global society and inhabit a single 'global reality', one implication of which is that educational reforms can travel and be analysed within a worldwide frame of reference.

In a separate publication (2009) Nicole Ortegón and I have proposed that there is an important historical antecedent and loose analogue to Knorr Cetina's description of currency markets in the World's Fairs/International Expositions of the end of the nineteenth and beginning of the twentieth centuries (e.g. the Universal Expositions in Paris in 1867, 1889 and 1900, as well as the Fairs held in St Louis in 1904, Chicago in 1893 and Philadelphia in 1876). The most successful of these events attracted tens of millions of visitors and featured exhibition halls in which various countries could exhibit their successes and most modern practices across many domains of human activity, including in the field of education. Ortegón and I argued that one of the extremely important elements of these expositions was to help construct a single global reality and to project forth a modern future. As Martin Lawn notes in the introduction to an edited volume that examined the education-related exhibits of the these events:

> A major significance of exhibitions was that they provided systems of classifications, and the models needed to illustrate them, which materialized the comparative process. Objects were placed in relation to each other by increasingly standardized systems of rules of measurement ... So, through this exhibitionary prism, hierarchies were established in the signs and sites of progress and modernity.
>
> (2009: 16–17)

Though they lacked the eat-lunch-at-your-desk, all-enveloping feel of the computer displays that fill up a currency trader's workspace, the technologies of museum display and their accompanying norms of spectatorship (Sobe, 2007) might be seen, in Knorr Cetina's terms, as composing a scopic system. The exhibits and what Lawn appropriately calls their 'systems of classification' supplied visitors with certain lenses and ways of thinking about school-related matters, among them the most modern and scientific pedagogic practices.

Knorr Cetina's comment that the 'audience may start to react to the features of the reflected, represented reality rather than to the embodied, pre-reflexive occurrences' (2008: 8) seems also to describe accurately what played out across nineteenth/twentieth-century international expositions considered as a series of interlinked events. In modelling educational futures, the world's fairs brought visitors and exhibitors into what one might call a 'house of mirrors' where everyone was observing each other. Despite not having a fraction of the velocity of currency traders' screens, the social and cultural exhibits at these fairs/expositions sometimes similarly evidenced an anticipated or actual reaction. An illustrative example of this kind of anticipation can be found in Spain's educational exhibits at the 1876 Centennial Exposition in Philadelphia. Their display cases not only housed an effort to present Spain as the spiritual mother of the Americas, but also included an attempt to mitigate the supposed perception that Spain was deficient and far behind other European nations in advancing the cause of popular education. The solution to this problem was to send neither charts nor devices nor building models (since all of these would have shown Spanish deficiencies). Rather, the solution was handsomely printed books. Archival records show that the Spanish Ministry of Education explicitly strategized in advance that, since these gilded and weighty tomes were printed in Spanish, they would have the additional advantage of being unreadable by the American jurors who would award the education exhibit prizes. Nor would the jurors know that these same volumes had in fact been exhibited at previous international expositions. And indeed, this tactic proved to be successful, for at the 1876 fair Spain received 93 awards in the education section, the largest number to any country after the United States (Pozo Andrés, 2009: 162–3). Thus, while the world's fairs/expositions did provide countries with a platform on which to display themselves, it is important to recognize that this was a platform set within the scopic system of international competition and comparison, which was at the same time a system through which modernity was debated and enacted.

The international exhibitions of the end of the nineteenth and early twentieth centuries purported to present a comprehensive, encyclopaedic survey of the world. And, despite the great swathes of territory and human experience that were excluded, these 'exhibitionary prisms' did much to construct the reality of a 'single world' as an all-encompassing, texturally even sphere within which codified distinctions and standardized differences could be established (in reference to concepts such as civilization, progress and modernity). It was in these spaces and within this setting that the worldwide 'universality' of professional pedagogic practices (at least the best practices thereof) might be convincingly represented to the visiting public. This would be visible not just to the educators who travelled to the expositions themselves but could also cause an impression among the hundreds/thousands of additional teachers who, through a multiplier effect, read about the expositions in the voluminous textual reporting that occurred on each event, particularly as Ministries of Education filed official reports and leading educators published their reflections and observations.

It is important to consider both networked and non-networked ways that global educational formations are assembled. Thus, for example, an exposition such as the 1915 Panama-Pacific International Exposition in San Francisco – at which Maria Montessori successfully demonstrated her kindergarten pedagogy (Sobe, 2004) – can be usefully viewed in network terms. Historians can, for example, excavate who visited what booths and collected what samples and took what texts and business cards back to their places/countries of origin. Yet, in another sense, there appears to have been a significant non-relational, non-network dimension to the importance of the expositions. This inhered in the totality of an event itself and in the visual and intellectual overload that imparted one-worldness notions and reinforced the idea that all teachers, in whatever country they were located, were joined as part of a great global educational project that had its own shared rules and regularities.

Now to today: even though the International Bureau of Expositions still operates out of Paris and even though expos continue through the present, this cultural form has lost the social significance it had one hundred years ago. We are more likely to find global scopic systems in the international news media than in exhibition pavilions. In the field of education, though, we have what appear to be increasingly successful, increasingly comprehensive and increasingly significant summative surveys of the world – an emerging global reflex system. Here I refer to PISA, TIMSS and TALIS: the scopic systems that generate the education global reflex systems of our time. Borrowing from Knorr Cetina, one might say that large international educational assessment projects of this sort act like an array of crystals that collect light and focus it on one point. They bring a vast array of activities, interests and events on to one shared, uniform surface. Describing currency trading desks, Knorr Cetina noted, 'when such a mechanism is in place, coordination and activities respond to the projected reality to which participants become oriented' (2008: 8). This is an observation that may already in some cases speak to the consequences that high-stakes accountability-oriented testing is having in educational settings around the globe. Or it may be an observation to hold out there in the field of education, if not as a prediction, at least as a vision of one of the possible futures that we face.

Of the three assessments mentioned, the OECD's TALIS project, or the Teaching and Learning International Survey, may be the most relevant to this discussion's interest in scrutinizing teacher professionalization in relation to the globalization of schooling. TALIS is premised on the idea that 'effective teaching and teachers are key to producing high performing students' and it gathers data on the learning environment and working conditions of teachers in schools. One purpose is to enable cross-country analyses that would allow countries 'to identify other countries facing similar challenges and to learn from other policy approaches'. The first TALIS cycle in 2008 involved 24 countries and focused on lower secondary education teachers. The TALIS 2013 cycle will involve more than 30 countries and also presents the option whereby countries can conduct the 2013 TALIS assessment in the same schools that participated in the 2012 PISA assessment.

Given the way that the PISA assessment has begun to play a role in shaping educational conversations around the globe, it is well worth paying attention to what kind of global exhibitionary prism TALIS creates. Going forward, we will want to pay considerable attention to how TALIS is brought into the politics of teacher professionalization. We will want to note whether, as a scopic system, TALIS makes headway in constructing the reality of a single world of teacher professionalism, one that would be texturally even with globe-spanning extra-local features – a global assemblage of the sort that Knorr Cetina describes for currency markets and that I have here proposed as an accurate descriptor of nineteenth/twentieth-century expositions. These two other examples suggest that the power of phenomena such as TALIS may lie in producing a reflection/projection of reality that policy makers and educators react to more than they react to the actual embodied reality of the here-and-now.

Concomitant with this, we might anticipate the further codification of distinctions and standardization of differences/deviation from educational 'best practices'. And, relatedly, we might also anticipate that, as actors in the school system reach out to the TALIS results as part of teacher professionalization (or, potentially, teacher de-professionalization), this will simultaneously involve a global-in-the-local reaching down and into the body of the teacher to discipline and govern his or her actions.

Teachers, teacher unions, policy makers, school administrators and academic researchers will be involved in these political negotiations. All involved should bear in mind that whatever becomes situated as 'global best practices' is not simply a matter of technical, empirical educational research but is also deeply entangled in the contingent and shifting cultural and social politics of education. All should also bear in mind that 'one-worldness' notions are not a neutral facet of a globalized world. The global needs to produced and sustained. A global reality of teacher professionalism needs to be produced as real. All the aforementioned parties have some role to play in shaping, furthering and resisting the global reflexivities and reflections that this entails.

References

Anderson, J.D. (1988) *The Education of Blacks in the South, 1860–1935*, Chapel Hill, NC: University of North Carolina Press.

Anderson-Levitt, K.M. (ed.) (2003) *Local Meanings, Global Schooling: Anthropology and world culture theory*, New York: Palgrave.

Beech, J. (2006) The theme of educational transfer in comparative education: a view over time, *Research in Comparative and International Education*, 1(1): 2–13.

Burbules, N.C. and Torres, C.A. (2000) Globalization and education: an introduction, in N.C. Burbules and C.A. Torres (eds) *Globalization and Education: Critical perspectives*, New York: Routledge, pp. 1–26.

Butchart, R. (2010) *Schooling the Freed People: Teaching, learning, and the struggle for Black freedom, 1861–1876*, Chapel Hill, NC: University of North Carolina Press.

Caruso, M. and Roldán Vera, E. (eds) (2007) *The Appropriation of Political, Educational, and Cultural Models in Nineteenth-Century Latin America*, Berlin: Peter Lang.

Chicagoland Researchers and Advocates for Transformative Education (CReATE) (2012) *Research Brief #1: Testing Today in Context: History, impact, and alternatives.* Available at http://dl.dropbox.com/u/2561000/CReATE-Testing-full.pdf (accessed 4 March 2012).

Dearborn, N.H. (1925) *The Oswego Movement in American Education*, New York: Teachers College, Columbia University.

Deleuze, G. and Guattari, F. (1987) *A Thousand Plateaus: Capitalism and schizophrenia*, Minneapolis, MN: University of Minnesota Press.

Fairclough, A. (2007) *A Class of Their Own: Black teachers in the segregated south*, Cambridge, MA: Harvard University Press.

Gautherin, J. (1993) Marc-Antoine Jullien ('Jullien De Paris') (1775–1848), *Prospects: The Quarterly Review of Comparative Education*, 23(3/4): 757–73.

Hollis, A.P. (1898) *The Contribution of the Oswego Normal School to Educational Progress in the United States*, Boston, MA: D.C. Heath.

Jullien, M.-A. (1816–17/1964) *Jullien's Plan for Comparative Education* (S. Fraser, trans.), New York: Teachers College Bureau of Publications.

Knorr Cetina, K. (2003) From pipes to scopes: the flow architecture of financial markets, *Distinktion*, 7: 7–23.

Knorr Cetina, K. (2008) *Microglobalization*, in I. Rossi (ed.) *Frontiers of Globalization Research: Theoretical and methodological approaches*, New York: Springer, pp. 65–92.

Knorr Cetina, K. and Bruegger, U. (2002) Global microstructures: the virtual societies of financial markets, *American Journal of Sociology*, 107(4): 905–50.

Lawn, M. (2009) Sites of the future: comparing and ordering new educational actualities, in M. Lawn (ed.) *Modelling the Future: Exhibitions and the materiality of education*, Oxford: Symposium Books, pp. 15–30.

Lipman, P. (2003) *High Stakes Education: Inequality, globalization, and urban school reform*, New York: Routledge.

Marcus, G.E. and Saka, E. (2006) Assemblage, *Theory, Culture & Society*, 23(2–3): 101–6.

Ogren, C.A. (2005) *The American State Normal School: An instrument of great good*, New York: Palgrave Macmillan.

Ong, A. and Collier, S.J. (2005) *Global Assemblages: Technology, politics, and ethics as anthropological problems*, Malden, MA: Blackwell.

Phillips, D. and Ochs, K. (2004) Researching policy borrowing: some methodological challenges in comparative education, *British Educational Research Journal*, 30(6): 773–84.

Popkewitz, T.S. (2005) *Inventing the Modern Self and John Dewey: Modernities and the traveling of pragmatism in education*, New York: Palgrave Macmillan.

Pozo Andrés, M. del (2009) The bull and the book: images of Spain and Spanish education in the world fairs of the nineteenth century, 1851–1900, in M. Lawn (ed.) *Modelling the Future: Exhibitions and the materiality of education*, Oxford: Symposium, pp. 153–82.

Rappleye, J., Imoto, Y. and Horiguchi, S. (2011) Towards 'thick description' of educational transfer: understanding a Japanese institution's 'import' of European language policy, *Comparative Education*, 47(4): 411–32.

Reed-Danahay, D. (2003) Europeanization and French primary education: local implications of supranational policies, in K.M. Anderson-Levitt (ed.) *Local Meanings, Global Schooling: Anthropology and world culture theory*, New York: Palgrave, pp. 201–18.

Resnik, J. (2006) International organizations, the 'education-economic growth' black box, and the development of world education culture, *Comparative Education Review*, 50: 175–95.

Riles, A. (2000) *The Network Inside Out*, Ann Arbor, MI: University of Michigan Press.

Rogers, D. (1961) *Oswego: Fountainhead of teacher education; a century in the Sheldon tradition*, New York: Appleton-Century-Crofts.

Sassen, S. (2001) *The Global City: New York, London, Tokyo*, Princeton, NJ: Princeton University Press.

Sassen, S. (2008) Theoretical and empirical elements in the study of globalization, in I. Rossi (ed.) *Frontiers of Globalization Research: Theoretical and methodological approaches*, New York: Springer, pp. 287–306.

Sobe, N.W. (2002) Travel, social science and the making of nations in early 19th century comparative education, in M. Caruso and H.-E. Tenorth (eds) *Internationalisation: Comparing educational systems and semantics*, Frankfurt am Main: Peter Lang, pp. 141–66.

Sobe, N.W. (2004) Challenging the gaze: the subject of attention and a 1915 Montessori demonstration classroom, *Educational Theory*, 54(3): 281–97.

Sobe, N.W. (2007) Attention and spectatorship: educational exhibits at the Panama-Pacific International Exposition, San Francisco 1915, in V. Barth (ed.) *Innovation and Education at Universal Exhibitions, 1851–2010*, Paris: International Bureau of Expositions.

Sobe, N.W. (2009) Entrelaçamentos e troca cultural na história da educação: mobilizando John Dewey no período entre guerras (Entanglements and intercultural exchange in the history of education: mobilizing John Dewey in the interwar era), *Revista Brasileira de História da Educação*, 21.

Sobe, N.W. and Ortegón, N.D. (2009) Scopic systems, pipes, models and transfers in the global circulation of educational knowledge and practices, in F. Rizvi and T.S. Popkewitz (eds) *Education and Globalism*, New York: National Society for the Study of Education (NSSE)/Teachers College Press, pp. 49–66.

Steiner-Khamsi, G. (2004) Blazing a trail for policy theory and practice, in G. Steiner-Khamsi (ed.) *Global Politics of Educational Borrowing and Lending*, New York: Teachers College Press, pp. 201–20.

4   The Shifting Boundaries of Teacher Professionalism

Education Privatization(s) in the Post-Socialist Education Space

Iveta Silova and William C. Brehm

Educators worldwide have been caught in the middle of complex globalization debates. One such debate has centered on the role of international education "experts"—usually of Western origin—in the construction and dissemination of "best practices" globally. Whether advising national governments or consulting for international development agencies (such as the World Bank, Organization for Economic Cooperation and Development or the United Nations), these "experts" have operated on the assumption that there exists a common and legitimate "blueprint" of educational policies and practices, which would lead (if implemented properly) to increased educational opportunities and improved educational quality worldwide. In the context of (neo)liberal globalization, they have been called upon to advise governments on such salient policy topics as education governance, teaching methods, curriculum reform, or (in the case of American international development assistance) anti-terrorism. More often than not, their advice has focused on the diffusion of global education policies and practices that, for many scholars in comparative education, have been central in analyses of the coercive spread of (neo)liberal education reforms such as stand-ardization of curricula, decentralization and privatization of schools, or the introduction of national educational assessment and international testing (Dale, 2000; Apple, 2006, 2009; Arnove and Torres, 2007; Robertson, 2007; Torres, 2009; Rizvi and Lingard, 2010).

From the post-socialist countries of Central Europe to the post-Soviet repub-lics of Central Asia to the formerly non-aligned—yet funded by the former Soviet Union—countries in Southeast Asia, policy makers have embraced these (neo)liberal educational reform "packages" to pursue an allegedly linear transition from communism to democracy (Silova, 2010: 5). In some cases, these reform "packages" were imposed by such "expert" organizations as the World Bank and Asian Development Bank; in other cases they were voluntarily borrowed by policy makers in the former socialist states who were fearful of "falling behind" internationally (Steiner-Khamsi and Stolpe, 2006: 189; see also Silova and Steiner-Khamsi, 2008). While contributing to the dissemination of (neo)liberal ideology, the implementation of new reform "packages" in various post-socialist contexts has inadvertently reinforced the power of international "experts," enabling them to speak for those who supposedly lack expert knowledge to "help" themselves. Furthermore, it has undermined the power of education professionals in national and sub-national settings, re-inscribing a dependency of local education communities on international "expert" knowledge (Rancière, 1991).

Directly affected by the "touch down" of global educational flows—whether education privatization, decentralization, or child-centered learning—school teachers have been affected the most. In the public eye, teachers embodied the success (or failure) that the post-socialist education transitions set out to achieve. Teachers were thus expected to reject "old" teaching practices (generally associated with teacher-centered approaches prevalent in the socialist past) and instead embrace "new" Western teaching methodologies and classroom management techniques that focused on child-centered learning. They became subject to a multitude of new policies and the accompanying national and international in-service trainings and professional development activities. Their professional lives no longer belonged to them, but were rather governed by globally circulating "norms" about curricula, textbooks, tests, and teaching methods. In this context, international "experts" were positioned to possess the "know-how" that local teachers were required to master. Instead of pursuing various opportunities for innovative teaching and learning in their own educational settings, teachers were expected to become merely "the implementers of reform policies designed and controlled by others" (Popa, 2007: 23; see also Lingard, 1995; Ginsburg, 1996).

While acknowledging the very real threats to teacher professionalism in the context of (neo)liberal globalization, this study explores how teachers have attempted to redraw—purposefully or not—their occupational boundaries in order to regain professional authority and autonomy by working within and between rapidly changing educational spaces. Embedded in a sociological discourse, the concept of "re-boundarying" acknowledges the power of sub-national actors in (re)negotiating the occupational boundaries that constitute the national education space, as well as (re)defining its content and orientation through their individual and collective daily work. Taking a broader perspective on teacher "professionalism," we specifically focus on instances of resistance and pursuit of alternatives among teachers as a professional group. From this perspective, teacher "professionalism" goes beyond the issues of teacher competency and accountability, to reflect rather "an expression of struggle over the control and purpose of schooling" (Lawn, 1989: 154).

By locating the discussion within the two different post-socialist contexts—Southeast/Central Europe and Southeast Asia—we approach the concept of occupational "re-boundarying" from two analytical angles. First, we explore how teachers navigate (neo)liberal education reforms in their daily lives by focusing on their participation in private tutoring activities. We argue that teachers may have accepted the logic of market-based education service provision (as reflected in their private tutoring activities), but have simultaneously used the newly created "private" space to evade and perhaps even defy multiple (neo)liberal regulations permeating their work in public schools, such as student-centered learning and curriculum standards. Second, and equally important, we suggest that the post-socialist education space itself presents a continuing challenge—and perhaps an alternative—to (neo)liberal capitalism. Neither resembling socialist pasts nor approximating (neo)liberal futures, the post-socialist education space contains a complex set of education phenomena in the early stages of its formation, where its fate "still belongs to the future, or rather, to one possible future" (Epstein, 1995: 331). It represents a state of "unfinished global transitions" where the boundaries between global and local (as well as public and private) imperatives are being constantly challenged and (re)negotiated.

Following a historical overview of the emergence of the international development "expert" (including the changing notions of "professionalism," "authority," and "expertise" in education development during the post-World War II and post-Cold War context), this chapter examines the changing notions of education professionalism in two post-socialist settings—Southeast/Central Europe and Southeast Asia. We purposefully chose to focus on these two seemingly disconnected contexts to highlight some of the common reactions and counter-actions triggered by the introduction of one of the most widespread (neo)liberal reforms worldwide—education privatization. Drawing on three studies on private tutoring conducted in Southeast/Central Europe and the former Soviet Union (Silova *et al.*, 2006; Silova, 2009) and Cambodia (Brehm *et al.*, 2012), we discuss how teachers navigate (neo)liberal reforms by embracing, resisting, and (re)defining education "expert" knowledge depending on the various education spaces they create and occupy at different times of their professional careers. An insight into their experiences thus opens an opportunity to examine the emerging formation of new ethical and political educational projects that not only comply with but also contest the (neo)liberal agenda.

The Emergence of the Education "Expert" in International Education

Firmly institutionalized in the areas of mass schooling and international development, the notion of the education "expert" has important historical roots. It is embedded in Western Enlightenment thought that emerged in the eighteenth century and grew based on the belief in the ability of human beings to apply rational, scientific analysis "to bring progress and prosperity to humanity" (Parpart, 1995: 223; see also Foucault, 1986). During the nineteenth century, the Enlightenment project led to the increased specialization of knowledge, which played a pivotal role in the creation of Western modernity and subsequently led to the division of the world into the knowing and the ignorant, the enlightened and the uninformed, and the developed and the developing. In this context, Western scientific knowledge was presented as universally valid and "experts" assumed a central role in collecting, transferring, and controlling scientific knowledge between West and East, as well as North and South (Parpart, 1995: 223).

The construction, collection, and transfer of "expert" knowledge occurred in different disciplinary fields, including comparative education. As early as the 1800s, Marc-Antoine Jullien (1775–1848)—who is frequently referred to as the "father" or "precursor" of comparative education—made one of the initial attempts to conceptualize the field of comparative education within the social science institution of modernity (Sobe, 2002). In particular, Jullien emphasized the importance of international travel that would enable Western observers to study education through systematic (and scientific) observation for the practical purposes of societal progress. He argued that such study would identify "deficiencies of the systems and methods of education and instruction" in various international contexts and thus enable the transfer of "improvements" from one country to another (quoted in Gautherin, 1993: 6). From this perspective, education was instrumental to the advancement of Western modernity:

> In the long run, education alone is capable of exercising a decisive and radical influence on the regeneration of man, the improvement of societies, true civilization, and the prosperity of states. Each generation, if entrusted to teachers worthy of their mission, should be the more perfect continuation of the generation it replaces. Thus would the human race advance with firm and confident step along the broad avenue of progress where the body social, wisely and strongly constituted, would no longer be a prey to the grievous upheavals, periodic crises, and fearful disasters that all too often lead to backsliding.
>
> (Jullien, quoted in Gautherin, 1993: 3)

While Jullien's experience may be seen as one of the initial (although not entirely successful) attempts to institutionalize comparative education within the modernity project, the theme of "progress" appears to have been systematically embedded in comparative education scholarship throughout the nineteenth and twentieth centuries. In the post-World War II context, the study of "foreign" education systems became a "tool" for achieving broader ends, directly "relating education to economic growth, social amelioration, and political development" (Noah and Eckstein, 1969: 116). Perhaps not coincidentally, the melioristic approach to comparative education further intensified during the period of the Cold War, when the study of "best practices" became paramount not only to ensure each country's educational competitiveness globally, but also to pursue other strategic interests—frequently expressed in the "concern for the plight of less fortunate people" (Noah and Eckstein, 1969: 38)—in non-aligned countries.

Whether working in the capitalist West or the socialist East (or South), education "experts" benefited from the "development turn" of the 1960s and 1970s (Steiner-Khamsi, 2006), positioning themselves on the frontier of the international development industry. In this context, each superpower had its own development assistance strategy that these "experts" advanced. Commenting on the comparative education activities during the Cold War, Holmes (1981) found that, regardless of various geopolitical contexts, British and American experts almost always favored the introduction of a decentralized system of educational administrators, whereas Soviet and German Democratic Republic experts always recommended the introduction of polytechnic education in countries they advised. Similarly, Steiner-Khamsi (2006: 26) observed that the US model of international development emphasized economic growth, decentralization, decreased public expenditures, and privatization, whereas the Soviet model focused on human capacity building, centralization, increased public expenditures, and collectivization. In these contexts, technical assistance strategies did not necessarily address local needs in various national and sub-national contexts, but rather reflected the existing political ideologies that the two superpowers advanced through international development efforts.

Notwithstanding differences in international development strategies and political ideologies, what both superpowers had in common was the underlying assumption of the inequality of intelligence among the "developed" and "developing" nations. Echoing the nineteenth-century myth of "progress," the development strategies of the superpowers reinforced the "old intellectual hierarchies" (Rancière, 1991: 109) through the division of the world into the knowing and the ignorant, the enlightened and the uninformed, the developed and the developing. According to this logic, people and countries in power were positioned at a (perceived) higher intellectual position than those on the receiving end, enabling them to justify the transfer of expertise from developed to developing countries. It is this presupposition of the inequality of intelligence that framed international development assistance by both the (capitalist) West and the (socialist) East.

And while the Cold War offered some (limited) alternatives in terms of the transferable "expert knowledge," the path towards modernity became reoriented exclusively toward Western ideals of market economy and political democracy after the socialist bloc collapsed in 1989. "Singular Western models" became the main yardstick for international development, while the sight of alternatives—"whether alternative capitalisms, alternative socialisms, or other utopias"—was lost (Burawoy, 1999: 309). In this context, international development efforts focused on identifying "best practices" that could be shared worldwide to help countries move down a linear, predictable path toward political democracy and market economy. Almost exclusively, these "best practices" reflected (neo)liberal ideals that were translated into such globally "travelling policies" as standardized curricula; decentralization, devolution, and privatization of schools; national educational assessment and international testing; and managerialism and rationalization of universities, among others. Backed by scientific data from robust experimental designs and empirically validated studies, international transfer of (Western) "expert" knowledge became a tool not only for solving national educational problems, but also for promoting educational development on a global scale through such initiatives as Education for All (EFA) and the Millennium Development Goals (MDGs). What remained unchallenged, however, was the foundational belief in the superiority of Western "expertise" and the underlying assumption that international development, led by Western "experts," would lead to a better world for all.

Manufacturing Crisis and Demand

While there is no agreement on whether the global spread of (neo)liberal reforms has been consensual or imposed,[1] international "experts" seem to have played an important role in not only identifying educational needs (and thus manufacturing the demand for the reforms), but also delivering the solutions. Commenting on international development in the African context, Samoff (1999) notes that education sector reviews (written by international "experts") appear to be "remarkably similar" in their analysis as well as in the presentation of the solution to the problem (p. 249). Written in a diagnostic style, these reviews identify problems (often expressed through "crisis" narratives) that need to be urgently remedied, thus manufacturing demand for (neo)liberal reforms with a sense of uncontested authority. Although highlighting commonalities of education sector reviews in Africa specifically, the quotation below is equally applicable to post-socialist contexts from Croatia to Kazakhstan to Cambodia:

> African education is in crisis. Governments cannot cope. Quality has deteriorated. Funds are misallocated. Management is poor and administration inefficient. From Mauritania to Madagascar, the recommendations too are similar: reduce the central government role in providing education; decentralize; increase school fees; encourage and assist private schools; reduce direct support to students, especially at tertiary level; introduce double shifts and multi-grade classrooms; assign high priority to instructional materials; favor in-service over pre-service teacher education.
>
> (Samoff, 1999: 250)

Not surprisingly, such education sector reviews produced a perception of a "crisis" situation that required an immediate international assistance, which involved the flow of foreign aid and the transfer of "expert" knowledge. In Central Asia, for example, international experts and agencies insisted that educational systems of Kazakhstan, Kyrgyzstan, Tajikistan, Turkmenistan, and Uzbekistan were approaching a "crisis situation" following the breakdown of the Soviet Union in 1991. This was clearly expressed in the titles of their numerous field reports—*A Generation at Risk: Children in the Central Asian republics of Kazakhstan and Kyrgyzstan* (Asian Development Bank, 1998), *Youth in Central Asia: Losing the new generation* (International Crisis Group, 2003), and *Public Spending on Education in the CIS-7 Countries* (Burnett and Cnobloch, 2003). While the notion of "crisis" had to be manufactured to a certain extent in the Southeast/Central European context to justify an increase in international aid into these countries, an actual crisis was well underway in the Cambodian context as illustrated in such publications as *Anatomy of a Crisis: Education, development, and the state of Cambodia, 1953–1998* (Ayres, 2000) and *Education and Fragility in Cambodia* (IIEP, 2011).[2]

What the rhetoric of "crisis" meant for education systems in the former socialist countries was that schools needed to be normalized—redefined, recuperated, and reformed—usually (but not exclusively) against the prevailing Western models (Silova, 2010, 2011). In this context, the West has been unproblematically presented as the embodiment of progress, whereas the East (and the South) emerged as underdeveloped, chaotic, and undemocratic. More importantly, solutions to the "crisis" situation were presented through the familiar narratives of "progress," "hope," and "salvation," which the West inevitably promised to bring to the newly emerging societies of the post-socialist regions. Following the influx of foreign aid in Cambodia in the 1990s, for example, the narratives of "hope" and "progress" appeared in reports commissioned or authored by the international development agencies: *Rebirth of the Learning Tradition: A case study on the achievements of Education for All in Cambodia* (Prasertsi, 1996), *A New Beginning: Children, primary schools and social change in post-conflict Preah Vihear Province, Cambodia* (Save the Children Norway, 2006), and "Expanding primary education access in Cambodia: 20 years of recovery" (Ratcliffe *et al.*, 2009). Describing the country as undergoing some level of "progress" was thus an attempt to attribute the (perceived) improvement to the very actions of the international development agencies.

As Lindblad and Popkewitz (2004) explain, these narratives of "progress" and "salvation" invoke a "social obligation to rescue those who have fallen outside the narratives of progress" (pp. xx–xxi). Furthermore, the promise of "salvation" for the "developing" post-socialist societies would be in abandoning the socialist past (or any other alternative) and embracing the logic of Western modernity, including the (neo)liberal education reforms. For example, reports from Southeast/Central Europe, the former Soviet Union, and Cambodia discuss "unqualified teachers," as well as a declining status of the teaching profession. In particular, the *Education and Fragility in Cambodia* report (IIEP, 2011) explains the reasons for these ills: "The poor salary, working conditions, and social status accorded to the profession have left many teachers disenchanted and aggrieved" (p. 17). The solutions offered to these problems—whether in Central Asia or Cambodia—revolve around notions of decentralization and deconcentration, whereby the national government passes control and authority to the sub-national and local levels.

In practice, this means a greater emphasis on "new public management," which encourages community-based accountability structures. Additionally, it calls on principals, head teachers, and headmasters to initiate formal accountability structures within their schools. In Cambodia and Central Asia, for example, the emphasis is as much on reducing disincentives (e.g. low teacher salaries) as creating incentives (e.g. performance-based pay) for improving the quality of education (see NEP, 2007; Steiner-Khamsi *et al.*, 2008). More often than not, these incentives are directly connected to teacher competencies in other areas—whether classroom management or teaching/learning methodologies—reflecting particular ideals and ideologies of (neo)liberal reforms. The assumption is that "progress" can be achieved through the right combination of (Western) education policies and practices, which should be diligently enacted by teachers. As Rancière (1991) warns, this logic leads to one outcome: "the integral pedagogization of society— the general infantilization of the individuals that make it up" (p. 133).

In the post-socialist contexts and beyond, the implementation of (neo)liberal education reforms thus entails a total (re)regulation of public education space, including the processes of bureaucratization and technicalization of teachers' work. Left unregulated are spaces outside of public education. And although one may expect the (neo)liberal "logic" to prevail in private education spaces, we argue that this is not necessarily the case. An examination of teachers' experiences in the domain of private tutoring reveals that there is a clear distinction between what is considered to be "good" or "proper" education in public and private education spaces. A closer examination of what happens in this "private" education space can thus reveal important insights into how teachers embrace, modify, or defy (neo)liberal reforms as they cross the boundaries between public (governable) and private (non-governable) education space.

Inside the Private (Tutoring) Space

A constant, multi-directional movement between the "public" and "private" education spaces inevitably creates many contradictions in teachers' lives. On the one hand, teachers work within an environment where user fees, incentive-based performance, and other market-based solutions are routinely used to engender better teaching (as measured by student outcomes). On the other hand, various regulatory schemes and codes of ethics discourage (and frequently forbid) teachers from turning education into a business within the public education space. The division of space into public and private not only separates what can and cannot be governed, but also creates an environment within which those who are governed—in this case, the teachers—internalize some of the very (neo)liberal logic used to order and regulate them, yet use it to pursue their own purposes. In some instances, for example, teachers use private tutoring in uniquely (neo)liberal ways to supplement their salaries with additional income. In other cases, however, they turn the (neo)liberal logic around to "correct" the shortcomings of public education, which they believe are stemming from the (neo)liberal reforms. Finally, and more importantly, teachers use private tutoring to reclaim their professional authority and thus (privately) defy the logic of (neo) liberalism outside the public school realm.

Using Private Tutoring to Supplement Low Salaries

Private tutoring is generally associated with income-generation activities among teachers who seek to supplement their low government salaries (Bray, 2007). The need to supplement salaries is often attributed to dilapidated government institutions, such as non-functioning tax systems, that make it difficult to properly fund public education. However, (neo)liberal policies have encouraged governments to reduce government expenditures on all public services, including education. While recognizing the potential inability of governments to create effective tax structures to pay for services such as public education, it is also necessary to acknowledge the equally important possibility that the lack of education expenditures may be one of the implications of (neo)liberal policies themselves. When education resources are limited and when education is perceived as a commodity, it is not surprising that teachers find private tutoring particularly advantageous.

In the context of Southeast/Central Europe and the former Soviet Union, private tutoring is primarily attributed to declining education expenditures that affect teacher salaries (Silova *et al.*, 2006; Silova, 2009). Immediately following the collapse of the former socialist bloc in 1991, most of the newly independent countries of Eastern Europe and the former Soviet Union experienced significant economic decline, which had a direct impact on education spending.[3] As public expenditure on education declined, private contributions were encouraged by government officials and international experts. Among the most adversely affected have been teachers. According to the studies of private tutoring conducted in 12 countries of Southeast/Central Europe and the former Soviet Union (Silova *et al.*, 2006; Silova, 2009),[4] teacher salaries were below the national wage average in Bosnia and Herzegovina, Croatia, Georgia, Kazakhstan, Kyrgyzstan, Lithuania, Slovakia, Tajikistan, and Ukraine. Although teachers' salaries were above the national wage average in the remaining countries, they were actually below the minimum subsistence level in Azerbaijan (69 percent of the minimum subsistence level) and barely exceeding it in Georgia (at 108 percent of the minimum subsistence level; Silova *et al.*, 2006; Silova. 2009). In many countries, teacher salaries declined so dramatically that they could no longer provide for average-sized families.

Similarly, there has been a broad consensus among Cambodian educators, union leaders, administrators, and society in general that teachers' salaries are insufficient to cover their expenses (Benveniste *et al.*, 2008). In 2007, for example, a primary teacher's base salary was US$44 per month, which made it difficult (if not impossible) for many teachers to afford the basic necessities of food, housing, and health care, as well as supporting any children or elderly family members (Benveniste *et al.*, 2008: 59).[5] Commenting on the implications of the "unlivable" wage," one teacher explained that her concern about the survival of her family became so great that it was difficult to focus on teaching: "Only [my] body comes to school, but [my] soul stays at home." This reflects both the overall economic decline and scarce allocation of government resources for education. In particular, education expenditure as a percentage of GDP constituted 2.3 percent in Cambodia, which is significantly below the world's average of 4.8 percent (European Commission, 2012). Despite the increases in education spending as a proportion of total government spending since the 1990s,[6] the percentage of recurrent expenditures devoted to teacher salaries had actually decreased from 78 to 60 percent between 1997 and 2005. As the report commissioned by the World Bank points out, "this is low in comparison with both developed and developing economies where the wage share ranges between 70–80 per cent" (Benveniste *et al.*, 2008: 74).

In both contexts, underpaid teachers have sought supplementary income in order to survive. In Cambodia, the majority of teachers (nearly 70 percent) have been supplementing their incomes by giving private lessons, driving motorbike taxis, working at the markets, farming, or in other ways (Benveniste *et al.*, 2008: 38). Similarly, teachers in Central Asia have been surviving by engaging in petty trading, farming, teaching in more than one school, and/or taking other jobs in addition to mainstream schooling (UNICEF, 2001: 80–1). To some extent, private tutoring has helped underpaid teachers to re-establish their economic independence by providing opportunities to generate additional income. For example, private tutoring is a common second occupation among Cambodian teachers, especially in urban primary schools (42 percent at the primary level and 87 percent at the lower secondary level). Earnings from private tutoring can represent approximately two thirds of the monthly average base salary with basic allowances (Benveniste *et al.*, 2008: 38). Similarly, more than half of the students

(64 percent) surveyed in Southeast/Central Europe and the former Soviet Union reported engaging in private tutoring activities (Silova *et al.*, 2006; Silova, 2009). The scope of private tutoring varied by country, with over 80 percent of sampled students in the Caucasus (Azerbaijan and Georgia) receiving tutoring, and below 60 percent of sampled students in the Balkans (Bosnia and Herzegovina), Slovakia, and Kyrgyzstan. In the context of market-driven reforms, many teachers have thus eagerly adopted the logic of "service provision," using private tutoring as a key income-generation activity (Silova and Bray, 2006).

What is important, however, is that private tutoring has been primarily associated with economic *survival*, and not necessarily profit making among teachers. For example, the majority of the respondents (63 percent) in the 2006 study agreed or strongly agreed with the statement that one of the main reasons for private tutoring was for teachers to receive additional financial income (Silova *et al.*, 2006). The proportion of the respondents agreeing with this statement was larger in the three countries with particularly difficult economic conditions— Mongolia (74 percent), Ukraine (74 percent), and Azerbaijan (71 percent). A study of private tutoring in Romania also confirmed that the majority of teachers regretfully referred to private tutoring in terms of "survival" and "making ends meet" (Popa, 2007: 136). Interviews with teachers interviewed in other geographic contexts echo similar sentiments:

> [It is] difficult in Cambodia: If we talk about [teacher] salary, it is low. Therefore, private tutoring must be pushed. It *must* happen.
>
> (Cambodian teacher)

> If my salary was sufficient to meet my basic needs, which are really modest, I would gladly stop this slave tutoring work.
>
> (Azerbaijani teacher)

Using Private Tutoring to Address the Perceived Shortcomings of Official Curricula

In addition to economic reasons, teachers engage in private tutoring to address the perceived shortcomings of public education. These shortcomings are generally associated with the implementation of (neo)liberal education reforms, including the reduction of education expenditures, the introduction of double- or triple-shift schooling, or the standardization of curriculum. Changes in structural issues such as school-day length, class size, and curriculum requirements thus generate dissatisfaction with public education and create the need for private tutoring. For example, the introduction of double- and triple-shift schooling in Cambodia during the 1990s entailed the reduction of the school day to 4–5 hours.[7] According to Cambodian teachers, this was simply not enough to cover the required curriculum. As one teacher explained, "If we teach for quality, students would fall behind the official curriculum; but if we teach to keep up with the curriculum, students would not receive quality education." Similarly, parents believe that school days are too short to cover the entire curriculum, explaining that "complete" education thus spans both public schools and private tutoring lessons: "You learn 50 percent in a government school and 50 percent in private tutoring." Despite the few reported cases of teachers purposefully "slowing down" content delivery to create a market for private tutoring (Bray, 1999: 55), the reduction of the school day nonetheless leads to a perceived need for more instructional time simply to provide requisite coverage of the national curriculum (Brehm and Silova, 2012).

Similarly, curriculum changes introduced in Southeast/Central Europe and the former Soviet Union since the 1990s were generally associated with an "overloaded" curriculum, which was a commonly criticized feature of Soviet schooling inherited in the post-Soviet context (Pitt and Pavlova, 2001; DeYoung *et al.*, 2006). As new knowledge and skills became desirable during the post-socialist period, new subjects (such as civics, information and communication technologies, and foreign languages) were added to the existing curriculum without major revisions of the existing curriculum content (DeYoung *et al.*, 2006). As a result, curricula became even more overloaded in terms of the number of academic subjects, while the hours spent on some of these subjects (e.g. history, physical education, or music) became significantly reduced. Furthermore, curricula remained largely scientific and subject-driven, with the primary focus on teaching facts rather than developing skills that would allow students to apply knowledge in various situations (Bagdasarova and Ivanov, 2009). Reflecting on curricula changes in her school, one Romanian teacher explained, "the curriculum is jam-packed with too much knowledge ... [leaving] no time to teach everything in my classes" (quoted in Popa, 2007: 153).

In addition to an "overloaded" curriculum, teachers were also expected to radically change their teaching styles. Teacher-centered instruction went out of fashion, while child-centered learning (such as collaborative learning and project-based group work) became increasingly encouraged by government official and international agencies. And although numerous in-service teacher-training programs took place, what the international "experts" did not foresee was that many of these "new" methodologies were not necessarily appropriate for the unique contexts of Southeast/Central Europe, the former Soviet Union, or Cambodia. Apart from a few "islands of innovations" (Niyozov, 2006: 224), often funded by international development agencies, many schools faced major difficulties in implementing new reforms. Commenting on education reform in Southeast/Central Europe and the former Soviet Union, a UNICEF report (2007) vividly summarized the local frustrations with the never-ending education reforms:

> Active learning is not an option in a small classroom where children are crammed three to every two-seater desk and the teacher has barely enough space to stand near a scratchy blackboard. Self-directed, project-based learning is not an option in a school without an atlas, a dictionary, an encyclopedia or room for children to work, or where homes have no books. Where two or even three shifts a day share the same classrooms, teachers cannot display work on walls and children cannot store work in progress in their desks ... Where Ministers and their agendas change every six months, where

several parallel reforms descend on schools at once, where some prestigious schools are declared "pilot" or "model" and receive computers or science labs while others have no running water, reform becomes no more than externally imposed, piecemeal change, a source of fear and unfairness, rather than renewal and opportunity.

(p. 48)

In this context, it is not surprising that many education stakeholders became concerned with the quality of education in public schools, thus turning to private tutoring to compensate for what they thought public schools could no longer provide. In Central Asia, the majority of surveyed private tutoring users reported that they took private tutoring because the school curriculum was overloaded (61 percent) and because they believed that school curricula did not cover everything required on university entrance examinations (58.5 percent). Furthermore, the surveyed students explained that they took private tutoring because they "wanted to learn more" (72 percent) (Silova, 2009). Of 12 countries participating in the private tutoring surveys (Silova *et al.*, 2006; Silova, 2009), an overwhelming majority (over 80 percent) agreed or strongly agreed with the statement, "the quality of mainstream education system should be such that no one would need private tutoring." By implication, decisions of students to take private tutoring may indicate their lack of satisfaction with the quality of education in mainstream schools. For example, almost 60 percent of respondents in Azerbaijan and over 50 percent in Georgia, Kyrgyzstan, and Tajikistan—the countries with the largest scope and highest intensity of private tutoring— believed that private tutoring was "the only way to get a high quality education."

Using Private Tutoring to Regain Professional Authority

Finally, there is evidence that teachers use private tutoring as a way to reclaim autonomy of their classroom because it has been overregulated—albeit decentralized—by the government. In this context, private tutoring presents a "private" education space, which is outside of government regulations and international "expert" advice. It is an education space where teachers themselves have the authority to determine what is "good" education for their students. A study on private tutoring in Southeast/Central Europe and the former Soviet Union (Silova *et al.*, 2006) highlighted that private tutoring presents an opportunity for teachers to engage in more innovative and individualized learning compared to what they are expected to do in mainstream schools. For example, some teachers argued that private tutoring enabled them to meet individual student needs more compared to their efforts in public schools. One teacher in Poland offered a stark comparison of the "public" and "private" education space: "a large number of students, little time, lots of material, no time for what's really the most important—developing a passion in students" (Silova *et al.*, 2006: 49). Other teachers added that private tutoring lessons allowed for more individual contact between students and teachers, as well as more opportunities for building students' self-esteem, developing their talents, and closing the existing educational achievement gaps.

Similarly, the existing research on private tutoring in Cambodia reveals that teachers use different instructional materials and methodologies to teach in private tutoring classes (Brehm and Silova, 2012; Brehm *et al.*, 2012, Brehm, 2013a). In particular, teaching materials are perceived to be of a higher quality than the government textbooks. Furthermore, these materials are chosen by teachers themselves to meet the specific needs of their students. One student elaborated on her education experience in public schools and private tutoring by noting the use of different teaching/learning materials: "In government classes teachers follow school textbooks, whereas in private tutoring teachers find lessons and exercises from many different sources." Importantly, students participating in private tutoring noted that curriculum content is often strategically split between classes in public schools and private tutoring lessons. When asked about the differences, students repeatedly explained that public school classes were primarily reserved for learning theory, whereas private tutoring allowed for practical application of theoretical concepts. In students' experiences, teachers used both more and better-quality examples in private tutoring lessons than in government school classes. The major distinction, however, revolved around the idea of splitting curricula into theory, which is typically taught during public school hours, and practical application, which is available during private tutoring lessons. One student gave a detailed description of how some teachers split curriculum content between public schools and private tutoring:

> Government class is mostly about giving introductions, theories, and a little bit of practice, while private tutoring has a lot of problem solving and practice … However, having private tutoring alone is difficult too … because practice alone is not enough. Learning theoretical introductions during school hours and practicing applications during private tutoring lessons is also necessary.

Additionally, we have observed teachers using different teaching/learning methodologies in public schools and private tutoring classes. During private tutoring lessons, for example, teachers generally use more one-on-one teaching strategies, while frequently avoiding group work. These pedagogical differences highlight the reality that the cost barriers to entry in private tutoring keep private tutoring classes small, allowing teachers the freedom to work with their students in new ways with new material. Teachers are also able to adjust their teaching methods depending on the student and have a greater ability to work with individual students, something that is impossible in public school classes where over 50 students sit in a 7 by 8-meter room. According to students, private tutoring lessons provide more opportunities for independent work and problem solving, whereas government school classes tend to group students by mixed ability to solve problems in groups more frequently. Similarly, high-ability students are less likely to help the teacher during whole-class instruction in private tutoring lessons, thus allowing more time for their own learning. Commenting on the class size, several students stated that private tutoring lessons also encouraged more active student participation in the learning process:

Attending private tutoring makes me brave and able to ask questions and learn better.

(Cambodian student)

Private tutoring classes are smaller and it is easier to ask questions.

(Cambodian student)

With so many students in government school classes, I sometimes feel shy to ask questions. This is not the case in private tutoring lessons.

(Cambodian student)

Overall, the participating students and parents unanimously agreed that private tutoring was a "good" and "necessary" part of the education system. None of the participants discussed private tutoring in negative terms; instead, the benefits of private tutoring were repeatedly discussed in terms of immediate academic success, future studies, or employment opportunities. As some students argued, attending private tutoring would help them "reach [their] goal in life," "get to high school," or "open up job opportunities." The majority of students emphasized that it is through private tutoring that they can acquire "all knowledge." In other words, the vast majority of the respondents believed that private tutoring was a necessary component of the education system without which complete (quality) education would be unattainable. More importantly, both Cambodian students and parents praised teachers for their efforts to maintain quality education through the extension of schooling into the "private" space.

What the preceding discussion reveals is that teachers used private tutoring as a mechanism to raise their professional status, which was undermined by the aggressive implementation of (neo)liberal reforms, including the increasing centralized control over school curricula, a growing emphasis on academic testing, or mounting demands for accountability. Stripped of their professional authority in the public school classroom, many teachers associated private tutoring with "the very notion of professionalism," including its "technical culture, a commitment to service ethic, and autonomy in planning and implementing their practice" (Popa and Acedo, 2006: 98). In other words, private tutoring served as a mechanism to maintain control over what teachers themselves believed constitutes "best practice." To some extent, it also became a space to challenge the globally "travelling" reforms and, perhaps, avoid these reforms altogether. Commenting on the rise of private tutoring in Romania, Popa and Acedo (2006) explain:

We interpret the process of private tutoring in terms of empowerment in an upbeat rather than defeatist fashion. We see this ("illegal") process of tutoring students as a little victory for teachers as individuals and as an occupational group, albeit on a minor scale, by offering an alternative to union struggles and electoral politics as a model: it creates some kind of protected zone.

(p. 109)

The Double Entendre of Privatization

The rise of private tutoring in post-socialist contexts offers a unique window into the complex nexus between (neo)liberal policy discourses, globalization, and local visions of education reform. In particular, there is an image of global policy "experts" and national governments pressing (neo)liberal reforms down into national education systems. These reforms—including standardization of curricula, outcomes-based accountability measures, decentralization and privatization of schools, and the introduction of national educational assessment and international testing—have contributed to de-professionalization of the teaching profession. As teaching becomes increasingly prescribed, regulated, individualized, and controlled through the introduction of (neo)liberal reforms, many educators become concerned about losing their professional authority in schools. At the same time, however, there is also evidence of teachers actively engaging with globalizing processes—as illustrated by the example of private tutoring discussed above—to press back against (neo)liberal reforms in unexpected and innovative ways.

As the examination of private tutoring practices in Southeast/Central Europe, the former Soviet Union, and Cambodia reveals, teachers have simultaneously embraced and defied the logic of (neo)liberal market-driven education reforms. On the one hand, private tutoring precisely reflects the logic of the market, turning education into a commodity, while contributing to the valorization of educational services. On the other hand, the non-public education spaces where private tutoring lessons are held enable teachers to reclaim their authority by defying some of the (neo)liberal education policy reforms implemented in public schools. In private tutoring lessons, teachers are able to use teacher-centered teaching methods, materials outside of the prescribed national curriculum, and not (necessarily) concentrate on national examinations. This skillful negotiation of what it means to support "private" education spaces creates a double entendre of privatization. While private tutoring itself is the outcome of the (neo)liberal privatization of public education, it is at the same time a "private" space where local knowledge trumps international "expertise." In a way, the private education space created by the international development industry has enabled teachers to redraw professional boundaries, allowing teachers to (privately) pursue their own visions of "good" education, while at the same resisting the Western educational reforms and "best practices."

A better understanding of how teachers cross the boundaries of the public/private (neo)liberal educational landscape opens possibilities for theorizing "private" space as a site of resistance and possibility, illustrating that local knowledge has not necessarily been undermined and de-professionalized but rather has been displaced from the governable space of public education into the private sphere. Despite being a "protected zone" from international regulation and national control, however, the reliance on the private education space has important occupational consequences. While strategically redrawing the occupational boundaries of post-socialist education space, teachers nevertheless continue to make individual choices to "survive" economically and professionally by engaging in private tutoring activities. In particular, the (neo)liberal logic of individualism offers a new territory for teacher professionalism to thrive; yet it remains an individual endeavor and therefore seriously affects occupationally anchored collectivity of teachers in the context of (neo)liberal globalization.

While recognizing complications that these new arrangements entail (for instance, the embrace of private space affects the social contract between governments and citizens; see Brehm, forthcoming 2013b), we nevertheless argue that these "private" education spaces play an important role in both pursuing local education interests and challenging the hegemony of (neo)liberal reforms. Similar to Sassen's (1991) argument about the "global city," private tutoring could be viewed as a de-nationalized national space, where global flows "touch down" in national territories and are serviced by local actors, but in ways that are oriented toward sustaining local visions of "quality" education and "good" life. As these visions flourish in "private" education spaces, they simultaneously challenge the hegemony of (neo)liberal reforms. The urgent task for researchers is thus to uncover the complicated "private" education spaces and examine how teachers redraw the boundaries between the global and the local (as well as the public and the private) in ways that enable them to reclaim professionalism and, equally important, redefine the global (neo)liberal agenda itself.

Notes

1   See, for example, the world culture debate in comparative education.
2   Cambodia experienced nearly three decades of civil unrest beginning in the 1970s, which resulted in genocide under the rule of Democratic Kampuchea (known as the Khmer Rouge).
3   While real public spending on education did not substantially change in some countries of Eastern and Central Europe (e.g. Poland, Lithuania), it fell by 77 percent in Azerbaijan and 94 percent in Georgia during the first part of the 1990s (Micklewright, 2000: 21; UNICEF, 1998). In some countries of Eastern Europe and the Baltics, trends in real spending were offset by declining numbers of children, so that per student expenditure was not affected (Micklewright, 2000). However, this was not the case in the Caucasus and Central Asia, which experienced population growth during that period of time (Micklewright, 2000). By the end of the 2000s, education spending as a percentage of GDP varied greatly across the region, with the majority of countries in the study spending around 4–6 percent of GDP on education (an average for OECD countries), while Azerbaijan, Georgia, and Kazakhstan spent below 3 percent of GDP (UNESCO Institute for Statistics, 2009).
4   The first study, *Education in a Hidden Marketplace: Monitoring of private tutoring* (Silova *et al.*, 2006), was conducted in 2004–5 and examined the scope, nature, and implications of private tutoring in nine former socialist countries, including Azerbaijan, Bosnia and Herzegovina, Croatia, Georgia, Lithuania, Mongolia, Poland, Slovakia, and Ukraine. The second study, *Private Supplementary Tutoring in Central Asia: New opportunities and burdens* (Silova, 2009), was conducted a year later (2005–6) and extended the geographical scope of the research to Kazakhstan, Kyrgyzstan, and Tajikistan in Central Asia. Follow-up data were collected in 2007–8 to examine various policy contexts and the changing government responses to private tutoring in the 12 countries in the study.
5   According to the World Bank report (Benveniste *et al.*, 2008), salaries increased after 16 years of experience by around 20 percent and after 28 years they increased by about 30 percent of the initial base salary. Salary levels also depend on the grade/subject

taught and the location of the school. For example, senior teachers in the sixth grade can earn US$80–100 per month (personal communication, March 31, 2011).
6   In Cambodia, government recurrent expenditures on education increased from approximately 13 percent in 2000 to nearly 18.5 percent in 2002 (European Commission, 2012). Between 2003 and 2007, the overall budget for education increased 29.5 percent in real terms, leading to an increased educational recurrent expenditure as a percentage of total government spending (from 11 percent in 1999 to 19.2 percent in 2007 back to 16.4 percent in 2009; as cited in Engel, 2011).
7   In 2005, approximately 81 percent of primary and 41 percent of lower secondary schools held two shifts (Benveniste *et al.*, 2008).

References

Apple, M. (2006) *Educating the Right Way: Markets, standards, god, and inequality*, New York: Routledge.
Apple, M. (2009) *Global Crises, Social Justice, and Education*, New York: Routledge.
Arnove, R.F. and Torres, A. (2007) *Comparative Education: The dialectic between the global and the local*, New York: Rowman and Littlefield.
Asian Development Bank (ADB) (1998) *A Generation at Risk: Children in the Central Asian republics of Kazakhstan and Kyrgyzstan*, Manila: ADB.
Ayres, D.M. (2000) *Anatomy of a Crisis: Education, development, and the state of Cambodia, 1953–1998*, Honolulu: University of Hawai'i Press.
Bagdasarova, N. and Ivanov, A. (2009) Private tutoring in Kyrgyzstan, in I. Silova (ed.) *Private Supplementary Tutoring in Central Asia: New opportunities and burdens*, Paris: UNESCO International Institute for Educational Planning (IIEP), pp. 119–42.
Benveniste, L., Marshall, J. and Araujo, M.C. (2008) *Teaching in Cambodia*, Washington, DC: World Bank.
Bray, M. (1999) *The Private Costs of Public Schooling: Household and community financing of primary education in Cambodia*, Paris: UNESCO International Institute for Educational Planning (IIEP).
Bray, M. (2007) *The Shadow Education System: Private tutoring and its implications for planners*, 2nd edn, Paris: UNESCO International Institute for Educational Planning (IIEP).
Brehm, W.C. (2013a) *Education, Equity, and Development in Cambodia: All education for some?* Submitted for publication by Gary Kawaguchi, Pannasastra University of Cambodia.
Brehm, W.C. (2013b) The post-conflict social contract in Cambodia: the effects of private tutoring in public education, *Globalisation, Education and Societies*.
Brehm, W.C. and Silova, I. (In press 2013) Hidden privatization of public education in Cambodia: equity implications of private tutoring, *Journal for Educational Research Online*.
Brehm, W.C., Silova, I. and Tuot, M. (2012) *The Public–Private Education System in Cambodia: The impact and implications of complementary tutoring*, Budapest: Open Society Institute.
Burawoy, M. (1999) Afterword, in M. Burawoy and K. Verdery (eds) *Uncertain Transition: Ethnographies of change in the postsocialist world*, Lanham, MD: Rowman and Littlefield, pp. 301–12.
Burnett, N. and Cnobloch, R. (2003) *Public Spending on Education in the CIS-7 Countries: The hidden crisis*. Available at www.cis7.org (accessed September 10, 2012).
Dale, R. (2000) Globalization and education: demonstrating "common world educational culture" or locating "globally structured educational agenda"? *Educational Theory*, 50(4): 427–48.

DeYoung, A., Reeves, M. and Valyaeva, K. (2006) *Surviving Transition? Case studies of schools and schooling in the Kyrgyz Republic since independence*, Greenwich, CT: Information Age Publishing.

Engel, J. (2011) *Rebuilding Basic Education in Cambodia: Establishing a more effective development partnership*, working paper, London: Overseas Development Institute.

Epstein, M. (1995) *After the Future: The paradoxes of postmodernism and contemporary Russian culture* (introduction by A. Miller-Pogacar, trans.), Amherst, MA: Massachusetts University Press.

European Commission (2012) *Analysis of the Continuous Decline of MoEYS Recurrent Budget Share in Recent Years*, presentation at the EDUCAM meeting, Phnom Penh, Cambodia, February 10.

Foucault, M. (1986) What is enlightment?, in P. Rabinow (ed.) *The Foucault Reader*, Harmondsworth: Penguin Books.

Gautherin, J. (1993) Marc-Antoine Jullien ("Jullien De Paris") (1775–1848), *Prospects: The Quarterly Review of Comparative Education*, 23(3/4): 757–73.

Ginsburg, M. (1996) Professionalism or politics as a model for educators' work and lives, *Educational Research Journal*, 11(2): 133–46.

Holmes, B. (1981) *Comparative Education: Some considerations of method*, London: George Allen and Unwin.

International Crisis Group (2003) *Youth in Central Asia: Losing the new generation*, Osh/ Brussels: ICG.

International Institute for Educational Planning (IIEP) (2011) *Education and Fragility in Cambodia*, Paris: UNESCO.

Lawn, M. (1989) Being caught in schoolwork: the possibilities of research in teachers' work, in W. Carr (ed.) *Quality in Teaching: Arguments for a reflective profession*, Lewes: Falmer Press, pp. 147–62.

Lindblad, S. and Popkewitz, T.S. (2004) *Educational Restructuring: International perspectives on traveling policies*, Greenwich, CT: Information Age Publishing.

Lingard, B. (1995) Rearticulating relevant voices in reconstructing teacher education, *South Australian Educational Leader*, 6(7): 1–12.

Micklewright, J. (2000) *Education, Inequality, and Transition*, Innocenti Working Papers, Economic and Social Policy Series no. 74, Florence: UNICEF Innocenti Research Center.

NEP (2007) *The Impact of Informal School Fees on Family Expenditures*, Philippines: ASPBAE.

Niyozov, S. (2006) Challenges to education in Tajikistan: the need for research-based solutions, in J. Earnest and D. Treagust (eds) *Education Reform in Societies in Transition: International perspectives*, Rotterdam: Sense Publishers, pp. 211–32.

Noah, H.J. and Eckstein, M.A. (1969) *Towards a Science of Comparative Education*, New York: Macmillan.

Parpart, J.L. (1995) Deconstructing the development "expert": gender development and the "vulnerable groups," in M. Marchand and J.L. Parpart (eds) *Feminism, Postmodernism, Development*, London and New York: Routledge, pp. 221–43.

Pitt, J. and Pavlova, M. (2001) Pedagogy in transition: from labour training to humanistic technology education in Russia, in S. Webber and I. Liikanen (eds) *Education and Civic Culture in Post-communist Countries*, Hampshire: Palgrave Macmillan, pp. 231–47.

Popa, S. (2007) *Defensible Spaces: Ideologies of professionalism and teachers' work in the Romanian private tutoring system*, unpublished doctoral dissertation, Pittsburgh, PA: University of Pittsburgh.

Popa, S. and Acedo, C. (2006) Redefining professionalism: Romanian secondary education teachers and the private tutoring system, *International Journal of Educational
Development*, 26: 98–110.

Prasertsri, S. (1996) *Rebirth of the Learning Tradition: A case study on the achievements of
Education for All in Cambodia*, Phnom Penh: UNESCO.

Rancière, J. (1991) *The Ignorant Schoolmaster: Five lessons in intellectual emancipation*,
Stanford, CA: Stanford University Press.

Ratcliffe, M., Patch, J. and Quinn, D. (2009) Expanding primary education access in
Cambodia: 20 years of recovery, in S. Nicolai (ed.) *Opportunities for Change: Education
innovation and reform during and after conflict*, Paris: UNESCO.

Rizvi, F. and Lingard, B. (2010) *Globalizing Education Policy*, New York: Routledge.

Robertson, S. (2007) "Remaking the world": neo-liberalism and the transformation of
education and teachers' labour, in L. Weis and M. Compton (eds) *The Global Assault
on Teachers, Teaching and their Unions*, New York: Palgrave, pp. 11–30.

Samoff, J. (1999) Education sector analysis in Africa: limited national control and even less
national ownership, *International Journal of Educational Development*, 19: 249–72.

Sassen, S. (1991) Spatialities and temporalities of the global: elements for a theorization,
Public Culture, 12(1): 215–32.

Save the Children Norway (2006) *A New Beginning: Children, primary schools and social
change in post-conflict Preah Vihear Province, Cambodia*. Available at www.norad.no/
en/tools-and-publications/publications/publication?key=138656 (accessed January 9,
2012).

Silova, I. (ed.) (2009) *Private Supplementary Tutoring in Central Asia: New opportunities
and burdens*, Paris: UNESCO Institute of International Educational Planning (IIEP).

Silova, I. (ed.) (2010) *Post-socialism is Not Dead: (Re)reading the global in comparative
education*, Bingley: Emerald.

Silova, I. (ed.) (2011) *Globalization on the Margins: Education and post-socialist transformations in Central Asia*, Charlotte, NC: Information Age.

Silova, I. and Bray, M. (2006) The context: societies and education in the post-socialist
transformation, in I. Silova, V. Budiene, and M. Bray (eds) *Education in a Hidden
Marketplace: Monitoring of private tutoring*, Budapest: Education Support Program
(ESP) of the Open Society Institute, pp. 41–60.

Silova, I. and Steiner-Khamsi, G. (eds) (2008) *How NGOs React: Globalization and education reform in the Caucasus, Central Asia and Mongolia*, Bloomfield, CT: Kumarian
Press.

Silova, I., Budiene, V. and Bray, M. (eds) (2006) *Education in a Hidden Marketplace:
Monitoring of private tutoring*, Budapest: Education Support Program (ESP) of the
Open Society Institute.

Sobe, N.W. (2002) Travel, social science and the making of nations in early 19th century
comparative education, in M. Caruso and H.-E. Tenorth (eds) *Internationalisation:
Comparing educational systems and semantics*, Frankfurt am Main: Peter Lang,
pp. 141–66.

Steiner-Khamsi, G. (2006) The development turn in comparative education, *European
Education: Issues and Studies*, 8(3): 19–47.

Steiner-Khamsi, G. and Stolpe, I. (2006) *Educational Import in Mongolia: Local encounters with global forces*, New York: Palgrave Macmillan.

Steiner-Khamsi, G., Harris-Van Keuren, C., Silova, I. and Chachkhiani, K. (2008) *The
Pendulum of Decentralization and Recentralization Reforms: Its impact on teacher
salaries in the Caucasus, Central Asia, and Mongolia* (background paper for UNESCO
Global Monitoring Report 2009).

Torres, A.C. (ed.) (2009) *Education and Neoliberal Globalization*, New York: Routledge.

UNESCO Institute for Statistics (2009) *Global Education Digest*, Quebec: UNESCO Institute for Statistics.

UNICEF (1998) *Education for All? The MONEE project*, Regional Monitoring Report No. 5, Florence: Innocenti Research Center.

UNICEF (2001) *A Decade in Transition*, Florence: UNICEF Innocenti Research Center.

UNICEF (2007) *Education for Some More Than Others? A regional study on education in Central and Eastern Europe and the Commonwealth of Independent States*, Geneva: UNICEF Regional Office for Central and Eastern Europe and the Commonwealth of Independent States.

Part II

Remaking Educational Formations and the National Education Space

5 Teachers' Work, Denationalisation and Transformations in the Field of Symbolic Control

A Comparative Account

Susan L. Robertson

Introduction

Currently there is unprecedented attention being directed at the 'quality' of school teachers in education systems around the world, and the part they should play in developing globally competitive knowledge-based economies (see OECD, 2001, 2005, 2009; Barber and Mourshed, 2007; Mourshed *et al.*, 2010; Bill & Melinda Gates Foundation, 2010a, 2010b; Bruns *et al.*, 2011; World Bank Group, 2011a; MacBeath, 2012). In a series of short videos featuring 'performers' and 'reformers' in education, the Organisation for Economic Co-operation and Development (OECD), in collaboration with global education consultancy firm, Pearson Education, profiles various aspects of what it regards as 'successful' teacher policies in countries as diverse as Singapore, Finland, Poland and Brazil. Yet closer scrutiny of the 'key facts' that are presented for these countries (for instance, the percentage GNP spent on education, teaching time, the presence of standards and accountability systems) suggests there is little in common regarding shared practices, raising questions about precisely what lessons are to be learned by whom.

The global consultancy firm, McKinsey & Company, sells its own version of what makes a top performing system and the part that teachers play in this. In two reports released in 2007 and 2010 on the best performing school systems, they point to studies conducted in the US, arguing that: 'the performance gap between students assigned three effective teachers in a row, and those assigned three ineffective teachers in a row, was 49 percentile points' (Barber and Mourshed, 2007: 12). This leads the McKinsey & Company authors to conclude that 'the main variation in student learning at school is the quality of the teachers' (p. 12), and from there to propose a significant injection of teacher professional development. The World Bank, too, has made equally strong claims regarding what they describe as the poor accountability of teachers in education systems, and the consequences this has for education and development. Their proposed solution? The implementation of policies that reshape the conditions of teacher employment, to include payment by results and shorter-term contracts.

This explosion in teacher policy commentary and initiatives has led one observer to note that, finally, teachers have made it on to the education policy agenda (Novoa, 2011). This new visibility for teachers ought to be welcomed, especially as in many countries teachers have confronted limited opportunities to place their concerns on the table. This is because of the dominance of neo-liberal policies which, beginning in the 1980s: (1) silenced teachers through arguments for school choice to overcome 'provider capture' (see Buchanan and Tullock, 1962; Buchanan and Wagner, 1977; Chubb and Moe, 1990); (2) placed learners, standards and accountability at the heart of the education enterprise (Hursh, 2005; Mulderrig, 2008; Sahlberg, 2007); (3) curtailed teachers' professional discretion and devalued teachers' expertise (Cochran-Smith, 2006); (4) limited the role of teacher unions (Stevenson, 2007); and (5) demonised teachers through negative media representations (Goldstein, 2011). Low-income countries have faced their own problems with ensuring quality classroom teachers; for instance, in Sub-Saharan Africa, HIV-AIDS has significantly reduced the numbers of teachers available to teach (Bennell, 2005), while Education for All policies have expanded access for learners and large classes for teachers (GMR, 2009). Such policies have particularly created new challenges in recruiting and retaining high-quality teachers within the system (see Zeichner, 2003; Compton and Weiner, 2008; MacBeath, 2012).

However, in making teachers visible it is evident this is no straightforward case of rehabilitation. To begin with, teachers appear as both villains and heroes in this new unfolding education policy drama: villains, as they are regarded as having failed students and their learning; heroes, as they are positioned as single-handedly (albeit with strong stage direction from the international agencies) able to turn around ailing international student performance scores and as a consequence set national economies on the path to economic growth. Making teachers visible means modernising teacher policies and practices to realise top-performing students fit for knowledge-based economies (OECD, 2005; Bruns *et al.*, 2011).

Yet it is the significantly expanded activity of a small group of international agencies, global education consulting firms and corporate philanthropic foundations, in the reframing and implementing of teacher policy agendas and governance tools, that is particularly striking and at the heart of this chapter. Not only does this signal a recalibration in the relationship between national governments and global agencies over the determination of teacher policy, but it raises the equally important question of how best to understand such developments within wider processes of globalisation. Like others in this collection, I will be drawing upon the work of Saskia Sassen (2003, 2006) and her arguments around the denationalisation of processes deep inside national territories and institutional domains – processes that are often ignored in many accounts of globalisation in favour of the more obvious. As she argues: 'When the social sciences focus on globalisation, it is typically not on these types of practices and dynamics but rather on the self-evident global scale' (Sassen, 2003: 2), such as the role of the International Monetary Fund (IMF), or the rise of the World Trade Organization (WTO). By denationalisation, Sassen is seeking to capture the ways in which processes that are 'localized in national, indeed subnational settings … involve transboundary networks and formations connecting multiple local or "national" processes and actors, or involve the recurrence of particular issues or dynamics in a growing number of countries' (Sassen, 2003: 1–2). Furthermore, not only are national states being transformed as they confront new geographies of globalising power, but there are 'new emergent privatised forms of authority for governing a range of specialised domains, and the circulation of private utility logics deep inside the public domain' (Sassen, 2006: 224).

For teachers whose work and workplaces have historically been sub-nationally organised, it is imperative that we examine the complex ways these scales are important sites for globalisation. Specifically, I will be exploring the ways in which the invocation of a global imaginary of shared risk and future, the emergence of new forms of transboundary relations, the relationally and interconnected nature of globalising teacher learning, and new forms of private authority, are characteristics of the globalising of teacher policies and practices. In order to examine the pattern and scope of these processes my analysis will be diachronic and synchronic. By diachronic I mean a historical approach that aims to register epochal changes. To this end, I briefly look back to an earlier phase of the global governance of teachers' work – from the 1960s to1990 – and the role in this of global agencies such as the International Labour Organization (ILO), United Nations Educational, Scientific and Cultural Organization (UNESCO) and the World Bank. By synchronic, I mean an examination of two political projects, the OECD's *Teaching and Learning International Survey* (TALIS), launched in 2007, and the World Bank's *SABER-Teachers*, launched in 2010, and the ways in which they seek to enrol national and sub-national sites in the globalising of teacher policy (World Bank, 2011b). Through the use of Bernstein's (1990, 2000) concepts of 'field of symbolic control', 'classification' and 'framing', as conceptual resources for identifying shifts in the nature of power and control, I chart the nature and extent of the denationalisation of teachers' work, the consequences for teachers as professionals, and how these processes might be contested. Finally, I wish to say something about my own positioning in this chapter – as an English-speaking Anglo-Saxon. The danger here is to offer a western, northern reading of the world of teacher policy, and in doing so, over-read and overdetermine their global influence. This is neither my intention, nor, I hope, the main outcome, though I recognise the dangers. Rather, I hope to direct attention to processes that are under-studied because they are being strategically rescaled and reframed, and to highlight the ways in which globalisation projects and processes are necessarily contingent, empirically dependent, and open to contestation.

The (Global) Governing of Teachers' Work – A Diachronic Account

Governing is a pedagogical relationship both in the broadest of senses of 'a fundamental social context through which cultural reproduction-production takes place' (Bernstein, 2000: 3), and, in its more narrow sense, of a pedagogical practice involving teachers and learners. Dale (2008) makes a similar point when he says:

> very basically, education is always part of what I call 'the social contract', the
> political goals of the wider society, its hegemonic project, to use a different

terminology. I shall refer to the way education is organised to make its contribution to the social contract as the ontology of governance … and that governance always has a pedagogic element.

(p. 1)

Governance as pedagogy refers to the consequences of the nature and form of the governance of education for identities and their social relations (Dale, 2008: 5). In examining the policies and programmes of the global agencies with regard to teachers and their work, we can also see a concern for governing in both these senses.

Three theoretical concepts from the work of Bernstein will be used to develop my analysis of transformations in the governing of teachers in national territorial spaces (see also Robertson, 2012). These are the concepts of 'field of symbolic control', 'classification' and 'framing' (Bernstein, 1990, 2000). By 'field of symbolic control' Bernstein (1990: 134–5) means those agents and agencies who specialise in discursive codes that they dominate. In the case of teachers' work, we can place here those agents and agencies who shape teacher policies and regulate teacher practices through the ways in which they determine what is thinkable and doable. I will be arguing that the denationalisation of teachers' work reflects a recalibration in power relations over the discursive codes in the field of symbolic control.

Bernstein (2000) refers to the what, who and how of governing using the concepts of 'classification' and 'framing'. By 'classification' Bernstein (2000: 6) means 'the what and who' of the social division of labour; for instance, the qualified teacher, assistant teacher, head teacher, Ministry official, and so on. Each of these categories has a particular identity, voice and consciousness produced through governing. 'Framing' (Bernstein, 2000: 12) is concerned with who controls what; in other words, whether the transmitter as opposed to the acquirer (the who) has control over the criteria for realising particular practices (the what). For instance, do teachers (as acquirers) claim professional expertise and therefore the right to determine the rules for realising classroom practices, or do the transmitters (such as the national state or international agencies) strongly frame teacher policies in turn limiting the possibilities for interpretation and enactment? These three concepts by Bernstein will be used as a means for looking at whether or not we can detect changing relations of power and control between teachers, the state and international agencies, over teachers and their work over time and space, and what this means for politics and democratic accountability.

Mundy (2007) argues that two mechanisms of global governance were key in the post-Second World War period: 'education as development' as a goal for modernising societies, and 'standard setting' (see also Robertson, 2012). These two mechanisms were aimed at promoting nation-state-building projects in the post-Second World War period: supporting the expansion and development of education in newly developed states of the south (via the UN Declaration of Human Rights and the mandate of UNESCO), and coupling these emerging states' trajectories to the developmentalist timeline of modernisation and its *telos* modernity (Ferguson, 2007: 188). The international organisations thus helped to structure a normative understanding of what educational development should be (levels, inputs, processes), and in tandem with bilateral agencies and a weak international federation of teacher unions and associations, sought to spur the development of education globally, modelled on the western world.

So what was the role of the global agencies with regard to teachers during this period? The World Bank's attitude was largely framed by their approach to financing education for development beginning in the early 1960s. From the start, the Bank's interest in financing education was viewed with a great deal of scepticism, not only as it represented a departure from work being carried out by the Bank, but also because it was viewed as a debilitating form of consumption, if not 'a bottomless pit' (Jones, 2007: 32–3). The Bank was soon guided in its decisions about education by the new economics of education, and in particular the view that education could be seen as an investment opportunity in 'human capital'. By way of contrast with the World Bank, UNESCO argued that education and culture mattered, and that education should be mobilised to foster a unifying global culture. UNESCO, therefore, took a much wider view of education for development. To this end, UNESCO tactically supported the promotion of human rights, and championed the 1948 Universal Declaration of Human Rights and fundamental education in an effort to drive up levels of literacy. UNESCO thus came to be associated with an explicit normative project in education around the idea of 'universality'. It was also an important standard-setting arm of the United Nations (Jones and Coleman, 2005: 53).

As standard setter, UNESCO was able to develop considerable expertise in education, with education planning a particular strength. With Bank funding it also set up a statistics branch – the UNESCO Division of Statistics – used to inform education development activities around the right to education. The main objective here was to provide member states with internationally comparable data in order to help them plan and develop national education and literacy programmes (Cusso and D'Amico, 2005: 202). And while the fundamental assumption was that the rest of the world would develop using a western model of education, national states and their teachers were encouraged to emulate other systems. As Cusso and D'Amico (2005: 200) argue, UNESCO tended to respect the diversity of national education systems, and did not publish rankings of countries based on statistical indicators, although technically these would have been possible. The locus of power and authority continued to lay with the Westphalian state (Sassen, 2006).

This can be seen in the ILO/UNESCO Recommendation concerning the Status of Teachers, which was adopted on 5 October 1966 (ILO/UNESCO, 2008: 8). In 146 paragraphs divided into 13 sections, the Recommendation set out the rights and responsibilities of teachers, including international standards for their initial preparation and further education, recruitment, employment, teaching and learning conditions, security of tenure, disciplinary procedures, participation in education decision making, and so on:

> [T]eaching should be regarded as a profession: it is a form of public service which requires of teachers, expert knowledge and specialised skills, acquired

and maintained through rigorous and continuing study … teachers should enjoy academic freedom in the discharge of professional duties to include the choice and selection of teaching materials … and that their salaries should reflect the importance to society of the teaching function.

(2008: 8)

However, these guidelines were to be the basis of a 'national' dialogue between teachers and national educational authorities and unions regarding teaching as a profession, in turn shaping national laws and practice. As a global Recommendation (unlike a Declaration), it was neither subject to national ratification and nor did it have national signatories. In Bernstein's (2000) terms, it was strongly classified in that it held a view of teachers with distinctive claims to identity and authority. However, it was weakly framed in that national settings (teachers, unions, education departments) were able to significantly shape, and realise, their own conceptions of the good teacher. Connell (2009: 215–16) points out that in the post-war period (until the 1990s), it was possible to identify a range of different conceptions of the good teacher around the globe; from the developmental state model in Australia where direct bureaucratic control was exercised over teachers, to indirect forms of rule over teachers to be found in countries such as the United Kingdom (Lawn and Grace, 1987). A burst of other possibilities emerged in the 1960s and 1970s for teachers as professionals, such as the reflexive practitioner, the critical pedagog, the teacher as scholar, and so on. These experiments were the outcome of strong currents of humanist, progressive and civil rights interests that were advanced throughout the 1960s and 1970s not only in the so-called developed economies, but more widely. However, by the early 1970s, these progressive currents were soon challenged by the stalling of economic growth, the worst economic crisis since the 1930s (Hobsbawm, 1994; Harvey, 2005), and the later advance of neo-liberalism as a political project.

Neo-liberalism and the Governance of Teachers

The advance of neo-liberalism as a counter-hegemonic project, and its subsequent materialisation in globally facing competition-states, reorganised public sectors to operate like quasi-markets, new forms of private authority, the construction of an education services sector open to trade, and an expanded agenda for international agencies, both challenged the transformed public sector education systems, and important features of teachers' work and workplaces (Robertson, 2000; Smyth *et al.*, 2000; Ball, 2007; Compton and Weiner, 2008; Connell, 2009). By the early 1990s, it was possible to see deep and far-reaching changes to teachers' work and in their workplaces in those countries that had fervently embraced market liberalism. Not only was the basis of teachers' professional expertise challenged, but those within the system were faced with an escalating set of demands around accountability, standards and performance. The net effect was to discourage high-quality applicants from entering teaching, or once in the system, to quicken their exit.

Yet, inn making this point, I do not want to imply that neoliberalism was an inevitable, or uncontested, political project. Rather, as Peck (2010) shows, there were major differences among neoliberals: between the idealist Chicagoans (led by Hayek, later to become the Chicago School led by Friedman) and the more pragmatic, European ordo-liberals. These differences centred on where to draw the line between the state and the market (Peck, 2010: 67). For as Peck (2010: 65) argues, neo-liberalism's curse has always been that it can live neither with, nor without, the state. The problem for liberal economists was how to deal with the fact that competitive free markets nevertheless tend to create monopolies, and that it is only the state that is able to legitimately introduce and regulate the conditions for competition. This did not stop the Chicago School from enthusiastically embracing the free market (arguing for minimal regulation by the state) as a means of organising social and economic life. The ordo-liberals preferred a more humanist form of the market, rooted in an understanding that the full capacities of the market could only be realised through their embedding in a robust legal and social order. These distinctions within neo-liberalism are important, for we will see when we look at governing teachers' work, that while, for example, the World Bank Group tends to view education problems and their solutions within a free market framework, the OECD's is predominantly an ordo-liberal outlook in that it keeps open a role for the state in managing the market.

However, as we will also see with the neo-liberalisation of teachers' workplaces, neoliberal projects tend to 'fail forward' (Peck, 2010: 6). What Peck means by this is that the manifest inadequacies of neo-liberalism tend to result in further rounds of neo-liberal intervention, of de- and re-regulation, of flows, backflows and undercurrents, aided by flanking mechanisms that create layerings and over-layerings (Peck, 2010: 17). As a consequence, the actually existing worlds of neo-liberalism are 'not pristine spaces of market rationality and constitutional order; they are institutionally cluttered places marked by experimental but flawed systems of governance, cumulative problems of social fallout, and serial market failure' (Peck, 2010: 31).

Teachers have lived, and continue to live, in these 'actually existing' worlds of neo-liberalising education systems that were being transformed by the 'different vectors, movements, and oscillations' (Peck, 2010: xvii) of neo-liberal projects and flanking mechanisms, including choice, vouchers, charters, devolved governance, global rankings, privatisation, public–private partnerships, management-by-audit, self-management and scenarios for the future reorganisation of education – the list goes on. Teachers also experienced a range of neo-liberal social interventions, and were confronted with their failures and fallout: reduced teacher wages, difficulties in recruiting teachers, significant attrition from the teaching profession, under-chosen schools leading to closure, high-stress teaching and learning environments, and high-stakes testing (Zeichner, 2010; MacBeath, 2012).

From early 2000 onwards, the OECD had become increasingly concerned with the emerging issues within the teaching profession, and their implications for pupil performance and the realisation of competitive knowledge economies. Yet their response was not to put neo-liberalism on notice, but to argue that teachers' work and workplaces needed to be renovated so as to generate

'21st century schools' learners. In a series of reports, the OECD (2005) pointed to major problems such as teacher shortages, teachers without teaching qualification, high teacher turnover rates, and poor teacher professional development. By 2007, the OECD had launched a major governing project, the *Teaching and Learning International Survey* (TALIS) – a data-gathering and benchmarking project on teachers around the world (OECD, 2011), which now joins the OECD's *Programme for International Student Assessment* (PISA) as an instrument for governing teachers, students and national education systems. By 2010, the World Bank had also launched its own teacher assessment and accountability instrument, SABER-Teachers, placing it into competition with the OECD and the ILO/UNESCO Recommendation concerning the Status of Teachers. In the following section, I review these two new governing projects, arguing that the OECD and the World Bank have used the crisis in teachers' work and workplaces as a means to legitimate its increased power in the field of symbolic control. While these technologies of rule are still in their infancy, the OECD has had some experience in finessing the nature of the discursive codes over time. Given, too, that the World Bank is likely to face increased hostility because of its unrelenting commitment to Hayekian/Friedmanite neo-liberalism, on the one hand, and crude representation of teachers as lazy and ineffective, on the other, this may well strengthen the influence of the OECD in the field of symbolic control.

The OECD, the World Bank and Teachers' Work – A Synchronic Account

In this section I now lay out the basis of a synchronic account of the transformations in teachers' work. I begin with the OECD, which in 2002 launched a major project reviewing teacher policy, drawing in 25 member states who committed substantial resources (OECD, 2005: 3). A final report, *Teachers Matter*, was published in 2005. This placed teachers' work, and the question of policy to regulate teachers, high on national agendas. Arguing that '[t]his OECD project provides probably the most comprehensive analysis ever undertaken of teacher policy issues at the international level' (p. 3) and that participating countries could learn from each other through 'sharing innovative and successful initiatives, and to identify policy options for attracting, developing and retaining effective teachers' (p. 3), the report was a reaction to wider issues surrounding teacher recruitment (image and status of teachers), the composition of the workforce (growing discipline issues among male students, academically weaker students entering teaching), the unequal geographic distribution of good teachers, declining salaries among teachers, and limited incentive structures that might recognise and reward good teachers.

In reviewing the response of member states to the OECD's *Teachers Matter* policy, Connell (2009: 214) argues that, while this agenda might suggest that governments might invest more resources into education systems, this was not the reality.

What *has* happened in Australia, as in other wealthy countries, is the construction of an imposing new apparatus of certification and regulation for teachers.

Statutory institutes have been created, and given the task of defining minimum standards for entry into school teaching; and the way they do this is already impacting on university teacher education programmes. They also have the task of defining more advanced levels of teacher quality – a key point on the Business Council's agenda – and the way they do this is likely to be a powerful influence on schools in the next generation.

Connell (2009: 214) argues that an important outcome of the *Teachers Matter* policy initiative is that it refashioned what was meant by 'the good teacher' – to be a competent teacher. Important too was the way 'the good teacher' is reclassified (as the competent teacher) and strongly framed (that is, that the elements that make up the competent teacher are highly specified) by the OECD.

TALIS is the OECD's instrument for promoting a reframing of teacher policy and practice inside national territorial borders. As argued earlier, TALIS emerged out of the OECD's teacher policy project and *Teachers Matter* report. The OECD states that TALIS is the result of collaboration between member states and the OECD. It has also engaged the Trade Union Advisory Council that sits within the OECD, and advises on labour issues. Only Mexico and Chile overlap between SABER-Teachers and TALIS. Unlike SABER-Teachers, which I will elaborate upon shortly, TALIS collects data from teachers and head teachers regarding their views on their learning environment and working conditions in schools. The questions range over school leadership, mechanisms for the reward of teachers, professional development, and teaching practices and beliefs. The questionnaires are thus translations of policy priorities.

Drawing on Bernstein (1990, 2000), we can see that TALIS strongly classifies and frames the good teacher as a competent, continuous learner; from collaborations in teaching to ensure learning from colleagues to engage professional development, and systems of appraisal and self-development. Taken together, these elements illustrate a shift away from 'education as development' to a 'learning as development' paradigm. But it also gains its power (reach/intensity) from the ways in which competitive comparison can leverage space, time and a development trajectory. While TALIS is low on hierarchy in that there are no composite figures ranking one country above another, its temporal sequencing (regular data collection/expanded repertoire), its development trajectory, and its capacity to link to other ranking technologies such as PISA, give the OECD greater leverage over governing teachers within national territorial boundaries, and in ways that connect teachers to global agendas, trans-boundary networks and new formations (Sassen, 2003, 2006). Its level of buy-in by member and non-member states (with the US joining TALIS 2013), and capacity to legitimate itself by arguing that the unions have been central to the process via the Trade Union Advisory Council[1] to the OECD (OECD, 2008), suggest fewer frictions than those confronting the World Bank's SABER-Teachers programme. That Education International (EI), which emerged out of two opposing federations in 1993 (and now representing 400 unions, 170 countries and 30 million global teachers), has been drawn into the creation of this global mechanism via the TUAC, also highlights the ways in which EI could be seen as incorporated into the global governance agendas for teachers on terms that are being driven by the OECD.

The OECD TALIS 2008 was spearheaded by the OECD's Indicators and Analysis Division (IAD), under the direction of Andreas Schleicher. TALIS is also a collaboration between member states of the OECD, and non-members. The first round of TALIS data collection took place in 2008 in 24 countries (17 OECD countries, 7 non-member countries). A second, more extensive, round of data is being collected from more than 30 countries/regions to be reported as 'TALIS 2013' in 2014. TALIS 2008 reported on data collected from 20 teachers teaching lower secondary school (level 2 of the 1997 revision of the International Classification of Education – ISCED 97) in 200 schools for each country participating in the survey. In the first design of the survey, options were presented to the participating countries, which included surveying a representative sample of teachers of 15 year olds who took part in PISA 2006 – PISA being also run by the IAD (OECD, 2009: 20).

In order to see the 'who' and 'what' of classification and framing, we need to look at the TALIS survey instruments as particular kinds of pedagogic devices. Broadly, TALIS 2008 collected data on: (1) the role and functioning of the head teacher; (2) how teachers' work is appraised and the feedback they receive; (3) teacher professional development; and (4) teachers' beliefs and attitudes about teaching. First, we can see the shift to 'learning as (individual) development' through their focus on various kinds of learning: ongoing professional learning, self reflection, feedback, and so on. We can also see from the discussion of the indices in the Annex (OECD, 2009: 268–75) the pedagogic principles at work. Teachers are asked to respond to a series of questions, for instance around teachers' beliefs, indicating how strongly they agree with the statement (1 = strongly disagree; 4 = strongly agree). In relation to teacher beliefs, there are two opposing indices: direct transmission (the implication here is a bad teacher) or constructivism (the implication here is a good teacher). Here the OECD (2009: 269) states: 'In short, constructivist beliefs are characterised by a view of the teacher as a facilitator of learning with more autonomy given to students whereas a direct transmission view sees the teacher as the instructor, providing information and demonstrating solutions.' In other words, the competent teacher facilitates the learning of the pupil through 'making knowledge', while direct transmission approaches to learning are conceptualised as 'taking knowledge'. That teachers are likely to need a combination of pedagogies depending on what needs to be taught is not thinkable in this framing.

Here we can see an important ontological and epistemological anchor that is central to the OECD's pedagogical project – that of constructivism. A central tenet of constructivism is that reality does not exist independently of the subjects who seek it. In other words, there is no other independent, pre-existing world (Olssen, 1996: 275). And as Olssen comments, ' it is not for the constructivists the objective world that limits or constrains what can be experienced or known' (p. 279). Constructivism as an epistemology thus presents all kinds of issues for teachers and assessment, particularly when we might see it as the teacher's duty to structure learning environments that facilitate the process of learning, which the society (and not the student) regards as having the greatest robustness. However, the attraction of constructivism for the OECD is that it fits with the ontology of neo-liberalism, of liberalism's concern for the individual. Teachers engaged in direct transmission are described as 'those who demonstrate the correct way to solve a problem', and who believe 'a quiet classroom is generally needed for effective learning'. The constructivist (read competent) teacher believes 'the role of the teacher is to facilitate students' own enquiry', and 'thinking and reasoning processes are more important than specific curriculum content'. In other words, the teachers' pedagogic practices that are presumed to materialise the competent learner for a knowledge-based economy place limits on the acquisition of scientific or disciplinary knowledge. It can be argued, therefore, that a constructivist teacher pedagogy, with its overemphasis on agency and 'social knowledge' as opposed to 'disciplinary' or 'scientific knowledge' (Rata, 2011: 2), links the wider political project of neo-liberalism to the emerging social base of production – the permanent, uncritical, learner for the competitive knowledge economy. More importantly, a constructivist teacher's pedagogy does not provide the resources for learners that might enable them to engage in critical reflection and political critique.

There is also a further challenge facing the authority of the OECD and its claim to expert knowledge on teacher policies, pedagogies and successful education systems. This comes in the form of counter-evidence that is presented by the case of Finland. In the OECD's PISA rankings, Finland ranks number one for student performance. However, the key elements the OECD proposes for teacher policies and high-performing schools are absent in Finland. More than this, Finland is also a high-growth economy, leading ex-World Bank staffer, Pasi Sahlberg (2007, 2010, 2011) to argue that successful economies such as Finland are successful precisely because they have completely different teacher policies from those favoured by the OECD. Finnish teachers spend fewer hours in class teaching than the OECD average, have considerable professional autonomy, are not engaged in formal systems of teacher evaluation, and do not receive merit pay. This has caused the OECD to alter its 'lesson learning' strategy through deploying the expertise of Pearson Education – the world's largest education firm (Ball, 2012: 124–8) – in marketing education products and services. A series of 'successful performer' videos (including Singapore, Poland, Ontario/Canada and Brazil) each carries a rather different story about how to build high-performing schools (Pearson Foundation, 2012). However, this has the effect of weakening the strength of the classification of 'high-performing schools' because the rules for realisation are made more open regarding which message the acquirer wants to take. This presents the OECD with a paradox in that it cannot fully control the outcomes of its own pedagogic practices. Added to this, evidence from its data-gathering activities (the place of Finland on PISA/Finland does not deploy any of the tools of the global reform movement) causes a weakening of the insulation that keeps the category of successful school/good teacher/high student performer in place.

The World Bank has also advanced a strong agenda around modernising the school and teachers' work, arguing that this is important for the development of knowledge-based economies. The World Bank Report, *Lifelong Learning for the Global Knowledge Economy* (*LLGKE*) (2003) sets out the account of the kinds of challenges knowledge economies present for education and training systems.

Schools and teachers pose particular problems for the Bank, in large part because teachers are seen as unionised and resisting change, and education systems are viewed as steeped in an organisational model of development that limits their capacity to respond to the wider challenges posed by globalising knowledge economies. The Bank's redesign of education favours a Hayekian free market model. However, it is also mindful that its earlier attempts at privatisation in the 1980s were particularly controversial. It has instead turned to public–private partnerships (PPPs) as an umbrella for advancing an agenda around state-funded vouchers and private sector provision (Lewis and Patrinos, 2011).

In their 2011 report, *Making Schools Work* (Bruns *et al.*, 2011), the Bank dedicates a lengthy fourth chapter (more than 60 pages) to the challenge of teacher accountability. A key argument is that education policy makers wishing to recruit, or 'groom', great teachers to raise the overall levels of learning among pupils confront the reality of education systems where there are weak or no incentives to alter performance. The report states: 'The vast majority of education systems are characterised by fixed salary schedules, lifetime job tenure, and flat labour hierarchies, which create rigid labor environments where extra effort, innovation and good results are not rewarded' (p. 142). Criticising the years of service/credential basis or teacher salaries and promotion they argue:

> The clear implication of available research is that most schools are recruiting and rewarding teachers for the wrong things, failing to encourage the capacities and behaviours that contribute most directly to student learning results, and unable to sanction ineffective performance.
>
> (p. 143)

A further issue emerges: the levels of expenditure on education and the percentage of this allocated to teacher salaries. Developing countries today spend an average of 5 per cent of GDP on education, and many countries are on track to increase this. The impact of this investment on their subsequent economic growth hangs largely on how they use the 4 per cent of GDP (80 per cent of total education spending) that goes to pay teachers. In a growing number of countries, the drive to improve student learning outcomes is translated into creative and sometimes radical policy reforms aimed at changing the incentives for teachers (Bruns *et al.*, 2011: 143).

The Bank's solution? Teachers should be paid, not by formal recognition of qualifications, or type of service, or geographic location; rather, they should be placed on contracts for specified periods of employment, with pay tied to student performance, thus establishing a link between teachers' employment conditions and accountability for results. Yet there is considerable variation among teachers in influencing learning, and many causes for this, ranging from teacher style to organisational issues, class size and wider social and economic factors, a point that the OECD work on teachers recognises (OECD, 2005). Pinning teacher pay to student performance establishes a link that suggests it is possible to distil that dimension of teacher performance that makes a difference, and that teachers are in control of this.

The question of teachers' pay structures and incentives linked to quality and outcomes is a major issue in policy agendas, with sharp differences of opinion and preferred research evidence between commentators. Charter Schools in the US have provided an interesting 'laboratory' for the Bank on generating evidence, as teachers employed by sector Charter Schools typically work on very different contracts from those in the public, and are viewed by the Bank as worthy of emulation. Charter School teachers are on individually negotiated contracts, are non-unionised, and are not tied to tenure. How have teachers fared in Charter Schools and do Charter Schools produce greater teacher professionalism and better learning outcomes? Johnson and Landman (2000) studied the experiences of teachers in six deregulated schools in the US – two state-sponsored Charter Schools, two in-district Charter Schools, and two public school-based management schools – all located in Boston and serving similar groups of students. Based on interviews with teachers and principals, supplemented by document analysis and informal observations, they concluded that the most autonomous schools – Charter Schools – are not necessarily the schools that enterprising teachers favour. Teachers in these schools voiced concerns about important features of their workplace – the scope and definition of their responsibilities, their role in school design and governance, their right to raise complaints and resolve problems, and assurances of job security and predictable pay. A longitudinal study of pupil performance in Charter Schools released in 2010 (CREDO, 2010) suggests that student outcomes are not necessarily likely to be better, despite the fact that many of the teachers in these schools are on untenured contracts. The CREDO study offers a group portrait that shows wide variation in performance. The study reveals that, although 17 per cent of Charter Schools nationwide provide superior education opportunities for their students, 50 per cent have results that are no different from the local public school options, and 37 per cent deliver results that are significantly worse than if these students had remained in traditional public schools.

This led Harvard academic Susan Moore Johnson to argue for a different set of proposals around teacher salary structures that are not tied to student outputs but constitute, rather, a career-based plan aimed at teacher development (Johnson and Papay, 2010). Similarly, in a presentation by the Finnish Ministry of Education to an OECD meeting in Japan in 2011, the Director General pointed out that, although Finland scores the highest on the OECD's PISA studies, and where their results are regarded as attributable to the quality of their teachers, teachers have less class time than the OECD average, have considerable professional autonomy, and also have a post-graduate degree. However, as the Director General pointed out, the Finnish system *does not* (their emphasis) use teacher evaluation, merit pay, census-based standardised tests or ranked schools (Sahlberg, 2011; see also Grek, 2009).

Despite this kind of evidence, the World Bank's Education Sector Strategy 2020 Report (2011a) notes that, over the next decade, the Bank will be further developing a System Assessment and Benchmarking for Education Results (now the Systems Approach for Better Education Results) (SABER) programme that will generate comprehensive information on education policies across the world. The basic contours of this knowledge-driven development model have already been established by the Bank, and, indeed, represent a significant component of Bank funding to education over the period 1998–2009.

The objective of the World Bank's SABER-Teachers project launched in 2010 is to collect quantitative data on teacher policies, to synthesise the results, and to use these for decision making in improving education (World Bank, 2011b). SABER-Teachers strongly classifies the 'good teacher' (defined by eight core policy goals), and uses strong framing rules by specifying ten core teacher policy areas, the specific questions to be asked in each of these areas, and evaluative/moral developmental trajectory – 'latent', 'emerging', 'established', 'mature' – to determine the extent to which the rules for realisation of the competent teacher are in place. Detailed questions about the terms and conditions of teachers' labour include: 'Is participation in professional development compulsory?', 'What is the burden of teacher compensation?', 'What labor rights do teachers enjoy?' and 'Are there monetary sanctions for teacher absenteeism?' These are surely political and economic questions around the use and exchange value of teachers' work, as well as signalling a growing level of surveillance over teachers and their time at work. There is also a strong moral and therefore cultural project at work as a result of the comparisons that will be made between countries, and between teachers. Countries will be compared with each other and will be able to learn from each other, while the evaluative/moral developmental trajectory provides both direction and levers for change. The focus is argued to be on the 'facts' of policy rather than teachers' 'experience' of policy – yet teachers will experience the outcomes of the changes that will ensue, and live in the worlds that emerge as a result. The Bank will also use its own organisational structures and consultants to gather data (World Bank, 2011b: 27), giving it significant control over the ongoing use and refinement of the system.

A diverse array of countries (13) was involved in the first round of SABER-Teachers data collection in 2010 – from Chile and Djibouti, to Egypt, Guatemala and New Zealand. While some of these countries are recipients of Bank aid, countries such as New Zealand have in the past been assigned the status of a laboratory for World Bank structural adjustment policies (Peck, 2010). A range of logics is at work as to who signs up to the project, and why. Yet, it also raises a wider set of issues for the Bank regarding its longer-term capacity to govern teachers globally. Its dependence on client states (rather than member states), its thinned legitimacy as a result of wider concerns over the Bank's activities in education, a commitment to market-liberalism in education that is not welcomed in many countries, its evident dislike of teacher unions and embrace of individual incentives, concerns over the link between aid and outcomes, and potential competition with the OECD's instruments may limit the geographical reach of this project, at least as a mechanism of global governance. Yet, where it is able to link aid to changes in policy concerning teachers, it will likely have major effects on the sector, including undesirable ones.

Teachers' Work, Denationalisation and Transformations in the Field of Symbolic Control

In this chapter I have argued that the global governance of teachers' work is not new in that it is possible to identify strongly classified, but weakly framed, mechanisms of governing in national and sub-national territorial states through standard setting and education development agendas over the period 1960s–1990. This is entirely consistent with arguments made by writers such as Sassen (2006) who point out that, in the post-Second World War Bretton Woods period, we witnessed significant processes of extending beyond the boundaries of the national state. However, this extension, broadly referred to as 'internationalisation', tended to reinforce, rather than weaken, national territorial boundaries. The processes that emerged from the 1980s onward, broadly referred to as globalisation, are however radically different. Nevertheless, as she also argues, 'the critical capacities for international governance and operations were developed in that process, which eventually become relodged into novel global assemblages' (Sassen, 2006: 12).

Similarly, with regard to teachers' work, the post-war technologies of governing have now been transformed into 'learning as development' while statistics are now used as a means of compiling, comparing, learning and performing what it means to be a globally successful school and teacher. And despite UNESCO's hesitation regarding comparing countries using statistics, it has also moved further in the direction being promoted by the OECD and the World Bank – of 'competitive comparison' (Robertson, 2012).

From the late 1990s onwards, we can see a significant transformation in the field of symbolic control, with the global agencies strongly classifying and framing conceptions of the good teacher to be realised in national education settings. In particular the statistical capabilities and augmenting projects of the OECD's IAD has placed it in a unique position to advance this project. However, the OECD's recent collaboration with the global education consulting firm, Pearson Education, will also inject significant funds and new forms of private authority into what was an intergovernmental set of relations and projects. UNESCO, the OECD, World Bank Group and the ILO all now collect, manage, evaluate and represent statistical data on teachers' work. These newer mechanisms of global governance now sit alongside the ILO/UNESCO Recommendation concerning the Status of Teachers, passed in 1966 – yet they encourage different kinds of conversations and engagements precisely because they have different logics of intervention as well as spatial and temporal politics.

In drawing upon my analysis in the previous sections, we can discern four distinct, though not disconnected, denationalising processes at work that are reconstituting the field of symbolic control over the governance of teachers. Concretely, these denationalising tendencies have the potential to further recalibrate the power and control of the global agencies, though I will argue that this process is both uneven and contested. These processes include the invocation of a global imaginary of both shared risk and a shared future; the emergence of new forms of transboundary relations that further erode the national; the relationally interconnected nature of global teacher learning; and the rise of new forms of private authority that sit beyond national spaces of representation and democratic accountability.

To begin, the invocation of 'risk' – of not having a 'modernised' teacher workforce fit for the twenty-first century, where teachers' use of properly weighed evidence facilitates the social knowledges of the students in ways that make a difference to the performance of every student – is linked to the project of realising 'world class' education systems for a globally competitive knowledge-based economy. That each country's investments in education and its teachers is about a future to be imagined, materialised and managed by global agencies like the OECD and the World Bank, aims to stand as the necessary legitimation for why power and control should be relocated. Furthermore, this shift is not behind the backs of national governments. Rather, (some) national governments have signed onto and funded, as well as facilitated, the collection of data, though clearly they are somewhat nervous about what different data-sets might reveal, and how these might be managed politically. Yet we also see here the limits placed on agencies, such as the World Bank, in having the capability to realise their ambition of controlling teachers through their determination of teacher policies. The Hayekian/Friedmanite neo-liberal ideology that has shaped the world view of its key advisers, a small epistemic community of economists of education, has never been able to exert the kind of influence on national governments that it would like (Mundy and Menashy, 2012). That this is the case, and that there are differences of view within the Bank over its policies and practices, could be politically exploited by critics.

Second, denationalisation processes are given direction, velocity and effect through the ways in which new, transboundary, relations between teachers, teacher policy advocates and continuing professional development providers are created and reinforced. Processes of re-boundarying, or re-bordering, are both the object and outcome of political projects aimed at weakening existing borders and their enclosed social activity and social relations (Robertson, 2011). Neo-liberalism, as a political project, has had as its core objective the selective elimination of existing boundaries around the movement of goods, services and finances at the level of the nation. Linking together existing systems, teachers and students, across national divides through large data-sets, breaks down national statistical and accounting systems. The global specification of what statistics are to be collected, how, when and in what time frames, as opposed to composing global statistics from national databases, is an example here. Similarly, drawing teachers into global narratives, video resources and opportunities for more global learning, reworks the nationally bounded nature of teachers' work and the notion of 'the good teacher'.

Third, the relationally interconnected nature of globalising teacher learning in national settings through competitive comparison (Robertson, 2012) undermines the notion of a national or a sub-national workforce. The reach of competitive comparison as a global tool is enabled by the ways in which hierarchical space, temporal rhythms and evaluative trajectories and scales are mobilised as complex modalities of power. As a powerful spatial framer and lever for allocating status, it pitches one country and its teachers against another in terms of a global hierarchical ordering of performers and underperformers. Through ratcheting up the temporal dimension to comparison, such as regular cycles of data collection, a new horizon for performance is targeted. This uses a horizontal place for comparison – over time – where one can learn to do better the next time, and the time after (or not), while keeping sufficient tension within the system. An evaluative/moral dynamic provides the basis of judging where a country lies on each teacher policy area, from 'not present' to 'fully developed', as we can see in the World Bank's work. Countries and teachers are to learn from this evaluative element about how to act more properly in ways specified by this framing of the good teacher. Embedding the governing strategy in national, regional and global projects, in turn amplifies its effects and therefore its power to shape outcomes. These global governing technologies are manifestations of a transformation in the field of symbolic control, in turn shifting sovereignty and authority away from the national and the teacher, to the global and global actors. Yet, at the same time, these projects are neither uniform in their classification and framings, nor likely materialisation in teacher practices.

Finally, a key outcome of this new denationalising global dynamic is the way in which the field of symbolic control is opened up to new forms of private authority, such as private consulting firms, corporate philanthropists and consultants. However, they exercise significant power in the reshaping of teachers' work in the absence of public accountability mechanisms. The OECD argues that Education International (EI), the global teacher education union, has given its approval to the development of TALIS. Yet, how is EI accountable in any democratic way to the classroom teachers that it is representing? What processes are in place for nationally located teachers to represent their claims and issues? And what of McKinsey & Company, or Pearson Education, whose responsibilities are to their shareholders and not teachers? Ironically teachers are visibly absent as professionals who have expertise, despite their noted visibility.

The denationalisation of teachers' work that is currently under way has resulted in the globalising of nationally oriented capabilities aimed at shifting the weight of gravity in the field of symbolic control in the direction of global agencies such as the OECD and the World Bank. Like all political projects, however, the outcomes will always be contingent, contested and open to transformation. That we can too easily see the frictions, fissures and failures in cohering logics at the level of discourse, let alone practice, suggests that these projects might well be stalled as much by their evident hubris as well as the air of nervousness that seems to be present with the rapid growth of private authority in these processes. However, what is important is enrolling classroom teachers in these debates. There is a lot to play for, and a lot to be lost. For if teachers are central to the learning and lives of students, helping teachers develop the capabilities to make a big global noise about a very big global issue is high priority. This is particularly as the kinds of teacher knowledge proposed, and working conditions, are deeply depoliticising.

Note

1   The Trade Union Advisory Council (TUAC) to the OECD was formed in 1948 as the trade union advisory committee to the European recovery programme, the Marshall Plan. When the OECD was finally established in 1962, morphing out of the Organisation for European Economic Co-operation (OEEC), the TUAC continued its work of representing unions in industrialised countries (affiliates come from 58 national trade unions) (OECD, 2008).

References

Ball, S. (2007) *Education plc*, London and New York: Routledge.

Ball, S. (2012) *Global Education Inc.*, London and New York: Routledge.

Barber, M. and Mourshed, M. (2007) *How the World's Best-performing Schools Come Out on Top*, New York: McKinsey & Company.

Bennell, P. (2005) The impact of the AIDS epidemic on schooling of orphans and other directly affected children in sub-Saharan Africa, *Journal of Development Studies*, 43(3): 467–88.

Bernstein, B. (1990) *The Structuring of Pedagogic Discourse: Class, codes and control*, London and New York: Routledge.

Bernstein, B. (2000) Pedagogy, Symbolic Control, and Identity: Theory, research, critique, revised edn, Oxford: Rowman and Littlefield.

Bill & Melinda Gates Foundation (2010a) *Working With Teachers to Develop Fair and Reliable Measures of Effective Teaching*, Seattle, WA: Bill & Melinda Gates Foundation.

Bill & Melinda Gates Foundation (2010b) *Learning About Teaching: Initial findings from the Measures of Effective Teaching Project*, Seattle, WA: Bill & Melinda Gates Foundation.

Bruns, B., Filmer, D. and Patrinos, H. (2011) *Making Schools Work: New evidence on accountability reforms*, Washington, DC: The World Bank Group.

Buchanan, J. and Tullock, G. (1962) *The Calculus of Consent*, Ann Arbor, MI: University of Michigan Press.

Buchanan, J. and Wagner, R. (1977) *Democracy in Deficit*, New York: Academic Press.

Chubb, J.E. and Moe, T.M. (1990) *Politics, Markets and America's Schools*, Washington, DC: Brookings Institution.

Cochran-Smith, M. (2006) Ten promising trends and three (big) worries, *Educational Leadership*, 63(6): 20–5.

Compton, M. and Weiner, L. (2008) *The Global Assault on Teachers, Teaching and their Unions*, New York: Palgrave.

Connell, R. (2009) Good teachers on dangerous ground: toward a new view of teacher quality and professionalism, *Critical Studies in Education*, 50(3): 213–29.

CREDO (2010) *Multiple Choice for Charter Schools*, Stanford, CA: University of Stanford.

Cusso, R. and D'Amica, (2005) From development comparison to globalization comparison: towards more normative international education statistics, *Comparative Education*, 41(2): 119–216.

Dale, R. (2008) *Educational Governance as Ontology and Pedagogy: New approaches to the impasse of educational reform for democracy and the social justice*, GES Working Paper, University of Bristol, August.

Ferguson, J. (2007) *Global Shadows: Africa in the neoliberal world order*, Durham, NC and London: Duke University Press.

GMR (2009) *Overcoming Inequality: Why governance matters*, Paris: UNESCO.

Goldstein, R. (2011) Imagining the frame: media representations of teachers, their unions, NCLB and education reform, *Education Policy*, 25(4): 543–76.

Grek, S. (2009) Governing by numbers: the PISA 'effect' in Europe, *Journal of Education Policy*, 24(1): 23–37.

Harvey, D. (2005) *A Brief History of Neoliberalism*, Oxford: Oxford University Press.

Hobsbawm, E. (1994) *Age of Extremes: The short twentieth century, 1914–1991*, London: Abacus.

Hursh, D. (2005) The growth of high stakes testing in the USA: accountability, markets and the decline of educational equality, *British Educational Research Journal*, 31(5): 605–22.

ILO/UNESCO (2008) *The ILO/UNESCO Recommendation concerning the Status of Teachers (1966), and The UNESCO Recommendations concerning the Status of Higher-Education Teaching Personnel (1997) with a Users Handbook*, Paris: UNESCO.

Johnson, S.M. and Landman, M. (2000) Sometimes bureaucracy has its charms: the working conditions of teachers in deregulated schools, *Teachers College Record*, 100(1): 85–124.

Johnson, S.M and Papay, J. (2010) *Redesigning Teacher Pay: A system for the next generation of educators*, Washington, DC: Economic Policy Institute.

Jones, P. (2007) *World Bank Financing of Education: Lending, learning and development*, 2nd edn, London and New York: Routledge.

Jones, P. and Coleman, J. (2005) *The United Nations and Education: Multilateralism, development and globalisation*, London and New York: Routledge.

Lawn, M. and Grace, G. (1987) *Teachers: The culture and politics of work*, Lewes: Falmer Press.

Lewis, L. and Patrinos, H. (2011) *Framework for Engaging the Private Sector in Education*, Washington, DC: The World Bank.

MacBeath, J. (2012) *The Future of the Teaching Profession*, Brussels: Education International.

Mourshed, M., Chijioke, C. and Barber, M. (2010) *How the World's Most Improved Systems Keep Getting Better*, New York: McKinsey & Company.

Mulderrig, J. (2008) Using keywords analysis in CDA: evolving discourses of the knowledge economy in education, in B. Jessop, N. Fairclough and R. Wodak (eds) *Education and the Knowledge-based Economy*, Rotterdam: Sense Publications.

Mundy, K. (2007) Global governance, educational change, *Comparative Education*, 43(3): 339–57.

Mundy, K. and Menashy, F. (2012) The role of the International Finance Corporation in the promotion of public private partnerships in development, in S. Robertson, K. Mundy, T. Verger and F. Menashy (eds) *Public Private Partnerships in Education: New actors and modes of governance in a globalizing world*, Cheltenham: Edward Elgar.

Novoa, A. (2011) Travelling, not arriving: an intellectual journey, in R. Sultana (ed.) *Educators of the Mediterranean … Up Close and Personal: Critical voices from south Europe and the MENA Area*, Rotterdam: Sense Publishers.

OECD (2001) *Knowledge Management in the Learning Society*, Paris: OECD.

OECD (2005) *Teachers Matter: Attracting, developing and retaining effective teachers*, Paris: OECD.

OECD (2008) *Labour and the OECD: The Role of the TUAC*, Policy Brief, Paris: OECD.

OECD (2009) *Creating Effective Teaching and Learning Environments: First results from TALIS*, OECD: Paris.

OECD (2011) *OECD Teaching and Learning International Survey (TALIS): TALIS 2013*, Paris: OECD. Available at www.oecd.org/document/40/0,4746,en_2649 (accessed 7 October 2011).

Olssen, M. (1996) Radical constructivism and its failings: anti-realism and individualism, *British Journal of Educational Studies*, 44(3): 275–95.

Pearson Foundation (2012) *Strong Performers and Successful Reformers in Education*. Available at http://pearsonfoundation.org/oecd (accessed 10 September, 2012).

Peck, J. (2010) *Constructions of Neoliberal Reason*, Oxford: Oxford University Press.

Rata, E. (2011) The politics of knowledge in education, *British Educational Research Journal*, 38(1): 103–24.

Robertson, S. (2000) *A Class Act: Changing teachers' work, globalisation and the state*, New York: Falmer Press.

Robertson, S. (2011) The new spatial politics of (re)bordering and (re)ordering the state-education-citizen relation, *International Review of Education*, 57: 277–97.

Robertson, S. (2012) Placing teachers in global governance agendas, *Comparative Education Review*, 56(4), in press.

Sahlberg, P. (2007) Education policies for raising student learning: the Finnish approach, *Journal of Education Policy*, 22(2): 147–71.

Sahlberg, P. (2010) Rethinking accountability in a knowledge society, *Journal of Educational Change*, 11(1): 45–61.

Sahlberg, P. (2011) *The Finnish Advantage: Good Teachers*, presentation to OECD Japan Government Seminar, Tokyo, June 28–29.

Sassen, S. (2003) Globalization or denationalization? *Review of International Political Economy*, 10(1): 1–22.

Sassen, S. (2006) *Territory, Authority, Rights*, Princeton, NJ: Princeton University Press.

Smyth, J., Dow, A., Hattam, R., Reid, A. and Shacklock, G. (2000) *Teachers' Work in a Globalizing Economy*, London and New York: Falmer.

Stevenson, H. (2007) Restructuring teachers' work and trade union responses in England: bargaining for change, *American Educational Research Journal*, 44(2): 224–51.

World Bank (2003) *Lifelong Learning for the Global Knowledge Economy*, Washington, DC: World Bank.

World Bank (2011a) *Learning for All: Investing in people's knowledge and skills to promote development: Education Sector 2020 Strategy Report*, Washington, DC: The World Bank Group.

World Bank (2011b) *SABER-Teachers: Objectives, rationale, methodological approach and products*, Washington, DC: The World Bank Group.

Zeichner, K. (2003) The adequacies and inadequacies of three current strategies to recruit, prepare and retain the best teachers for all students, *Teachers College Record*, 105(3): 490–519.

Zeichner, K. (2010) Competition, economic rationalization, increased surveillance, and attacks on diversity: neo-liberalism and the transformation of teacher education in the US, *Teaching and Teacher Education*, 26(8): 1544–52.

6 The OECD and the Global Re-Regulation of Teachers' Work

Knowledge-Based Regulation Tools and Teachers in Finland and England

Risto Rinne and Jenny Ozga

Introduction

This chapter focuses on the effects on teachers' work of new forms of regulation, as examples of ideas and political technologies that travel globally and touch down in ways that seek to steer specific national and sub-national forms of teacher professionalism. We explore the macro-processes of policy steering – paying particular attention to the role of the OECD – and responses to those steering processes in terms of their possible effects on professional identities and practices in Finland and England. Our main concern is to highlight the ways in which the OECD's knowledge-based regulation tools (KBRTs) attempt to promote orthodox professional practice and increased standardisation of professional formation and development. It is important to stress that the strength and power of a KBRT lies in its apparently objective nature, in the attractiveness of the space of negotiation and debate that it creates, where experts, policy makers and other knowledge brokers meet and position themselves, and in its capacity to define the terms of that engagement. According to Pons and Van Zanten (2007) there are three main elements of KBRTs: (1) they reflect particular 'world visions' that represent the agenda-setting capacities of particular interests; (2) they represent a particular and politically oriented set of beliefs concerning legitimate policy in a given domain; and (3) they represent a wide and growing network of actors who are constantly drawn into the process of intelligence gathering, audit and meditative policy making (Jacobsson, 2006).

We draw here on the history of OECD's Programme for International Student Assessment (PISA) to identify possible developments in relation to OECD's recently inaugurated *Teaching and Learning International Survey* (TALIS) and to highlight the ways in which these forms of regulation act on national systems. In making this analysis, we draw on the work of Carvahlo (Carvahlo *et al.*, 2009; Carvahlo, 2012) and others in order to clarify and underline the ways in which these instruments alter the logic of education governance. The first section explains our approach to analysis of the influence of the OECD; we then move to a discussion of the TALIS survey and its place in the overarching OECD 'project', and then consider theories of professionalism and work, along with brief accounts of teachers' work in Finland and England, before concluding with a consideration of the possible impacts of the OECD's interest in the teaching profession on teachers' work more generally.

Policy Technologies and KBRTs

Although international organisations (IOs) – the World Bank, the EU and the OECD – have different agendas, there are significant shared approaches to policy for education and learning, delivered through a range of instruments that can be targeted at national policies: they can promote, develop and disseminate policies, coordinate, set standards, supply technical assistance and offer financial inducements. Initially, education was quite a low priority for the OECD, which focused in its origins on economic statistics and predictions. Over the decades, however, education has become an increasingly central target of OECD knowledge production and administration. The Centre for Educational Research and Innovation (CERI) was founded as early as 1968, and the Education Committee in 1970. Education indicator projects came into wider use in the 1980s, influenced by the so-called Indicators of National Education Systems (INES) project that opened the way for the comparative 'Education at a Glance' indicators and later for PISA. The Education Directorate was created in 2002. The transition towards the 'knowledge-based economy' and the centrality of the production of human capital as a key resource placed education in the foreground of OECD policy. Most recently, the OECD's activity has been strongly focused on learning policy, in which not only institutionalised formal education but also informal and non-formal learning comes within the OECD ambit (Rinne, 2004a, 2004b; Niukko, 2006) and reflects a growing interest in promoting lifelong learning.

The production of forms of comparative data has a long history. It can be seen in the development of the International Association for the Evaluation of Educational Achievement (IEA) in Hamburg from the 1950s when external experts on data production started to bring national systems into view. The IEA has continued its work, but it has been displaced by the OECD's growing interest in measuring outcomes from education, which led to the creation of the Programme for International Student Assessment (PISA) in 1997. For more than a decade PISA data has provided states with system data to steer and reshape their education systems:

> As national systems can be re-imagined in new ways because of the velocity and scope of data, so, on a larger scale, can Europe be imagined [into existence] as well. The construction of Europe as a legible, governable, commensurate policy space has been made possible by data flow, spurred by targets and indicators across a range of policy areas in Europe. Comparison for constant improvement against competition has come to be the standard by which public systems are judged.
>
> (Lawn, 2009)

The OECD has become a kind of global 'benchmarker' of standards that are of the utmost importance in relation to positional competition as well as reputational competition between nation-states and their education institutions (Lauder *et al.*, 2006: 41; see also Rinne *et al.*, 2004a, 2004b; Robertson *et al.*, 2006). The OECD is the largest and most credible data producer and source of comparative statistics as well as of economic and social data. It has recently (2011) initiated several new comparative international assessment programmes, for example the Programme for the International Assessment of Adult Competencies (PIAAC) – the most comprehensive international survey of adult skills undertaken to date. The Assessment of Higher Education Learning Outcomes (AHELO), initiated in 2011–12, tests what students in higher education know and are able to do upon graduation. More than a ranking, AHELO is a direct evaluation of student performance. The OECD claims that AHELO: 'will provide data on the relevance and quality of teaching and learning in higher education. The test aims to be global and valid across diverse cultures, languages and different types of institutions.' In justifying the AHELO, OECD states that:

> Governments and individuals have never invested more in higher education. No reliable international data exists on the outcomes of learning: the few studies that do exist are nationally focused. Available rankings reflect neither the quality of teaching and learning nor the diversity of institutions.
> (OECD, 2012)

These developments are widely recognised and are the subject of many commentaries (see, for example, Hopmann and Brinek, 2009), while PISA provides a source of data for an infinite number of secondary analyses. However, questions about what these technologies of comparison mean, what their aims are and how they influence political processes are relatively neglected. These policy technologies, in the words of Lascoumes and Le Galès, are best understood as having the purpose:

> of orienting relations between political society (via the administrative executive) and civil society (via its administered subjects) through intermediaries in the form of devices that mix technical components (measuring, calculating the rule of law, procedure) and social components (representation, symbol).
> (2007: 6)

Comparison, and comparative data, in this analysis, becomes a governing form (Novoa and Yariv-Mashal, 2003): benchmarking, according to Nóvoa (2010: 270), is 'a process that constructs educational realities as much as it describes them … Through the arrangement of categories and classifications, a definition of the "best" system is proposed.'

The process of attraction into comparative data production – established through participation in PISA – creates a space in which national and transnational experts and policy makers interact in ways that allow the nation-states to be seen as independent and voluntary participants (Grek *et al.*, 2009; Mäkinen, 2011), while encouraging 'best practice' and policy learning that enables national adaptation of the OECD 'script'. The key principles that the OECD has established are, following Carvahlo (2012): (1) that regular surveys establish the 'truth' about national education systems; (2) that improving national systems can only be achieved with reference to the pace and direction of change elsewhere; and (3) that international comparisons can fully represent the complexity of educational experience. KBRTs such as PISA are thus much more than information-gathering tools about specific issues – they are sets of practices in which experts are recruited to work with policy makers to examine modern state structures, governing procedures and choices; and to elaborate standards that define and therefore make up governing practices. Collective scrutiny requires the development of agreements about rules and standards, which in turn support the propagation of transparency and 'best practice'. These are knowledge-based regulatory forms that both support and grow out of changing governing practices – especially those associated with soft regulation. Jacobsson (2006: 208–9) identifies three sets of interconnected forms of governing activity associated with soft governance: regulative (formal laws and directives), inquisitive (auditing and ranking) and meditative (where experiences are compared and ideas shared). Meditative governing practices build on regulation and auditing, but they encompass them, and offer a space in which the OECD encourages policy learning, presents models of good practice and encourages nations to be 'good pupils' (as in the case of Finland – see Simola *et al.*, 2009).

In summary, then, we see KBRTs such as PISA as part of a particular definition of the role of education in contemporary (knowledge) societies that promulgate specific models for the regulation of the education sector.

From Learners to Teachers: The TALIS Survey

The *Teaching and Learning International Survey* (TALIS) programme is one of the most recent OECD instruments that may become the flagship KBRT for education policy moving beyond PISA. The need for constant monitoring of student assessment is now firmly established; attention is shifting to learning and teaching practices in school and to teacher education and training. This new focus has to be understood in the context of changes in production, in society and in labour markets. The crisis of Fordism prompted critique of education as failing to answer the needs of rapidly changing economies and redefined labour markets. This was associated with increased emphasis on inculcating flexibility and adaptability in all human life. Flexibility and flexible learning were also connected with organisational change and the growth of ICT (see Jessop, 2008: 30–1). The knowledge economy agenda disrupted nationally embedded and institutionalised practices and norms in education/learning. The preferred attitudes and dispositions promoted by current policies and encouraged by new knowledge practices are coherent across the range of educational institutions and beyond them, from early childhood throughout adult working life (itself extended). This agenda also brings a shift in governing practices in education within the nation-state, from national and institutionally based governing to governing through networks of new actors, along with individual self-governance, informed by constant self-evaluation of performance, steered through the benchmarking and competitive performance regimes of transnational organisations, including the OECD. This, combined with relentless pressure to produce capital-friendly conditions underpinned by low public spending and low taxes (Jessop, 2002), along with the equally relentless pressure to maximise value for money in the public sector, prompted efforts to re-regulate the place of school and its core work force, teachers.

This translates into a new emphasis on the teacher as exemplar and monitor of learning processes and is clearly exemplified in the European Commission's response to the OECD's TALIS, produced by DG Education and Culture:

> As schools become more autonomous, with open learning environments, teachers assume greater responsibility for the content, organisation and monitoring of the learning process, as well as for their own personal career-long professional development. Furthermore, as with any other modern profession, teachers have a responsibility to extend the boundaries of professional knowledge through a commitment to reflective practice, through research, and through systematic engagement in continuous professional development from the beginning to the end of their careers.
>
> (Scheerens, 2010: 12)

A further strong factor in focusing attention on teachers is the very influential report for the McKinsey Global Institute (Barber and Mourshed, 2007), which asserted that 'the quality of an education system cannot exceed the quality of its teachers' and that 'the only way to improve outcomes is to improve instruction'. This statement is heavily referenced in TALIS-related publications and frames the DG Education and Culture's engagement with TALIS by connecting this prioritisation of teacher quality to concerns about achieving the Lisbon 2020 goals. Indeed, EU member states, responding to the TALIS agenda and the OECD's prioritisation of policy for the profession, agreed to work together in specific areas of teacher education policy ensuring a continuum of teacher education, encouraging all teachers to be autonomous learners in their own career-long professional development, to make the teaching profession a more attractive career choice and ensure that teacher recruitment, placement, retention and mobility policies maximise the quality of school education.

Teacher educators are now charged with responsibility for promoting, during initial teacher education, early career support and continuous professional development, 'the acquisition of the competences that teachers need, such as teaching transversal competences, teaching heterogeneous classes, and collaborating with colleagues and parents' (Scheerens, 2010: 14). All of these developments indicate the shaping of the policy agenda for teachers, which is then reflected in the key issues investigated by TALIS, and in the reading of the data and its translation into a frame for further development.

The first cycle of TALIS took place in 2008 in 24 countries: Australia, Austria, Belgium (the Flemish community), Brazil, Bulgaria, Denmark, Estonia, Hungary, Iceland, Ireland, Italy, Korea, Lithuania, Malta, Malaysia, Mexico, the

Netherlands, Norway, Poland, Portugal, Spain, the Slovak Republic, Slovenia and Turkey. England and Finland were not involved in the first round of TALIS but they are participants in the second round, in 2013. TALIS is claimed to be the new 'evidence base on education' and to provide a 'powerful insight into working conditions of teachers and teaching and learning practices in schools' (OECD, 2011b: 2–3). The OECD states that TALIS is an instrument to 'help countries to improve policies for developing a high-quality teaching profession' and it is presented as 'a collaborative endeavour between governments, an International Consortium, the OECD and the Teachers' Unions' (Ischinger, 2009; OECD, 2011a, 2011b: 2–3). The first cycle focused on lower secondary education teachers. TALIS 2013 has a wider scope: it has 30 countries or regions as participants. TALIS 2013 also gives participating countries the option to survey teachers in elementary and upper secondary schools. Furthermore, countries are able to conduct the TALIS 2013 in schools that participate in PISA 2012, thus creating very powerful data that link teacher and pupil performance. The guiding principles that shaped the development of the 2008 survey strategy were policy relevance: clarity about the policy issues and a focus on the questions that were most relevant for participating countries were regarded as essential, as were international comparisons. It was also regarded as essential that the results should yield information that could be used to develop indicators and the survey should yield information that is valid, reliable and comparable across participating countries.

TALIS 2008 focused on key aspects of what the survey refers to as the 'learning environment' that were held to influence the quality of teaching and learning in schools. These were (1) the leadership and management of schools – the roles adopted by school leaders, given increasing accountability and devolution of educational authority; (2) the appraisal of teachers' work in schools and the form and nature of the feedback they receive, as well as the use of outcomes from these processes to reward and develop teachers; (3) the professional development that teachers undertake and its connection to appraisal systems, support from school leaders and impact on classroom practices; and (4) the profiles of countries with regard to teaching practices, activities, beliefs and attitudes, and how these vary according to teacher background characteristics. The focus on changing learning environments is visible in the concern to investigate – and then promote – 'a modern view of teachers' that identifies their activities beyond the classroom, for example:

> cooperating in teams of teachers, building professional learning communities, participating in school development, and evaluating and changing working conditions. Those activities shape the learning environment at the school level, i.e. school climate, ethos and culture, which directly and indirectly (via classroom level processes) impact student learning.
>
> (OECD, 2008: 33)

While the OECD's discussion of the results tends to emphasise leadership and learning environments, a close reading reveals that TALIS was prompted by concerns not only about management and leadership of education and schooling, but also about teacher morale and retention. TALIS may be read as a response to growing concern in many OECD countries that teachers are leaving the profession prematurely and that many teachers are not willing to work regimes that are over-regulated (Gray *et al.*, 2011: 131–2).

The discussion of the findings of TALIS 2008 in the OECD's report on TALIS (OECD, 2011b) emphasises that, while teaching is viewed as a relatively stable career with strong job security, this may also create a risk of inertia and lack of flexibility (OECD, 2009: 29). In fact, the discussion reveals considerable concerns within the OECD about the meaning and achievement of the whole edifice of performance measurement. To some extent PISA can be read in this discussion as a prisoner of formal schooling, while with TALIS, PIAAC and AHELO, OECD seeks to break the bonds of the formal school system and build comparative data on the possibilities and limitations of lifelong and life-wide learning and thus locate the reconstruction of teachers – the making of 'new' teachers for the 'new world order' (Maguire, 2010: 60) – within a wider framework beyond the school. This fits with the wider policy discourse on the re-engineering or re-professionalisation of teaching, which seeks to create the 'world-class' teacher, who is not so much a pedagogue as a professional classroom manager and an expert on the provision of 'high quality client services in more areas for less time' and who is 'flexible according to needs' (Maguire, 2010:62; see also McWilliams, 2008: 35).

Such models of teaching are linked directly to enhancing school autonomy (OECD, 2006). In many education systems, schools have been granted greater autonomy in recent years and the power to make decisions has been decentralised (OECD, 2008). The OECD's TALIS analyses stress that teachers are more and more regarding students as active participants in the process of learning and of acquiring knowledge and do not see the teacher's main role as the transmission of information and the giving of correct solutions. This is, according to TALIS, most often the case in northwest Europe, Scandinavia, Australia and Korea and least visible in southern Europe, Brazil and Malaysia (OECD, 2009: 88). The OECD also notes that teachers across countries are identifying more with 'constructivist' models of teaching, where the teacher is more of a facilitator than a direct transmitter of knowledge. This is most evident in northwest Europe, Scandinavia, Australia and Korea and not so evident in Italy and Malaysia (OECD, 2009: 120).

At the same time, the investigation through the TALIS survey of teacher appraisal and feedback systems indicates that these do not have a negative impact upon teachers, according to the OECD. However some 'inappropriate' systems do have negative impacts and negative consequences, especially those systems that misalign incentives and rewards (Lazear, 2000; OECD, 2009: 158). A wide range of systems in the countries surveyed emphasise different outcomes and different aspects of teachers' work. Yet, the great majority of teachers in these varied systems consider the appraisal and feedback they receive to be 'mostly beneficial' to their work as teachers, to be quite fair, and to increase both job satisfaction and, to a lesser degree, job security. In fact, given the benefits of systems of appraisal and feedback, the greatest concern raised by the OECD relates to countries that lack such systems (OECD, 2009: 158). Yet independent research has identified feelings of insecurity, fear and reduced satisfaction in work when a new performance assessment system is introduced in education. An emphasis on accountability can be assumed in some instances to imply strict and potentially punitive measures and thus have a negative impact upon teachers, their appreciation of their jobs and their work as teachers (Smyth *et al.*, 2000; Butt and Gunter, 2007; Gray *et al.*, 2011).

To summarise, we believe that TALIS and the other survey developments such as PIAAC and AHELO represent a profound shift from learners to teachers in the OECD's repertoire of policy technologies and knowledge-based regulation tools: teachers are now of central importance to the OECD's strategic priorities for improving the performance of education and learning systems. However, in contrast to PISA's relatively straightforward (though not uncontested) focus on test performance as the driver of the KBRT, it is much more difficult to trace the relationship between the definition of the newly acknowledged educational 'problem' of teachers and the data or evidence being gathered by TALIS to clarify and solve this problem. Rather, it seems that the data are diverse and contradictory and do not offer a simple guide to action. We turn now to look at teacher regulation in two different contexts, Finland and England, to explore further the terrain within which this form of regulation seeks to 'touch down'.

New Model Teachers? The Emergence of Professional Learning Communities

We do not intend here to review the long and tortuous history of professionalism as a concept and its application to teachers. In brief, we see teachers as an occupational group that is caught in a continuous process of negotiation and renegotiation of its claims to professional status, seeking to engage in a power practice, as Larson (1977: 22) puts it: 'Professionalism is a power practice, an attempt to achieve closure by producing a commodity whose acquisition and distribution is assiduously monopolised by the professionals themselves.'

But teaching is a power practice that is especially vulnerable to intervention because of the nature of the 'commodity' whose acquisition and distribution is a focal point of struggle (see, for example, Seddon *et al.*, this volume; Connell, 1985; Lawn and Ozga, 1988; Kivinen and Rinne, 1994; Lawn, 1996; Maguire, 2010). Recent redefinition of the terms under which teachers could seek to claim authority have included, in many different national systems, the adoption of standards, registration requirements, codes of ethics and university level pre-qualifying requirements, and these have been used to apparently raise the status of the profession while also ensuring that the professions can effectively be managed and their performances increasingly controlled by government (Ball, 1998; Harrison and Pollitt, 1994; Stronach *et al.*, 2002).

In this perspective, a key issue is the interplay between the capacity that teachers have to mobilise their resources in order to claim professional status, and the prevailing conditions that influence that capacity. In the historically embedded structures of schooling within national systems, this capacity was strongly influenced by the scope permitted by the state to the professional workforce as its employees responsible for dealing with social problems. Education/

schooling was oriented towards 'persistent problems' within capitalism: preparation of the workforce, disciplining identities to ensure social order and cohesion, and legitimising social ordering despite the continued existence of inequalities. Education policy and the capability of national education systems, exercised through the teaching workforce, mediated contradictory imperatives without ever solving – or, indeed, directly recognising – the problems and tensions they created (for example, between meritocracy and equality, or between targeted and inclusive provision) (Dale, 2009). Teachers carried the tensions created by the contradictory imperatives of their work into their professionalising strategies, while national narratives sought, with greater or lesser degrees of success, to gloss the contradictions raised by their claims for status, autonomy and a fairer allocation of educational opportunities.

The new, global learning agenda de-centres national education 'projects' and also displaces the school, as policy makers adopt global prescriptions (emerging, as did PISA, from networks of experts that cross policy-knowledge boundaries) (Normand, 2011) that advocate the importance of freeing organisations from traditional structures, empowering teachers through collaboration, and developing cultures that value shared responsibilities and values, using the concept of the professional learning community (PLC) (Weindling, 2005; Stoll *et al.*, 2006). This concept is directly derived from ideas in the economics of knowledge concerned with releasing creativity and energy and with building knowledge sharing, generation and retention into organisational processes (Foray, 2004). These 'learning communities' apparently engender relations of trust, transparency and openness within organisations that are claimed to be conducive to 'real' learning, which is further supported by situated theories of learning, advocating the promotion of teacher learning through reflection and social interaction. The professional community of teachers is envisaged as including a focus on student learning, shared values and vision, collective responsibility, reflective professional inquiry, collaboration and group and individual learning (Stoll *et al.*, 2006).

Recent research supports the idea that participation in a professional learning community leads to changes in teaching practices as teachers become more student-centred (Vescio *et al.*, 2008). In addition, the teaching culture apparently becomes more collaborative. The TALIS survey drew on this literature to represent some of the key characteristics of professional learning communities, specifically school characteristics such as a cooperative climate and evaluation and feedback mechanisms. Data derived from the survey support the definition of collective professional development as a context for continuous professional development. Thus ideas derived from school effectiveness research combine with the shift in policy makers' concerns towards the teaching profession to reinforce the definition of the 'problem' of teacher professionalism in relation to the need for cultural change. This in turn supports prescriptions of collaborative work and situated, active learning that enrol the profession in a project of continuous improvement within professional learning communities that monitor their own continuous learning.

While this may be the emergent OECD agenda, delivered through TALIS, the project may be a good deal more complex than the installation of comparative and competitive national testing. There are three factors that contribute to the complexities in operating this policy technology that seeks to attract and enrol participating countries and frame the logic of their engagement. The first is the strength – in some contexts, at least – of embedded national practices of teacher education and development. The second relates to the lack of clear direction from the 'evidence' of TALIS. Once the logic of PISA was accepted, the process of response to the results of testing was relatively easy to install. The logic of creating professional learning communities is rather less clear, as the TALIS data reveal different orientations to teaching, both 'constructivist' and 'transmission', and also reflect a very wide variation in levels of training, and in conditions of work (data about these are barely discussed in the OECD reports). Moreover, the impact of leadership – one of the OECD's favourite elements of school success – on teaching quality is not demonstrated clearly in the TALIS data. The third is the context of neo-liberal policy logic, which drives down public spending, strengthened in some cases by deepening economic crisis, but seeks quick, technical fixes to the long-term, strategic issue of developing human capital. These factors may make both the attraction of professional communities and the related 'meditative' stage of the governing process (Jacobsson, 2006) more difficult to achieve. In the next section, we briefly consider two cases, Finland and England, which are participating in TALIS 2013, in order to identify the degree of fit between the global prescription for teaching quality and the assumptions and practices on the ground in two contrasting contexts.

Teachers in Finland and England

Finland is a small Nordic country with approximately 5.3 million inhabitants, only 4.3 per cent of whom are immigrants, while the corresponding percentage in (for example) England is 11.3 per cent. At the individual level the main objective of Finnish education policy is to offer all citizens an equal opportunity to receive education, regardless of age, domicile, financial situation, gender or mother tongue. At the national level a major objective of Finnish education policy is to achieve as high a level of education and competence as possible for the whole population.

In the post-war era, the cornerstones of Finnish education and social policy were inclusion and universalism. In the education system selection into different paths occurred only after the completion of comprehensive schooling at 15 years of age. All education including the tertiary sector is public, and until recently was completely publicly funded and free of charge. The social democratic type of welfare state in place in Finland since the Second World War was equally inclusive. However, from the last recession at the beginning of the 1990s, there have been considerable cuts in the welfare state, shifting the emphasis to a more selective and market-oriented direction. In the field of education, schools in basic education have been reduced and parental choice has been introduced, creating a (quasi) school market (Rinne *et al.*, 2011; Seppänen *et al.*, 2011).

In Finland teachers are very united and almost all are members of the same Trade Union of Education in Finland (OAJ), which includes class teachers and subject teachers, primary school teachers and secondary school teachers. Both Finnish teachers and the union are quite conservative rather than radical. Finland is also unique compared to almost any other country in that teachers and their work are highly trusted, and lightly regulated and controlled. The status of teachers is high and there are no problems in recruiting young people to teacher training. The status measured by salaries, however, is not very high but in the middle level. Teachers have also won their long professional struggle for an academic university education to the level of a Master's degree (Aro *et al.*, 2011; Statistics Finland, 2011).

The clear majority – 69 per cent – of teachers is female. The bulk of the teachers are 30–59 years old. There are smaller numbers of younger teachers, as university studies generally take 5–6 years. Not all teachers continue to work in the profession until the normal retirement age (63 years) (Aro *et al.*, 2011). Most teachers work full time (94 per cent) and hold tenured posts as municipal civil servants. Full-time teachers are members of their respective trade unions almost without exception (Eurydice, 2010: 161–3).

The Finnish teaching profession has been seen historically as one of the most important (semi)-professions in society and considerable resources have been invested in teacher education. Because teachers have been trusted as professional experts in education they have also been entrusted with considerable pedagogical independence in the classroom and schools have likewise enjoyed substantial autonomy in organising their work within the limits of the national core curriculum. Recruitment to the profession in Finland is highly selective: only 10 per cent of applicants to teacher education programmes are admitted, which implies that those accepted are highly motivated and multi-talented students with very good academic skills. Young Finnish teachers, in particular, are well acquainted not only with various teaching methods but also with education research; many of them, moreover, appear to be well prepared and motivated to develop their professional skills through further education and training (Välijärvi *et al.*, 2007: 48–9).

Finnish teachers and schools are not very strongly assessed, evaluated, regulated or controlled. In fact inspection has been abolished and there are no national testing systems of student behaviour and achievement. After the deregulation and decentralisation of education in 1990s, the new globally introduced system of school assessment was legislated for but in fact it is very weak and loosely used in practice. It can be argued that there is a distinctive national Finnish Model of Quality Assurance and Evaluation (QAE) in compulsory education, which differs very strongly from the mainstream of international and global evaluation policies.

The key elements are (Simola *et al.*, 2009, 2010):

1   QAE information is intended first and foremost for administration and decision making at national and municipal levels – and only secondly for other interest groups, i.e. pupils and their parents;
2   the purpose of QAE in education is to develop – not to control, sanction or allocate resources;

3   sample-based assessments of learning are favoured over mandatory national testing of the whole age cohort;
4   there is no basis for or need to publish school-based ranking lists.

One of the main reasons for high trust in Finnish teachers and their comparatively high status can be traced to teacher education and its academicisation in the post-war era in Finland. As Aro *et al.* (2011) argue, the key changes were to move teacher education into the universities, to create separate Faculties of Education and to weaken the idea of teachers as 'model citizens', but rather define them as academic professional experts. Competition for places increased, the selection of teacher training students tightened: it became more difficult to enter into the academic route for teaching than to enter university to study other subjects. The point was to highlight the scientific prestige of teacher training, to make it scientifically comparable to other academic fields and to make teacher training curricula more 'research oriented'. Finally, pressures for harmonisation according to the European model (the Bologna process) and to reduce teacher education standards have been very limited in their effects as the influence of the OAJ remains strong and it remains committed to the principle that teachers be educated to Master's level.

In more general terms, it is important to understand that in Finland the comprehensive school is both a system and a pedagogical philosophy. The system very strongly emphasises the principles of reducing inequality of educational opportunity and of integrating all children and young people of the age group in the same classes, and it is organised in ways that represents a particular pedagogical philosophy and practice. Philosophical principles are an intrinsic part of this system that guarantees equal educational opportunities to everyone independent of his or her social, gender, regional and ethnic origin. Finnish education policy has been largely premised on equity and democracy (Välijärvi *et al.*, 2007: 38).

In relation to supranational influences, Niukko (2006), Rinne (2006) and Kallo (2009) have conducted research on the role of the OECD in Finnish education policy. Finland seems to have been the 'model pupil' of OECD education politics, at the level of the policy texts, but remains in fact rather slow in implementing any proposed reforms. The Ministry of Education seems to offer three explanations for the role of being a 'model pupil' at the level of rhetoric only: the need to find more international information, the need to legitimise its own planned reforms with the OECD's recommendations and to reduce uncertainty related to the future (Kallo, 2009: 295–7; Mäkinen, 2011).

Ironically, its capacity for delayed response to the OECD's recommendations is undoubtedly linked to Finland's success in PISA, which has been very important in Finnish education politics. In the early 1990s there was heavy criticism of the Finnish comprehensive school and the principles of 'too much' equality and even stronger critiques of academic teacher education. After the PISA results criticism of the comprehensive school and of academic teacher training ended and university teacher training has become 'glorified'. It is believed that academic teacher education as well as the devotion of Finnish teachers to their work are the explanatory factors behind the PISA success (see Aro *et al.*, 2011).

England presents a considerable contrast to Finland, not only in terms of scale (England has over 60 million inhabitants), but also in relation to the extent of regulation of the teaching force, and the absence of a national 'project' for education that goes beyond achieving 'world classness' (Ozga, 2011). There is no parallel with Finland's comprehensive provision and overarching education 'project' of inclusion and equality. Indeed, recent research suggests that it is no longer possible to talk of a 'system' of education in England, but rather provision there should be understood as a set of sub-systems, operating more or less independently, or organised in networks (for example, in 'chains' of Academies with one sponsor) (Lawn, 2012). Indeed, the distinguishing feature of schooling in England is its diversity – at least in London and larger conurbations – where the creation of a market responsive to parental choice and a strong belief in the benefits of modernising education, in line with an imaginary of effective, competitive business practice, has led to the coexistence of different routes through schooling, which are located in institutions with widely contrasting funding regimes, relations with central and local government curricula and pedagogies.

There are many consequences associated with this reshaping of the landscape of educational provision: for our purposes the focus here is on the impossibility of seeing the teaching workforce in England as a unified entity. School workforces are officially categorised as those of 'state-funded' schools (Academies and 'free' schools) and those for the Local Authority-maintained sector (i.e. traditional public sector provision, largely comprehensive but strongly affected by the proliferation of alternative provision that enjoys higher levels of resource from government and the private sector). This differentiated provision produces parallel universes of varied working conditions, training routes and qualifications, and of rewards and career progression in teaching. Increased diversity is a reflection of the pursuit of 'transformational change in the school workforce' (DfES, 2002), initiated by New Labour in England in the 1990s and still in process under the Conservative-Liberal Democrat UK coalition government that took office in 2010.

That change – although generating a wide range of policy initiatives – is strongly driven by a technicist view of teaching in which problems of underperformance are 'fixed' through the widespread deployment of teaching assistants (219,800 or 2 per cent of the teaching force in 2011). This focus on teaching assistants and an expanded school support staff reflects a policy drive for teachers to focus on core tasks (especially teaching literacy and mathematics) combined with the opening up of a pool of labour that is further expanded by de-regulation of routes to qualified teacher status (QTS). Related developments include the growth of appointments of head teachers (principals) from outside education (DfES/PricewaterhouseCoopers, 2007). Indeed the number of teachers who might be classified as local council employees has recently reduced for the first time in over a decade (by 10,000 in the year 2011–12), in part because of the growth of Academies, where principals are not regulated by statutory agreements and who are free to use their resources to buy in services (including 'super teachers' working across a pool of schools, or flexible workers contracted by an agency).

De-regulation of QTS is attractive to policy makers because it breaks the compact between the state and the profession that guaranteed recognition of the professionality of teachers and weakens their capacity for solidarity in defence of their professional status, their pay and conditions of work. At the same time employer flexibility is increased through the opening up of progression possibilities from teaching assistant to teacher, and lines of demarcation are increasingly blurred. Modernisers have argued since the 1990s that the creation of clear career pathways within different sectors of the workforce (e.g. for headship, or subject leaders) will combat what they see as a problem of stagnation in the (previously rather undifferentiated) profession, release energy through enhancing competition for reward, and attract the right kind of people (from business or with other wider experience) into teaching (DfES, 2002; Butt and Gunter, 2007). Modernising initiatives have also resulted in radical changes in initial teacher training and teaching practices. The drive for greater accountability within the teaching profession has led to greater 'intensification and prescription of training regulations' (Brown and McNamara, 2001). In relation to wider pedagogic practices, there has been a trend towards acceptance of fashionable models of learning (e.g. 'multiple intelligences') and standardisation of curricula to meet targets and performance levels using a standard three- or four-part lesson 'delivery' format (Gewirtz, 2007).

Commentators vary in their assessment of 'fast' policy for modernisation of the profession, some emphasise the harmful consequences for teachers. They include the substantial personal costs of the combination of 'fast' and 'performative' policies, for example the deep levels of exhaustion reported by teachers across education sectors, with teachers continually struggling to work within what they see as fragmented, results-driven systems. These analyses also draw attention to the production of performative selves (McNamara and Stronach, 2002; Ball, 2003), as teachers try to negotiate competing teaching discourses represented by their personal beliefs and formal accounts – government, ITT institution and school. Performativity is 'a culture and mode of regulation that employs judgements, comparisons and displays as means of incentive, control, attrition and change – based on rewards and sanctions (both material and symbolic)' (Ball, 2003: 216). However, other commentators emphasise new opportunities for recognition, self-affirmation and enhanced status for teachers (Gewirtz, 2006: 19).

Our own previous research, with others, suggests the culture of teaching influences the effects of these performative regulatory frameworks. Studies into the effects of performance management and quality assurance practices on teachers' work in a number of national systems, including Finland and England, suggest that, in countries with coherent and integrated practices and pedagogies, teachers are better able to adapt to external pressures and constructively mediate them. However, in England, influences external to the school loom large alongside more embedded practices and influence the context of teaching and, to a very considerable extent, define the meanings of those same activities (Gray *et al.*, 2011: 148–9; Ozga, 2011). Certainly in England, the government's determination to reduce public sector funding is combined with a relentless emphasis on international competitiveness, and together this results in the translation of the OECD's prescriptions for teacher quality as 'workforce remodelling' that seeks to produce a 'new professionalism'(ATL, 2010) as a technical fix, rather than a cultural shift. In this context, in contrast to Finland, constant critique of 'underperforming' teachers by policy makers has eroded public confidence, while the teacher workforce is offered a 'new professionalism' that maintains an obsessive focus on meeting targets and punitive inspection models (Baxter, 2012 forthcoming), while also referencing the OECD discourse of enhanced professionalism and the need for professional learning communities. The result is a corrosive breakdown of trust between teachers and government, illustrated in increased problems of retention and morale.

Conclusion

KBRTs attempt to de-contextualise policy steering by presenting apparently objective data as knowledge for policy that seeks to establish a definition of a 'problem', the terms in which it may be discussed, and its preferred solution. The OECD has created a massive edifice of data collection and comparison that has changed the ways in which we think about schooling within countries and across the globe. Through this technologisation, OECD seeks to establish a particular governing logic. But the real difficulty for policy makers is that these logics, which seek to appear natural and self-evident, are not enough to sustain the shift in focus towards teachers. The logic of the instrument seeks direct connections between teacher quality and pupil/system performance, but the logic may not move in the direction that the OECD wants to go. For example, although the success story of PISA for Finland is well established and heavily referenced in recent policy texts from the Department for Education (DfE) in England, there is no evidence of the widespread policy transfer of Finnish publicly provided, unregulated, uncontrolled and unevaluated provision, along with its expensive academic teacher training system into the English context – or, indeed, anywhere else. The costs are prohibitive, even before taking into account the need to adapt and adjust to national conditions. Yet TALIS indicates there is continued commitment to new policy technologies, which seek 'convergence towards the tool' (Carvahlo, 2012) through regulation, but also search for means of governing 'at a distance' through constant learning in self-regulating, self-disciplined professional communities. This is an idea that has little purchase at the level of the nation, although, ironically, it may prove an effective resource for organised teachers, in their attempts to manage change 'from below' (Bates and Carter, 2007). As we have argued, the data from TALIS reflect the difficulty of constructing a KBRT from comparative data about teachers: the shaping and impetus of the instrument are far from clear, nor is there a strong, agreed narrative around 'performance'. As Marilyn Strathern put it: Teaching 'cannot be made fully transparent simply because there is no substitute for the kind of experiential and implicit knowledge crucial to expertise' (Strathern, 2000: 313).

In our earlier discussion, we stressed that policy steering in education is increasingly driven by on knowledge-based regulation tools (KBRTs) that attempt to promote orthodox professional practice and increased standardisation of teaching, combined with the promotion of self-regulated learners and professionals. We argued that the strength of a KRTB lies in its apparently objective nature, in the attractiveness of the space of negotiation and debate that it creates, and in its capacity to define the terms of that engagement. After reviewing the emergent KBRT of TALIS, we suggest that there are real weaknesses in translating these KBRTs, as tools based on the model of performance testing of PISA, to teachers and teaching. The main reasons for this difficulty are the incoherence of the narrative of teaching quality/excellence emerging from the data, which reflect the continuing strength of embedded teacher practices and relations, whether they be of autonomous public professions in Finland, or highly regulated, segmented education workers in England. The continuing importance of the nation-state as an actor in these developments means that the OECD faces a challenge in creating an attractive space of negotiation for the mediation of the interaction between itself and the national nation-state, which remains a key player in this governing regime (Jacobsson, 2006). Thus, although globalisation and supranational organisations such as OECD may be developing sophisticated KBRTs, 'the myth of the powerless state' (Ball, 1998: 67–8) is challenged by the complexity of regulation in these times. Nation-states, as Jacobsson (2006) puts it, continue to be actors, and in some policy cases, at least, their scripts remain open to interpretation, and resistant to, or obstructive of, global governing logics.

References

Aro, M., Rinne, R. and Järvinen, T. (2011) *WP3 National Report Finland*, GOETE – Governance of Educational Trajectories in Europe, CELE, University of Turku.

Association of Teachers and Lecturers (ATL) (2005) *Evidence Submitted to the Enterprise and Learning Committee Teacher Workload Agreement by the Association of Teachers and Lecturers (ATL)*, London, ATL.

Ball, S.J. (1998) Big policies/small world: an introduction to international perspectives in education policy, *Comparative Education*, 34(2): 119–30.

Ball, S.J. (2003) The teacher's soul and the terrors of performativity, *Journal of Education Policy*, 18(2): 215–28.

Barber, M. and Mourshed, M. (2007) *How the World's Best Performing School Systems Come Out on Top*, New York: McKinsey and Company. Available at www.mckinsey.com/clientservice/socialsector/   resources/pdf/Worlds_School_systems_final.pdf (accessed 20 December 2011).

Bates, J. and Carter, B. (2007) Workforce remodeling and the limits to 'permanent revolution': some responses of English headteachers. *International Electronic Journal for Leadership in Learning*, 11(18). Available at www.ucalgary.ca/~iejll (accessed 20 December 2011).

Baxter, J. (2012) What counts as excellence in inspection in England? Shifting Criteria. Paper to the European Conference of Educational Research (ECER), Cadiz, 19 September 2012.

Brown, T. and McNamara, O. (2001) Initial and continuing development of teachers, in M. Askew and M. Brown (eds) *Teaching and Learning Primary Numeracy: Practice policy, and effectiveness*, Southwell: BERA.

Butt, G. and Gunter, H. (eds) (2007) *Modernizing Schools: People, learning and organisations*, London: Continuum.

Carvahlo, L.M. (2012) The fabrications and travels of a knowledge-policy instrument, *European Education Research Journal* (special issue on PISA), 11(2): 172–88.

Carvahlo, L.M., Costa, E. and Barrosso, J. (2009) *Integrative Report on the Reception of PISA*, KNOW&POL Integrative Report on Orientation 3. Available at www.know-andpol.eu (accessed 12 February 2012).

Connell, R. (1985) *Teachers' Work*, London, George Allen and Unwin.

Dale, R. (2009) Contexts, constraints and resources in the development of European education space and European education policy, in R. Dale and S. Robertson (eds) *Globalisation and Europeanisation in Education*, Oxford: Symposium Books, pp. 23–43.

Department for Education and Skills (DfES) (2002) *Transforming the School Workforce Pathfinder Project*, London: DfES.

Department for Education and Skills (DfES)/PricewaterhouseCoopers (2007) *An Independent Study of School Leadership*, London: DfES.

Eurydice (2010) *Eurybase: Organisation of the education system in Finland 2009/2010*, Brussels: European Commission. Available at http://eacea.ec.europa.eu/educa-tion/eurydice/documents/eurybase/eurybase_full_reports/FI_EN.pdf (accessed 19 December 2010).

Foray, D. (2004) *The Economics of Knowledge*, Boston, MA: MIT Press.

Gewirtz, S. (2006) Towards a contextualized analysis of social justice in education, *Educational Philosophy and Theory*, 38: 69–81.

Gewirtz, S. (2007) *Changing Teacher Roles, Identities and Professionalism: Full research report*, ESRC End of Award Report, RES–139–25–0182, Swindon: ESRC.

Gray, J., Croxford, L., Strombaek Pedersen, C., Rinne, R., Silmäri-Salo, S., Simola, H. and Mäkinen-Streng, M. (2011) Teachers' perceptions of quality assurance and evaluation, in J. Ozga, P. Dahler-Larsen, C. Segerholm and H. Simola (eds) *Fabricating Quality in Education: Data and governance in Europe*, London and New York: Routledge, pp. 127–49.

Grek, S., Lawn, M., Lingard, B., Ozga, J., Rinne, R., Segerholm, C. and Simola, H. (2009) National policy brokering and the construction of the European education space in England, Sweden, Finland and Scotland, *Comparative Education*, 45(1): 5–21.

Harrison, S. and Pollitt, C. (1994) *Controlling Health Professionals*, Milton Keynes: Open University Press.

Hopmann, S. and Brinek, G. (eds) (2009) *PISA According to PISA – Does PISA Keep What It Promises?* Vienna: University of Vienna Press.

Ischinger, B. (2009) Foreword, in OECD (eds) *Creating Effective Learning and Teaching Environments: First results from TALIS*, Paris: OECD.

Jacobsson, B. (2006) Regulated regulators: global trends of state regulation, in M.L. Djelic and K. Sahlin-Andersson (eds) *Transnational Governance*, Cambridge: Cambridge University Press.

Jessop, B. (2002) *The Future of the Capitalist State*, Cambridge: Polity Press.

Jessop, B. (2008) A cultural political economy of competitiveness and its implications for higher education, in B. Jessop, N. Fairclough and R. Wodak (eds) *Education and the Knowledge-Based Economy in Europe*, Rotterdam: Sense Publishers, pp. 13–39.

Kallo, J. (2009) *OECD Education Policy: A comparative and historical study focusing on the thematic reviews of tertiary education*, Jyväskylä: FERA.

Kivinen, O. and Rinne, R. (1994) The thirst for learning, or protecting one's niche? The shaping of teacher training in Finland during the 19th and 20th centuries, *British Journal of Sociology of Education*, 15(4): 515–28.

Larson, M.S. (1977) *The Rise of Professionalism: A sociological analysis*, Berkeley and London: University of California Press.

Lascoumes, P. and Le Galès, P. (2007) Understanding public policy through its instruments: from the nature of instruments to the sociology of public policy instrumentation, *Governance*, 20(1): 1–21.

Lauder, H., Brown, P. Dillabough, J.-A. and Halsey, A.H. (eds) (2006) *Education, Globalization & Social Change*, Oxford: Oxford University Press.

Lawn, M. (1996) *Modern Times: Work, professionalism and citizenship in teaching*, London: Falmer.

Lawn, M. (2009) *In a Comparable State: Making an exhibition of ourselves in European education*, paper presented at the 'State and Education 1759–2009' conference, Ministry of Education, Lisbon, Portugal, 4–5 June.

Lawn, M. (2012) *A Systemless System of Education*, Working Paper 6 of the Governing by Inspection project. Available at www.governingbyinspection.com (not yet active).

Lawn, M. and Ozga, J. (1988) Schoolwork: interpreting the labour process of teaching, *British Journal of Sociology of Education*, 9(3): 323–36.

Lazear, E. (2000) Performance pay and productivity, *The American Economic Review*, 90(5): 1346–61.

McNamara, O. and Stronach, I. (2002) Working together: the long spoons and short straws of collaboration, in O. McNamara (ed.) *Becoming an Evidence-based Practitioner*, London: RoutledgeFalmer, pp.155–68.

McWilliam, E. (2008) Making excellent teachers, in A. Phelan and J. Sumsion (eds) *Critical Readings in Teacher Education: Provoking absences*, Rotterdam: Sense Publishers, pp. 33–44.

Maguire, M. (2010) Towards a sociology of the global teacher, in M.W. Apple, S.J. Ball and L.A. Gandin (eds) *The Routledge International Handbook of the Sociology of Education*, London and New York: Routledge, pp. 58–68.

Mäkinen, S. (2011) *International Organizations' Instruments Towards the Internationalization of Higher Education in Finland and in China in the 21st Century*, Research plan. Turku: CELE.

Niukko, S. (2006) *'Yhteistyötä ilman riskejä'? OECD:n rooli Suomen koulutuspolitiikassa* (Co-operation Without Risks'? The role of the OECD in Finnish education policy), dissertation, University of Turku.

Normand, R. (2011) *Gouverner la réussite scolaire. Une arithmétique politique des inégalités*, Berne: Peter Lang.

Nóvoa, A. (2010) Governing without governing: the formation of a European educational space, in M.W. Apple, S.J. Ball and L.A. Gandin (eds) *The Routledge International Handbook of the Sociology of Education*, London and New York: Routledge, 264–273.

Novoa, A. and Yariv-Mashal, T. (2003) Comparative research in education: a mode of governance or a historical journey? *Comparative Education*, 39(4): 423–38.

OECD (2006) *Improving School Leadership: Policy and practice in OECD countries*, Paris: OECD.

OECD (2008) *TALIS 2008 Technical Report*, Paris: OECD.

OECD (2009) *Creating Effective Teaching and Learning Environments: First results from Talis*, Paris: OECD.

OECD (2011a) *About the Organisation for Economic Co-operation and Development (OECD)*, Paris: OECD. Available at www.oecd.org/pages/0,3417,en_36734052_36734103_1_1_1_1_1,00.html (accessed 20 September 2011).

OECD (2011b) *TALIS 2013: Teaching and learning international survey*, Paris: OECD.

OECD (2012) Testing student and university performance globally: OECD's AHELO. Available at www.oecd.org/edu/ahelo (accessed 30 May 2012).

Ozga, J. (2011) Governing narratives, 'local' meanings and globalising education policy, *Education Inquiry*, 2(2): 305–18.

Pons, X. and van Zanten, A. (2007) *Knowledge Circulation, Regulation and Governance:*

Literature review (part 6), Louvain: EU Research Project, Knowledge and Policy in Education and Health Sectors (KNOW&POL).

Rinne, R. (2004a) Suomalainen korkeakoulupolitiikka ylikansallisessa talutusnuorassa? (Finnish higher education policy in the context of transnational controls?), in J. Löfström, J. Rantala and J. Salminen (eds) *Esseitä historiallis-yhteiskunnallisesta kasvatuksesta* (Essays on the historical and social development of education), Helsinki: Centre for Studies on Education Research and Development.

Rinne, R. (2004b) Searching for the rainbow: changing the course of Finnish higher education, in I. Fägerlind and G. Strömqvist (eds) *Reforming Higher Education in the Nordic Countries: Studies of change in Denmark, Finland, Iceland, Norway and Sweden*, New Trends in Higher Education, Paris: International Institute for Educational Planning (IIEP), pp. 89–135.

Rinne, R. (2006) Like a model pupil? Globalisation, Finnish educational policies and pressure from supranational organizations, in J. Kallo and R. Rinne (eds) *Supranational Regimes and National Education Policies: Encountering challenge*, Research in Educational Sciences 24, Turku: Finnish Educational Research Association, pp. 183–216.

Rinne, R., Kallo, J. and Hokka, S. (2004a) Liian innokas mukautumaan? OECD:n koulutuspolitiikka ja Suomen vastauksia (Too eager to comply? OECD education policies and the Finnish response), *Kasvatus*, 35(1): 34–54.

Rinne, R., Kallo, J. and Hokka, S. (2004b) Too eager to comply? OECD education policies and the Finnish response, *European Educational Research Journal*, 3(2): 454–85.

Rinne, R., Simola, H., Mäkinen-Streng, M., Silmäri-Salo, S. and Varjo, J. (2011) *Arvioinnin arvo. Suomalaisen perusopetuksen laadunarviointi rehtoreiden ja opettajien kokemana*, Turku: Suomen kasvatustieteellinen seura.

Robertson, S.L., Xavier, B. and Dale, R. (2006) GATS and the education service industry: the politics of scale and global reterritorialization, in H. Lauder, P. Brown, J.-A. Dillabough and A.H. Halsey (eds) *Education, Globalization and Social Change*, Oxford: Oxford University Press, pp. 228–46.

Scheerens, J. (2010) *Teachers' Professional Development: Europe in international comparison. An analysis of teachers' professional development based on the OECD's Teaching and Learning International Survey (TALIS). A secondary analysis based on the TALIS dataset*, Luxembourg: Office for Official Publications of the European Union.

Smyth, J., Dow, A., Hattam, R., Reid, A. and Shacklock, G. (2000) *Teachers' Work in a Globalising Economy*, London: Falmer.

Seppänen, P., Rinne, R. and Sairanen, V. (2011) Suomalaisen yhtenäiskoulun eriytyvät koulutiet. Perusopetuksen sisäiset valinnat esimerkkinä Turun koulumarkkinat (The Finnish comprehensive school in the context of diversity), *Yhteiskuntapolitiikka* (in press).

Simola, H., Rinne, R., Varjo, J., Kauko, J. and Pitkänen, H. (2009) Quality assurance and evaluation (QAE) in Finnish comprehensive schooling: a national model or just unintended effects of radical decentralisation? *Journal of Education Policy*, 24(2): 163–78.

Simola, H., Rinne, R. and Varjo, J. (2010) Vasten valtavirtaa: Kontingenssi, polkuriippuvuus ja konvergenssi suomalaisen perusopetuksen laadunarviointimallin kehityskuluissa (Against the flow: contingency, path dependence and convergence of primary school quality assessment models), *Hallinnontutkimus*, 29(4): 318–34.

Statistics Finland (2011) Statistics Finland's PX-Web databases. Helsinki. Available at http://pxweb2.stat.fi/database/StatFin/databasetree_en.asp (accessed 14 September 2011).

Stoll, L., McMahon, A. and Thomas, S. (2006) Identifying and leading effective professional learning communities, *Journal of School Leadership*, 16(5): 620–40.

Strathern, M. (2000) Audit Cultures: Anthropological studies in accountability, ethics and the academy, London: Routledge.

Stronach, I., Corbin, B., McNamara, O., Stark, S. and Warne, T. (2002) Towards an uncertain politics of professionalism: teacher and nurse identities in flux, *Journal of Education Policy*, 17(1): 109–38.

Välijärvi, J., Kupari, P., Linnakylä, P., Reinikainen, P., Sulkunen, S., Törnroos, J. and Arffman, I. (2007) *The Finnish Success in PISA – and some reasons behind it 2. PISA 2003*, University of Jyväskylä: Finnish Institute for Educational Research.

Vescio, V., Ross, D. and Adams, A. (2008) A review of research on the impact of professional learning communities on teaching practice and student learning, *Teaching and Teacher Education*, 24(1): 80–91.

Weindling, D. (2005) *Teachers as Collaborative Professionals: A survey of ATL members*, London: Association of Teachers and Lecturers.

7 Local Tradition, International Engagement

Challenges for the Asian Professoriate

Anthony Welch

Worldwide, the professoriate faces a series of significant challenges: the ageing of the profession, effects of increasing commercialization, fragmentation of the profession, and the effects of globalization and transnational delivery. One assessment of these changes, some years ago, summarized them as follows: 'Commodified, Virtualised, Globalised and Postmodernised; the professoriate stands at the crossroads of an uncertain future' (Welch, 2005: 1).

In what follows, a sketch of key changes to higher education in key parts of Asia, and the implications for the professoriate, is followed by three specific instances of the ways in which the boundaries of academic work practised by the professoriate in Asia are being challenged. Each of the instances discussed below reveal ways in which academic work, and the work of academics, is being re-bordered. It is argued that, while all three examples cited represent forms of re-bordering, some constitute more powerful re-territorializing than others, in what is a highly dynamic context. The Chinese knowledge diaspora forms a powerful transnational network that can act to breach national borders, as well as advance transnational research networks at both ends of the knowledge bridge. (For returnees, however, some re-adaptation to local ways may be needed, upon re-entry to the domestic workplace.) Islamic networks, centuries old, are both regional and trans-regional; each represents a challenge to traditional national borders of academic practice. The final example cited, the Association of South East Asian Nations (ASEAN), has regionalism as its defining feature, yet it is argued that it remains, as yet, a weaker element in South East Asia than in Europe. Countries such as Malaysia, India and Indonesia, for example, only gained independence from colonialism in the years immediately after the end of the Second World War (1945), and expended much energy in the initial decades in developing a national system, notably in higher education. Hence, while regionalism is now being discussed actively within certain higher education circles, it is at a less mature stage of development, relative to Europe, with its longer history of both statehood and transnational collaboration.

The Changing World of Asian Higher Education – Implications for the Professoriate

For much of Asia, the challenges to the traditional work of the professoriate are substantial. Massification, privatization (including of public sector institutions), poor salaries, reduced funding, at least in per-student terms, limited regulatory capacity and an ageing profession are changing the contours of academic work. The following section sketches the contours of these contextual developments and challenges; three examples are then treated, illustrating how re-territoriali-zation is breaching national borders at differing levels of intensity.

Now embracing 31 per cent of the world's student total, massification has changed the landscape of higher education in much of developing Asia over the past decade or two, including for the professoriate. Just the scale of a single system, China, reflects the scope of massification – with almost 30 million students currently enrolled in higher education, and over 2,300 regular higher educa-tion institutions (HEIs), China's faculty now totals over one million: 1,075,989 in 2008 (Yan, 2010). In the other regional giant, India, enrolments have also risen strongly, since independence: from 263,000 in 1950–1, in 30 universities and 750 affiliated colleges, to 11 million students in 230 universities and 17,000 degree-granting affiliated colleges and non-affiliated university-level institutions by 2005 (Kaul, 2006: 22; Welch, 2012a). In Indonesia, the world's most populous Muslim majority nation, total enrolments are estimated to be around 4 million, of which perhaps 200,000 are within Islamic HEIs (state and private).

This rapid expansion of systems within South East Asia, South Asia and East Asia has presented major challenges to their governance and regulatory capacity, and also to equity, with a widening gap between rich and poor having greatest effects on access to higher education by the poor, particularly in rural areas (ADB, 2010a, Welch, 2011a, 2012a). Enrolment growth in selected Asian states over the period since 1980 is summarized in Table 7.1. While all the selected coun-tries reveal strong growth in enrolments over the period, differences, including between the two regional giants, are a striking feature.

This trend of vigorous enrolment growth across much of the region has not been matched by equivalent growth in state support, or faculty numbers, however. At least in per-student terms, state support has declined, if differentially. Once again, China provides a clear illustration of a widening gap between enrolments and state support – over the 1998 to 2003 period, for example, enrolments rose by 230 per cent. By comparison, the rate of increase in state funding was little more

Table 7.1 Student enrolment in higher education in selected countries of the Asian region

Country	1980	1998	2004	2007	2007/1980 as %
Indonesia	543,175	–	3,551,092	3,755,187	691
Malaysia	57,650	443,000	731,077	748,797	1299
Thailand	361,400	1,814,000	2,251,453	2,469,808	683
Viet Nam	114,701	810,000	1,328,485	1,590,000	1386
China	1,662,796	7,364,000	18,090,814	25,346,279	1515
India	3,545,818	–	11,852,936	14,862,962	419

Source: compiled from Welch (2012a: 5).

than six tenths as high, over the same period – 140 per cent (Sun and Barrientos, 2009: 192; Zhao and Sheng, 2008; Wu and Gao, 2010; Welch, 2012a).

For the Chinese professoriate (used throughout this analysis to denote the totality of the academic profession, not merely those holding the professorial title), for example, this failure to adequately support massification entailed significant changes to their working lives (Shen, 2008). An immediate effect was on workloads. Staff/student ratios worsened substantially over the period – from 1:7.24 in 1995 to 1:17.93 in 2006 (Welch, 2011b: 67). In Viet Nam, too, student numbers, which increased thirteenfold between 1987 and 2009, were by no means matched by the rise in the number of faculty, which was just threefold. In the face of this widening gap, staff/student ratios there also worsened dramatically – from 1:6.6 in 1987 to 1:28 in 2009 (ADB, 2010b). Unsurprisingly therefore, Viet Nam's ambitious higher education agenda for the next decade includes a target to train 20,000 new Ph.D.s by 2020; in part to respond to a significant anticipated shortage of well-qualified academic staff (World Bank, 2008; Dang, 2009). This widening gap between spiralling enrolments and limited state support, while also evident in other parts of the world, notably in the Anglo-American systems, is widespread in the Asian region (ADB, 2009; Welch, 2012a).

Other massification effects have also had an impact on the Asian professoriate. A particular set of challenges that arises relates to staffing: to replenish an ageing professoriate, and train sufficient numbers of well-qualified faculty to satisfy spiralling demand, without reducing quality. For South East Asia, China and India, the problem of replenishment is exacerbated by long-standing problems of brain drain, whereby the best and brightest often leave to study abroad, and do not always return (Kapur and McHale, 2006; Welch and Zhang, 2008; Welch and Cai, 2010; Welch and Hao, 2011; Welch, 2012a). Further aggravating the situation, major destination countries such as Australia, Canada and the USA have, in recent decades, each developed sophisticated migration schemes, targeted at the high-skilled, that act as a draw card to graduates, especially from the Asia-Pacific region. An increasing trend is observable of well-qualified graduates from the Asia-Pacific, undertaking research degrees in Anglo-American systems, and then moving into academic posts in those countries (Hugo, 2004; Guo and De Voretz, 2006; Welch, 2010b). But even within Asia, there are enormous disparities, with systems such as Hong Kong and Singapore, with their wealth, highly developed infrastructure and active global recruitment strategies, far more able to attract a genuinely global academic workforce to fill local staff shortages. For countries such as Indonesia, the Philippines or Viet Nam (and for Cambodia and Laos, even more so) this remains a distant goal. Their own diaspora may represent a more practical alternative, although even this can be complex at times (Welch, 2010d).

A further related challenge stems from funding constraints. Given that, as indicated above, governments throughout the region have failed to match enrolment growth with equivalent rises in state support, the predictable outcome has been strong growth in private higher education. As a specialist in finance of higher education argued recently, the consequences were 'a shortage of revenue to accommodate both the increasing costs of instruction and research, as well as (and exacerbated by) the increasing revenue needs of rising enrollments' (Johnstone, 2009: 1; Varghese, 2004; IMHE, 2010).

This has led to specific consequences for the professoriate. In effect, massification has led to privatization, of two different but related forms. The first consists in the often poorly regulated expansion of the private higher education sector, which in the Philippines embraces some two thirds of all HEIs, and in India 75 per cent (ADB, 2008: 45; Agarwal, 2009: 91). Even in socialist Viet Nam, the private sector has been expanding, and current targets are for a further massive expansion by 2020 (Hayden and Khanh, 2010; HERA, 2010; Welch, 2010d). A combination of limited state capacity and domestic politics has meant that in India, for example, it has long been the practice to found a private college and hope that the state will fund it. As a result of such practices, by 2006 43 per cent of HEIs and 30 per cent of student enrolments were in private unaided institutions (Agarwal, 2009: 72, 81, 91). Leading to similar effects in the Philippines has been the common practice by politicians to found a private HEI, however poorly supported, as part of their legacy. In Indonesia, an entire category of HEIs is termed *tidak terakreditasi* (not accredited) (Welch, 2011a: 38). The balance of public and private HEIs in selected Asian states is summarized in Table 7.2.

While at one level, this growth trend is simply a response to demand, leading Levy among others to dub such institutions 'demand-absorbing' (Levy, 1986; Altbach and Levy, 2005), the growth of a substantial private sector, some of which lies outside national accreditation procedures, has implications for both the quality of higher education overall, and for the working conditions of the professoriate. For example, the common practice of moonlighting, whereby poorly paid faculty at public sector HEIs are also employed part-time at private sector HEIs, at night or weekends, in effect weakens teaching quality, research output and time-commitment at the former, while only shoring up the latter

Table 7.2 Numbers and types of HEIs in selected Asian states, 2007

Country	Public Degree	Subtotal	Private Degree	Non-degree	Subtotal	Total
Indonesia	–	81	–	–	2,431	2,512
Malaysia	18	58	22	519	541	599
Philippines	424	1,776	1,363	2,045	3,408	5,184
Thailand	66	66	54	401	455	521
Viet Nam	305	305	64	–	64	369
India (2006)	245	4,493	80	13,400	13,480	17,973
China (2009)	–	1,983	–	–	334	2,317

Sources: ADB (2008: 45); Agarwal (2009: 91); Ministry of Education (People's Republic of China) (2010).

Note: for India, the total includes Aided, Unaided and Deemed universities.

(which often exhibit much lower entry criteria, a restricted range of offerings, and lower proportions of well-qualified teaching staff, particularly those holding doctoral degrees). In effect, the growth of the private sector regionally is largely at the expense of quality, with few private HEIs contributing substantially to overall national innovation, or to basic research production (Altbach and Levy, 2005; Levy, 2002, 2010; Altbach and Salmi, 2011).

But the growth of the private sector relative to the public is not the only effect of reduced state funding. Under pressure to shore up their bottom line, public HEIs are also feeling the push to diversify their income sources. Hence, another trend resulting from the widening gap between spiralling enrolments and limited state support in the higher education sector has been the privatization of public sector HEIs, many of which in Thailand, China and elsewhere rest on weak financial foundations (Welch, 2012a). This, too, is having a significant effect on the professoriate in many parts of Asia. In India, Indonesia and Thailand, some major public universities quadrupled the income deriving from fees within a matter of years, while numbers of nationally reputable public HEIs in Indonesia have introduced a 'special path' (*Jalur Khusus*) that reserves a proportion of places on high-demand courses to those with the ability to pay high fees (*Tempo*, 2003; *Jakarta Post*, 2004; Welch, 2006, 2011a; *Bangkok Post*, 2008). A key strategy adopted by numerous public HEIs in the region has been to develop what are variously called 'extension', 'diploma' or 'executive' courses (*Kompas*, 2002; Welch, 2011a, 2012a). Such courses have much lower entry criteria than regular courses, but are far more expensive. For the small proportion of faculty who are involved (usually from high-demand areas such as business, IT, or perhaps languages), the courses can be quite lucrative, but once again, the effect is to depress quality, as well as time available to students at the mother institution and time for research. Given that it is often the same staff from the parent institution who teach such 'extension' courses, a further effect is to bifurcate the profession, into the small proportion who can take advantage of such opportunities, and the large majority who cannot. Often poorly regulated, the courses have been widely criticized and have generated many complaints from dissatisfied 'customers', but since some public universities in Thailand now report that 60 per cent of their income derives from such activities, and some individual faculties (usually Economics or Business) as much as 75 per cent, the practice is likely to continue (Poapangsakorn, 2008). The fact that not all income derived from such fee-based activities is rigorously accounted for has raised concerns about transparency, or corruption, in higher education. This adds to local and international concerns about corruption in higher education in Indonesia, Viet Nam and elsewhere in the region (Transparency International, 2010; Welch, 2006, 2007, 2011a, 2011b).

These are some key indications that the lifeworld experienced by faculty in much of Asia is not merely changing, but is very distinct from that taken for granted in the West. Another index is seen in faculty salaries. For the professoriate in much of developing Asia, academic salaries, like public sector wages more generally, have long been inadequate to the maintenance of a middle-class lifestyle. While from 2005, the State Taxation Administration listed Chinese university faculty as a high-income group, and they have traditionally also gained significant non-salary benefits such as housing, and subsidized food and entertainment, in practice academic salaries for most Chinese faculty remain modest, albeit rising significantly over the last decade or so (Yan, 2010: 104). In much of South East Asia, with the notable exception of Singapore, the same is true. Hence, many faculty are engaged in additional work, whether moonlighting at a private university, running a small business, undertaking consultancy work (where possible), private tutoring, or some combination of the above. In turn, this has an impact on the commitment and energy they can devote to their mother institution, the public HEI that is their principal employer (if not always the principal source of income).

National/Regional/Global – Renegotiating Educational Space

Whereas most of the reforms instituted, and the regulation of the system, were traditionally bounded by the borders of the state, this is no longer the case. And it is just here that the context indicated above matters, as the following analysis reveals. It is not just the obvious impacts of the regional financial crisis of the late 1990s that swept through the economies of South East Asia, and the more recent global financial crisis beginning around 2008, that have highlighted the importance of external effects on higher education within the South East Asian region, but also the rise of regional and trans-regional consortia in higher education (Denman, 2010; Welch, 2011b), the implanting of offshore campuses (McBurnie and Ziguras, 2007; Welch, 2012c), and the effects of greater mobility – of students, staff and programmes. The Islamic context for higher education in several ASEAN states, most notably Malaysia and Indonesia, forms a further significant element, as seen below. Each of the following examples illustrates elements of the breakdown of the former national boundaries to higher education, albeit not to the extent that the breathless pronouncements of several hyper-globalists, including regional scholars such as Kenichi Ohmae (1991, 1995) have argued.

China's impressive drive to recruit talent from throughout the world forms the first example of how educational space is being re-formed, with implications for the traditional given of the nation-state, including in education (Welch, 2010c). The drive to deploy overseas talent, both Chinese and non-Chinese, in the service of the domestic higher education system and national innovation more generally, has been underpinned by ambitious national and provincial level schemes, institutional strategies and a significant reorientation of policy at the national level (Zweig, 2006; Zweig *et al.*, 2008; Welch and Cai, 2010; Welch and Hao, 2011).

While such strategies, and the legislative instruments and specific schemes that give them force, are national in setting, the reach of these schemes is worldwide, and embraces both high-skilled Chinese in various parts of the world, as well as non-Chinese. In practice, overseas Chinese are far more likely to be chosen, with some schemes registering more than 95 per cent of recruits of such background (Cai, 2012). A major pull factor for overseas Chinese consists of China's world-leading economic growth rates, averaging around 10 per cent per annum since 1990, which is creating significant opportunities at home. A second pull factor consists of China's drive to develop an innovative society, with a consequent emphasis on science and technology and human resource development, including via higher education. Push factors include the global financial crisis (GFC), which reduced opportunities in a number of the most developed countries, as budgets for higher education were reduced and jobs in universities and associated research facilities declined (*Global Higher Education*, 2011; Welch and Hao, 2011). Figure 7.1 charts rising return rates over the past decade and a half, as more high-skilled Chinese abroad took the opportunity to return home.

For such schemes to prosper, earlier policy settings, which had demonized Chinese who had studied abroad, especially outside the USSR or Eastern Europe, as "running dogs" of imperialism and traitors' (Rhoads, 2011: 6; see also Ye, 2001; Bieler, 2004), needed to be amended.

For the Chinese knowledge diaspora too (a growing proportion of an estimated total diaspora of between 35 and 50 million worldwide), such changed policy settings create new and desirable opportunities to cooperate with mainland colleagues. China's revised policy, instituted in 2001, changed direction from *huiguo fuwu* (Return and Serve the Homeland) to the more flexible *weiguo fuwu* (Serve the Homeland); it has seen the development of a wide array of key Overseas Talent Recruitment schemes, targeting the large pool of high-talent overseas Chinese. As indicated above, provinces (especially the wealthier, most developed provinces in China's east) have instituted parallel programmes, while leading national universities have introduced non-resident fellowship schemes, sometimes termed *yaling moshi* (dumbbell model). The wide array of such schemes, and their responsible agencies or ministries, summarized in Welch and Cai (2010), have now been further modified by at least two new elements. The *2011 Plan*, instituted by the Ministry of Education (MoE), is scheduled to commence in 2012, and to replace the *985 Project* from 2013. The State Administration of

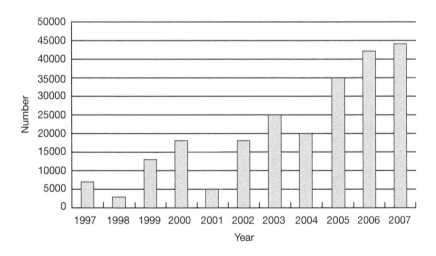

Figure 7.1 Rising rates of returnees, China 1997–2007

Sources: National Bureau of Statistics (2008); Welch and Cai (2010).

Foreign Expert Affairs (SAFEA) has also recently developed a new programme entitled the *Top Foreign Experts Project*.

The much-touted knowledge economy (World Bank, 2002) is in principle borderless. In practice, there are many barriers to the free flow of knowledge and of high-skilled labour. Nonetheless, the Chinese example above clearly underlines the growing importance of the huge pool of high-skilled Chinese talent for the development of Chinese higher education, and research and development more generally. This is in turn tied to the changing character of Chinese migration, which is now increasingly high-skilled in character. Of Silicon Valley's Asian population in the late 1990s, for example, many held at least a Master's level qualification. For both mainland Chinese and Taiwanese residents, the figure was particularly high: 86 per cent and 85 per cent, respectively (Kapur and McHale, 2006: 113). For China-born migrants to Australia (which shows the highest net brain gain of all OECD countries (Docquier and Marfouk, 2006)), the proportion of high-skilled migrants was more than 50 per cent. Of long-term Chinese immigrants to Australia, over eighty per cent currently fall within the three highest occupational categories, while significant numbers have moved into academic posts, usually after taking their Ph.D. at an Australian university (Welch and Zhang, 2006, 2008; Yang and Welch, 2010). It is precisely these individuals who can form important knowledge and cultural bridges between China and host nations, with potential benefits for both sides. One such individual explained the strength of such shared cultural bonds:

(When I returned) … my feeling was, (like) when the child had been away from home for a long time, the parents welcomed their child as a guest. My Alma Mater wants me to return and conduct workshop or seminar for the students. If time permits, I am very happy to, and I think I am committed to doing so.

(Welch and Zhang, 2008: 8)

Another indicated the elements of that close, shared culture appreciatively:

When I talk with my former colleagues, we still communicate as old friends and colleagues. However, when I came back and talked to the junior staff or junior scientists, they paid very high respect to me. Obviously, this is because of the philosophy, the thousands of years of Confucianism.

(Welch and Zhang, 2008: 9)

While in practice there are impediments on both sides that inhibit maximal use of such individuals, the increasing recognition of their blend of skills, capacities and networks forms a powerful transnational knowledge trajectory. Complex questions of culture, knowledge and identity, and renegotiation of former national boundaries to knowledge flows, are evident within such networks.

In practice, while such networks are increasing in scale and scope, with increasing effects on the Chinese innovation system, there are some complications that remain to be solved, notwithstanding the almost universal desire to serve their homeland, evinced by the Chinese knowledge diaspora (Welch and Zhang, 2008; Yang and Welch, 2010). Some individuals in the diaspora indicated that the extent to which *guanxi* (the complex network of relationships that is an integral component of Chinese life) still dominated academic life was a concern that made them hesitant to involve themselves (further) with the domestic system. Others indicated that there were not (yet) specialists in their particular area (a situation that some decided to resolve, by returning to China each year, and running short courses at major universities there). Some women pointed to their greater difficulties in negotiating a system that was still largely patriarchal, and hierarchical. Still others lamented that, despite initial enthusiasm evident in visits from Chinese delegations, or in their return visits to the homeland, there was little follow-up after the visit, something they found frustrating: 'I met one high-level delegation from China. The delegation head assured me that China needed quality personnel like me. But where can I find the bridge for building the linkage? There is no answer' (Welch and Zhang, 2008: 11).

Clearly, while shared ethnicity, and a shared language and culture, transcended national borders, creating a new knowledge space with important benefits for both sides, practical exigencies limited their effectiveness, at times (Welch and Cai, 2010; Yang and Welch, 2010). There is no doubt, however, that China in particular treasures its overseas talent, and is keen to deploy them in the service of the homeland, where they are having a greater and greater impact. Within Asia, both China and India, the two regional giants, have a considerable advantage here, in having a large and highly educated diaspora at their disposal; but the evidence is that China has developed more effectively, to deploy this resource.

A second example of transnational knowledge networks, and associated flows of students and staff within and beyond South East Asia, is actually centuries old, but the scale and reach of such flows are increasing, and again illustrate the power of globally mobile ideas, and the regional and trans-regional dimensions of such flows. The tendrils of Islamic higher education in South East Asia, which are centuries old, extend not merely through Indonesia, Brunei and Malaysia (where, unlike Indonesia, Islam is the state religion), the southern Philippines and southern Thailand, but also to the Middle East. Some signs of transnational regulation have recently been instituted, but are seen by some as more symbolic than substantial. Regional networks and partnerships, however, represent a more powerful trend, particularly between Malaysia and Indonesia.

Islamic higher learning can lay claim to having been among the earliest forms of higher learning in the region now known as South East Asia (Azra, 2004). Imported from the Middle East, for some considerable time numbers of the brightest and most committed scholars from what is now Indonesia and Malaysia have travelled to centres of teaching and scholarship in the Middle East, both Mecca and notably the venerable Al-Azhar in Cairo (Welch, 2012b). That this remains the case is readily attested to by recent visitors to the Al-Azhar campus (including the author), although the Arabic language can constitute a barrier, as young Indonesians and Malaysians acknowledge. This long-standing pan-Islamic epistemic current imparts a significant trans-regional element to Islamic higher education in South East Asia, including links between specific HEIs in

Thailand's predominantly Muslim south, and Al-Azhar (largely in the form of visits). Narathiwat University, in southern Thailand, for example, formed an agreement with Egypt's venerable Al-Azhar University, to bring a teacher from Al-Azhar to teach Islamic Studies to students at Narathiwat. The agreement also offered 80 places to Thai students to study at Al-Azhar. Thai students' scholarships were provided by the Egyptian government.

Further pan-Islamic developments in recent years specifically illustrate the theme of regulation and re-regulation – albeit in a complex fashion, as some of the preceding analysis of the South East Asian context indicated. The formation of the Federation of the Universities of the Islamic World (FUIW), the Islamic Body for Quality and Accreditation (IBQA), the Draft Strategy on the Promotion of University Education in the Islamic World, the development of an Islamic higher education area, and the Islamic Conference of Ministers of Higher Education and Scientific Research are the major examples of moves towards establishing a pan-Islamic form of higher regulation in higher education (ScienceDev, n.d.: 16; UWN, 2010; Welch, 2012b). But how substantial such moves are in practice is another question – some have argued that they are more important rhetorically than in reality. The IBQA, for example, has been criticized by some (including some Malaysians) as more a marketing tool for Malaysian higher education, than a substantive organization to enhance quality assurance across the world of Islamic higher education.

But there are also strongly regional elements to Islamic higher education. Some of these same HEIs in southern Thailand, such as the Princess of Naradhiwas University, have institutional agreements with a University in Brunei Darussalam, and also engage in visits to sister institutions in Malaysia. Another agreement, between Yala University and the University of Brunei Darussalam (UBD) includes staff and student exchanges, as well as joint research, and training programmes and conferences. Students from Yala were able to study for one semester at the UBD, with all costs (including accommodation) to be covered by the UBD. Plans were also mooted for a conference on Islamic education in South East Asia.

Other elements of Islamic higher education within South East Asia that transcend the national include Malaysia's attempts to develop its higher education system into an Eduhub, as part of which it has been strongly advertising its appeal to Muslim students, from both the region and elsewhere. Trading on its status as a Muslim culture, and instruction in the international languages of Arabic and English, has helped market Malaysian higher education. While by no means all international enrolments at Malaysian HEIs were Muslim, by 2007 Indonesia had replaced China as the largest regional source of international students, while Bangladesh was the third largest source country. Malaysia's Minister of Education, Mohamed Khaled Nordi, has advertised Malaysian higher education strategically to the 43 million young people in the Middle East and North Africa (MENA) countries that he estimated were eligible to enter higher education. While higher motives were explicitly mentioned – 'We're providing access to our higher education, places in our universities, because we believe that this is one way of contributing towards the development of our fellow Muslim countries' (*Bernama*, 2009) – more strategic motives were equally apparent:

You will see that there will be a consistent and constant effort by Malaysia, especially my ministry, to come over to this region to establish closer ties with governments and officials responsible for higher education so that they will always consider Malaysia whenever they decide to send their students for further studies.

(*Bernama*, 2009)

The final example illustrates moves from national to regional forms of organization and regulation of higher education but, at the same time, reveals the limits to such moves. The Association of South East Asian Nations (ASEAN) includes several elements focused specifically on higher education, the best known of which is the ASEAN Universities Network (AUN). The Southeast Asian Ministers of Education Organization (SEAMEO) also operates a Regional Institute for Higher Education and Development (RIHED). At the same time, the capacity constraints and other issues listed earlier, in practice, limit the effectiveness with which regionalism can operate in higher education (Welch, 2012d). For several ASEAN member states, domestic limits to institutional governance, regulatory capacity, quality, corruption and financial constraints all inhibit more robust engagement in regional initiatives, including in higher education. Here again, wealthier and more developed systems such as Singapore are far better placed than much less developed systems such as Laos or Cambodia.

Another significant part of the explanation consists in an understanding of the limits of regionalism, and the robustness and effectiveness of regional institutional architecture, within ASEAN more generally. As Jayasuriya (2003), among others, has pointed out, ASEAN regionalism is at a less mature point, relative to Europe, hence instituting regulatory regionalism (including in higher education) 'will prove difficult in a region where there is scant evidence of a history of policy coordination and, moreover, where levels of economic development and the organisation of … systems differ considerably' (pp. 209–10). For Jayasuriya, ASEAN regionalism has largely been triumphalist in character, and has too often been focused on '"formal regional institutions" … to the detriment of the understanding of the domestic political mainsprings of regional governance' (Jayasuriya, 2003: 199).

These limits constrain the effectiveness with which regional architecture in higher education operates. Initiatives include an attempt to develop a South East Asian higher education common space, via a harmonization process (Aphijanyatham, 2010). An Exploration of a Common Space conference was followed by recommendations from the 3rd Director General/Secretary General/ Commissioner for Higher Education in South East Asia Region meeting, held in Bangkok in January 2009. Although progress has thus far been limited, a Malaysia-Indonesia-Thailand (MIT) student mobility project, coordinated by the respective national higher education organs and SEAMEO RIHED, commenced in 2010, with a proposed cohort of 150 students. Some scholarships are also offered to support enrolment by students from one ASEAN member country, in programmes offered by another. Overall, however, and notwithstanding certain achievements in regional higher education initiatives, both domestic and regional constraints limit the effectiveness with which regulatory regionalism can harmonize what are in practice very disparate systems, and strongly local elements.

The analysis above has argued and illustrated connections and tensions between the local, the regional and the global in higher education in South East Asia, several of which have implications for the re-territorialization of the professoriate. The rise of diasporic knowledge networks in one sense expands and challenges the notion of the nation-state, and its capacity to regulate higher education. Predicated upon notions of culture and identity (Welch, 2010d), such networks necessarily introduce new elements and networks into higher education, and research and development more generally. The implications of a worldwide Chinese professoriate, with close professional networks of scientific exchange, are significant not merely for China, and for major host countries such as the USA, Canada and Australia, but are increasingly of world importance. Islamic higher education within South East Asia also illustrated long-standing pan-Islamic dimensions that were at once regional and trans-regional. These too are growing, but their influence on the global knowledge system is less certain, given the relatively peripheral place of HEIs within the Islamic world. The final example reflected upon the character of regionalism and regional architecture in South East Asian higher education and rehearsed some of the issues raised in the opening section on the particular qualities of higher education within the region, including several elements affecting the professoriate. It is clear that, while aspirations for regional harmonization are significant, they are yet to be matched by achievement. Asian regionalism, particularly within ASEAN, has not yet matured to the extent that Europe has, with its sophisticated and relatively well-funded mobility schemes for the professoriate, and EU research funding schemes.

What is raised by each of the above examples, and more generally in the analysis, is the broader challenge to methodological nationalism in educational analysis (as in the social sciences more generally (Smith, 1983)). While methodological nationalism has been argued to be evidence of the nation-state being seen as 'the natural and necessary representation of the modern society' (Chernilo, 2008: 1; see also Wimmer and Glick Schiller, 2002), its equivalent in educational research has been the assumption of the nation-state as the natural unit of both analysis and reflection (Welch, 2010c). In a post-colonial context, in which some South East Asian states have only been free of foreign forces for a few decades, and in the case of Viet Nam, significantly less, nationalism and the associated architecture of the modern state, including regulatory architecture in higher education, comprise a developing discourse, beset on one hand by conflicting local demands domestically and on the other by an emerging, if still immature, regionalism. While the region aspires to develop its own forms of regionalism, including in higher education, it will be some time before it develops the domestic and regional regulatory capacity to occupy some of the space currently occupied by domestic arrangements – themselves still facing a number of challenges, as the analysis above indicated.

This is also true for the professoriate, many of whom in Asia still face a challenging context, characterized by limited autonomy, and poor wages and working conditions, within systems of higher education that are still relatively peripheral in world terms. But there is huge variation, with Singapore and Hong Kong, with their advanced infrastructure and global faculty, far more integrated into the world knowledge system than systems such as Laos, Burma or Cambodia. In this context, it is not useful to speak of an Asian professoriate, *sui generis*, but rather of a graduated series of contexts, each with a different setting, and differing implications for the professoriate, and the knowledge spaces they strive to create.

References

Agarwal, P. (2009) *Indian Higher Education, Envisaging the Future*, Delhi: Sage.

Altbach, P. (ed.) (1999) *Private Prometheus*, Westport, CT: Greenwood Publishing.

Altbach, P. and Levy, D. (eds) (2005) *Private Higher Education: A global revolution*, Amsterdam: Sense Publishers.

Altbach, P. and Salmi, J. (eds) (2011) *The Road to Academic Excellence: The making of world class research universities*, Washington, DC: World Bank.

Aphijanyatham, R. (2010) *East Asian Internationalisation of Higher Education: A key to regional integration*, Bangkok: SEAMEO RIHED, Programme Report No. 25, December.

Asian Development Bank (ADB) (2008) *Education and Skills: Strategies for accelerated development in Asia and the Pacific*, Manila: Asian Development Bank.

Asian Development Bank (ADB) (2009) *Good Practice in Cost-sharing and Financing in Higher Education*, Manila: Asian Development Bank.

Asian Development Bank (ADB) (2010a) *Poverty, Inequality, and Inclusive Growth in Asia: Measurement, policy issues, and country studies*, Manila: Asian Development Bank.

Asian Development Bank (ADB) (2010b) *Viet Nam: Preparing the Higher Education Sector Development Project (HESDP)*, Manila: Asian Development Bank. Available at www.adb.org/Documents/Reports/Consultant/VIE/42079/42079-01-vie-tacr-03.pdf (accessed 10 September 2010).

Azra, A. (2004) *The Origins of Islamic Reformism in Southeast Asia: Networks of Malay Indonesia and Middle Eastern 'Ulaama' in the seventeenth and eighteenth centuries*, Sydney: Allen and Unwin.

Bangkok Post (2008) Learning curve: educators worry over lack of quality control, *Bangkok Post*, 28 July.

Bernama (2009) Malaysia to boost Muslim progress through education, *Bernama*. Available at www.bernama.com/bernama/v3/news_lite.php?id=381479 (accessed 29 July 2009).

Bieler, S. (2004) *'Patriots' or 'Traitors': A history of American-educated Chinese students*, London: M.E. Sharpe.

Cai, H. (2012) Deploying the Chinese knowledge diaspora: a case study of the 111 Project at Peking University, in K. Yu and A. Stith (eds) *Competition and Cooperation Among Universities in the Age of Internationalization*, Shanghai: Shanghai Jiao Tong University Press.

Chernilo, D. (2008) *Methodological Nationalism: Theory and History*, paper presented at the Annual Conference of the International Association of Critical Realism, King's College, London, July 2008.

Dang, Q. (2009) *Recent Higher Education Reforms in Viet Nam: The role of the World Bank*, Working Paper 13, Danish Pedagogical University, October.

Denman, B.D. (2010) *Invisible Colleges and International Consortia in Higher Education*, paper presented at the IMHE/OECD 2010 Conference, Higher Education in a World Changed Utterly: Doing More with Less, Paris, 13–15 September.

Docquier, F. and Marfouk, A. (2006) International migration by educational attainment (1990–2000), in C. Ozden and M. Schiff (eds) *International Migration, Remittances and the Brain Drain*, London: Palgrave Macmillan, pp. 151–200.

Global Higher Education (2011) Austerity budgets, fiscal squeezes, and territorial obligations: the end of an era, *Global Higher Education*, 1 November.

Guo, S. and De Voretz, D. (2006) Chinese immigrants in Vancouver: quo vadis? *Journal of Immigration and Integration*, 7(4): 425–47.

Hayden, M. and Khanh, D. (2010) Private higher education in Viet Nam, in M. Hayden, G. Harman and D. Khanh (eds) *Reforming Higher Education in Viet Nam*, Amsterdam: Springer, pp. 215–25.

HERA (2010) *Higher Education Reform Agenda*, Ha Noi: Ministry of Education.

Hugo, G. (2004) Demographic trends in Australia's academic workforce, *Journal of Higher Education Policy and Management*, 27(3): 327–43.

IMHE (2010) 2010 General Conference, Higher Education in a World Changed Utterly: Doing More with Less, Paris, 13–15 September, Available at www.oecd.org/edu/imhe/generalconference (accessed 20 September 2012).

Jakarta Post (2004) State universities open door to the rich, *Jakarta Post*, 8 April.

Jayasuriya, K. (2003) Introduction: governing the Asia Pacific – beyond the 'new regionalism', *Third World Quarterly*, 24(2): 199–215.

Johnstone, B. (2009) Worldwide trends in financing higher education: a conceptual framework, in J. Knight (ed.) *Financing Higher Education: Access and equity*, Rotterdam: Sense Publishers, pp. 1–54.

Kapur, D. and McHale, J. (2006) *Give Us Your Best and Brightest: The global hunt for talent and its impact on the developing world*, Washington, DC: Centre for Global Development.

Kaul, S. (2006) *Higher Education in India: Seizing the opportunity*, Working Paper No. 179, Delhi: Indian Council for Research on International Economic Relations. Available at www.icrier.org/pdf/WP_179.pdf (accessed 20 September 2012).

Kompas (2002) Kian marak, program ekstensi di Universitas Indonesia, honorarium dosen lebih menjanjikan (More and more extension programmes at University of Indonesia, lecturers secure greater financial benefits), *Kompas*, 3 October.

Levy, D. (1986) *Private Higher Education: Studies in choice and public policy*, Oxford: Oxford University Press.

Levy, D. (2002) *Unanticipated Development: Perspectives on private higher education's emerging roles*, State University of New York, Albany. Available at www.albany.edu/department/eaps/prophe/publication/paper/PROPHEWP01_files/PROPHEWP01.pdf (accessed 14 July 2003).

Levy, D. (2010) *East Asian Private Higher Education: Reality and policy*, discussion paper. Available at http://siteresources.worldbank.org/INTEASTASIAPACIFIC/Resources/EastAsianPrivateHigherEducation.pdf (accessed 15 September 2012).

Levy, D. (2012) Two monologues: Wall Street versus Occupy Wall Street, *International Higher Education* (blog). Available at www.insidehighered.com/blogs/world-view/two-monologues-wall-street-vs-occupy-wall-street-india#disqus_thread (accessed 6 June 2012).

McBurnie, G. and Ziguras, C. (2007) *Transnational Education: Issues and trends in offshore higher education*, London: Routledge.

Ministry of Education (People's Republic of China) 高等教育学校 (机构) 数 (Number of Higher Education Institutions). Available at www.moe.edu.cn/publicfiles/business/htmlfiles/moe/moe_2812/200906/48836.html (accessed 15 May 2010).

Ohmae, K. (1991) *The Borderless World: Power and strategy in the interlinked economy*, London: Fontana.

Ohmae, K. (1995) *The End of the Nation State: The rise of regional economies*, London: HarperCollins.

Poapangsakorn, N. (2008) *Implications for Financing Higher Education in Thailand*, paper presented at the Financing Higher Education and Economic Development in East Asia conference, DPU University Bangkok.

Rhoads, E. (2011) *Stepping Forth into the World: The Chinese educational mission to the United States 1872–1881*, Hong Kong: Hong Kong University Press.

ScienceDev (n.d.) *Towards the Islamic Higher Education Area*. Available at sciencedev. net/Docs/ISESCO_document_2.doc (accessed 29 October 2011).

Shen, H. (2008) Progress of the academic profession in mainland China, in Research Institute for Higher Education (RIHE) (eds) *The Changing Academic Profession in International Comparative and Quantitative Perspective*, Hiroshima: RIHE.

Smith, A.D. (1983) Nationalism and classical social theory, *British Journal of Sociology*, 34(1): 19–38.

Sun, F. and Barrientos, A. (2009) 'The equity challenge in China's higher education policy, *Higher Education Policy*, 22(2): 191–207.

Tempo (2003) Jalur Khusus. Menembus Kampus Ternama, *Tempo*, 1 June, pp. 54–5.

Transparency International (2010) *Corruption Perceptions Index 2010*. Available at www. transparency.org/policy_research/surveys_indices/cpi/2010/results (accessed 28 August 2012).

University World News (UWN) (2010) Islamic states: boosting scientific cooperation, *University World News*, 31 October. Available at http://top-colleges.onlineschoolnet. com/2010/10/31/ISLAMIC-STATES-Boosting-higher-education-cooperation-University-World-News (accessed 12 March 2011).

Varghese, N. (ed.) (2004a) *Private Higher Education*, IIEP Policy Forum No. 16, Paris: UNESCO/IIEP.

Viet Nam News (2002) Officials fall in school scandal, *Viet Nam News*, 7 October.

Welch, A. (2005a) Challenge and change: the academic profession in uncertain times, in A. Welch (ed.) *The Professoriate: Profile of a profession*, Amsterdam: Springer, pp. 1–19.

Welch, A. (2005b) From peregrinatio academica to the global academic: the internationalisation of the profession, in A. Welch (ed.) *The Professoriate: Profile of a profession*, Amsterdam: Springer, pp. 71–96.

Welch, A. (2006) Blurred vision: public and private higher education in Indonesia, *Higher Education*, 54(5): 665–87.

Welch, A. (2007) Ho Chi Minh meets the market: public and private higher education in Viet Nam, *International Education Journal*, 8(3): 35–56.

Welch, A. (2010a) Viet Nam, Malaysia and the global knowledge system, in L. Portnoy, S. Bagley and V. Rust (eds) *Higher Education and International Competitiveness*, Chicago, IL: Chicago University Press, pp. 143–60.

Welch, A. (2010b) Culture and identity, in R. Connell, C. Campbell, M. Vickers, A. Welch, D. Foley and N. Bagnall, *Education, Change & Society*, Oxford: Oxford University Press, pp. 130–67.

Welch, A. (2010c) Nation-state, diaspora and comparative education: the place of place, in D. Mattheou (ed.) *Changing Landscapes, Topographies and Scenarios: Schooling systems and higher education*, Amsterdam: Springer, pp. 285–308.

Welch, A. (2010d) Internationalisation of Vietnamese higher education: retrospect and prospect, in G. Harman, M. Hayden and T. Pham (eds) *Reforming Higher Education in Viet Nam: Challenges and priorities*, Amsterdam: Springer, pp. 215–26.

Welch, A. (2011a) *Higher Education in South East Asia: Blurring borders, changing balance*, London and New York: Routledge.

Welch, A. (2011b) The dragon, the tiger cubs and higher education, in D. Jarvis and A. Welch (eds) *ASEAN Industries and the Challenge from China*, London and New York: Palgrave Macmillan, pp. 39–122.

Welch, A. (2012a) *Counting the Cost: Financing higher education for inclusive growth*, Manila: Asian Development Bank.

Welch, A. (2012b) Seek knowledge throughout the world: mobility in Islamic higher education, *Research in Comparative and International Education* (special issue on Academic Mobility).

Welch, A. (2012c) Contributing to the Southeast Asian knowledge economy? Australian offshore campuses in Malaysia and Vietnam, in A. Nelson and I. Wei (eds) *The Global University: Past, present and future perspectives*, London and New York: Palgrave Macmillan, pp. 45–73.

Welch, A. (2012d) Regionalism and the limits of regionalism in Indonesian higher education, in D. Neubauer and J. Hawkins (eds) *Regionalism in Asia-Pacific Higher Education*, London and New York: Palgrave Macmillan.

Welch, A. and Cai, H. (2010) Enter the dragon: the internationalisation of Chinese higher education, in J. Ryan (ed.) *China's Higher Education and Internationalisation*, London: Routledge, pp. 9–33.

Welch, A. and Hao, J. (2011) Returnees and diaspora: twin sources of innovation for Chinese higher education, *Frontiers of Chinese Education*, in press.

Welch, A. and Zhang, Z. (2006) The Chinese knowledge diaspora: communication networks among overseas Chinese intellectuals in the globalisation era, *Bijiao Jiaoyu Yanjiu*, 26(12): 31–7 (in Chinese).

Welch, A. and Zhang, Z. (2008) The Chinese knowledge diaspora: communication networks among overseas Chinese intellectuals, in D. Epstein, R. Boden, R. Deem, F. Rizvi and S. Wright (eds) *Geographies of Knowledge, Geometries of Power: Framing the future of education: World yearbook of education 2008*, London: Routledge, pp. 338–54).

Wimmer, A. and Glick Schiller, A. (2002) Methodological nationalism and beyond: nation-state building, migration and the social sciences, *Global Networks*, 2(4): 301–34.

World Bank (2002) *Constructing Knowledge Societies*, Washington, DC: World Bank.

Wu, D. and Yu, K. (2011) In the red? Debt levels at higher education institutions in China, *Asia Pacific Asia Review*, 12(3): 329–36.

Yan, F. (2010) The academic profession in China in the context of social transition: an institutional perspective, *European Review*, 18(1): 99–116.

Yang, R. and Welch, A. (2010) Globalisation, trans-national academic mobility and the Chinese knowledge diaspora: an Australian case study, *Discourse* (special issue on Transnational Academic Mobility), 31(5): 593–607).

Ye, W. (2001) *Seeking Modernity in China's Name: Chinese students in the United States 1900-1927*, Stanford, CA: Stanford University Press.

Zhao, L. and Sheng, S. (2008) *Fast and Furious: Problems of China's higher education expansion*, EAI Background Brief No. 395, Singapore: East Asia Institute.

Zweig, D. (2006) Learning to compete: China's efforts to encourage a 'reverse brain drain', in C. Kuptsch and E.F. Pang (eds) *Competing for Global Talent*, Geneva: International Institute for Labour Studies, pp. 187–213.

Zweig, D., Chung, S-F. and Han, D. (2008) Redefining the brain drain: China's diaspora option, *Science Technology and Society*, 13(1): pp. 1–33.

8   What is College Lecturers' Work?

Possibilities for Professionalizing College Lecturers in South Africa

Stephanie Matseleng Allais

Introduction

The work of college lecturers in South Africa has been shaped in different ways by serial policy reform. Under apartheid these institutions were low-status technical colleges offering theoretical training for an apprenticeship system that produced mainly white male artisans. Various reforms have attempted to 'transform' the colleges into 'dynamic', 'responsive' vocational institutions which policy makers will make a substantial contribution to reducing youth unemployment and contribute to economic 'productivity' and competitiveness (e.g. DHET, 2012). Now known as Further Education and Training (FET) colleges, they are the focus of considerable policy attention, with government having announced intentions for massive expansion of the sector (National Planning Commission, 2011; DHET, 2012).

This chapter explores the possibilities for autonomous professionalism for college lecturers in South Africa, drawing on Eliot Freidson's (2001) idea of professionalism as a 'third logic' of the labour market, juxtaposed with the different logics of the free market and bureaucratic labour markets. I explore international trends in technical and vocational education and training (TVET),[1] and locate South African policy developments in this context, considering explicit and implicit narratives about the work of college lecturers and the implications for professionalism.

Neoliberalism and the Global 'Turn to TVET'

South Africa's preoccupation with reform of vocational education and 'skills' policy is very much part of an international trend. Policy focus on TVET internationally has intensified in recent years, as the World Bank, a long-time critic, has started advocating building TVET systems. Aid money and technical assistance to developing countries from a variety of international organizations has increased. At the same time, the policy focus has shifted from traditional notions of building technical skills to a focus on skills as the basis for entrepreneurship. Both developments, I argue, have their roots in neoliberalism.

The idea of education as the solution to economic problems has been central to neoliberalism (Brown *et al.*, 2011). Reforms in wealthy countries have stripped away much of the safety net of welfare states, and structural adjustment programmes in poor countries demolished miniscule existing welfare provision and prevented the growth of more, as governments shifted from attempting to ensure employment to controlling inflation regardless of the effect on employment (Harvey, 2005). The neoliberal policy consensus has been that, while governments cannot guarantee employment, they can and should assist individuals to become 'employable' or to develop 'marketable skills'. Neoliberalism, argues Hein Marais (2011: 137–8), drawing on Gillian Hart (2006):

> represents a new modality of government predicated on interventions to create the organizational and subjective conditions for entrepreneurship – not only in terms of extending the 'enterprise model' to schools, hospitals, housing estates, and so forth, but also in inciting individuals to become entrepreneurs themselves.

Unemployment is redefined as a learning problem that can and should be solved by individuals (Novoa, 2002; Brown *et al.*, 2011). Educational institutions must become more entrepreneurial, and provision of vocational education must be market-based (even if this means state providers functioning within a market or quasi-market), as the market is seen as the best mechanism to distribute goods and services.

Rising levels of youth unemployment together with rising levels of school completion may lie behind increasing policy interest in post-school educational provision, including TVET. Qualification inflation, as individuals are compelled to invest in ever higher levels of education in order to gain a foothold in the labour market, combined with casualization, inevitably means that individuals undertake education programmes with little relationship to the workplaces that they find, or hope to find, themselves in. The growing disconnection between 'requirements' of the world of work and the educational qualifications held by individuals may be implicated in the growing international rediscovery of TVET. The rediscovery of TVET may also be the result of neoliberal emphasis on pro-enterprise policy – in many instances new 'skills' policies channel finances into the private sector, or enable the private sector to gain subsidized ownership of one of the few remaining unprivatized sectors in many countries. Alongside this is a preoccupation with 'vocationalizing' general education, as schools and universities are under pressure to produce learners with 'relevant' skills (Grubb and Lazerson, 2006).

Simon McGrath (2012) suggests that TVET reform internationally over the past 15 years, particularly in developing countries, has been guided by what he refers to as a global 'TVET toolkit'. This 'toolkit' includes systemic reform focused on giving more power to employers, often through competence-based qualifications and/or qualifications frameworks; quality assurance systems; outcomes-based and 'institutionally-neutral' funding; and managed autonomy for public providers. These are all mechanisms aimed at creating and supporting regulated markets in TVET, in the hope that this will enable individuals to gain skills that can lead to jobs or work.

Competence-based training and qualifications frameworks, which initially emerged in the English-speaking liberal market economies where there are poor linkages between education programmes and workplaces, are intended to improve 'relevance', by developing qualifications comprised of employer-defined competencies. In other words, the starting point for thinking about education is a description of the needs and practices of the workplace. They are also part of quality assurance and marketization policies, as learning outcomes and qualifications are intended to be used as performance measures against which governments (and the private sector) can contract providers and evaluate their performance, breaking up what is perceived as 'monopolization' of provision by public providers (Raggat and Williams, 1999). Starting with the National Vocational Qualifications (NVQs) in the United Kingdom, spreading to the competence-based reform of vocational education in Australia, and a National Qualifications Framework (NQF) in New Zealand, the emphasis has been on government regulating vocational education through reforming and regulating a 'market of qualifications' comprised of employer-specified competencies (Phillips, 1998; Allais *et al.*, 2009).

This 'market of qualifications' approach to vocational education stands in strong contrast to TVET systems in coordinated market economies, such as the German dual system, which focus on education for well-regulated and protected occupations (Rauner, 2007; Iverson and Stephens, 2008; Brockmann, 2011). In the latter approach, TVET is 'integrated into a comprehensive education system, and is designed to develop the ability to act autonomously and competently within an occupational field', and aims to develop vocational competence and identity (Brockmann, 2011: 120–1). In the former approach, employer-specified competencies tend to lead to narrow skills training for fragmented work processes in the immediate job at hand (Winch, 2011). Intellectual functions (planning, coordinating, evaluating, controlling) are sharply separated from execution (Clarke, 2011). The competence-specification approach seems to lead to narrow and low-status vocational education that most people try to avoid. It also seems to lead to endless cycles of reform, trying in vain to get closer to an elusive idea of what employers *really* want in the workplace, and the constant reorganization of government agencies and quasi-governmental agencies (Keep, 2007; Allais, 2010; Brockmann *et al.*, 2011). Teaching or training in TVET are lower-status occupations, with low-level or no regulated qualifications and insecure conditions of employment, as compared with those in the coordinated market economies (Young, 2008; Wheelahan, 2010; Gamble, 2011).

The former, liberal market economy approach, has dominated the developing world, partly because poorer countries invariably are dominated by informal markets, with few well-regulated and stable occupations. They have weak states and weak education systems, and, particularly in Africa, extremely weak TVET systems. The package of reforms contained in the 'TVET toolkit', particularly outcomes-based qualifications frameworks and quality assurance systems, have great appeal because they are focused on *regulation* of provision, rather than trying to build and improve providing institutions, and are positioned as leading to 'employability', rather than employment. The growth of qualifications frameworks, competence-based training and labour competence frameworks continues, despite lack of evidence of success – there are almost no documented achievements of this model in the developing world, other than the proliferation of paper qualifications and competence statements that are never actually awarded to anyone (Allais, 2010). The growth of qualifications frameworks in Europe may reflect the growing influence of neoliberal policies, and the breakup of the social pacts that enabled strong vocational education and well-regulated occupations, or, more optimistically, it may reflect a substantially different notion of a qualifications framework.

South Africa provides a particularly interesting area of study, as neoliberal reforms have, in many instances, been presented as part of democratization and the transformation of apartheid legacies, thereby enhancing their legitimacy, and perhaps enabling faster and more extreme liberalization than would otherwise have been possible. The South African NQF is a particularly extreme version of a policy that has, in other countries, been introduced in fewer sectors of the education system, and with far more limited goals. Further, different government departments' implementation of neoliberal public sector reform, as well as their institutional logics and legacies, have refracted global trends in very particular and often contradictory ways. The following section explores these dynamics through an analysis of policy documents and processes, as well as information from key informants in the college system.

The South African Dual Transition and the 'Turn to TVET'

In 1994, capturing imaginations around the world, and with the support of the majority of the population, South Africa managed a 'miracle' transition from racist authoritarianism to democracy. South Africa was one of many 'transitional' states in the early 1990s experiencing a parallel transition, democratization of the state on the one hand, and liberalization of the economy on the other hand, with the consequence of increased economic inequality together with the institutionalization of formal democracy. However, perhaps because of the unique horror of the apartheid system, the unique global support for the anti-apartheid movement, and the euphoria of the defeat of apartheid, the dual transition was less in the spotlight, and the extremely rapid transition from a highly regulated and relatively isolated economy to a highly neoliberal economy (Marais, 2011) was masked by the transition to democracy.

The South African economy, dominated by a minerals and energy complex, has a weak industrial sector based on low-skilled and unskilled work (Fine and Rustomjee, 1996). Unemployment is extremely high – between 20 and 40 per cent of the population, depending on whether one uses the 'narrow' or 'broad' definition (Makgetla, 2010). Less than half of South African adults had some kind of income-generation strategy in the mid 2000s (Makgetla, 2010; Marais, 2011). Youth unemployment is particularly high: one in eight adults under 25 years of age has a job (National Treasury, 2011).

TVET is seen as an important part of the solution to this problem, together with policies such as youth wage subsidies and increasing 'labour market flexibility'[2] (National Planning Commission, 2011; National Treasury, 2011; DHET, 2012).

But unlike wealthy countries where 'social exclusion' refers to a minority (although increasing) section of the population, in South Africa this strategy is invoked as a solution to the problem that the *majority* of the population are outside the labour market. The TVET sector that is supposed to deal with this problem is a small and weak sector of the education system: the headcount enrolment in the college system in 2010 was 326,970 learners; this includes all years of study, and many students enrolled for short (three-month) programmes (DHET, 2012). In other words, South Africa provides an extreme example of an international trend: the attempt to use education policy, and particularly vocational education policy, to solve economic problems. The likelihood of policy makers' goals being achieved in South Africa is circumscribed by the inherent weakness of the reform approaches, the weakness of providing institutions, and contradictory pulls from government departments. These are discussed below, after some brief contextual information.

The History of the System

Under apartheid, as well as in colonial pre-apartheid South Africa, work-related curricula were associated with low-achieving learners and the control of 'social deviancy' (Badroodien, 2004). The system was highly racialized, low status, fragmented and separated from the rest of the education system (Gamble, 2003). The strongest part of it, artisan training, was aimed at white men, conducted through state-owned enterprises and the colleges (McGrath, 1996; Gamble, 2004a; McGrath *et al.*, 2004). College lecturers taught a nationally prescribed curriculum in three-month blocks, preparing learners for national examinations, which, coupled with work experience for the remainder of the year, were requirements for sitting a trade test and becoming a qualified artisan. The certificates offered were known as N1, N2 and N3 – or the 'N' courses. The few colleges open to black people offered mainly short programmes that led to narrow skills (Badroodien, 2004; DHET, 2009).

By the 1980s, the colleges provided a route to a qualification for those who did not complete their secondary education. With the addition of languages, students could obtain a certificate that was regarded as the same as the senior secondary qualification obtained in schools, known in South Africa as the Matric, although at a level that did not lead to university entrance (Umalusi, 2006). Colleges also offered post-secondary education, with three certificates, commonly referred to as N4–N6. These certificates, with the addition of a prescribed amount of work experience, resulted in the awarding of the National N Diploma.

In the 1990s, racially based admissions ended. The student population shifted dramatically, from 60 per cent white and 18 per cent African students in 1990, to 12 per cent white and 75 per cent African by 2000 (DHET, 2009). A large number of these students had a Matric, despite the fact that the colleges were officially offering an alternative to this qualification, and a declining number of them had work placement through an apprenticeship, as state-owned enterprises were corporatized, and started focusing more on profit than training. The colleges were, then, increasingly serving as full-time post-school institutions, instead of functioning in parallel with the school system by providing part-year courses for people on apprenticeships. This trend has continued, in large part because South Africa has no public post-school offerings outside the university system, and only a small fraction (less than 20 per cent) of learners who obtain a Matric qualify to apply for degree study at a university.

Two Masters

The negotiated settlement that led to the first democratic elections in 1994 placed substantial authority for much of the education system, including the colleges, in the hands of provincial governments. At a national level, education and training were split between a Ministry of Education and a Ministry of Labour, with the former responsible for schools, adult education, colleges and universities, and the latter in charge of what was called 'skills development'. The Department of Labour developed a levy-grant system through which employers were taxed 1 per cent of their payroll. Sectoral Education and Training Authorities (SETAs) were set up in different areas of the economy, to distribute grants back to employers upon receipt of training plans and reports (Republic of South Africa, 1997). The system was intended to create an incentive for employers to train, and also to enable the aggregation of information about the training needs of each sector. The SETAs could also apply to be quality assurance bodies for educational provision in their respective economic sectors.

While the colleges were officially under the Ministry of Education, and directly under provincial governments, they were also expected to engage with the skills development system of the Department of Labour and, for the first time, to teach courses other than the N1–N6 courses, as well as to develop curricula and assessment for new courses. This may not have become a problem, if there had not been substantial difference in policy implementation by the two Ministries. Key to the differences was the National Qualifications Framework.

The NQF, the Department of Labour and the 'Entrepreneurial College'

A National Qualifications Framework (NQF) introduced in 1995 was intended as a key tool to reform the education and training system as a whole by replacing all existing qualifications in the country with a set of new outcomes-based qualifications and part qualifications (unit standards) designed by new stakeholder-based structures (Republic of South Africa, 1995; SAQA, 2000a, 2000b). The new qualifications and unit standards would be registered by a newly created South African Qualifications Authority (SAQA) on the NQF. This system – the design and registration of outcomes-based qualifications – was intended to change *all* learning programmes and curricula, at all levels, in all sectors. Quality assurance bodies, according to the original policies, would be accredited by SAQA. Educational providers would apply to quality assurance bodies to be accredited to offer or assess specific qualifications and unit standards. Assessors would be 'registered' by quality assurance bodies, to assess specific unit standards and qualifications.

Although heavily derived from similar reforms in New Zealand, Australia and, more indirectly, the UK, the NQF was described as a tool to transform and democratize the apartheid education system through learning outcomes. Official documents emphasized its roots in the labour movement,[3] downplaying international policy borrowing (Allais, 2007). Clothed in the rhetoric of the liberation movement, a contractualized model of reform was introduced: institutions, including the public colleges, were supposed to become entrepreneurial, offering qualifications desired by businesses, and marketing themselves to learners. This was intended to create 'a demand-led enterprise training policy' (Kraak, 2004: 126) through which a regulated market of provision of training would become responsive to employers' needs. Funding would be directed to training providers through employers commissioning relevant training for their staff, in order to claim back their skills levy. Like much TVET reform internationally, and in common with New Public Management-style public sector reform,[4] public and private providers were to be treated the same, with funding from learner enrolments for programmes that they had been accredited by quality assurance agencies to offer. While official documentation emphasized individual empowerment in a discourse of democratization (SAQA, 1997, 2000a), the logic of providing better information to learners as consumers of training was embedded in a discourse of self-help and entrepreneurialism, unquestioningly adopting assumptions of neoclassical economics (Allais, 2011).

The Ministry of Labour announced that the old apprenticeship system would be entirely replaced by a new system of 'learnerships', offered through newly developed outcomes-based national qualifications registered on the NQF. The 'N' courses would no longer have a role in the system. Colleges were expected to apply to SETAs for accreditation to offer programmes against new qualifications. SETAs in turn were applying to SAQA for accreditation to be quality assurers.[5] Colleges started using the new qualifications and unit standards, and attempted to be accredited by SETAs, each with different bureaucratic requirements, in order to 'be responsive' to employer needs, although this was still only a small part of their work.

'Managed Autonomy' for Colleges under the Department of Education

Initial reform of the colleges appeared to support the policy direction described above. By 2003 the 152 technical colleges had been restructured into 50 multi-campus FET colleges. These new FET colleges were given substantially increased autonomy, through the FET Colleges Act of 2006, which gave councils wide-ranging powers, including hiring lecturers directly (Republic of South Africa, 2006). All of this was supposed to enable colleges to function as responsive providers in the new policy environment.

But the reform logic was not followed through. Colleges continued to offer the 'N' courses – while the apprenticeship system was designated as due to end, it was still officially in the process of being phased out. The Department of Education developed a new curriculum, and a new national qualification for the colleges to offer, called the National Certificate (Vocational), to replace the 'N' courses.

This new qualification, formally phased into the colleges from January 2007, was supposed to be broader and more substantial than the old courses for the apprenticeships system, teaching 'high level conceptual knowledge' (DHET, 2009: 11). But there was continuity with the old system: a nationally specified curriculum and a national examination, contrary to the qualifications model of the NQF.[6] The curriculum is an outcomes-based one, which makes considerable demands on college educators, but, in contradiction with this, there is a national examination, which, coupled with textbooks, leads to an implicit syllabus.

Thus, two different sets of 'boundaries' emerged for the work of college lecturers. On the one hand, college lecturers were supposed to be entrepreneurially minded sellers of qualifications, designers of curricula and assessment, and sophisticated navigators of a highly complex accreditation, qualifications and quality assurance system, through a system based on contractualization and competition. On the other hand, they were supposed to teach a prescribed curriculum, leading to a national examination, through a state-funded system, managed by a national Department of Education.

Coming Together?

The original design of the NQF, as well as much of the quality assurance system built around it, largely collapsed, and was completely changed in 2009, just before a dramatic (if perhaps rhetorical) shift in the broader political and economic realm, away from the neoliberal notions of a regulatory state, and towards a (perhaps rhetorical) project of a 'developmental state', claimed by the government that came to power in 2009. This government replaced a government led by the same political party, the African National Congress (ANC). However, dramatic shifts within the configuration of party leadership enabled the new government to associate itself with substantial shifts in economic and political policy (Marais, 2011). A newly created Department of Higher Education and Training is headed by a Minister who is also General Secretary of the South African Communist Party, as well as a member of the ruling ANC. The creation of this Ministry has, for the first time, located the entire post-school education and training system in a single Ministry, including workplace-based training, and the complex host of institutions surrounding the levy-grant system. For the first time colleges are separated from the school system: schools are now the responsibility of a newly created Department of Basic Education.

Education policy changes have been signalled: official statements have indicated a far greater role for central government and building stronger institutions as a key focus. The role of provinces in relation to colleges is in the process of being phased out, and proposed amendments to existing legislation will transfer college lecturers back to being state employees (DHET, 2012). The apprenticeship system and the 'N' courses have been officially reinstated. SETAs are losing their authority to accredit providers, and quality assurance is far more centralized, through three Quality Councils (Republic of South Africa, 2008). But there are also continuities: much of the policy rhetoric currently emanating from the new department, as well as from the rest of government, is still located in the discourse of 'human resource development' in service of a 'knowledge economy' as a solution to economic problems, and training as a solution to social exclusion. The FET colleges, in a dramatically expanded and substantially improved form, remain positioned as key to realizing this vision.

This is the shifting context in which attempts are being made to professionalize college lecturers through qualification policy.

The National Attempt to 'Professionalize'

A recently conducted survey (National Business Initiative, 2011) describes college lecturers as mainly between 25 and 50 years old, fairly evenly matched between men and women. English is the most widely spoken language as a first or second language, but over two-thirds of the respondents speak an African language as a first or second language. The most commonly held qualification (just over 20 per cent of a large sample of respondents) was the National N Diploma, which lecturers would have obtained if they had completed all the college courses – N3 to N6 – and undergone work experience. A further 12.8 per cent had only lower-level certificates offered in the colleges (the N3 to N6 certificates). Just over 20 per cent had a Bachelor's degree, of which 5.2 per cent were a Bachelor of Technology. A mere 2.7 per cent had completed an apprenticeship or passed a trade test, while 16.4 per cent had some other artisan/trade/technician qualification. Some 15.3 per cent of the respondents reported that they were or had once been registered artisans; of these, four-fifths were still registered. The majority had between one and ten years' teaching experience; only 5.3 per cent were in their first year of teaching. The majority had no relevant work experience in industry or business. Of course this picture varies dramatically across fields. For example, in IT, Construction and Engineering, the vast majority of lecturers are men, and the IT lecturers are generally younger than the other lecturers (National Business Initiative, 2010). The staff most likely to have industry experience are those who teach learnerships or programmes paid for through the skills-levy system, as opposed to those who teach the mainstream (NCV or N) college courses (DHET, 2012).

In the past, most college lecturers were drawn from business and industry (DHET, 2009). Many had technical qualifications coupled with practice and experience in the workplace, particularly those involved in delivering engineering courses. Some had educational qualifications through technikons – tertiary institutions that have recently been renamed universities of technology. Lecturers teaching mathematics or languages were frequently recruited from the school system.

Both the former Department of Education and current Department of Higher Education and Training have been attempting to contribute to the 'professionalization' of lecturers through qualification policy. In the recent past qualifications were regulated through the Department of Education, as part of the regulation of qualifications for schoolteachers.[7] Now, for the first time, specific and separate policy is being developed for college lecturers (DHET, 2011). An early version of this policy argues that 'college lecturers ought to be autonomous and reflective professionals *in addition to being employees'* (DHET, 2009: 9; my emphasis). Policy documents argue that ensuring appropriate arrangements for delivery, certification and recognition of lecturers' qualifications will make it easier for them to progress along a formal education career path (DHET, 2009, 2011). Institutionalizing, formalizing and improving educator training, and regulating the qualifications of lecturers, are the main ways in which this 'professionaliza-tion' is envisaged. Proposals currently being debated include a suite of university-based teaching qualifications for college lecturers, although with considerable differences in proposals for lecturers teaching general and academic subjects, lecturers teaching vocational subjects, and lecturers teaching practical compo-nents of courses.

In 2010 a new course, worth 30 credits (120 credits is roughly a year's full-time study), was piloted, known as the Vocational Education Orientation Programme. It was offered by a few universities and universities of technology, and aimed to provide an introduction to the TVET institutions and policies (the colleges but also the broader 'skills' policies), to assist lecturers in working with the prescribed curricula, and to assist them with pedagogy as well as with management and administrative tasks (DHET, 2011).

These qualification policies constitute the closest form of an official narra-tive about college lecturer professionalism in South Africa. But policies, prac-tices and systems also present implicit invisible narratives that create boundaries of possibility for the nature of work and, hence, of professionalism. Freidson (2001) argues that professions are occupations in which workers, rather than consumers or managers, control work, because work relies on judgements based on specialized knowledge and cannot, therefore, be standardized, rationalized or commodified, and is inaccessible to those lacking the training and experi-ence. He juxtaposes professions with work that is rule governed and controlled by managers in a large bureaucracy (whether the state or a firm), and work that is at the 'mercy of the market'. These three logics are provided as ideal types, to provide an analytical framework with which to examine occupations, and not exact descriptions of particular professions. The shifting TVET policy in South Africa described above seems to have mainly moved the focus of college lecturers somewhat between the logic of the bureaucracy and the logic of the market, with little possibility for autonomy in their work. The following sections consider this in more detail, in relation to the knowledge base of college lecturers as well as their conditions of employment and the labour process.

Knowledge Base and Boundaries

John Beck and Michael Young summarize the essential common traits of professions:

> an exceptional measure of collective collegiate autonomy over their condi-tions of professional training, certification of professional competence, and conditions of work and practice; a knowledge base defined by the profes-sions *themselves*; and professional training which also involved intensive

socialisation into the values of a professional community and its standards of professional integrity, judgement, and loyalty – in other words, the creation of a professional habitus.

(2005: 188)

Clearly, a key issue with regard to professionalism is the extent to which the occupation in question has a monopolized domain of practice controlled through university-acquired knowledge. Jeanne Gamble (2010: 5), drawing on Freidson (1994) and Andrew Abbot (1988), explains the dilemma with regard to schoolteachers: pedagogy is and always will be contested. This means there is no coherent 'story' to offer to the outside world. Many dominant educational ideas, such as progressivism, blur the distinction between curriculum and pedagogy, as well as blurring the divide between the everyday world and the classroom (Muller, 2000; Egan, 2002; Young, 2008). And, to the extent that teaching is seen as a female, caring and nurturing occupation, parents tend to believe they know about pedagogy.

Knowledge about vocational pedagogy is even more weakly developed than pedagogy in general. Work experience is frequently seen as more important than 'theoretical' study in colleges, and ideas like Etienne Wenger's (1999) 'community of practice' are invoked by policy makers and researchers to emphasize the importance of informal learning, juxtaposed with formal instruction. All of this means that dominant pedagogical theories leave little room for vocational lecturers to establish boundaries between their expert practice and the world of laypeople. At the same time, subject matter expertise of college lecturers is weakly developed, and it does not, as is the case for many schoolteachers, have a base in a strongly developed disciplinary body of knowledge.[8] All of these factors contribute to college lecturers being positioned as rule-governed state employees, to an even greater degree than is the case for teachers.

The dominant alternative, competence-based training, in South Africa mainly introduced through NQF-type qualifications, positions itself as freeing lecturers from the boundaries of work defined by the bureaucracy – it suggests an alternative in which they are free to design their own curricula and assessment. In many cases colleges have been attracted to this route as it seems closer to the world of work. This perceived higher degree of autonomy does not, though, offer a basis for professionalism; instead it throws lecturers to the market. Consumers, here employers, dictate to lecturers what they should be teaching. And because there is no coherent knowledge base and no separate teaching of theoretical knowledge, but rather a constantly shifting response to employers' alleged needs, derived from analysis of jobs, this approach leads to low skills and low-status vocationalism, upholding the commonly held idea that vocational curricula are 'dumbed down' versions of general academic curricula (Gamble, 2004b). In other words, lecturers are saved from the bureaucracy only to be thrown to the market (and, given that it is a regulated market, this involves a considerable amount of processes and systems that bound work in different ways).

What is the alternative? Following Freidson's and Gamble's logic, subject matter expertise is the key to establishing a knowledge base and boundaries of practice.

No one tries to 'professionalize' university lecturers, although political and economic systems could be seen as 'proletarianizing' them (for example, Newfield, 2010). University lecturers in South Africa, as in many countries, do not require formal training as educators. Their disciplinary specialization *is* their professional knowledge. It is this, and not their knowledge about how to impart knowledge, that gives them power over their own knowledge base, as well as boundaries from laypeople. Gamble (2010: 12) cites Schulman (1986: 6) as pointing out: 'The highest university degrees of "doctor" and "master", which were traditionally used interchangeably, both entitled recipients to be called a teacher.' This should not be read as an argument that any kind of 'teacher training' is a waste of time. Introduction to debates about pedagogy, as well as practical strategies, and the philosophy and sociology of education may, as Antonio Gramsci argued, provide a basis for a strong sense of vocation and identification with the profession (Entwistle, 1979). But as Gamble (2010), drawing on Beck (2008, 2009) argues, the current emphasis on standards and practice fragments and deprofessionalizes, leaving no basis for a distinctive form of expertise, and creating work that is bounded and framed by short-term market needs.

The draft policy on lecturer qualifications (DHET, 2011) speaks at length about the importance of subject matter expertise. However, 'disciplinary learning' is included as one of five types of learning needed by college lecturers, the others being 'pedagogical learning', 'practical learning', 'fundamental learning' (which refers to a second South African language and computer literacy) and 'situational learning'. Further, disciplinary learning is defined as including *both* subject matter expertise and the study of education. And as pointed out above, universities in most cases do not have the same specializations as what is taught in college qualifications – for many college subjects there is no natural equivalent discipline in the universities; they also have very little expertise in vocational pedagogy, to say nothing of the other types of learning imagined by policy makers. It could be the case that, once universities start training lecturers, they will start to develop research and expertise. However, another bleaker possibility is that they will hire college lecturers and retired teachers on short-term contracts in order to meet government training targets, and push lecturers through inadequately designed courses, with little effect on practice, and with no long-term benefits for the profession; South Africa has considerable experience in this sad practice with regard to schoolteachers (Taylor, 2011).

Part of the problem is the weakly organized voice of lecturers within the sector. This relates directly to conditions of employment and the nature of work.

Conditions of Employment and the Labour Process

As mentioned above, college lecturers were previously employed by provincial departments of education under the Employment of Educators Act, which governs the employment of schoolteachers, and shifted by the FET Colleges Act so that currently the majority of lecturers are employed directly by colleges; however, these lecturers were still paid directly by the state. A minority[9] of lecturers is employed by colleges and paid by colleges; these tend to be lecturers hired through learnerships and programmes funded through the skills-levy systems.

Salary negotiations take place through the Education Labour Relations Council, the bargaining council for teachers, in a bargaining unit specific to the colleges. Lecturers are represented by the South African Democratic Teachers' Union (SADTU) and the Combined Trade Union: Autonomous Teacher Unions.[10] These are unions that predominantly organize schoolteachers. Employers are represented by both the Department of Higher Education and Training and the FET Colleges Employers' Association. Although many lecturers are not unionized, agreements reached in the bargaining council apply to all lecturers.

Unionization of schoolteachers is a contentious issue in South Africa, particularly with regard to debates about professionalism, and particularly because of apartheid history and the liberation struggle. SADTU, which represents nearly two-thirds of schoolteachers and is predominantly black, is seen as the union that champions teachers' bread and butter issues, while NAPTOSA (the National Professional Teachers' Organization of South Africa), smaller and representing mainly white teachers, although by now with a fairly substantial number of black members, has historically separated itself from a tradition of striking, and prided itself on supporting teachers' professional development. However, in recent years NAPTOSA members have joined SADTU in strikes, and SADTU actively talks about teacher professionalism. While these debates have relevance to the college sector, the voice of college lecturers is dwarfed in these unions by their small numbers relative to schoolteachers, and low levels of unionization in the colleges.

There is currently no professional council for college lecturers. Schoolteachers and college lecturers in South Africa are required to register with the same professional council, the South African Council of Educators (SACE). The majority (68.8 per cent) of college lecturers are registered, some on an interim basis as they do not meet all the formal qualification requirements (National Business Initiative, 2011). SACE is a weak voice even within the school system (De Clercq, 2011). Its voice in the college sector is particularly insignificant.

Amendments to legislation are currently under way, whereby the lecturers currently paid by the state will become state employees, and the minority, employed and paid by colleges, will remain as college employees. There is currently contestation about whether the transferred majority will be employed through specific legislation, as schoolteachers are, or as general public servants, through the Public Service Act (NAPTOSA, 2011). The latter arrangement will shift collective bargaining to the bargaining council for all public servants for state-employed lecturers, and the remainder, employed by the colleges, will remain in the Education Labour Relations Council. Many lecturers are employed on short-term contracts (around 35 per cent by some counts); there is currently a collective agreement to improve conditions of service of contract staff. This is a product of a single bargaining council, and the conditions of employment for these lecturers may well become more precarious if current proposals are implemented.

All of this, then, amounts to non-independent conditions of employment, a minority being largely at the mercy of the market as entrepreneurs selling courses, and with most lecturers being largely controlled by the state. But this majority can also be seen as employed through a kind of hybrid model: even when the state is the formal employer, current policies allow colleges to renew contracts based on learner enrolments. Enrolment-based funding is introduced to make colleges 'responsive'; in practice it ensures that workers who are formally 'controlled by the state' are in fact 'at the mercy of the market'.

Possibilities for Professionalism

College lecturers are in a weak position: largely un-unionized, with little autonomy over conditions of employment, with no professional association to speak of, and in the lowest-status corner of a profession that is the focus of considerable public criticism and government attempts at regulation and control. Policies thus far implemented have in practice shifted lecturers back and forth between the 'logics' of the bureaucracy and the market; employment policies, as well as the lack of a clear knowledge base, make it difficult to see possibilities for Freidson's notion of autonomous professionalism.

Judyth Sachs (2001) distinguishes between what she calls 'managerialist professionalism', which comes from employing authorities who want to 'improve education' by making teachers more 'professional', usually translating as more 'effective' and frequently including 'less likely to strike'; and 'democratic professionalism', which emerges from the profession itself, concerned about status and pay. The absence of an organized voice, either through a union or professional council, makes the former type of professionalism more likely to be the result of the current regulation through qualification process. The danger is that this type of professionalism tends to focus on behaviour, as Linda Evans (2011) shows in relation to the UK, rather than on the attitudes and 'intellectuality' of teachers – the factors discussed above as necessary for autonomous professionalism. Jenny Ozga (1995) argues that performance- or standards-based reforms in fact *de-professionalize* teachers, because they reduce their autonomy, and Sachs (2003) argues similarly that:

> professionalism under the guise of standards becomes a tool for employers demanding more of teachers. The implementation of a standards framework puts teachers in a double bind. If they do not have a set of publicly documented standards like other 'professions', then they are seen not to have the same professional status as those professions who do have these codified frameworks.
>
> (p. 184)

Andy Hargreaves (1992) also points out that work intensification in teaching makes it less likely that teachers can improve their knowledge base, as they have no time to keep up with their field. Undertaking professional development activities based on government specified standards may contribute to the intensification of lecturers' work, unless participation in standards-based professional development is seen as an integral part of teachers' work and time allocated for this to occur. This is why, as Freidson (2001) argues, it is a mistake to emphasize associations or codes of ethics in attempts to 'professionalize', without addressing more fundamental issues of conditions of employment and autonomy over work. In South Africa in particular, a further consideration is the context in which lecturers work. As Yael Shalem and Ursula Hoadley (2009: 130) point out, in relation to school teachers, 'to keep pushing a more stringent regulative framework might bring about more of the current low morale, but will not provide the real oxygen that the system needs'. The catch-22 is that until lecturers are more organized, and until the knowledge fields that they draw on are better developed, there is little possibility for the development of the latter type of democratic professionalism.

What the future roles of the colleges will be is still not entirely clear, besides government intent to massify the system. Given that South Africa is not going to shift from a liberal economy, and that we are not going to have regulated occupational labour markets in the near future, despite the rhetoric about a shift away from neoliberalism, it is likely that the best hope for colleges is to offer increasingly higher levels of education, in association with universities. This may be playing into the qualification inflation trap; learners may still not get jobs. But the workplace cannot be the only preoccupation of colleges; their starting point must also be providing an education of intellectual integrity, regardless of the needs or lack of needs of the labour market. This is a particularly important role in South Africa, as most people have received an inadequate education. It means, though, protecting vocational education from the *immediate short-term* needs of employers and from a *narrow* labour market focus. It also means a focus on increasing subject matter expertise, as well as the capacity to conduct research, and allowing time for this in the working day of a college lecturer.

The best and most plausible prospect for this is for lecturers themselves to play a role in the development of such a knowledge base, working with university-based researchers. This will not, though, be a quick project, and will need considerable support from the state in terms of funding modalities and employment conditions that support long-term institutional and professional development.

Notes

1 Terminology varies across countries and is highly contested; here I am using the term 'technical and vocational education and training' to include all mid-level technical and vocational education, as well as what is sometimes called 'skills training', that is focused on preparing learners for the workplace.
2 As Ha-Joon Chang (2010) points out, these are quintessentially neoliberal policies, as they are premised on the idea that it is the cost of labour, bolstered by institutional arrangements like trade unions and collective bargaining, which leads to unemployment; he also reminds us that 'labour market flexibility' is a euphemism for job insecurity.
3 The apparent 'win-win' policy solution, whereby the NQF was positioned as representing all things to all people, perhaps derives from South Africa's version of 'third way politics', as the union policy developers involved in the NQF were very influenced by the idea of 'post-fordism' and the idea of economic competitiveness through a more highly skilled labour force (Von Holdt, 1991; Samson, 1999; Desaubin, 2002).

4 New Public Management broadly refers to public sector reform focused on forcing state institutions to operate 'as if' they were in a market, or to compete in markets, through a greater element on 'results' (Hood, 1995; Pollitt, 1998). This entails a range of mechanisms to monitor performance, such as performance indicators and appraisals (Phillips, 1998), as well as the introduction of economic standards for the evaluation of governance (Wolf, 2010). Because of the emphasis on contractualization, it has, in many instances, resulted in an increased regulatory role of the state (Hudson, 2010).

5 As Keep (2007) points out in relation to the UK system, focusing TVET reform on regulation of qualifications tends to lead to a proliferation of 'arms-length' government agencies; as mentioned in the previous endnote, this is in many instances the logical consequence of New Public Management-style public sector reform.

6 It was only the weakest parts of the education system (vocational education, professional training, community development, skills training, adult education) that attempted to comply with the qualifications and quality assurance model of the NQF. The formal education and training system did not (Allais, 2012). For example, universities did not use the new qualifications developed through stakeholder structures, but registered their existing qualifications on the NQF. The quality assurance body for all general and further education and training, Umalusi, which had a considerable influence on the college system as it moderated the external examinations and issued certificates to learners, refused to participate in the quality assurance system of the SETAs (Umalusi, 2007). Many policies of SAQA were ignored; nor did lecturers and teachers in universities and schools get trained and registered as 'assessors', despite official SAQA policy pronouncements (SAQA, 2001).

7 *Criteria for the Evaluation of Qualifications for Employment in Teaching Posts in Post-School Education* (internal national education department document), *Criteria for the Evaluation of Qualifications for Employment in Education, 1995–1999*, and the revised policy *Criteria for the Recognition and Evaluation of Qualifications for Employment in Education based on the Norms and Standards for Educators, 2000*.

8 Although of course much contemporary curriculum policy for schools dilutes this relationship.

9 NAPTOSA (2011) suggests that there are currently 8,557 lecturers in the system, of which 5,685 are college appointed but state employed, and 2,872 are college appointed and employed.

10 This includes the second largest teacher union, NAPTOSA (the National Professional Teachers' Organization of South Africa) as well as several smaller unions.

References

Abbott, Andrew (1988) *The System of Professions: An essay on the division of labour*, Chicago, IL and London: University of Chicago Press.

Allais, Stephanie (2007) *The Rise and Fall of the NQF: A critical analysis of the South African National Qualifications Framework*, doctoral thesis, University of the Witwatersrand.

Allais, Stephanie (2010) *The Implementation and Impact of Qualifications Frameworks: Report of a study in 16 countries*, Geneva: International Labour Office.

Allais, Stephanie (2011) 'Economics imperialism', education policy and educational theory, *Journal of Education Policy*, 27(2): 263–74.

Allais, Stephanie (2012) Why solving on-going problems with the NQF matters, in Helene Perold, Nico Cloete and Joy Papier (eds) *Shaping the Future of South Africa's Youth: Rethinking post-school education and skills training*, Cape Town: African Minds., pp. 9–28.

Allais, Stephanie, Raffe, David, Strathdee, Rob, Young, Michael and Wheelahan, Leesa (eds) (2009) *Learning from the Early Starters*, Employment Sector Working Paper no. 45, Geneva: ILO.

Badroodien, Azeem (2004) Technical and vocational education provision in South Africa from 1920 to 1970, in Simon McGrath, Azeem Badroodien, Andre Kraak and Lorna Unwin (eds) *Shifting Understandings of Skills in South Africa. Overcoming the Historical Imprint of a Low Skills Regime*, Cape Town: HSRC Press, pp. 20–45.

Beck, John (2008) Governmental professionalism: re-professionalising or de-professionalising teachers in England, *British Journal of Educational Studies*, 56(2): 119–43.

Beck, John (2009) Appropriating professionalism: restructuring the official knowledge base of England's modernised teaching profession, *British Journal of Sociology of Education*, 30(1): 3–14.

Beck, John and Young, Michael (2005) The Assault on the professions and the restructuring of academic and professional identities: a Bernsteinian analysis, *British Journal of Sociology of Education*, 26(2): 183–97.

Brockmann, Michaela (2011) Higher education qualifications: convergence and divergence in software engineering and nursing, in Michaela Brockmann, Linda Clarke and Christopher Winch (eds) *Knowledge, Skills and Competence in the European Labour Market: What's in a vocational qualification?*, Abingdon and New York: Routledge, pp. 120–35.

Brockmann, Michaela, Clarke, Linda and Winch, Christopher (eds) (2011) *Knowledge, Skills and Competence in the European Labour Market: What's in a vocational qualification?*, Abingdon and New York: Routledge.

Brown, Phillip, Lauder, Hugh and Ashton, David (2011) *The Global Auction: The broken promises of education, jobs, and incomes*, Oxford and New York: Oxford University Press.

Chang, Ha-Joon (2010) *23 Things They Don't Tell You About Capitalism*, London: Allen Lane.

Clarke, Linda (2011) Trade? Job? Or Occupation? The development of occupational labour markets for bricklaying and lorry driving, in Michaela Brockmann, Linda Clarke and Christopher Winch (eds) *Knowledge, Skills and Competence in the European Labour Market: What's in a vocational qualification?*, Abingdon and New York: Routledge, pp. 102–19.

De Clercq, Francine (2011) Teacher professionalism in South African education: the dearth of professional voices, Cape Town.

Desaubin, France (2002) *Politics and Strategy of the Labour Movement in South Africa: A crisis of 'strategic' and 'social' unionism*, doctoral thesis, Australia National University.

Department of Higher Education and Training (DHET) (2009) *The Draft National Policy Framework for Lecturer Qualifications and Development in FET Colleges in South Africa*, Government Gazette, Notice 1194 of 2009, Pretoria: DHET.

Department of Higher Education and Training (DHET) (2011) *Policy on Professional Qualifications for Vocational Education Lecturers*, draft discussion document, October, Pretoria: DHET.

Department of Higher Education and Training (DHET) (2012) *Green Paper for the Post-school System*, Pretoria: DHET.

Egan, Kieran (2002) *Getting It WRONG from the Beginning: Our progressivist inheritance from Herbert Spencer, John Dewey, and Jean Piaget*, New Haven, CT and London: Yale University Press.

Entwistle, Harold (1979) *Antonio Gramsci: Conservative schooling for radical politics*, London: Routledge and Kegan Paul.

Evans, Linda (2011) The 'shape' of teacher professionalism in England: professional standards, performance management, professional development and the changes proposed in the 2010 white paper, *British Educational Research Journal*, 37(5): 851–70.

Fine, Ben and Rustomjee, Zavareh (1996) *The Political Economy of South Africa: From minerals-energy complex to industrialisation*, Boulder, CO: Westview Press.

Freidson, Eliot (1994) *Professionalism Reborn: Theory, prophecy and policy*, Cambridge: Polity Press.

Freidson, Eliot (2001) *Professionalism: The third logic*, Oxford: Polity Press.

Gamble, Jeanne (2003) *Curriculum Responsiveness in FET Colleges*, Cape Town: HSRC Press.

Gamble, Jeanne (2004a) *Tacit Knowledge in Craft Pedagogy: A sociological analysis*, doctoral thesis, University of Cape Town.

Gamble, Jeanne (2004b) A future curriculum mandate for further education and training colleges: recognising intermediate knowledge and skill, in Simon McGrath, Azeem Badroodien, Andre Kraak and Lorna Unwin (eds) *Shifting Understandings of Skills in South Africa: Overcoming the historical imprint of a low skills regime*, Cape Town: HSRC Press, pp. 175–93.

Gamble, Jeanne (2010) *Teacher Professionalism: A literature review*, report commissioned by the Joint Education Trust, Johannesburg.

Gamble, Jeanne (2011) *The Professional Development of VET Lecturers/Teachers: Possible options for UCT*, a briefing document commissioned by the Dean of Humanities, University of Cape Town.

Grubb, Norton and Lazerson, Marvin (2006) The globalization of rhetoric and practice: the education gospel and vocationalism, in Hugh Lauder, Phillip Brown, JoAnne Dillabough and A.H. Halsey (eds) *Education, Globalization, and Social Change*, Oxford: Oxford University Press, pp. 295–307.

Hargreaves, Andy (1992) *Changing Teachers, Changing Times: Teachers' work and culture in a post modern age*, New York: Teachers College Press.

Hart, Gillian (2006) Beyond neoliberalism? Post-apartheid developments in historical and comparative perspective, in Vishnu Padayachee (ed.) *The Development Decade? Economic and social change in South Africa, 1994–2004*, Cape Town: HSRC Press, pp. 13–32.

Harvey, David (2005) *A Brief History of Neoliberalism*, Oxford and New York: Oxford University Press.

Hood, Christopher (1995) The 'New Public Management' in the 1980s: variations on a theme, *Accounting, Organizations and Society*, 20(2/3): 93–109.

Hudson, Christine (2010) Transforming the educative state in the Nordic countries, in Anja A. Jakobi, Kerstin Martens and Klaus Dieter Wolf (eds) *Education in Political Science: Discovering a neglected field*, Routledge/ECPR Studies in European Political Science, London: Routledge, pp. 56–70.

Iverson, Torben and Stephens, John D. (2008) Partisan politics, the welfare state, and three worlds of human capital formation, *Comparative Political Studies*, 45(4/5): 600–37.

Keep, Ewart (2007) The multiple paradoxes of state power in the English education and training system, in Linda Clarke and Christopher Winch (eds) *Vocational Education: International approaches, developments and systems*, Oxford: Routledge, pp. 161–75.

Kraak, Andre (2004) The National Skills Development Strategy: A new institutional regime for skills formation in post-apartheid South Africa, in Simon McGrath, Azeem Badroodien, Andre Kraak and Lorna Unwin (eds) *Shifting Understandings of Skills in South Africa: Overcoming the historical imprint of a low skills regime*, Cape Town: HSRC Press, pp. 116–57.

McGrath, Simon (2012) Vocational learning for development: a policy in need of a theory?, *International Journal for Educational Development*, 32(5): 623–31.

McGrath, Simon (1996) *Learning to Work? Changing discourses on education and training in South Africa, 1976–96*, doctoral thesis, University of Edinburgh.

McGrath, Simon, Badroodien, Azeem, Kraak, Andre and Unwin, Lorna (eds) (2004) *Shifting Understandings of Skills in South Africa: Overcoming the historical imprint of a low skills regime*, Cape Town: HSRC Press.

Makgetla, Neva Seidman (2010) The international economic crises and employment in South Africa, in John Daniel, Prishani Naidoo, Devan Pillay and Roger Southall (eds) *New South African Review 1*, Johannesburg: Wits University Press, pp. 65–86.

Marais, Hein (2011) *South Africa Pushed to the Limit: The political economy of change*, Cape Town: UCT Press.

Muller, Johan (2000) *Reclaiming Knowledge* (ed. Philip Wexler and Ivor Goodson), London and New York: RoutledgeFalmer.

NAPTOSA (2011) Submission: *Further Education and Training Colleges Amendment Bill, 2011*, submitted to Portfolio Committee on Higher Education, 23 August 2011.

National Business Initiative (2010) *Survey of Information Technology, Construction and Engineering Lecturers in Further Education and Training Colleges*, Pretoria: DHET.

National Business Initiative (2011) *Lecturer Supply, Utilisation and Development in the Further Education and Training College Subsystem*, Johannesburg: National Business Initiative.

National Planning Commission (2011) *National Development Plan: Vision for 2030*, Pretoria: Republic of South Africa, Presidency.

National Treasury (2011) *Confronting Youth Unemployment: Policy options for South Africa*, discussion paper for public comment, Pretoria: Republic of South Africa, National Treasury.

Newfield, Christopher (2010) The structure and silence of the cognitariat, *Edu-factory Web Journal*.

Novoa, Antonio (2002) Ways of thinking about education in Europe, in Antonio Novoa and Martin Lawn (eds) *Fabricating Europe: The formation of an education space*, Dordrecht: Kluwer Academic.

Ozga, Jenny (1995) Deskilling a profession: professionalism, deprofessionalisation and the new managerialism, in Hugh Busher and Rene Saran (eds) *Managing Teachers as Professionals in Schools*, London: Kogan Page, pp. 21–37.

Phillips, David (1998) *The Switchment of History: The development of a unitary qualifications framework*, doctoral thesis, University of Wellington.

Pollitt, Christopher (1998) Managerialism revisited, in B. Guy Peters and Donald J. Savoie (eds) *Taking Stock: Assessing public sector reforms*, Montreal: Canadian Centre for Management Development.

Raggat, Peter and Williams, Steve (1999) *Government, Markets and Vocational Qualifications: An anatomy of policy*, London and New York: Routledge.

Rauner, Felix (2007) Vocational education and training: a European perspective, in Alan Brown, Simone Kirpal and Felix Rauner (eds) *Identities at Work*, Dordrecht: Springer.

Republic of South Africa (1995) *South African Qualifications Authority Act*, Pretoria: Government Gazette.

Republic of South Africa (1997) *Green Paper on a Skills Development Strategy for Economic and Employment Growth in South Africa*, Pretoria: Department of Labour.

Republic of South Africa (2006) *Act No. 16 of 2006: Further Education and Training Colleges Act, 2006*, Pretoria: Government Gazette.

Republic of South Africa (2008) *National Qualifications Framework Act, vol. 524*, Pretoria: Government Gazette.

Sachs, Judyth (2001) Teacher professional identity: competing discourses, competing outcomes, *Journal of Education Policy*, 16(2): 149–61.

Sachs, Judyth (2003) Teacher professional standards: controlling or developing teaching?, *Teachers and Teaching*, 9(2): 175–86.

Samson, Melanie (1999) Undressing redress: a feminist critique of the South African National Qualifications Framework, *Discourse: Studies in the Cultural Politics of Education*, 20(3): 433–60.

SAQA (1997) *SAQA Bulletin*, 1(1).

SAQA (2000a) *The National Qualifications Framework: An overview*, Pretoria: SAQA.

SAQA (2000b) *The National Qualifications Framework and Standards Setting*, Pretoria: SAQA.

SAQA (2001) *Criteria and Guidelines for the Registration of Assessors*, Pretoria: SAQA.

Schulman, Lee S. (1986) Those who understand: knowledge growth in teaching, *Educational Researcher*, 15(2): 4–14.

Shalem, Yael and Hoadley, Ursula (2009) The dual economy of schooling and teacher morale in South Africa, *International Studies in Sociology of Education*, 19(2): 119–34.

Taylor, Nick (2011) *Priorities for Addressing South Africa's Education and Training Crisis*, a review commissioned by the National Planning Commission, Johannesburg: JET Education Services.

Umalusi (2006) *Apples and Oranges? A comparison of school and college subjects*, Pretoria: Umalusi.

Umalusi (2007) *The 'F' Word: The quality of the 'fundamental' component of qualifications in general and further education and training*, Pretoria: Umalusi.

Von Holdt, Karl (1991) Towards transforming SA industry: a 'reconstruction accord' between unions and the ANC?, *South African Labour Bulletin*, 15(6): 17–25.

Wenger, Etienne (1999) *Communities of Practice: Learning, meaning and identity*, Cambridge: Cambridge University Press.

Wheelahan, Leesa (2010) *Why Knowledge Matters in Curriculum*, Abingdon and New York: Routledge.

Winch, Christopher (2011) Skill: a concept manufactured in England?, in Michaela Brockmann, Linda Clarke and Christopher Winch (eds) *Knowledge, Skills and Competence in the European Labour Market. What's in a vocational qualification?*, Abingdon and New York: Routledge, pp. 85–101.

Wolf, Klaus Dieter (2010) Normative dimensions of reform in higher education, in Anja A. Jakobi, Kerstin Martens and Klaus Dieter Wolf (eds) *Education in Political Science: Discovering a neglected field*, Abingdon and New York: Routledge, pp. 178–90.

Young, Michael (2008) *Bringing Knowledge Back In: From social constructivism to social realism in the sociology of knowledge*, London and New York: Routledge.

9 State Interventions for University Restructuring

The Construction of Academic Practice and Identity in Public State Universities in Mexico

Omar García Ponce de León, Virginia Montero Hernández, María Luisa Zorrilla Abascal, Manuel Francisco Aguilar Tamayo and John S. Levin

Latin America continues to be one of the regions in the world with the highest levels of both poverty and inequality (Reimers, 1994; Bonal, 2004). While funding for public higher education has declined significantly in Latin American countries since the 1980s, universities were pressured to engage in processes of structural reform to accommodate global pressures and neoliberal economics (Torres and Schugurensky, 2002; Bonal, 2004). During the last half of the twentieth century, federal governments in Latin American countries began to create policies and programs to restructure higher education and foster social progress through knowledge construction. Programs for university change aimed to alter the organizational culture and structures of higher education institutions. The modernization of higher education in Mexico initiated during the late 1990s illustrates the ways in which traveling policies are adopted by national agencies and government to reorganize the political, economic, social, and educational landscape.

The demands of productivity and accountability emphasized by international agencies such as the Organisation for Economic Co-operation and Development (OECD) led the Mexican government and national agencies to formulate change initiatives to transform higher education institutions. A fundamental component in this restructuring was the formulation of policies targeting full-time faculty members and their practices. This chapter describes the ways in which academics navigated and responded to the regulations and policies aimed to modernize public universities. In the first part of the chapter, we discuss the origins of higher education restructuring and the programs aimed to professionalize academics. We review literature to explain the ways in which the federal government adopted traveling policies (i.e. forms of educational accountability derived from globalizing trends) to create professionalizing programs and reconfigure existing organizational conditions of the public university in Mexico. The second part of the chapter analyzes empirical data to explain the re-boundarying work that faculty members and university officers have done since the end of the 1990s to translate globalizing trends in educational policy into local practices.

We view academics' re-boundarying work as a series of negotiations and practices to satisfy demands of institutional restructuring and professionalization. At the end of the chapter, we draw some conclusions about the role of federal programs in the reconfiguration of academic practice and faculty identity.

Adoption of Traveling Policies: Context and Origins of Re-Boundary Work in Mexico

Through the twentieth century, Mexican higher education developed with a strong focus on teaching and professional service. From its origins until the early 1990s, the goal of the Mexican university was nation building and professional training. As global trends influenced the definition of federal agendas, the Mexican federal government began to implement new programs to professionalize academics and change the organizational landscape of universities to respond to knowledge economy demands. University restructuring that began during the late 1990s became a turning point that challenged traditional practices to introduce a new pragmatic and scientific orientation.

Since its origins in 1910, the mission of the National University in Mexico was to train specialists in traditional professions, foster a national identity, and create an intellectual elite; it was not until the late 1920s, under a pragmatic-oriented climate, that scientific research emerged as a critical component of the university's functioning (Burke, 1977). According to Kent (1993), the traditional orientation of public universities in Mexico was characterized by (a) inflexible modes of organization, (b) a focus on teaching, (c) heavy reliance on administrators to represent institutional power, and (d) low emphasis on the value of disciplines to organize academic life. The traditional Latin American university did not focus on the consolidation of knowledge communities but the reproduction of existing professions (e.g. administrators, physicians, teachers, lawyers, accountants) through the implementation of a Napoleonic organizational model instead of departmental structure (Ornelas and Post, 1992).

By 1950, reform debates began not only as an internal matter at universities but also as a theme for national concern. The elitist character of the national university in Mexico triggered discomfort among members of the population. As a result, during the late 1960s, advocates for university reform demanded a critical, popular, and democratic university (i.e. open admissions to universities, greater subsidies from the federal government, and no tuition increases). To answer the public's demands, in 1970 Mexican president Luis Echeverría articulated the need to modernize higher education and increase the number of higher education institutions; however, he made no specific proposals for the modernization of universities.

During the period of unregulated expansion of higher education initiated during the 1970s (Gil-Antón, 2003), state public universities allowed the enrollment of a massive number of students without planning the type of educational services to offer to this new community of learners. It is estimated that, from 1960 to 1992, nine faculty members were recruited daily and only 10 percent of them were researchers as well as instructors (Gil-Antón, 1994). By the 1990s, the majority of professors working at public state universities held only a bachelor's degree. As a result of unregulated expansion, in 1996, there was a total of 18,093 full-time professors working at public universities: 8 percent of that population had completed a doctoral program; 32 percent had a professional specialization (e.g. pediatrics or psychological therapy); and 60 percent had attained a bachelor's degree (Vidales *et al.*, 2006). The unregulated expansion of higher education engendered low student attainment, lack of accredited programs, use of outmoded instructional techniques, and minimal research (Guevara-Niebla, 1992).

The restructuring of higher education during the late 1980s and early 1990s aimed to address the detrimental conditions of education created by years of unregulated expansion and ill-defined purposes and structures of higher education institutions (Guevara, 2004). The period of university restructuring that began during the late 1990s consisted of the implementation of federal policies and programs to regulate academic work, the professionalization of faculty members, and organizational functioning at universities (Rodríguez, 2000; Silva, 2000; Ibarra-Colado, 2002; Porter, 2003). The restructuring of higher education in Mexico coincided with globalizing pressures during the 1990s. In 1994, Mexico was included as a member of the OECD and, as a member, was expected to address the economic, social, and environmental challenges of globalization. To comply with the new demands, Mexico opened its economic systems toward international trade and formulated agreements with countries and regions such as North America, the European Union, Japan, and several Latin American countries (OECD, 2006). In addition to these new forms of economic participation at the international level, Mexico was expected to create an educational system aimed to promote economic and social advancement. However, since 1996, the OECD has released reports listing the deficiencies of higher education in Mexico and offered recommendations for its improvement (OECD, 2006).

These international engagements occurred in a context characterized by subordination of universities to state and federal mandates and policies and included universities' organizational rigidity based on their traditional practices and culture. The federal government's attempts to restructure higher education in Mexico occurred in the midst of a process of educational decentralization initiated during the early 1990s. This was a political strategy to reduce the number of political conflicts at the center of the country and legitimize the authority of the State. Educational decentralization was not motivated by authentic motivation to delegate authority to regional state authorities. The central government maintained strong normative power on fundamental matters and delegated specific responsibilities to regions, which had to operate through weak local agencies that did not have capacity to both manage and finance educational issues (Ornelas, 2003). Within a context of seeming educational decentralization, the restructuring of higher education became a process highly controlled by federal and state governments. Thus, although state universities were legally autonomous institutions (i.e. they make their own decisions with regard to personnel, curriculum, and research), their pathways of transformation and everyday operations were dictated through centralized processes (Kent, 1993). Yet, government intervention in university affairs was prompted by international and national developments that had affected decision-making processes since the 1980s and placed constraints on institutional autonomy (Ordorika, 1996, 2003).

As a result of the ambiguous process of decentralization, the restructuring of higher education operated through a non-unified policy framework formulated within Federal agencies such as the Ministry of Education and the National Council for Science and Technology (*Consejo Nacional de Ciencia y Tecnología*, CONACYT). Kent (1993) argues that there are two policy orientations working simultaneously to modify the organizational life of universities and the characteristics of the academic profession in Mexico. On the one hand, the Ministry of Education introduced accountability principles to promote institutional self-evaluation and external peer review of academic disciplines and teaching practices. On the other hand, CONACYT created guidelines to allocate funds to graduate programs and research based on the results of evaluation by external peer committees. The competing agendas and lack of communication between national agencies have hindered the formulation and implementation of policy aimed to restructure higher education in Mexico (Porter, 1999).

The modernization of higher education institutions in Mexico has been a difficult process to be realized due to long-established practices and organizational values, as well as ambiguous federal and state mandates and decision-making processes. The result has been the coexistence of two rationales that operate simultaneously: an old rationale that is strongly embedded in the everyday life of institutions and includes traditional academic practices such as an emphasis on teaching; and a new rationale promoted externally by the federal government and sustained through neoliberal practices imported from other countries (Kent, 1993).

Programs for University Restructuring

As part of federal initiatives for university restructuring, the Ministry of Education required that public universities increased the number of full-time faculty members with a universally validated professional model of postsecondary education (e.g. research oriented, high degree output, participation by faculty in international scholarly exchange, and publication networks) (Gil-Antón, 2003). Two major federal programs aimed to promote academic professionalization have persisted since their creation in the late 1980s and the 1990s.The first program was the National System of Researchers (*Sistema Nacional de Investigadores*, SNI), a program regulated by CONACYT. Created in 1984, SNI aimed to stimulate research activities by rewarding scientific participation and productivity of Ph.D. holders who belong to either federal or state universities, both in the public and private sectors (CONACYT, 2011). Applicants who obtain positive outcomes in the process of evaluation are granted the appointment of "national researcher," which translates into a financial reward (one received on a monthly basis as a supplement to faculty's base salary) and public prestige for the individual.

In addition to SNI, another major federal program that targets academic practices was implemented in 1996 to foster faculty's professionalism and committed participation both in teaching and research activities (Vidales *et al.*, 2006). The Faculty Enhancement Program (*Programa para el Mejoramiento del Profesorado*, PROMEP) identifies four central activities for faculty: research, teaching, tutoring, and service. The program was expected to last ten years (from 1996 to 2006); however, PROMEP continues to the present. On the one hand, the program encourages the creation of a new professional profile (*Perfil PROMEP*) and the remediation and increase of graduate studies for faculty members (those without advanced degrees). On the other hand, PROMEP aimed to promote collaborative and multidisciplinary work by requiring faculty members to formalize the creation of research groups (*Cuerpos Académicos*) and networks (*Redes*) both at national universities and abroad (Chavoya-Peña, 2001). Based on the characterization and regulation formulated by PROMEP, in Mexican public universities, a *Cuerpo Académico* is expected to be a group of full-time faculty who work in the same department, have diverse disciplinary backgrounds, share research interests, and work together to design research projects and apply for federal grants to conduct research. PROMEP encourages and rewards both individual and group productivity by supporting faculty to engage in graduate education (specifically among those faculty who have not obtained a master's or doctoral degree) and to conduct research projects on an individual and collaborative basis.

Conceptual Considerations: Discourse, Social Practice, and Identity

We use a poststructuralist approach to make sense of the relationship between the implementation of federal programs for university restructuring that began in the 1990s and the construction of the professional identity and practice of faculty members. Three conceptual principles shape our framework. First, educational policies and strategic programs to regulate higher education institutions are specific types of discourses that influence the ways in which faculty members shape their identity and practice. A discourse refers to a set of knowledge power relationships aimed to create taken-for-granted definitions and categories by which governments rule and monitor their populations and by which members of communities define themselves and others (Foucault, 1972, 1980). Individuals' everyday actions and identity formation are shaped by the discourses with which they are engaged (Luke, 1995; Dressman, 2008). Second, faculty members' everyday practices and interactions with others at higher education institutions facilitate both the reproduction of and change to institutional discourses. Both the maintenance of and change to institutional discourses are based on people's engagement in cultural practices, which involves the selective use of cultural resources to define individuals' identities and strategies of action (Swidler, 2001). Through their capacity of self-reflection, individuals both select and dismiss elements of an institutional discourse to construct their everyday lives, including their participation in organizations, and define their personal projects (Swidler, 2001; Ortner, 2006). Third, faculty members develop a professional identity based on their use of specific institutional discourses available to them (Gee and Green, 1998). Individuals' engagement in socio-cultural practices facilitates the process of identity formation by providing them with cultural materials to understand who they are and how they can behave (Levinson and Holland, 1996; Rockwell, 1996, 1999).

Methodological Approach and Sample

As part of a case study approach, we analyzed academics' narratives and federal policy documents to understand the ways in which full-time faculty members made decisions to comply with federal programs and everyday activities as professionals. The empirical data presented in this chapter are part of a larger collaborative research project in which Mexican and US scholars examine the patterns of construction of academic practices within three public state universities in Mexico. This three-year project is funded by CONACYT. The study of the Mexican context is a first step in a series of collaborative projects aimed to explain the construction of academic professions in different countries. We excluded part-time faculty because there are no federal policies or programs formulated to either define or regulate the practice of part-time faculty at public state universities.

There are five types of higher education institutions in Mexico: research centers, federal public institutions, state public institutions, technological public institutions, and private institutions (Galaz-Fontes and Gil-Antón, 2009). Our research site was a state public university. We use quotations taken from a series of semi-structured interviews with full-time faculty members (n = 12) in a state public university in the west-central part of Mexico. The *Universidad de la Región Centro* (a pseudonym, hereafter URC) was founded in 1937 and it became an autonomous university in 1956. According to the last institutional report by university officers, by the 2008–9 academic year, the student population (including undergraduate and graduate students) was 50,256. In the same academic year, there were 1,605 faculty members with a graduate degree working at the undergraduate and graduate level. The number of full-time faculty members who engaged in teaching, research, service, and student tutoring was 791 (out of the 1,605 faculty members with a graduate degree). Part-time faculty focused on teaching undergraduate courses; this faculty subgroup did not engage in service or research. Only 336 full-time faculty members were members of the National System of Researchers (SNI). Full-time faculty associated with some of their colleagues to create a total of 156 *Cuerpos Académicos*, as demanded by PROMEP.

We interviewed 12 full-time faculty members from four disciplinary areas established in the university's organizational structure: natural and exact sciences, administrative and social sciences, engineering and technology, and education and humanities. There were more male than female full-time faculty members (eight males; four females) since the male population in the academic body at URC was larger. We use pseudonyms to refer to our informants. The interview protocol explored six broad areas: (a) personal and professional background, (b) characteristics of the organizational context (both at the university and faculty level), according to faculty members' perceptions, (c) the ways in which faculty perceive and think of the normative and policy framework that regulates their academic work, (d) faculty's work-related attitudes, goals, and expectations, (e) forms of self-definition, and (f) the ways in which faculty organized and performed their professional responsibilities (teaching, research, and service).

We examined participants' narratives inductively, identifying patterns and linkages across the data as a strategy to create a coherent explanation of the events studied (Erickson, 1986). We identified four categories of analysis: the values and prescriptions embedded in federal programs, academics' understandings of federal programs, the strategies of action they enacted to perform their professional practice and respond to federal programs' regulations, and their self-perceptions and explanations about themselves as professionals.

Findings: Faculty Members Navigating Professionalizing Programs

The process of modernization that began during the 1990s to make Mexican universities academically competitive at the international level is a process that full-time faculty members experienced in a particular way. Three broad conditions characterize faculty members' experience with the research-oriented professionalizing programs at the university. The historical construction of higher education policy and organizational conditions in Mexico has mediated faculty members' acceptance of federal programs as legitimate means to modernize the university. Although full-time faculty members viewed PROMEP and SNI as programs that exerted considerable influence on the development of their academic practice and professional career at the university, they did not approve of the role of federal programs in university restructuring entirely, due to the lack of appropriate working conditions that support authentic processes of professionalization.

Reluctant Acceptance: Legitimization and Patterns of Self-Identification

Faculty members' compliance with federal programs was characterized by a sense of reluctant acceptance. On the one hand, faculty accepted and assimilated the language and symbolism embedded in federal programs to be legitimized as members of the academic community in Mexico. On the other hand, faculty criticized the institutional strategies to implement federal programs and regretted that they had to participate in those programs to maintain a consistent income. Full-time faculty participated in those programs to achieve job security and improve their low salaries. The scores that full-time faculty members achieve in the process of evaluation linked to federal programs such as SNI influence the increase or decrease of earnings they can obtain. Since the base salary of full-time faculty members is fairly low (i.e. approximately 1,000 US dollars per month), faculty endeavor to obtain high evaluation results that enable them to increase the amount of their additional earnings. Furthermore, positive assessment outcomes led faculty members to gain a specific kind of official acknowledgment that maximized their opportunity to apply, in the future, for research grants.

URC faculty participation in the evaluation processes related to PROMEP and SNI was not necessarily translated into higher levels of academic competitiveness for universities. URC faculty members found fault with the underlying assumptions and mechanisms of implementation of federal programs. Programs were viewed as remedial strategies to ameliorate academics' incomes rather than strategies to strengthen the academic culture and organizational functioning of the public university. An Engineering faculty member illustrates the URC faculty's typical perception of federal programs:

> I think these programs should not exist … [U]niversity faculty should be able to have a decent salary and to perform their activities under optimal conditions. The reality is far away from that ideal. The government does not have enough money to increase faculty members' salary; thus, this kind of programs [PROMEP and SNI] is created to make academics compete for resources on the basis of individual achievements … [T]his situation is pretty pitiable.
>
> (Edison, male, Faculty of Electrical Engineering)

Although the implementation of federal programs was an initiative to stimulate a research-oriented academic culture, scholarly productivity, and faculty professionalization, the implementation of programs such as PROMEP and SNI turned out to be, according to the views articulated by faculty members, only a compensatory strategy to increase academics' income. Federal programs were national initiatives to respond to the demands of the knowledge economy in the international context; however, the ways in which federal programs operated on a daily basis did not translate into authentic possibilities for faculty members to reach high levels of scholarly productivity and academic competitiveness. Universities do not have optimal conditions to stimulate research activities (e.g. lack of specialized libraries, limited or non-existent access to specialized databases, deficient access to the internet, lack of specialized laboratories and equipment, lack of offices for all faculty members, and no capacity to pay teaching assistants and graduate student researchers). Due to the lack of infrastructure to generate research activities at public state universities, faculty members viewed federal programs as mechanisms to receive a reasonable salary to satisfy life demands and to cover some needs of infrastructure (e.g. access to bibliographical resources, office supplies, and computer equipment and software) to do their work at the university.

Although faculty members did not view PROMEP and SNI as crucial elements to improve academic life at universities, they emphasized that these programs were highly influential in their self-definition as professionals. All faculty members in our sample noted that becoming a member of SNI was a central condition of viewing themselves as academics. Newton has worked at URC for over 40 years; he is a senior faculty member and, in the main, devoted to institutional service. Newton's narrative illustrates faculty members' ambivalence of their perceptions of and feelings toward federal programs, a phenomenon identified in previous studies about the academic profession in Mexico (Galaz-Fontes and Gil-Antón, 2009):

A central requirement to remain at the university is to become a member of SNI. If we say that we are researchers, we have to prove it. How can we demonstrate that we are researchers? Well, we need to be evaluated by either the institution or an external agency: SNI plays that role. I think SNI helps us obtain formal acknowledgment about what we do and who we are; it enables us to prove that we are researchers.

(Newton, male, Faculty of Physics)

All faculty members agreed that it was necessary for them to comply with the requirements established by federal programs to be considered as professionals and to be able to apply for research grants either by themselves or as members of a collaborative research group. URC faculty members acknowledged that SNI and PROMEP were formal mechanisms through which their status as researchers and teachers was legitimized within the professional community and the institutional context. Although faculty members were interested in conducting research and undertaking scholarly work, they found serious difficulties in engaging in large research projects and publishing, given their working environment.

To summarize, professionalizing programs were both accepted and rejected by faculty members. Acceptance was based on faculty members' possibility to increase their base salary. Faculty members' rejection of the program stemmed from the federal government's unrealistic expectations that both PROMEP and SNI would create academically competitive universities without creating optimal working conditions (e.g. increased salaries, better technological infrastructure, and equipped laboratories).

Socialization into Modernization: Meeting Institutional Standards

Faculty members knew that becoming a member of the academic community at URC involved learning about how to participate in evaluation processes to become members of SNI and PROMEP. The process of university restructuring included the socialization of faculty members into the evaluation criteria and administrative procedures established by federal programs. Pascal has worked at URC for three years. In comparison to Newton, Pascal has been at URC for a relatively short period of time; however, during this period he has come to realize the central role that federal programs play in academics' job security and salary:

We [as academics] always try to reach the highest institutional standards, which means to become a member of SNI. With regards to the balance between the teaching and research aspects of our work, the university requires that we [faculty members] become PROMEP professors. The demand is so huge that if one does not participate in either SNI or PROMEP, one can be fired. I know it well because in the Faculty of Physics and Mathematics some professors were dismissed because they were neither PROMEP nor SNI.

(Pascal, male, Faculty of Engineering)

Although our informants acknowledged that it was mandatory to learn and meet the requirements established by federal programs to be able to keep their jobs and achieve tenure, they viewed these requirements as unnecessary forms to regulate their work. Faculty viewed their work agenda as highly prescriptive, based upon a series of benchmarks defined by federal programs. SNI required faculty members to reach high levels of research productivity no matter what kind of organizational conditions faculty had in their workplace or what other academic functions (i.e. teaching and service) they had to perform. PROMEP, in some contrast, required high levels of productivity and effectiveness not only in research but also in teaching and service. Therefore, socialization into the faculty role at the university included learning how to comply with different tasks and demands. URC faculty members explained the ways in which they organized their workload and schedule in order to meet the demands of federal programs:

> To meet PROMEP's requirements, we [academics] try to do all the activities we are asked to do [research, teaching, and service]. If we are doing some overload, we have to find a seemingly balanced way to report all the things we are required to do. One has to do the math to have a total of forty hours [per week]. If one is working more than forty hours, one cannot report that. In theory, we devote approximately two hours to service, five hours to student tutoring, fifteen hours to research and approximately eighteen to teaching … The kind of balance in the number of hours we devote to work does not occur on a daily basis; however, in our reports we have to pretend that such balance is really happening.
>
> (Adalia, female, Faculty of Sciences and Engineering)

The extra number of hours faculty members invested in order to comply with program requirements was related to the necessity to engage in bureaucratic processes, apply for grants, prepare teaching materials, and design courses. Federal programs did not take into consideration the series of peripheral activities faculty had to undertake in order to accomplish their main academic functions (i.e. teaching, research, and service). URC faculty members regretted the ways in which programs such as SNI and PROMEP forced them to create fictional accounts about the ways in which they performed their everyday practices. Evaluation reports, which consisted of specific formats, included inaccurate descriptions about the time allocated to the various activities of full-time faculty members. All faculty members noted that it was difficult to attain the demands of their institutions and federal programs through a 40-hour working week. URC faculty members emphasized that they were compelled to invest extra hours of work in order to fulfill federal programs' benchmarks:

> I have to give classes fifteen hours per week, that's the requirements at this university … [I]t is difficult to establish a specific number of hours for research. All the time we are either in front of your computer or outside thinking about a research problem … [I] think all the time about my research and there is always a moment in which I have to start writing all that thinking. Maybe

there are more than twenty hours per week devoted to research, around two hours devoted to service, and the rest of time includes student advising … [I] have to organize my time to have the outcomes needed. I have to give three hours of classes every day to comply with PROMEP … [H]owever, devoting more time to research will bring more benefit for me.

(Rosaline, female, Faculty of Biology)

Similar to the US context, the core content of academic work for a typical full-time faculty member at a university includes teaching, research, and service (Rhoades and Slaughter, 1997; Honan and Teferra, 2001). Although the distribution of percentages allocated to each academic function can vary according to the size and orientation of the university (Boice, 1992; Massey, 1997; Gappa *et al.*, 2007), academics are required to participate both in teaching and research with the same degree of efficiency (Fairweather, 1989, 2002). In the Mexican context, the demands are similar to those in the US: university regulations and federal programs such as SNI and PROMEP require full-time faculty members at public state universities to engage in research, teaching, and service. Yet, our faculty sample indicates that full-time faculty members face considerable frustration in performing all their professional duties due to the inefficient organizational conditions at state public universities.

Overall, URC faculty members did not view SNI and PROMEP as programs articulated effectively with other components of the organizational structure of the university. SNI and PROMEP targeted individuals without paying careful attention to the organizational conditions in which academics work or the processes through which they achieved productivity. To obtain the financial rewards and official acknowledgment through SNI and PROMEP was an individual endeavor rather than a project supported by the university in which faculty members worked.

Competing Agendas: Management of Individual and Collective Productivity

SNI and PROMEP demanded commitment to individual and group productivity. On the one hand, SNI rewards academics who show high levels of individual productivity. On the other hand, PROMEP is a program that seeks to promote not only effective teaching and individual academic productivity, but also collective work and group productivity through the creation of *Cuerpos Académicos* and *Redes* to conduct research projects. Therefore, in order to comply with program requirements, URC faculty members had to work both in groups and individually.

URC faculty did not view the creation of *Cuerpos Académicos* as a genuine practice aimed to strengthen the academic competitiveness of the university. Faculty explained that PROMEP's demand for collegial work consisted of a series of regulations and administrative procedures that discouraged rather than promoted authentic forms of multidisciplinary and collaborative work. Participation in *Cuerpos Académicos* allowed faculty members to publish with other colleagues, apply for research grants as a team, and receive federal funds to perform academic activities (e.g. conference attendance); however, in some cases the development of collegial interactions was not exclusively based on the motivation to create knowledge, but on the necessity to share financial resources and publish together as a strategy to achieve positive scores in the evaluation process.

Criticisms about the authenticity of PROMEP's goals regarding collegial work were not exclusive to our sample; other studies have found similar responses and perspectives from faculty. In his study of the northern university in Mexico, Valles (2009) indicates that, during a five-year period, full-time faculty members at this institution preferred to consolidate their work on an individual basis; however, they had to engage in the dynamics of bureaucratization and formalization of collegial work through their affiliation to a specific *Cuerpo Académico* in order to compensate for the lack of financial resources to conduct research. Similarly, faculty members at URC talked about participation in *Cuerpos Académicos* and *Redes* as an imposed group dynamic that did not encourage authentic collaborative and multidisciplinary work:

> I think the idea of collaborative work that PROMEP promotes is not helpful … [W]hat is not good is that collaborative work is linked to money. We can choose a research topic together to apply for money as a group and be acknowledged as a *Cuerpo Académico*, even when the topic is not socially relevant.
>
> (Newton, male, Faculty of Physics)

Faculty members' participation in *Cuerpos Académicos* was distorted not only by the economic stimulus linked to it but also by the excessive regulation and bureaucratization that resulted from the process of undertaking collaborative work. Group dynamics and productivity were subordinated to detailed principles of accountability. As collective actors, *Cuerpos Académicos* were expected to report the origins and processes of their creation as a group, what their goals were, what kind of management techniques they implemented to achieve their goals, and what products they were going to generate. URC faculty experienced PROMEP's accountability and mandatory reports as a form of control that forced them to transform their collaborative work into another field of bureaucratization rather than an authentic opportunity to engage in reflection with other colleagues. As a result, faculty members did not always experience membership in a *Cuerpo Académico* as a self-motivated component of their professional practice:

> We already had some forms of collaborative work but now we have to report everything and formalize it. PROMEP requires us to have meeting summaries every time we get together. We did not consider it necessary to do that before. Now we have to show some kind of formal evidence that proves that we worked as a research group … [I]t is stressful to comply with all the formal requirements. As a *Cuerpo Académico*, at the end of the year

we have to deliver a report about all the activities we did … [W]e cannot give a general report; it has to be a detailed summary of everything. It is kind of ridiculous.

(Emily, female, Faculty of Humanities)

Although there are exceptional cases of authentic collaboration through the formulation of *Cuerpos Académicos*, URC faculty did complain about the regulations and bureaucratic processes attached to participation in them and to productivity.

Achievement Versus Compliance: Expressions of Agency

In spite of the accountability principles implemented through federal programs and the connection between scholarly productivity and salary, faculty members endeavored to navigate institutional standards and organizational challenges to perform academic activities that were rewarding for them. There were three types of academic achievement faculty members at URC reported: knowledge creation that was relevant to modify educational practices and address social demands; teaching and tutoring that encouraged student mobility toward other national or international institutions; and, authentic forms of collaborative work. The development of research projects through collaboration was linked to academics' efforts to consolidate knowledge communities aimed to examine and address particular fields of inquiry through both disciplinary specialization and multidisciplinary work. URC faculty described their commitment to knowledge creation as part of their personal motivation and desire to contribute to the betterment of educational conditions. Carlos was a full-time faculty member who earned his doctoral degree in the field of higher education. He had been working at URC for 11 years. His research focus was on the development of strategies to teach the history of higher education. Carlos emphasizes his commitment to engage in research and to contribute in the development of new instructional approaches and programs:

I have done a lot of field research: case studies. Derived from my research activities, I have had the opportunity to work as a consultant for the Ministry of Education, specifically in issues related to the process of curriculum design in the subject of history … [I] like to participate in the national congress about the teaching of history … [I] enjoy being in contact with other researchers and practitioners who are interested in the teaching of history from elementary school to higher education. It is through the collaboration with other research networks that we try to analyze the curriculum of history and how to educate future historians.

Although the imperative to achieve positive scores was an ongoing concern, faculty members preserved their enthusiasm about learning, research, and teaching. Several full-time faculty emphasized that they enjoyed their jobs and the opportunity to provide social service. The notion of giving back to society was part of the ideological component of faculty who achieved academically in spite of the regulations and poor salaries in the academic profession:

> I really enjoy working with my students and help them as much as I can. I love preparing my classes and my research ... [W]e are trying to develop technology for our nation. Nobody in the country really does this. We are manufacturing a specific type of technology to reduce the dependency of our country in terms of systems for data acquisition. I learned a lot when I went to US and Europe. Now I want to share that knowledge with my students ... [I] was offered a job in the US. They offered 120,000 annually. I said, "No, thanks," I thought, "I want to help Mexican students" ... [I] think I am an idealist. I am not working as faculty because of the money. I know I cannot make money as a professor.
>
> (Adalia, female, Faculty of Sciences and Engineering)

URC faculty members' social commitment was a strong factor that motivated them to maintain their academic endeavors in spite of the challenging working conditions and the lack of a supportive context for the implementation of federal programs.

Faculty members reported achievement of research productivity and social impact through the construction of authentic forms of collaborative work. In most cases, faculty members differentiated collaborative work from *Cuerpos Académicos*. Collaborative work was described by full-time faculty as those self-directed and self-motivated forms of collegial interaction aimed to deepen the study and understanding of a topic that was relevant for participants. Although some faculty acknowledged that *Cuerpos Académicos* could encourage authentic collaboration among them, the mandatory nature of *Cuerpos Académicos* was experienced as an imposition that discouraged productive interaction among academics. Participation in *Cuerpos Académicos* and compliance with the reports required by *Cuerpos Académicos* were demanding and in many cases difficult to maintain along with individual projects:

> In my other forms of collaboration [those I developed voluntarily], I started working with some of my colleagues by accident and because we realized we shared similar research interests ... [M]y relationship with them has not been predetermined or imposed ... [I] belong to a *Cuerpo Académico* but in that respect, I do not see a major benefit other than obtaining some kind of economic benefit. What I have done is to maintain my other forms of collaboration, which has been beneficial not only for me but also for my students. Through the communication and work I have with other professors both in Mexico and the US, I have been able to provide my students with opportunities to travel to other places to study.
>
> (Newton, male, Faculty of Physics)

Faculty members valued collaborative work and managed to work with their colleagues to improve their own learning opportunities and professional experiences; they enjoyed the opportunity to work with others when the conditions of collaboration were not imposed. The possibility to select and decide, on a personal basis, the style of collaboration was fundamental to achieve authentic productivity with colleagues to construct knowledge:

> [T]his department is really supportive ... We have good communication; we work a lot; and it is easy to make agreements among us ... [A]t present we work as a *Cuerpo Académico*; however, we used to work collaboratively before. We have always worked together because we liked to be in that way. However, in previous years, we did not view the necessity to do an official report about what we were doing as a team ... [W]e also work with international colleagues from France or Argentina. We have created international exchange to improve our experiences in teaching, research, and academic mobility.
>
> (Emily, female, Faculty of Humanities)

Motivation to learn, interactions with others, and the provision of service were important factors that allowed URC faculty members to achieve academic outcomes within their challenging working conditions. Professionalizing programs did not motivate radical transformations in the level of academic competitiveness of the university; however, the programs influenced faculty members' perceptions about themselves, their work context, and their professional practice.

Conclusions

The implementation of federal programs for Mexican university restructuring during the late 1980s and 1990s was part of the government's adoption of traveling policies that emphasized new understandings about the role and assessment of academic productivity within a knowledge-based economy. Similar to other initiatives of change in higher education (Porter, 2003), the implementation of federal programs such as SNI and PROMEP has been mandated without paying careful attention to existing organizational conditions. Mexican universities are expected to engage in knowledge construction and the transfer of knowledge as part of university restructuring; however, the existing cultural, political, or organizational conditions are not entirely supportive of the achievement of the goals established by federal programs (Brunner, 1989). Previous studies about the implementation of federal programs in Mexico show that the adoption of evaluation models and research activities to construct knowledge has not been accomplished entirely; thus, the restructuring of the public state universities continues to the present (Fortes and Lomnitz, 1994; Díaz-Barriga, 2007).

The strengths of federal programs as institutional discourses that can regulate the manner in which individuals define themselves and their patterns of behavior are evident in the efforts to transform the academic profession in Mexico (Foucault, 1972, 1980). The influence of professionalizing programs has been crucial in the definition of academics' everyday practices and self-understandings.

The importance of other factors such as disciplinary specialization, departmental cultures, or institutional types in shaping the construction of the academic profession has been (Clark, 2001), in the Mexican context, overshadowed. Full-time faculty members at state public universities are a different "species" of professionals from those found at Mexican universities during the 1960s and 1970s. The university professor has transitioned from an instructor with a bachelor's degree who focused on teaching into an academic with a doctoral degree who has to engage in teaching, research, and service effectively.

The development of academics as central figures in higher education institutions in Mexico is a recent phenomenon triggered by the implementation of professionalizing programs (Galaz-Fontes and Gil-Antón, 2009). Although the formulation and implementation of federal programs has been defective, government initiatives for university restructuring have influenced the configuration of the academic profession in Mexico. Full-time faculty members participate in federal programs to accomplish professional legitimization within the national discourses of modernization. Faculty members' professional status is legitimized through their participation in the evaluation processes that federal programs demand. Therefore, faculty members' identity formation and self-worth as professionals are subordinated to their capacity to meet principles of accountability and bureaucratic administration required by programs such as SNI and PROMEP. Although faculty members criticize the characteristics and forms of implementation of federal programs, they agree to comply with programs' regulations to receive a satisfactory income and be granted funding opportunities to conduct research. Faculty members' participation in federal programs is based on a sense of reluctant acceptance, which represents faculty members' ambivalent feelings toward federal policies, including the capacity to negotiate institutional and personal goals.

Faculty members' reluctant acceptance was part of the re-boundarying work to shape their professional practice. The characteristics of academic professionalism and professionalization in Mexico were redefined based on the ways in which faculty members made sense of, and endeavored to meet, the institutional standards of federal programs. First, academics' self-understanding as professionals was linked to their capacity to meet accountability measures through their everyday performance and productivity. Second, socialization into the academic community and the university as an organization included the ability of faculty members to achieve (a) positive assessment outcomes that guarantee a consistent income and job security, (b) the effective management of multiple activities and deadlines within poor working conditions (i.e. ineffective bureaucratic structures, ambiguous organizational missions, and discretional action), and (c) continual individual and collective productivity. Within the context of federal programs and accountability demands, the notion of professionalism among Mexican faculty was, and continues to be, a contested terrain. Professionalization at public state universities in Mexico has become a process of continual negotiation among federal demands, local conditions, and individual interpretations about what it is to be faculty at a public state university.

While faculty members are discontent with the ways in which federal programs regulate their practice, they also suggest that there are opportunities for authentic academic work in public state universities. Full-time faculty members apply for grants, either individually or collectively, and they engage in intellectual work and obtain resources aimed to provide undergraduate and graduate students with initial training to do scientific research. Since federal agencies such as CONACYT are the main sources of financial support for full-time faculty members working at universities, the competition to gain research grants is intense among faculty members across the nation. The majority of state universities do not have funds to offer faculty members opportunities to develop consistent research projects. Within a highly competitive quest for resources and stable incomes, faculty members have to find strategies that make them more marketable or desirable within the national context. Participation in SNI and PROMEP provides faculty members with the opportunity to become marketable or legitimate, or both, by acquiring the symbols of prestige and practices of compliance embedded in federal programs. As a result, professionalization has also become a process through which faculty members become more profitable and marketable within their professional community.

The adoption of traveling policies in Mexico has encouraged changes in the ways in which faculty negotiate their professional concerns, demands, and discourses. Although the meaning of the academic profession in Mexico has changed to respond to international demands, it is clear that higher levels of academic competitiveness at public state universities will not be accomplished if academics' working conditions remain the same. It is also unlikely that the modernization of higher education in Mexico can be based on the individual achievement of those faculty members who choose to participate in professionalizing programs such as SNI and PROMEP.

References

Boice, R. (1992) *The New Faculty Member: Support and fostering professional development*, San Francisco: Jossey-Bass.

Bonal, X. (2004) Is the World Bank education policy adequate for fighting poverty? Some evidence from Latin America, *International Journal of Educational Development*, 24: 649–66.

Brunner, J.J. (1989) La educacion superior y la formación profesional en America Latina, *Revista Mexicana de Sociología*, 51(3): 237–49.

Burke, M.E. (1977) The University of Mexico and the revolution, 1910–1940, *The Americas*, 34(2): 252–73.

Chavoya-Peña, M.L. (2001) Organización del trabajo y culturas académicas: estudio de dos grupos de investigadores de la Universidad de Guadalajara, *Revista Mexicana de Investigación Educativa*, 6(11): 79–93.

Clark, B.R. (2001) Small worlds, different worlds: the uniquenesses and troubles of American academic professions, in S.R. Graubard (ed.) *The American Academic Profession*, New Brunswick, NJ: Transactions, pp. 21–42.

CONACYT (2011) *Sistema Nacional de Investigadores*. Available at www.conacyt.gob.mx/SNI/Paginas/default.aspx (accessed June 10, 2011).

Díaz-Barriga, A. (2007) Los sistemas de evaluación y acreditación de programas de educación superior, in A. Díaz-Barriga and T. Pacheco-Méndez (eds) *Evaluación y cambio institucional*, México Distrito Federal: Paidós, pp. 55–145.

Dressman, M. (2008) *Using Social Theory in Educational Research: A practical guide*, New York: Routledge.

Erickson, F. (1986) Qualitative methods in research on teaching, in M.C. Wittrock (ed.) *Handbook of Research on Teaching*, New York: Macmillan, pp. 119–60.

Fairweather, J.S. (1989) Academic research and instruction: the industrial connection, *Journal of Higher Education*, 60(4): 388–407.

Fairweather, J.S. (2002) The mythologies of faculty productivity: implications for institutional policy and decision making, *Journal of Higher Education*, 73(1): 26–48.

Fortes, J. and Lomnitz, L.A. (1994) *Becoming a Scientist in Mexico: The challenge of creating a scientific community in an underdeveloped country*, University Park, PA: Pennsylvania State University.

Foucault, M. (1972) *The Archaeology of Knowledge* (A. Sheridan-Smith, trans.), New York: Harper and Row.

Foucault, M. (1980) *Power/Knowledge* (C. Gordon, E.C. Gordon, L. Marshall, J. Mepham, and K. Soper, trans.), New York: Pantheon.

Galaz-Fontes, J.F. and Gil-Antón, M. (2009) La profesión académica en México: un oficio en proceso de reconfiguración, *Revista Electrónica de Investigación Educativa*, 11(2): 1–31.

Gappa, J.M., Austin, A. and Trice, A.G. (2007) *Rethinking Faculty Work: Higher education's strategic imperative*, San Francisco, CA: Jossey-Bass.

Gee, J.P. and Green, J.L. (1998) Discourse analysis, learning, and social practice: a methodological study, *Review of Research in Education*, 23: 119–69.

Gil-Antón, M. (1994) *Los rasgos de la diversidad: Un estudio sobre los académicos mexicanos*, México Distrito Federal: UAM-A.

Gil-Antón, M. (2003) Big city love: the academic workplace in Mexico, in P.G. Altbach (ed.) *The Decline of the Guru: The academic profession in developing and middle-income countries*, New York: Palgrave Macmillan, pp. 23–51.

Guevara, P.G. (2004) *Mujeres académicas: El caso de una universidad estatal mexicana*, México Distrito Federal: Plaza y Valores Editores.

Guevara-Niebla, G. (ed.) (1992) *La catástrofe silenciosa*, México: Fondo de Cultura Económica.

Honan, J.P. and Teferra, D. (2001) The US academic profession: key policy challenges, *Higher Education*, 41(1/2): 183–203.

Ibarra-Colado, E. (2002) La "nueva universidad" en México: transformaciones recientes y perspectivas, *Revista Mexicana de Investigación Educativa*, 7(14): 75–105.

Kent, R. (1993) Higher education in Mexico: from unregulated expansion to evaluation, *Higher Education in Latin America*, 25(1): 73–83.

Levinson, B.A. and Holland, D.C. (1996) The cultural production of the educated person, in B.A. Levinson, D.E. Foley, and D.C. Holland (eds) *The Cultural Production of the Educated Person: Critical ethnographies of schooling and local practice*, New York: State University of New York Press, pp. 1–54.

Luke, A. (1995) Text and discourse in education: an introduction to critical discourse analysis, *Review of Research in Education*, 21: 3–48.

Massey, W.E. (1997) Uncertainties in the changing academic profession, *Daedalus*, 126(4): 67–94.

OECD (2006) *OECD Thematic Review of Tertiary Education: Country background report for Mexico*, México Distrito Federal: Ministry of Education in Mexico.

Ordorika, I. (1996) Reform at Mexico's National Autonomous University: hegemony or bureaucracy, *Higher Education*, 31(4): 403–27.

Ordorika, I. (2003) The limits of university autonomy: power and politics at the Universidad Nacional Autónoma de México, *Higher Education*, 46(3): 361–88.

Ornelas, C. (2003) Las bases del federalismo y la descentralización en educación, *Revista Electrónica de Investigación Educativa*, 5(1): 1–18.

Ornelas, C. and Post, D. (1992) Recent university reform in Mexico, *Comparative Education Review*, 36(3): 278–97.

Ortner, S. (2006) *Anthropology and Social Theory. Culture, power, and the acting subject*, London: Duke University Press.

Porter, L. (1999) Crisis in the government of our public universities, *Revista Electrónica de Investigación Educativa*, 1(1).

Porter, L. (2003) *La universidad de papel: Ensayos sobre la educacion superior en México*, México Distrito Federal: Centro de Investigaciones Interdisciplinarias en Ciencias y Humanidades.

Reimers, F. (1994) Education and structural adjustment in Latin America and sub-Saharan Africa, *International Journal of Educational Development*, 14(2): 119–29.

Rhoades, G. and Slaughter, S. (1997) Academic capitalism, managed professionals, and supply-side higher education, *Social Text*, 51: 9–38.

Rockwell, E. (1996) Keys to appropriation: rural schooling in Mexico, in B.A. Levinson, D. Holland, and D. Foley (eds) *The Cultural Production of the Educated Person*, New York: State University of New York Press, pp. 301–24.

Rockwell, E. (1999) Recovering history in the study of schooling: from the Longue Durée to everyday co-construction, *Human Development*, 42(3): 1–10.

Rodríguez, R. (2000) La reforma de la educación superior: señas del debate internacional a fin de siglo, *Revista Electrónica de Investigación Educativa*, 2(1): 69–86.

Silva, A.A. (2000) *Estado, políticas y universidades en un periodo de transición: Análisis de tres experiencias institucionales en México*, Guadalajara: Fondo de Cultura Económica.

Swidler, A. (2001) *Talk of Love: How culture matters*, Chicago, IL: University of Chicago Press.

Torres, C.A. and Schugurensky, D. (2002) The political economy of higher education in the era of neoliberal globalization: Latin America in comparative perspective, *Higher Education*, 43(4): 429–55.

Valles, A.C. (2009) *La práctica de investigación y el PROMEP*, paper presented at the 9th Congreso Internacional Retos y Expectativas de la Universidad.

Vidales, G.U., Sahagún, G.A. and Oca, J.R. (2006) *Programa de Mejoramiento del Profesorado: Un primer análisis de su operación e impactos en el proceso de fortalecimiento académico de las universidades públicas*, PROMEP. Available at http://ses4.sep.gob.mx/pe/promep/PROMEPanalisis1.pdf (accessed September 26, 2007).

10   Learner-Centred Education and Teacher Professionalism at the Local–Global Nexus

Michele Schweisfurth

Learner-centred education (LCE) has been a recurring theme across a range of countries, both as a national reform policy and in more localised teaching innovations. This chapter will focus on LCE as a travelling policy. The analysis draws selectively on a deliberately eclectic range of conceptual literature, including: literature from comparative education on policy borrowing; educational literature that interrogates LCE pedagogy from different disciplinary positions; and concepts from literature on teacher professionalism and identity. It also refers to the extensive research literature on LCE's problematic implementation in developing countries.[1] While LCE has been used extensively and often successfully with adult learners, and although it is sometimes implemented through bottom-up innovations, this chapter will focus on how government policy reforms in learner-centred directions interact with questions of teacher identity and professionalism in schools, with particular reference to developing countries.

LCE's promoters argue that it has many benefits over traditional didactic methods, including learning effectiveness, the capacity for critical thinking and learner emancipation, and preparation for life and work in a globalising, changing and diverse world. However, where LCE is a new idea, particularly in resource-poor contexts, there is historical and comparative evidence of implementation challenges across many contexts. Existing teaching patterns do not change easily, even where there is enthusiasm for LCE. The implementation of LCE relies heavily on teachers' capacities and agency, and thwarts the usual evaluation and accountability measures that are used to judge and impose standards of teaching. With advocates across the global to local continuum, and yet with such an evidently problematic record of implementation, LCE is an informative case study within which to consider teacher professionalism in the current context of pluri-scalar change forces in education.

The chapter will first consider LCE as a travelling policy, and its space at the intersection of the local and the global in a context of policy convergence. It will then explore each of the three main narratives we find in the literature regarding LCE's purposes and how these relate to teacher professionalism and accountability. Finally, it will consider some of the implementation difficulties specific to developing countries regarding LCE practice. How these can be understood in relation to the questions of teacher identity and teacher agency will be examined, drawing out the implications for support for teachers' professional development in such contexts.

Learner-Centred Education as a Travelling Policy

In the contemporary educational policy milieu, ideas of all kinds are constantly being transferred, translated and transformed across national and other boundaries (Cowen, 2006). In other words, they are moved from one context to another; they are adapted to the new context; and they are, over time, changed profoundly in their new setting as they are indigenised through the actions of local implementers. In turn, they help to transform the education system into which they have been imported. As Phillips and Ochs (2003) hypothesise in their model of educational policy 'borrowing', the impetus for transfer is based on a combination of factors, often a mixture of internal dissatisfaction concerning educational quality and outcomes; negative external evaluations and subsequent pressures; and the eternal politically motivated quest for something to fix the real and imagined problems, preferably quickly and visibly. LCE has been a particularly popular policy option internationally, especially in the developing world.

It is partly about who promotes LCE – at the global level, UNESCO and UNICEF, for example (UNESCO, 2008; UNICEF, n.d.), are very active in this regard. The foundations for this UN agency engagement with LCE are the implications for educational policy and practice of international agreements such as the UN Convention on the Rights of the Child (see, for example, Article 12 on the importance of the views of the child, Article 13 on the freedom of expression, and Article 29 on the development of each child's individual potential). UNICEF's Child-Friendly Schools initiative, for example (UNICEF, 2004), and UNESCO's Associated Schools Project Network (UNESCO, n.d.) explicitly promote learner-centred education. The UNICEF initiative is endorsed by almost all governments, and the ambition is to 'scale up' to make more, or preferably all, schools in a given country to be child-friendly (and, therefore, teaching to be learner-centred) (www.unicef.org/lifeskills/index_7260.html). Similarly, the Associated Schools Project Network is explicit in its desire to influence policy nationally as well as to work at the level of schools (www.unesco.org/new/en/education/networks/global-networks/aspnet/about-us/mission/).

Further international agreements on Education for All (EFA) facilitated by UN agencies enshrine notions of quality with learner-centredness embedded in them, such as the Dakar Framework for EFA (UNESCO, 2000), which advocates 'stimulating, participatory learning environments' (paragraph 70). This framework is endorsed and applied widely throughout the international community. Additionally, structural adjustment packages dictating the conditions for multilateral aid to developing countries have in some cases included curriculum reform measures with implications for teaching methodology (Chisholm and Leyendecker, 2009). At the national and bilateral level, a number of aid agencies have historically encouraged the implementation of LCE in developing countries; in the 1990s, policy documents from national aid agencies, including the UK, Danish, American, Canadian and Norwegian departments, advocated LCE (Tabulawa, 2003).

How far such advocacy has amounted to coercion or conspiracy is a subject of much debate. In the contemporary politics of global governance and aid, the discourse is about 'partnership' rather than outsiders setting conditions, but the subtle workings of influence are powerful in contexts where one partner has resources that the other partner needs. In any case, as the section below notes, there are powerful internal drivers that help to fuel the movement of LCE policy. Ultimately, the impetus for reform towards LCE is not entirely foreign: the attraction of LCE is 'a combination of top-down pressures and bottom-up desires' (Chisholm and Leyendecker, 2009: 691).

Learner-Centred Education: Three Narratives of Purpose and Professionalism

LCE as a travelling policy is inherently attractive, for at least three distinct sets of reasons, all of which make it a desirable policy for governments to pursue when they are attempting to raise educational quality and outcomes, and are concerned to be seen to be moving in 'modern' directions. LCE has been described as a 'policy panacea' (Sriprakash, 2010). Analysis of the vast literature on LCE (Schweisfurth, 2012) reveals three broad narratives regarding why LCE is important for learners, all of which encourage the policy to travel across borders, as governments 'borrow' policies in line with national priorities.

First, one line of reasoning is that people, by virtue of their essential natures and shared biology, learn more effectively when they have more control over their learning, and are guided in the process, rather than having a fixed curriculum imposed on them in set ways. Set broadly within perspectives from psychology, we might call this the cognitive perspective. A second contention is that a key purpose of LCE is to free people from oppressive forms of control, controls that are manifested in knowledge which limits their thinking and prospects, and pedagogical approaches which keep them subjugated to the wills of those with power. These are the emancipatory arguments for LCE. In this view, LCE is believed to help break down traditional teacher–learner power relations, and thus prefigure a more equitable social order. It is also seen to develop the critical thinking skills that lead to freedom from oppression, and therefore underpins the development of democratic citizenship. With the global growth in the numbers of democratic political regimes, there is an increasing concern for education's role in facilitating democratic citizenship, and LCE is seen as an appropriate vehicle. Third, we find LCE advocated as an appropriate preparation for contemporary and future life. The main version of this preparatory narrative is found in some contemporary policy documents where queries about the changing nature of the knowledge and skills required for future working life in a changing economic world order raise the need for flexible and personal forms of learning and skills of metacognition and research. LCE is seen as the best preparation for the future, where 'economic success is increasingly based upon the effective utilisation of intangible assets such as knowledge, skills and innovative potential as the key resource for competitive advantage' (ESRC, 2005). All OECD countries have, or are moving towards, knowledge economies (OECD, 1996), and middle-income countries are rapidly catching up; naturally low-income countries would not want to be left behind in these developments. The flexibility and responsiveness, research skills and imagination demanded by the knowledge economy of the future are said to be best nurtured by LCE.

Each of these narratives bears a particular relationship to the question of teacher professionalism and accountability. If governments have the desire and intention to hold teachers accountable to pedagogical reforms in the direction of LCE, they will meet challenges in these attempts, within each of these narratives. These challenges create spaces within which teachers can embrace, resist or reframe LCE policy within the scope of their own agency as well as giving consideration to other 'competing imperatives' (Alexander, 1995; Schweisfurth, 2002) that they face in their professional lives. The cognitive narrative is achievement-oriented, in that it aims to improve learning and therefore learning outcomes. However, the more individualised nature of teaching and learning in an LCE framework suggests that the traditional means of holding teachers accountable to outcomes, through comparing examination results, are meaningless. Yet, in many systems, including those ostensibly moving towards greater learner-centredness, common assessment remains a major driver of the education system, and is perceived as the favoured indicator of the quality of student learning, teacher skill and school management. Inspection is also problematic as a means to judge effectiveness in the LCE classroom: it is considerably easier to watch one teacher teaching than to observe large numbers of children learning. Within this narrative, teacher professionalism would have to include the capacity to judge the needs of each individual learner and to facilitate access to appropriate and stimulating resources and activities to meet these needs: these are challenging capacities to judge externally. They also sit uneasily with the realities of classroom life in developing countries, where classes of 80 are not uncommon, and with cultures that value collectivism over individualism.

The second narrative is about emancipation – obviously a hopelessly complex outcome to measure in order to assess teachers' LCE skills. But more importantly, this is not so much an achievement or outcome-oriented approach as a way of working where process is as important as outcomes and where a teacher's 'higher moral purpose' (Sockett, 1993) is the driving force. Teachers motivated to use learner-centred approaches from within this narrative are likely to perceive themselves as accountable to a higher order than policy, and may indeed be critical of the authorities who would like to hold them accountable. It is their own moral compass that guides their work, with a focus on egalitarian classroom relationships, respect for the rights and dignity of learners, and the cultivation of transformational skills through critical thinking about learning as well as through it.

The third narrative, preparation, is based on a particular model of what the economic future looks like. This particular vision of the future is neither certain nor empirically verifiable in the present, and holding teachers accountable for individuals' contribution to economic growth is not reasonable. The potential confounding variables between the classroom-based learning of a cohort of children, on the one hand, and their contribution to a nation's economy as working adults, on the other, make teachers' responsibility for this connection nearly impossible to trace.

If LCE is a policy 'script' (Alexander, 1995), then no matter how tightly framed, it will still be enacted by teachers and each performance will vary. It is only if LCE is reduced to a set of observable teaching techniques – belying the richness of each of the three narratives – that teachers might be held accountable to this practice. This opens the door to the thinnest, most rhetorical forms of implementation: children sitting in groups without actually collaborating; pupils being consulted about trivial matters without having any say in substantial matters of the curriculum; apparently individualised learning plans based on a narrow range of options and driven by common assessment; and whole-class discussions framed tightly by teacher control and dominated by the more vociferous and able learners. Ultimately, in the case of the professionalism of the teachers implementing LCE, no matter how we tell the story of LCE's benefits, the nature of the pedagogical changes demanded requires trust and autonomy, rather than accountability – what Hoyle (1975) might have termed 'extended professionalism'. Trust has its own benefits over accountability: it is a means of reducing uncertainty and is a basis for sound and productive relationships through cooperation and communication (Tschannen-Moran and Hoy, 2000). However, as discussed below, the nature of teacher identity and professionalism is not universal, and this is one of several issues constraining the implementation of LCE in developing country contexts.

Implementation of LCE in the Developing World

Along with the three broad narratives of advocacy, there is another, very different, narrative regarding LCE. This, too, raises major questions about teacher professionalism. Despite its international and national endorsement, LCE policy implementation by teachers at the classroom level has proven to be extremely problematic in developing country contexts. A recent analytical overview of 72 articles that have appeared in the *International Journal of Educational Development* in the past 40 years, including small-scale studies from across the Global South as well as regional meta-analyses, pointed to, above all, a history of implementation 'riddled with failures grand and small' (Schweisfurth, 2011: 425). Regardless of why policy makers or others might want teachers to improve the quality of their teaching through LCE, the policy, more often than not, does not take hold. Researchers report 'tissue rejection' (Harley *et al.*, 2000) and teacher 'failure' to make the 'paradigm shift' (Tabulawa, 2003). Considering the lengthy history of LCE's provenance as a policy import to the developing world, the evidence of problems is compelling, and yet evidently overlooked time after time. The problems of implementation might, on the one hand, be attributed to the nature of the process. 'Policy sociology has shown that policy and curriculum implementation does not follow the predictable path of formulation–adoption–implementation–reformulation' (Chisholm and Leyendecker, 2008: 196).

In addition, there are specific reasons for these 'failures', in relation to the nature of this travelling policy, and the contexts in which it is being implemented. Research reveals a range of factors. First, in developing countries in particular, resources are scarce, and teaching didactically from whatever textbook is available is the path of least resistance. Traditional, teacher-centred methods demand little other than one book and some chalk. Research on teachers' views reveals that they themselves often attribute implementation issues to a lack of resources, with expectations cited as being unreasonable (e.g. Jessop and Penny (1998) on The Gambia and South Africa). Second, as well as not taking teachers' views on resources or other concerns into consideration, policy proclamations are often generally unrealistic in the goals they set for changing practice, or the timeframe within which they expect these to be achieved (e.g. Dyer (1994) on India, and Jansen (1989) on Sub-Saharan Africa). Third, teacher training – both pre-service and in-service – is rarely effective in replacing the traditional methods teachers have personally experienced and used with learner-centred approaches. Short in-service courses do not impact sustainably on teachers' practice, and even teachers enthused during training tend to revert to tried-and-tested methods, often from their own learning experiences, when left to their own devices (e.g. Vavrus (2009) on Tanzania). Teaching methods are not simply learned techniques: they are an expression of a teacher's self, and they are born out of cultural socialisation. This question of cultural appropriateness of LCE is the fourth issue. For example, in countries where unquestioning respect for elders is central to the lived culture, LCE's emphasis on learner freedom is in stark contrast to cultural norms (e.g. O'Sullivan (2004) on Namibia), and the emphasis on the individual is at odds with collectivist tendencies in some cultures, where group cohesion and achievement are emphasised (e.g. Kanu (2005) on Pakistan). Finally, once teachers are in schools, even those who have become committed to LCE during their training, they find other pressures working against this practice, such as inspection regimes that reward authoritarian classroom management and coverage of a fixed curriculum. One of the most common 'own goals' appears in contexts as diverse as China and South Africa. In a range of cases, governments have attempted to introduce LCE policy while maintaining a common examination regime that is based on a fixed body of knowledge, which determines students' life chances, and to which teachers are held accountable for good results by inspectors, parents and other stakeholders.

Teacher Professionalism, Motivation and Identity in Developing Countries

Of particular significance to this volume is the question of teacher professionalism, and how that fits into this mix of factors. While essentialising or generalising across the majority world is dangerous, there is evidence that teacher professionalism is understood differently across many contexts in the developing world, as compared to the notions of extended/unrestricted professionalism (Hoyle, 1980) embedded in the LCE narratives. As Barrett (2008: 496) notes: 'Research on teacher identity can provide insights on the "stories" of how teachers respond to and are agents for change in both their professional and social contexts.'

Research findings have pointed to a complex range of factors in and descriptors of teachers' professional identities in such situations. A number of assumptions need to questioned regarding, for example, teachers' motivations for entering the profession; the nature of their preparation for teaching; and how they perceive their roles in terms of their relationships with learners and the extent of their professional autonomy. Constructions originating from Western understandings of what it means to be a teacher, particularly a learner-centred one, do not sit easily with local realities. Local variations of the culture of teacher professionalism will also affect the ways that teachers exercise resistance or avoidance when unfamiliar policies with origins in other contexts are imposed from above.

Studies indicate, for example, that motivations for entering the teaching profession in poorer countries are not necessarily shared with teachers in other parts of the world. There is evidence from a number of studies (including a four-country study by Coultas and Lewin (2002)) that, for many, teaching is not a first-choice profession, and that candidates often enter tertiary-level teacher preparation programmes because their secondary school examination results do not qualify them for their preferred option. This inevitably influences how far they are likely to be committed to pedagogical change generally, and the challenges posed by the alien demands of LCE are likely to be unpalatable.

The process of teacher education in many contexts does not prepare students for learner-centred classrooms. It is often itself authoritarian in delivery (Harber, 2004) – even when it is preaching LCE doctrine – and theoretical rather than practical (e.g. Altinyelken (2010) on Uganda). Once they are employed, there is evidence that teachers' motivation is hampered by lack of appreciation by authorities for the challenges of their role, and a sense of personal insecurity with new methods. A study of teachers' attitudes in Zambia, Papua New Guinea and Malawi (VSO, 2002) highlights the fragility of teacher motivation, their indignation at the poor and unreliable remuneration they receive, and their strong sense of being subject to a 'blame culture' in which they are scapegoats for policy and social failings. It is this last factor that teachers find the most demotivating: their lack of voice, and the willingness of those outside the profession to undermine or undervalue their efforts. The study demonstrates that one of the first things to go when teachers feel unmotivated is their willingness to try new approaches in the classroom. Additionally, in many cases in the developing world, teachers are teaching in a second language in which they are not fluent. This hampers their sense of efficacy and is likely to make them conservative in how they manage classroom discourse: when working in an uncomfortable language, teachers 'save face' by asking questions to which they know the answers, rather than open questions that might take them into territory they do not understand (Brock-Utne and Holmarsdottir, 2004).

Studies of teacher identity in Sub-Saharan Africa (Jessop and Penny, 1998; Stuart, 2002; Barrett, 2008) have pointed to the importance of both the relational aspects of teaching, where teachers' concerns and motivations lie primarily in their relationships with children, and the instrumental, where job security is a primary factor in contexts of few formal employment options. While we might assume that the teachers most concerned with their relationships with children might be ripe for LCE, it has been observed that 'relaters claim an interest in aspects of competence pedagogy, whilst demonstrating a restricted understanding of educational purpose as following the syllabus and preparing children for examination success' (Barrett, 2008: 504). In other words, the kindest thing you can do for the children you want to help and nurture is to prepare them for examinations – not particularly conducive to LCE experimentation. With more experienced teachers, there is a tendency, rhetorically, to defer both to traditional pedagogy (the local) and to newer, more learner-centred approaches (the global) without reflexively resolving the tensions between them. The notion of the reflective practitioner – another discursive panacea in the educational change literature – does not map readily on to the context of teacher professionalism everywhere.

Even where teachers are motivated through their own sense of professionalism or the training they receive to implement LCE, on the job they are likely to face barriers that conflict with these beliefs, sometimes in the form of inspector, manager or parental expectations (as is the case where examination results set the standards of effectiveness). Learners themselves may resist such changes, if they are aware that knowing examination content is the most important learning they can do to improve their life chances (Vavrus, 2009). Teachers, as is human nature, will seek coherence across these change forces and their professional lives and identities (Giddens, 1991). But given the many tensions and conflicts between the global and local, the old and new, and the experienced and taught, and given few opportunities to reflect safely on their resolution, paradigm shifts are unlikely.

These are broad generalisations that research evidence suggests hold up across much of the Global South, Sub-Saharan African in particular. However, there are exceptions everywhere, and the precise nature of these tensions and how they are lived and resolved (or not) by individual professionals or how they are expressed collectively varies across different contexts. South Africa makes an interesting example in many of these regards, illustrating both the general and the particular. During the apartheid era, curricula were racially specific and were designed to reinforce divisions by preparing learners from different groups for their 'rightful' place in society. In the optimism of the era immediately post-apartheid, education policy, in globally unprecedented ways, was framed in a discourse of emancipation. Outcomes-based education (OBE) – itself a travelling policy – was adopted to replace the existing curricula, and LCE principles were embedded in the policy framework. In a sudden and profound transition from the previous educational regime, policy dictated that: 'The curriculum, teaching methods and textbooks … should encourage independent and critical thought, the capacity to question, enquire, reason, weigh evidence and form judgements, achieve understanding, recognise the provisional nature of most human knowledge and communicate clearly' (Department of Education, 1995: 22). However, in the aftermath of policy proclamations, it quickly became apparent that change at the classroom level was less consensual or straightforward, for many of the reasons indicated above, despite wide support from the profession in principle. Particularly, the case in the South African context was the problem of policy's intensive change and inaccessible language – teachers struggled to interpret policy, even where they endorsed its spirit, and misunderstandings were (and remain) rife (Nykiel-Herbert, 2004; Todd and Mason, 2005). The 'provisional nature of knowledge' cited above, for example, demands a reflexive understanding of philosophy and epistemology from teachers whose own education had been designed to prevent such depth of reflection. The transitions demanded a reframing of professional role and identity, from teacher to facilitator: in itself a substantial challenge, as in any context. In South Africa, the challenge was compounded by a culture of politicised resistance in schools, dating back to the apartheid years, which in the post-apartheid era morphed into an unhappy constellation of violence and apathy widely cited as the breakdown of the culture of teaching and learning (November *et al.*, 2010). Misinterpretations of the demands of OBE absolved teachers of the need to teach actively, with knowledge and effort situated discursively by them in the learner (Nykiel-Herbert, 2004), and a culture of entitlement among teachers after years of underprivilege reinforced this stance (November *et al.*, 2010). Fortunately, there are well-researched exceptions to these generalisations in the 'new' South Africa, which illustrate the agency of education professionals even where the prevailing culture of teaching and learning and professionalism do not support it. Christie (1997), for example, has documented the very different culture in 'resilient schools', where strong management, teacher commitment and supportive mechanisms have teachers resisting not so much government policy but the prevailing barriers and resistance to government policy. This, Christie argues, is school-based, rather than an outcome of policy change or centralised training initiatives, and less about implementation of LCE and more about sustaining meaningful and orderly teaching and learning more generally: the ultimate learner-centred achievement in this particular context.

Beyond the Impasse

Studies point to teacher isolation in terms of how far they are supported in changing their practice in learner-centred directions. Where new LCE policy fails for any of the myriad reasons that research has revealed, what we often find are recriminations based on teachers' roles in the process. As with all changes to pedagogy:

> if progress is slower than we would like, then it is assumed that the prescriptions are not being correctly operationalised by the teachers, rather than that the prescriptions need to be re-assessed and perhaps reconceived by those who train the teachers and provide the frameworks of policy and resource within which they work.
>
> (Alexander, 2008: 2)

In other words, the prescriptions themselves regarding LCE need to be considered carefully: are they feasible and appropriate for the physical and human resource context? Is the prescription at odds with local and educational cultures? Comparative research indicates that many teachers believe that positive support would help them to be motivated to make pedagogical changes (VSO, 2002). There are glimmers of evidence about what does seem to work in terms of encouraging change that is seen as positive by both the agents of policy (policy makers and external agents) and the agents of implementation (teachers). Joined-up thinking is needed across policy, training, evaluation and support functions, and the efforts must be sustainable across time. Given the importance of modelling in teachers coming to terms with pedagogical change, it is also apparent that, if policy communications, teacher education and in-service support are learner-centred with an understanding of teachers as learners, there will be greater coherence in the change process (Schweisfurth, 2011). Given the multiple, complex foundations of LCE, teachers would need to be 'remade' professionally, rather than simply trained, in order to be able to rise to its demands; this requires a reflexive engagement with the tensions between the global and the local. As we have seen, teacher accountability to LCE is not a meaningful proposition, and thus it requires trust between teachers and other stakeholders to reach shared understandings of what LCE can and should achieve, and how.

The alternative or complement to finding ways of improving teachers' take-up of policy is greater acceptance of how travelling policies such as LCE are translated and reconceived by professionals in different contexts, within a framework of minimum standards with local variations (Schweisfurth, 2012). For example, teachers' professional identities and cultural norms of power distance might demand more formal manifestations of relationships with pupils, and a more authoritative demeanour, than Western conceptions of child-centredness idealise. This need not violate fundamental principles of mutual respect and the upholding of basic rights. As Cowen (2006) reminds us about travelling policies: 'as it moves, it morphs'. Grafting policy shifts with origins in other professional cultures on to teaching realities in developing countries might usefully take this into consideration from the outset.

We might think of LCE as something of a 'Trojan Horse'. It is easy, with a global eye, to admire its rich potential, and to welcome the benefits that it promises. It is wheeled easily into a new context, driven by the powerful combination of global governance, bilateral efforts and local aspirations, with the winds of modernity at its back. The coalition army nested inside is intended to battle poor-quality and meaningless education, the dangers of authoritarianism, and underdevelopment. But when opened, an undisciplined rabble of ragtag recruits is unleashed, and enters into conflict with local capacities, cultural and classroom practices, and teachers' professional identities. Whether or not the remaking of teacher professionalism, which is required for LCE as it is currently conceived, is feasible or even desirable, what is evident is that 'quick fix' importations are not working.

Note

1   The term 'developing countries' is problematic for a number of well-rehearsed reasons (e.g. Phillips and Schweisfurth, 2006), including the difficulty of dividing the world's nations into two categories; the multiple parameters of development, upon which a given country might have different indications; and the internal differences between richer and poorer regions or individuals in a given country. However, given the particular resource constraints and pressures experienced in nations at the lower end of the human development index scale, the shorthand 'developing countries' will be used, with apologies, to indicate contexts relevant to this discussion.

References

Alexander, R.J. (1995) *Versions of Primary Education*, London: Routledge.

Alexander, R.J. (2008) *Education for All: The quality imperative and the problem of pedagogy*, Brighton: Consortium for Research on Educational Access, Transitions and Equity

Altinyelken, H. (2010) Curriculum change in Uganda: teacher perspectives on the new thematic curriculum, *International Journal of Educational Development*, 30: 151–61.

Barrett, A. (2008) Capturing the *différance*: primary school teacher identity in Tanzania, *International Journal of Educational Development*, 28: 496–507.

Brock-Utne, B. and Holmarsdottir, H. (2004) Language policies and practices in Tanzania and South Africa: problems and challenges, *International Journal of Educational Development*, 24: 67–83.

Chisholm, L. and Leyendecker, R. (2008) Curriculum reform in post-1990s sub-Saharan Africa, *International Journal of Educational Development*, 28: 195–205.

Chisholm, L. and Leyendecker, R. (2009) Curriculum reform in sub-Saharan Africa: when global meets local, in R. Cowen and A. Kazamias (eds) *International Handbook of Comparative Education*, Dordrecht: Springer.

Christie, P. (1997) Schools as (dis)organisations: the 'breakdown of the culture of learning and teaching' in South African schools, *Cambridge Journal of Education*, 28: 283–300.

Coultas, J. and Lewin, K. (2002) Who becomes a teacher? The characteristics of student teachers in four countries, *International Journal of Educational Development*, 22(3–4): 243–60.

Cowen, R. (2006) Acting comparatively upon the educational world: puzzles and possibilities, *Oxford Review of Education*, 32(5): 561–73.

Department of Education (South Africa) (1995) *White Paper on Education and Training*, Pretoria: Department of Education.

Dyer, C. (1994) Education and the state: policy implementation in India's federal policy, *International Journal of Educational Development*, 14(3): 241–53.

ESRC (2005) *Knowledge Economy in the UK*. Available at www.esrcsocietytoday.ac.uk/ESRCInfoCentre/facts/UK/index4.aspx?ComponentId=6978&SourcePageId=14971#0 (accessed 14 March 2006).

Giddens, A. (1991) *Modernity and Self-Identity: Self and society in the late modern age*, Stanford, CA: Stanford University Press.

Harber, C. (2004) *Schooling as Violence: How schools harm pupils and societies*, London: Routledge.

Harley, K., Barasa, F., Bertram, C., Mattson, E. and Pillay, S. (2000) 'The real and the ideal': teacher roles and competences in South African policy and practice, *International Journal of Educational Development*, 20: 287–304.

Hoyle, E. (1975) Professionality, professionalism and control in teaching, in V. Houghton, P. McHugh and M. Colin (eds) *Management in Education: The management of organisations and individuals*, London: Ward Lock Educational, in association with Open University Press.

Hoyle, E. (1980) Professionalization and deprofessionalization in education, in E. Hoyle and J. Megarry (eds) *World Yearbook of Education 1980*, London: Kogan Page, pp. 42–57.

Jansen, J. (1989) Curriculum reconstruction in post-colonial Africa: a review of the literature, *International Journal of Educational Development*, 9(3): 219–31.

Jessop, T. and Penny, A. (1998) A study of teacher voice and vision in the narratives of rural South African and Gambian primary school teachers, *International Journal of Educational Development*, 18(5): 393–403.

Kanu, Y. (2005) Tensions and dilemmas of cross-cultural transfer of knowledge: post-structural/postcolonial reflections on an innovative teacher education in Pakistan, *International Journal of Educational Development*, 25: 493–513.

November, I., Alexander, G. and van Wyk, M.M. (2010) Do principal-educators have the ability to transform schools? A South African perspective, *Teaching and Teacher Education*, 26: 786–95.

Nykiel-Herbert, B. (2004) Misconstructing knowledge: the case of learner-centred pedagogy in South Africa, *Prospects*, 34(3): 249–65.

OECD (1996) *The Knowledge-based Economy*, Paris: OECD. Available at www.oecd.org/dataoecd/51/8/1913021.pdf (accessed 20 September 2012).

O'Sullivan, M. (2004) The reconceptualisation of learner-centred approaches: a Namibian case study, *International Journal of Educational Development*, 24: 585–602.

Phillips, D. and Ochs, K. (2003) Processes of policy borrowing in education: some explanatory and analytical devices, *Comparative Education*, 39(4): 451–61.

Phillips, D. and Schweisfurth, M. (2006) *Comparative and International Education: An introduction to theory, method and practice*, London: Continuum.

Schweisfurth, M. (2002) *Teachers, Democratisation and Educational Reform in Russia and South Africa*, Oxford: Symposium.

Schweisfurth, M. (2011) Learner-centred education in developing country contexts: from solution to problem? *International Journal of Educational Development*, 31: 425–32.

Schweisfurth, M. (2012) *Learner-centred Education in International Perspective*, London: Routledge.

Sockett, H. (1993) *The Moral Base for Teacher Professionalism*, New York: Teachers College Press.

Sriprakash, A. (2010) Child-centred education and the promise of democratic learning: pedagogic messages in rural Indian primary schools, *International Journal of Educational Development*,30: 297–304.

Stuart, J. (2002) College tutors: a fulcrum for change?, *International Journal of Educational Development*, 22(3–4): 367–79.

Tabulawa, R. (2003) Pedagogical classroom practice and social context: the case of Botswana, *Comparative Education*, 39(1): 7–26.

Todd, A. and Mason, M. (2005) Enhancing learning in South African schools: beyond outcomes-based education, *International Journal of Educational Development*, 25: 221–35.

Tschannen-Moran, M. and Hoy, W.K. (2000) A multidisciplinary analysis of the nature, meaning and measurement of trust, *Review of Educational Research*, 70(4): 547–93.

UNESCO (2000) *The Dakar Framework for Action. Education for All: Meeting our collective commitments*, Paris: UNESCO.

UNESCO (2008) *First Collection of Good Practices for Quality Education*. Available at http://unesdoc.unesco.org/images/0016/001627/162766e.pdf (accessed 10 December 2011).

UNESCO (undated) *Mission*, UNESCO Associated Schools. Available at www.unesco.org/new/en/education/networks/global-networks/aspnet/about-us/mission (accessed 28 March 2011).

UNICEF (2004) *Child-friendly Schools*. Available at www.unicef.org/lifeskills/index_7260.html (accessed 14 March 2012).

UNICEF (undated) *Education*, UNICEF UK. Available at www.unicef.org.uk/UNICEFs-Work/Our-mission/Childrens-rights/Education (accessed 12 December 2011).

Vavrus, F. (2009) The cultural politics of constructivist pedagogies: teacher education reform in the United Republic of Tanzania, *International Journal of Educational Development*, 29: 303–11.

Voluntary Service Overseas (VSO) (2002) *What Makes Teachers Tick? A policy research report on teachers' motivation in developing countries*, London: VSO.

11 The Doubts and Uncertainties of French Educators in the Face of Travelling Policies

Romuald Normand

Introduction

As the saying goes: '*Plus çà change, plus rien ne change*' (the more things change, the more nothing changes). Compared to other nations, French educators seem not much influenced by travelling policies and their effects on education systems (Ozga and Jones, 2006). Their vision is largely embedded in the national context and the main developments in the building of a European space of education (Lawn and Novoa, 2002) have been largely ignored by the French education community. Managerialism and the market, as political technologies developed in other countries, are often seen in France as carrying unwelcome neo-liberal principles into the public sphere. During recent decades, ministers of education, from both the Left and the Right, have attempted to implement reforms, but they have failed to change the structures of education and school organization, leading the former leftist minister Claude Allègre to characterize the French system as a 'mammoth' (Derouet and Normand, 2011). Furthermore, awareness of globalization was slow to emerge until the beginning of the 2000s, when French policy makers, after several official reports, decided to increase their involvement in the Lisbon agenda. In government, the PISA survey became the touchstone of reforms and it remains at the centre of official and even scientific rhetorics (Mons, 2008; Baudelot and Establet, 2009).

At local level, French educators face difficulties in moving away from the central idea of the comprehensive school. Their attachment to the democratic ideal of the common school entails high expectations of the State and impedes the exploration of alternative possibilities and visions. Furthermore, education is an arena of highly disputed politics in France because in it are embedded other issues at stake in public debate: citizenship and multiculturalism, knowledge and culture, religion and Islamism, equality and freedom, the public and the private. As a result, it is difficult to reach a collective agreement about reforms while permanent ideological battles divide the Left and the Right, but also Left leaders themselves. Lobbies and interest groups also remain influential in policy making. Associations, trade unions and, more recently, think tanks are very active in promoting and contesting reform. In 2003–4, despite the launching of a Great Debate by the Haut Conseil de l'Evaluation de l'Ecole (High Council of School Assessment), consensus has been difficult to achieve among divergent visions of education (Thélot, 2005). However, at the heart of the State, high-ranking policy makers had worked behind the scenes in bipartisan committees and shadow meetings to promote a framework of New Public Management (Bezès, 2009). In fact, changes in the French education system stem primarily from a shift in the structure of the State and this process is largely influenced by policy borrowing from the European Union and supra-national organizations (Christensen and Laegreid, 2007). However, inside the system, educators do not experience these changes except through discontinuities and disarticulations encountered in their professional lives (Goodson and Hargreaves, 1996; Bezès *et al.*, 2011).

This chapter aims to explore the uncertainties and doubts of educators in the face of these transformations and discuss how they maintain assumptions and practices that are firmly embedded in the narrative of the comprehensive school. After emphasizing the sense of legacy and the importance of values and justice in the vision of French educators, I explain why it is so difficult for them to accept school restructuring and professionalism influenced by travelling policies. I describe how they try to resist policy making that can be described nevertheless as 'ambiguous' and 'erratic'. Conclusions will then be drawn about the impact of current reforms on the system of professions in France.

The Endless Narrative of the Golden Age of the Comprehensive School

Before analysing changes in the institutional environment and conditions of work of French educators, it is necessary to investigate the historical and cultural background that structures their educational vision. In France, the history of public schools is not distinct from the foundation of the Republican State and reflects its values and principles of justice. This explains why globalization, because it questions the place of the State and its future, creates many fears and anxieties among educators. For most of them, education is a question of legacy: the values and conception of knowledge inherited from the French Revolution and Republican roots have to be protected from 'barbarian invasions'. For many, education is the basis of national citizenship, a means of collective emancipation distinct from private interests and local powers and the best way to reduce social inequalities. Historically, this legacy explains the long quest for the democratization of access for working-class pupils and the collective attachment to the comprehensive school model. However, in the last two decades, the Republican vision of equality, meritocracy and elitism has been contested while the project of the '*collège unique*', or common school, which represented progressive hopes, failed.

Some Principles Defining the School System of the Republican State

The first high schools and the first body of inspectors were created during Bonaparte's consulate. Napoleon's great education reform while emperor was the creation of the Imperial University and legislation expressed the State's monopoly in the governance of primary and secondary schools. Progressively, the State forced municipalities to be responsible for primary education through Acts designed by the ministries of Guizot (1833) and Falloux (1850). The Falloux Act recognized the duality of the French education system (in other words the coexistence of public provision, funded by the State, and private Catholic provision), but it also gave considerable recognition to the Catholic religion to combat emergent socialist ideas. This contradicted the Enlightenment ideas advanced by the French Revolution. In the 1880s, the creation and the confirmation of the Third Republic entailed a long-lasting transformation in the educational vision of the State. The successive Acts of the Minister Jules Ferry (1881–2) established schooling as free, compulsory and secular (*laïque*). Henceforth all pupils had access to primary education and they had to be instructed on an equal basis with no distinction made for their cultural and social backgrounds. The '*hussards noirs de la République*' (literally, the shock troops of the Republic – the primary school teachers) had to remain neutral in respecting each child's freedom of conscience, in recognizing all religions with the same impartiality but in restricting their influence to outside the schools and classrooms. For the Republican policy makers, close to Protestant elites, this was a spectacular revenge against the old monarchist and conservative groups who had tried to diminish the influence of the legacy of the French Revolution. The policy of the '3Rs' and the dominance of French language throughout the school system were also means to counteract the local influence of the Church and the Nobility and their hostility to Republican ideals.

Ever since then the Republican school has been considered as a sanctuary where the values and knowledge of the Enlightenment could be transmitted to new generations in order to make them citizens. This vision was shared by influential intellectuals such as Ferdinand Buisson and Emile Durkheim, the founder of the French educational sciences and sociology. In considering education as 'the methodical socialization of a generation', Durkheim explained that the schoolmaster had to be placed at the centre of the classroom and had to use the authority given by the State to reinforce the pupil's sense of belonging to the Nation. The schoolmaster was viewed as a 'secular priest' in the 'Republican Church'. Learning the sense of rules, the spirit of discipline and the independence of free will were the main aims of the Republican school in creating a new citizen (Durkheim, 1934). Today, these principles are shared by the majority of French teachers, who consider, with Durkheim, that classrooms (and schools) must be protected from the (bad) influences of families and local groups.

The other aspect of this Republican legacy concerns the status of educators and their position as State civil servants. In the traditional conception of bureaucracy, the civil servant is indifferent to the user's personal attributes; he or she has to maintain the impartiality of the State without considering inherited status and social position. This professional ethic is shared by many French educators: indifference to pupil difference is considered to be a democratic and moral attitude that maintains Republican ideals. In addition, the respect for hierarchy shown by civil servants, who are accredited and recruited by a professional body on the basis of their high levels of performance in selective examinations, is understood as an appropriate means of maintaining the authority and legitimacy of the State.

But French teachers, as a professional group, also control their working conditions, and assert their expertise in school subjects as the basis of their 'pedagogical freedom' to decide for themselves what is important in teaching and learning.

Elitism Between Meritocracy and Equality: A Necessary Fiction

The extension of the public school system is intrinsically linked to the mode of selection and fabrication of the elite. From '*classes préparatoires*' (prep schools) to '*grandes écoles*' (public colleges), the Republican State continued the tradition initiated by the Ancient Régime through selection of the best students after the baccalaureate and their recruitment as top civil servants for administration and public companies. The training of the Republican elite coincided with the creation of particular professional groups (State bodies) who today occupy positions of power in French society despite much criticism of their privileges and self-reproduction (Bourdieu, 1996). This 'State nobility' was largely influential in the maintenance of restricted access to the elite while the universities, with insufficient public funds and infrastructure, were compelled to accept large numbers of students who had completed the baccalaureate and to manage high failure and drop-out rates. Despite this big division between the few and the many, and despite decades of political quests for equality of opportunities, a highly divisive system has been maintained. Ideas of meritocracy and equality are so embedded in public consciousness that it is difficult, even for educators, to admit to the existence of a large gap between the 'winners' and the 'losers'. They continue to assert that schooling recognizes talent according to pupil efforts in learning, despite evidence of a biased competition from the beginning of schooling and achievement results that are largely related to parental background and resources.

However, equality of opportunities remains a 'necessary fiction' in the French education system because it corresponds to principles of justice supporting a democratic society (Derouet, 1992; Dubet, 2004). In Republican narratives, everybody has the capacity to perform and to improve their social position through the school system. Performance and merit are seen as virtues of excellence: achievement follows from self-empowerment, effort and reflexivity, reflecting a collective belief that diplomas and jobs are accessible to those who deserve them. However, in fact the school system is incapable of reducing the impact of social inequalities on pupil achievement. Since the 1960s, the sociology of education has demonstrated that the distribution of test results and the formation of elites are determined by social background. But, despite the school system's failure to reduce gaps between pupils, the principle of meritocracy is the norm by which school practices and the guidance of pupils are appraised by educators. This collective attachment to merit explains the maintenance of national examinations and '*concours*' or testing regimes, through which, because of the equivalence of school conditions, the best pupils are tested and selected in a 'Republican' competition.

This principle also explains why PISA findings are accepted so uncritically by progressive educators who want to change schools and to make them more egalitarian. Far from being considered as benchmarks imposed on nation-states, PISA data are used to demonstrate that France is more unequal than other countries because of its elitism and its incapacity to improve the achievement of the most deprived pupils. This argument against Republican elitism is largely advanced by such sociologists as Christian Baudelot and Roger Establet, two former Marxists, who have an impact on discourses held by leftist trade unions and political parties (Baudelot and Establet, 2009). But this egalitarian argument is also used by the Right to advocate reforms, even if its vision is different. More broadly, PISA has become a discourse for policy makers who use it to justify change in the education system as necessary without questioning the conditions of production or political aims of this international survey (Greek, 2010). The traditional conception of elitism and meritocracy is also contested by sociologists such as François Dubet and Marie Duru-Bellat, who are close to the progressive Left and advocate a reform of the comprehensive school (Dubet *et al.*, 2010).

The Dead End of School Democratization: The 'Collège Unique' *at Stake*

Beyond the debate on elitism and meritocracy, French educators express concern about the impact of schooling on the democratization by knowledge and the building of citizenship. The idea of the '*école unique*', capable of providing 'fair' selection of working-class pupils and allowing them access to secondary education, dates from the project of the 'Compagnons de l'Université Nouvelle' (Companions of the New University) (Derouet, 2001a; Garnier, 2007). After the First World War, this group of leftist intellectuals decided to reduce early selection and to promote the comprehensive school for all. But they faced resistance from the Right, which was hostile to the process of democratization. This political project was taken over by the Popular Front and the Langevin-Wallon Plan, and met success through the creation of the '*collège unique*' in 1975. This policy ended early selection and unified the curriculum. It was influenced by trade unions and by pedagogical movements, but also by the OECD's recommendations to increase access of working-class pupils to upper-secondary schooling and higher education. As in the English case, the '*collège unique*' held all the leftist hopes for the promotion of equality of opportunities through an education system for all (Simon, 1991; Prost, 2004). As a consequence, admission to secondary education was extended to underprivileged children while in the mid-1980s the Ministry of Education fixed a new target of '80% of a generation to take the baccalaureate' (Derouet, 2001b). In fact, it was a 'false democratization': segregation and social inequalities remained high in terms of pupil selection and access to different types of baccalaureate.

At the end of the 1980s, progressive educators and policy makers recognized that democratization had failed to reduce inequality of opportunities among pupils and students. Drop-out rates had increased in secondary education and the inflation of diplomas within higher education had decreased their value (Duru-Bellat, 2006). The policy of 'Education Priority Areas', implemented in 1981 to reduce the achievement gap between deprived suburban schools and mainstream schools, did not work despite additional resources provided by the State (Meuret, 1994; Moisan and Simon, 1997; Kherroubi and Rochex, 2002). Social exclusion and urban segregation were reinforced by the development of middle-class strategies of accessing private schools or skirting round catchment areas to escape from poor school conditions in teaching and learning (van Zanten, 2001). The *'collège unique'* was in 'crisis' despite the Ministry's attempts to start a small-scale diversification in school provision (for example, through some optional courses to better focus teaching on pupils' learning) while maintaining the official rhetoric the child had to be placed at the centre of the education system (Rayou, 2000). In fact, teachers were not well prepared to adapt their teaching and cope with new arrivals from the working class and with second-generation immigrants. In 1989, the *'instituts de formation des maîtres'* (teacher training colleges) were founded to support the teaching profession and help it to better match new professional requirements. But this policy failed to promote changes in practice and the dissemination of a mixture of didactics and philosophy did not impact on school achievement. During the 1990s the education debate remained controversial among educators and it set 'Republicans' and 'Pedagogues' in opposition to one another, particularly through the public controversy between two influential leftist intellectuals in the media: Alain Finkielkraut, philosopher and professor at the Ecole Polytechnique, and Philipe Meirieu, pedagogue and professor at the University of Lyon. The former defended the maintenance of the Republican legacy: a traditional transmission of knowledge based on academic disciplines, the affirmation of authority and Republican values inside the classroom. The latter advocated a stronger focus by teachers on learning, opening the school to civil society and parents, school improvement and innovation, cultural diversity and partnerships. This debate revealed the importance of philosophical disputes among public leaders (for example, in the controversy about banning the *hijab* in schools), rather than practical concerns about learning and teaching conditions (Normand, 2009).

Between Doubts and Uncertainties: The Elusive Reform of the French Comprehensive School

Compared with England, France has been quite slow to reform its comprehensive schools. At the same time as James Callaghan, then the British prime minister, spoke at Ruskin College in October 1976 demanding that the model be changed, the French Ministry of Education was implementing it. It is only in 2005 that the French basic skills framework was created, in contrast with other countries where it had been well established for many years. There are major gaps between educational reforms in France and the movement of globalization. Knowledge transfer and policy borrowing among French policy makers is real but slow and the national and public school system operates like a powerful government machine that absorbs global standards and dilutes them into a 'Republican patchwork'. The central government does not help educators to understand the significance and direction of reforms even if some tools, knowledge and programmes are borrowed from foreign countries that have already implemented accountability and school choice policies. The European Union also has a major influence in the restructuring of the French comprehensive school. The majority of educators are not very aware of this policy borrowing and they feel helpless and doubtful when confronted with the Ministry's decisions and actions (Robert and Tyssens, 2007). The Ministry itself does not implement a coherent national strategy and this makes changes more difficult to understand at local level.

The Basic Skills Framework and its Problematic Translation among Educators

Although French political leaders, such as Jacques Delors or Edith Cresson, were at the heart of the European space of education and training, their actions were ignored for a long time by the community of French educators. When the LMD (bachelor (licence)/master/doctorate) system was implemented in French higher education, after the conference at the University La Sorbonne (1998), and the Bologna process was launched, many educational scientists did not understand how their working conditions could be influenced by European decision making (Charlier and Croché, 2003). Today, the issue of Europe is so controversial that French policy makers prefer to minimize the role of the Lisbon strategy in the restructuring of the French education system. Among educators, the idea of lifelong learning is largely ignored and very often assimilated into further vocational training, which means that it is not, in their view, part of the main mission of State public schools. In the official rhetoric, considerable emphasis is placed on equality of opportunities, school-time scheduling, Republican values, the duty of remembrance based on national history, school guidance, personalized learning and basic skills, but there is no mention of the European context, except in relation to foreign languages. In the Ministry's guidelines many directives and recommendations embed a mix of national strategy and policy frameworks borrowed from global and European developments.

A good example is the French '*socle commun de connaissances et de compétences*' (framework of basic skills). This framework was implemented in the 2005 Act and promoted by the High Council of Education. It is considered as the basic building block in the implementation of accountability policy linking curriculum and assessment. It includes knowledge standards, skills and values that each pupil has to master by the end of compulsory schooling. The basic skills framework is structured in seven main areas: French language, foreign languages, mathematics and sciences, ICTs, humanist culture, social and civic skills, and autonomy and initiative. This structure is very close to the European key-competencies framework for lifelong learning. However, scrutiny of some items reveals the subtle translation made by French officials. The item 'learning to learn', which emphasizes pupil experience and the context of learning, was translated into 'humanist culture' and focused on school subjects such as history, geography and literature. The 'sense of initiative and entrepreneurship', which includes creativity, innovation and risk-taking, was turned into 'autonomy and initiative', emphasizing socialization (the building of a citizen) and guidance. These differences demonstrate the particular cultural and societal visions of French policy makers and educators. These remain largely unaffected by values and norms travelling through globalization. This example also provides evidence about the importance of the French conception of teaching, which preserves an emphasis on transmission of (subject content) knowledge. This uneasy compromise between different norms makes it difficult for educators to grasp the meaning of reform when they are confronted, in training sessions, official conferences or school meetings, with a framework that combines a Republican vision of the comprehensive school and features of accountability and standards policies that have been implemented elsewhere. These difficulties are intensified by the tools designed by the Ministry of Education to support teachers and to facilitate the 'appropriation' of the basic skills framework. Each teacher has to complete a '*livret de compétences*' (skills booklet) on a regular basis through which pupils' achievement has to be recorded. There are two reasons for the creation of this tool. First, pupil guidance is an important issue in the French comprehensive school tradition and educators feel more concerned about pupils' career choices than their conditions of learning. Second, educators are quite indifferent to assessment: formative assessment is not well developed and national tests are so poorly designed and so infrequent that they do not impact on teaching practices. At best, teachers spend their time reporting scores to their inspectors without being involved in team work and collaborative assessment practices.

The Crisis of the Comprehensive School Despite Some Limited Changes

The basic skills policy, despite some obstacles, defines a new accountability regime for the French State school system and imposes a new vision previously promoted by supra-national organizations and the European commission. However, the bureaucratic and centralized French system does not fit the dominant conceptions and policy requirements shared by global experts and policy makers: assessment, school improvement, personalized learning and leadership (Thrupp and Willmott, 2003; Thrupp, 2005). Nevertheless the wider context of welfare state 'reform' impacts on school organization and the identities of professional educators, as well as on their working conditions (Gewirtz, 2002). In France, because the public school system has been so culturally linked with the State apparatus, the transformation of the teaching profession is probably harder to accept than in other countries (Malet, 2008). The restructuring of the French education system can be observed from different perspectives. At the top, the 2001 Act modified public finances and budgets (LOLF: *Loi organique relative aux lois de finance*). It transformed public policies through the introduction of a 'culture' of performance and responsibility within the State administration and civil services. Now, administrative units have to report their expenses and to respect the standards of New Public Management: economy, effectiveness and efficiency. In education, this policy influences progressively the monitoring of programmes within the public school system while audit procedures are enlarged. Schools have to design school development plans and targets. After a discussion, an 'administrative' contract is signed between the head teacher and local authorities. However, for the moment, this is not directly linked to the school budget. Benchmarks used to assess and compare schools are designed by the Ministry of Education according to a top-down process. At school level, there is not much feedback and support in the use of these data, and no consequences for professional practices. Educators, however, consider this policy to be a significant reduction of public expenditure on education, which increases their workload and ignores their day-to-day professional challenges.

The other major change stems from the beginning of a diversification in policy for the recruitment to schools of pupils from deprived backgrounds and from a shift in the governance of education priority areas. School choice policy in France is still very much in limbo. However, the New Right government chose to abolish school catchment areas to create incentives for choice among parents. The effect is an increase in inequalities between schools because schools in deprived areas cannot stem the flight of pupils who can move to more favoured schools. There is much criticism of these developments from sociologists and Left-wing activists (Obin and van Zanten, 2008; Blanchard and Cayouette-Remblière, 2011). However, school choice is limited because the move from one school to another is restricted to special conditions (scholarship holders, siblings, medical care, etc.) and schools in great demand have no room for additional pupils. Furthermore, there is no system of league tables as in England. Families develop strategies according to school reputation, judged with reference to such issues as discipline, violence and social climate rather than through a scrutiny of pupils' test scores (van Zanten, 2009). Even if this school choice policy borrows some experiences from other countries (for example, the USA and England), and even if it is inspired by New Right ideology, the consciousness of inequalities among people and educators and their attachment to the State impedes the full implementation of quasi-market regulation. School choice is certainly promoted by New Right politicians as a means to reduce social exclusion and urban segregation and to enhance parents' democratic participation.

However, the national programme of '*internats d'excellence*' (boarding schools of excellence) created in 2008 is a good example of the compromise reached by the government to reconcile its neo-conservative and Republican principles. These 12 schools at national level recruit voluntary teachers and gifted pupils from priority education areas and select them according to their school performance. Pupils are supported by a rich learning and teaching environment so that they are well prepared for access to selective prep schools after the baccalaureate (i.e. those schools that allow access to colleges or '*grandes écoles*' after two years of preparation). But unlike the US charter schools, funding is not dependent on an increase in performance and these schools welcome gifted pupils even if they come from deprived areas. So teachers and the schools are not expected to improve results, but only to provide a good environment for pupils. This system is considered primarily as a means to enhance school meritocracy and to reduce social inequalities. In parallel, the new policy for education priority areas decreased their number but also restructured them into '*réseaux "ambition réussite"*' (education action networks). The main objectives of the programme are to increase cooperation between primary schools and lower-secondary schools, to reduce truancy and drop-out rates, to promote multiple-partnership on pupil guidance, to stimulate pedagogical innovations and to support teaching with pedagogical assistants. However, the achievement gap between pupils has not been reduced even if the rates of retention have decreased because head teachers and inspectors put pressure on teachers. Teaching practices did not change except through the development of a vague 'diagnosis' of pupil learning needs. The school structure and organization remained the same with limited team work and concerns about personalized learning (Malet and Brisard, 2005).

The establishment of a 'pedagogical board' and 'pedagogical experiments' represents the most recent attempt by the Ministry to enhance school improvement. The former consists in gathering teachers through a quarterly meeting to reflect about school development planning and cooperation. The appointment of teachers (mainly coordinators of school subjects and class teachers) is the responsibility of the head teacher, but teachers can also attend the meeting on a voluntary basis. In fact, this 'pedagogical board' functions as a sort of small assembly where appointed teachers feel that they are on duty and elected teachers feel they must represent the interests of their peers (they talk about issues related to their school subject or aspects of reforms criticized by trade unions). The head teacher has no means by which to convince teachers to be more involved outside the classroom or to share experiences and practices with their colleagues. The legitimacy of, and responsibility for, teaching belongs to teachers who value a high sense of professional autonomy and consider that they are accountable only to their inspector. 'Pedagogical experiments' are developed through flexible management of the school timetable. Each school has the opportunity to retain some teaching hours for an 'experiment' to launch new projects, to sustain school improvement, to develop partnerships, to create collective thinking on teaching practices, to support pupils in their personalized learning, and so on. This 'eligibility to experiment' is controlled and assessed by local authorities and schools have to respect precise requirements in order to get funded. The Ministry distinguishes between 'experiments' and 'innovations'. Innovations depend on teachers' sense of creativity and initiative. Experiments must be designed through a protocol and a contract and are systematically assessed by the inspectors. Many experiments are not focused on teaching and learning in the classroom and they often have little connection to pupil achievement. They do not modify the school structure and they are managed by a handful of voluntary, motivated and 'heroic' teachers.

Challenges to Educators: A New Professionalism?

The gradual abandonment of the comprehensive school is resisted by educators. They are critical of the basic skills framework and claim the State is abandoning its ideal of equality and Republican principles to implement a neo-liberal project in education (Careil, 2002; Laval, 2003). Reforms provoke diverse reactions ranging from protest to civil disobedience, and trade unions, while they oppose market and business, seem divided about the attitude to adopt. The absence of clarity among policy makers and some of the ideological visions held by former ministers of education did not help to reconcile educators and policy making. The future of the profession is now at stake.

New Public Management is being implemented throughout the public services and the status and career prospects of civil servants are being revised. Even if these developments create outright opposition among educators, they will have important consequences for their working conditions in the near future. Performance management, audit, flexibility, contracts and partnership progressively replace the ideas of administration, monitoring, status and mission that are familiar to educators. The performing school is becoming a reality in programmes for education priority areas that are used as political experiments by the French Ministry of Education.

From Protest to Civil Disobedience: French Educators in Great Confusion

Some recent successful French films on schooling illustrate how the imaginary of past schooling remains very powerful in the minds of both public and educators. The film *Etre et avoir* (To be and to have), which described the daily life of a school teacher and his pupils in a rural primary school, was very popular at the box office. *Entre les murs* (Between the walls) described the difficult interactions between a teacher and his pupils in a deprived lower-secondary school, and the impossibility for him of transmitting his knowledge and empowering pupils to learn French. The book written by the teacher narrating his troubled experience also enjoyed success. Even the performance of Isabelle Adjani, a famous actor, playing the role of a teacher in *La Journée de la jupe* (The day of the skirt) and asserting Republican principles against the challenging views of Muslim pupils, was very popular. All these events keep alive a certain patrimonial vision of the Republican school shared by many educators through notions of authority, culture, 'savoirs' (academic knowledge), rules, 'laïcité' (State secularism), citizenship and national identity. The rejection of multiculturalism, the assertion of equality and the attachment to the transmission of knowledge contribute to shaping professional groups and to maintaining their defence of the Republican school and its values. This defence is undertaken by associations and institutions lobbying for the protection of school subjects (French, mathematics, history or philosophy) in a demanding national curriculum, the salvation of grammar and spelling, the maintenance of a duty of remembrance in textbooks, and the prohibition of veils and religious objects inside schools.

However, the trade unions appear divided between tradition and modernization. The Syndicat National des Enseignements du Second degré-Fédération Syndicale Unitaire (SNES-FSU), the most important leftist union, hostile to reforms, acts to maintain the teaching profession's 'established rights'. It supports the democratization ideal through the transmission of academic knowledge and increased participation in compulsory schooling from ages 16 to 18. It considers that the basic skills framework dilutes the school culture in managerial skills and it argues for increased public funding and reduced class sizes. The Syndicat Général de l'Education Nationale-Confédération Démocratique Du Travail (SGEN-CFDT), its direct opponent, accepts the need for a certain amount of reform and, although it is fighting for equality of opportunities, it demands school improvement more focused on learning, diversification of school provision and the involvement of parents, better recognition of ethnic and racial segregation and the development of assessment. This difference can also be perceived between the teachers of primary education, more focused on learning, and those of secondary education who claim an expertise in school subjects related to academic disciplines. Trade unions are also very active in the dissemination of information among members, which helps teachers to be aware of their rights, of the decisions of the Ministry and of debates on education issues. They also provide advice for teachers' personal and professional careers and this gives them much influence in the school community.

But the two sides are unified in the defence of education as a public service and they often join other trade unions to protest through strikes and demonstrations against 'reform' of the welfare state (Geay, 1997). In fact, historically, teachers' trade unions were strongly involved in the struggle for social rights in alliance with the working class. This tradition of conflict was maintained until the beginning of the 1980s, but then the CFDT adopted a reformist stance and renounced its utopia of working-class self-government. Even if they had abandoned their ideology of class struggle, teachers' trade unions were united up to the beginning of the 1990s in defence of Republican principles, although they were more and more focused on wages and purchasing power, the protection of status and the revaluation of careers. However, in 1992, a deep schism had a great impact on the trade union landscape. The Fédération de l'Education Nationale (FEN), which was internally governed by the Syndicat National des Instituteurs (SNI), representing primary teachers and close to the Socialist Party but also associated with pedagogy and secularism, was challenged by its leftist wing, the SNES, representing secondary teachers and close to the Communist Party and the ultra-Left. Of course, this schism had consequences for trade union unity in confronting policy making and their divisions discredited trade unionism among members and also provided opportunities for successive governments to implement their reforms. This disagreement led to the emergence of other movements of protest, short-lived and less coordinated and less recognized by the Ministry, through national and informal teaching committees during strikes, or through websites and blogs that criticized policy making. This diversification led also to a diminution of membership and focused trade union officials on developing services for members to support them in the management of their careers and compensate for the shortcomings of the State in this area.

In the last two decades, the relationship between trade unions and the Ministry of Education has broken down. One explanation is the Ministry's strategy to diminish the influence of trade unionists (and of the general inspectors) in policy making and increase the role of external advisors and consultants. The breakdown can also be explained as a consequence of the attitudes and decisions of several Ministers. Educators did not like to be compared to a 'mammoth' by Claude Allègre. They did not accept Luc Ferry's project of transferring guidance advisors and school nurses from the State to local authorities (the project was abandoned). They opposed the reduction of posts and the reform of high school planned by Xavier Darcos and the conflict has been enlarged to the issue of pupil empowerment. This expresses a sort of tradition of protest culture that has reached high school pupils and is today a component of the youth experience (Cortéséro and Derouet, 2010). These pupils, through associations close to the Left, often join student protests when they feel that their rights or the principle of equality of opportunity are threatened by reforms of the baccalaureate, or by increases in university fees or reductions in finance for schooling. These forms of street protest are less expressive of a political involvement alongside trade unions or political parties and are better understood as more spontaneous and playful demonstrations related to imaginaries of May 1968. They operate as rites of passage and of inclusion in the community of pupils, but some of these demonstrations are becoming sites of violence towards the police by organized groups from suburban areas who challenge the authority of the State and appropriate consumer goods that they cannot normally access.

Moreover, the absence of dialogue and the culture of protest did not enable a compromise between the Ministry and trade unions. Mistrust of the Ministry has increased among educators who consider they have been humiliated and victimized by a government and policy makers incapable of explaining the significance of reforms and driven by ideology. Indeed some teachers at primary school level created a movement of 'civil' disobedience after a teacher had refused to apply official instructions requiring him to develop personalized learning in his classroom. He replaced the personalized learning programme with a theatre lesson and had been reprimanded by the inspectors.

In 1998, the reform of the Instituts Universitaires de Formation des Maîtres (IUFMs) (academic institutes of teacher training) generated important criticism and protest among educators. These institutes, created by the Act of 1989, were considered as places for the transformation of professional practices among teachers to help them in facing the challenges of the democratization of the education system and in making use of education research findings (particularly in didactics) to reduce school failure. This training, a legacy of the professional culture of the primary education, which replaced the tradition of the Ecoles Normales d'Instituteurs, faced numerous criticisms because of its incapacity to change pedagogical practices in schools. However, these training places were strongly defended by educators because they remained autonomous from the universities and because they were linked to professionals and to a contextualized research, unlike the universities that focused on academic content and the training of the research profession. The reform, which aimed at incorporating the IUFMs in the universities, was severely criticized on the grounds that it diminished the importance of educational sciences in the training of new teachers, it reinforced the weight of disciplines, and above all it deleted the year of induction that allowed trainees to enter progressively into the profession. For budgetary reasons, and because of his mistrust of educators, the Minister Xavier Darcos introduced this change in such a way as to catch trade unions, school subject associations and pedagogical activists off their guard. This conception of training, which also led to dismissals of new teachers and gaps in recruitment in scientific disciplines, is likely to be revised after the publication of a very critical report from the Senate.

The Restructuring of a Profession: Towards the Performing School?

The restructuring of the education profession has begun but it is not yet visible to educators. Currently, there is a public debate about changes in teacher assessment. Until now, teachers were assessed through pedagogical and administrative grades. The pedagogical mark is awarded by the inspectorate and depends on the quality of teaching during an inspector's classroom visits (every five or seven years, or three or four times during a teacher's career). The administrative mark is awarded by the head teacher and it assesses teacher initiative, punctuality and assiduity. These marks are framed by a scale negotiated beforehand between the Ministry and trade unions. Inspectors and head teachers thus have no means to influence the advancement of teachers' careers, which depend on seniority. The government's aim is to individualize and personalize teacher assessment and to delegate more power to the head teacher. The Bill (January 2012, *proposition de loi no. 4151*) plans to implement a 'professional interview' between the teacher and the head teacher on an annual basis and an assessment supported by four criteria: capacity to support each pupil's progress, mastery of skills in the school subject, professional practices through collective action within the school (relationships with parents, involvement in the school project), and the quality of the teacher's work related to conditions of learning and sharing Republican values. On this basis the head teacher would decide what level of salary increase each teacher deserves. The Bill has produced vivid reactions among trade unions and school subject associations, who claim it is an attack on public services and the introduction of a managerial ideology.

This hostility towards managerialism is not only shared by trade unionists who oppose the implementation of an intermediary hierarchy in schools, the development of assessment and the introduction of performance. The majority of inspectors and head teachers conceive their roles as administrators, servants and representatives of the State, and not as managers. In their minds, management is a matter for the private sector and they often argue that schools cannot be compared to private companies. Because of their mistrust of business and the market, they feel uneasy with New Public Management and they criticize the Ministry's desire to develop a 'culture of performance'. The inspectorates, in particular, face serious challenges. The government aims to reinforce head teachers' local powers and to diminish the inspectors' influence in the regulation of primary and secondary schools. The shift from a hierarchical and centralized State structure to a regional and self-regulated one transforms the mission of the inspectorate. While it moves towards audit, it has to shift from control to support. But it is losing its monopoly in assessment. The Ministry is currently designing new indicators and new software to develop monitoring and benchmarking at school level. After the mess created by the implementation of poorly designed and biased national assessments at primary school level, the High Council of Education called for the creation of an agency separate from the Ministry. So, even if the inspectorate remains an independent entity, its power could be reduced in the future. For head teachers and teachers, this professional restructuring has already began in schools involved in new programmes for education priority areas named, respectively, 'CLAIR' and 'ÉCLAIR'. Although they are claimed as 'experiments' by the Ministry, they anticipate major changes in school organization and management. A function of 'leader' has been created: this position is officially described as 'prefect of studies' (a Napoleonic term for the person who secured discipline and studies in religious colleges!). Despite this anachronism, the function entails the recognition of new professional positions at the intersection of administration, classrooms and pastoral care (three separate and quasi-autonomous sectors in the current loosely coupled organization of French secondary schools). This reform was vividly denounced by the body of Conseillers Principaux d'Education (officers of pastoral care in secondary schools), who are mediators between the school administration and the teaching staff in charge of discipline, attendance and citizenship. These officers and their trade union considered this new function of leader as a threat to their status, missions and future as a profession. The trade union invited its members to occupy these posts in order to not leave them to external members outside the professional body. This criticism was relayed by a trade unionist discourse, particularly from the SNES, who denounced the risk of '*caporalisation*' (petty officiousness) created by the development of an 'intermediary hierarchy' and a 'managerial drift'. Head teachers also have autonomy in the recruitment of staff after their proposals have been accepted by their local authority. Then, they build teams according to their managerial objectives but they have to demonstrate progress in their schools' performance.

Conclusion

French educators feel abandoned by the State. Each day, they observe the effect of the reduction of public expenditure on their conditions of work (an increase in school size and workload, less support for deprived pupils and reduction of training schemes). This explains why François Hollande, the Socialist candidate for President, has just promised to create 60,000 teaching posts, while President Sarkozy announced that the State would replace only one civil servant in two after retirement. The Left will strategically defend education as a public service that has to be kept away from the market and privatization. But leaders of the Socialist Party already consider what type of 'Third Way' they will implement. The think tank Terra Nova, which expresses the proposals of the Socialist Party, produced a manifesto during the electoral campaign that emphasized the need to reform the teaching profession, to promote social inclusion and to develop networks and partnerships. François Dubet, the French sociologist well known for his ideas close to the modernist Left and defender of the modernization of the comprehensive school, wrote Terra Nova's report with other anonymous colleagues, perhaps some top civil servants. The Right promotes performance management, more autonomy for schools and the pursuit of previous policies. Its teacher training policy (ending the integration of teacher training colleges into university departments, and reduction of a year in the preparation of novice teachers) was received with hostility by the profession. But despite these ideological oppositions, the basic skills framework and the new accountability are not challenged. Furthermore, the PISA survey's conclusions are well accepted by political parties and trade unions who consider it is a good diagnosis of inequalities from which new policies could be designed and implemented. The government, but also its main opponent, the Socialist Party, are using the findings in a strategic way to claim for the need for such urgent reforms as the reduction of drop-outs or the implementation of a strategy in literacy. The idea that PISA data serve the European Open Method of Coordination and provide benchmarks that reinforce competition between Member States (with considerable impact on national policies) is not really visible in the French public debate on education. As the German writer Goethe argued in his *Maxims and Reflections* (1842), Frenchmen and mathematicians are alike: whatever you say to them, they translate it into their own language, and forthwith it is something entirely different.

References

Baudelot, C. and Establet, R. (2009) *L'Elitisme républicain: l'école française à l'épreuve des comparaisons internationales*, Paris: Seuil/République des idées.

Bezès, P. (2009) *Réinventer l'Etat: Les réformes de l'administration française (1962–2008)*, Paris: PUF.

Bezès, P., Demazière, D., Le Bianic, T., Paradeise, C., Normand, R., Benamouzig, D., Pierru, F. and Evetts, J. (2011) New Public Management et professions dans l'État: au-delà des oppositions, quelles recompositions?, *Sociologie du Travail*, 53(3): 293–348.

Blanchard, M. and Cayouette-Remblière, J. (coord.) (2011) Penser les choix scolaires, *Revue Française de Pédagogie*, 175: 5–88.

Bourdieu, P. (1996) *The State Nobility: Elite schools in the field of power*, Stanford, CA: Stanford University Press.

Careil, Y. (2002) *Ecole libérale, école inégale*, Paris: Syllepses.

Charlier, J.-E. and Croché, S. (2003) Le processus de Bologne, ses acteurs et leurs complices, *Education et Sociétés*, 12(2): 13–34.

Christensen, T. and Laegreid, L. (2007) *Transcending New Public Management: The transformation of public sector reforms*, Aldershot: Ashgate.

Cortéséro, R. and Derouet, J.-L. (2010) Institution et socialisation politique des jeunes, *Education et Sociétés*, 25: 5–6.

Derouet, J.-L. (1992) *Ecole et justice: De l'égalité des chances aux compromis locaux*, Paris: Métailié.

Derouet, J.-L. (coord.) (2001a) Les inégalités d'éducation: un classique revisité, *Education et Sociétés*, 5: 5–91.

Derouet, J.-L. (2001b) La sociologie des inégalités d'éducation à l'épreuve de la seconde explosion scolaire: déplacements des questionnements et relance de la critique, *Education et Sociétés*, 5: 9–24.

Derouet, J.-L. and Normand, R. (2011) The hesitation of French policy makers in identifying a Third Way in Education, *Journal of Educational Administration and History*, 43(2): 141–63.

Dubet, F. (2004) *L'école des chances: Qu'est-ce qu'une école juste?*, Paris: Seuil/République des idées.

Dubet, F., Duru-Bellat, M. and Vérétout, A. (2010) *Les sociétés et leur école: Emprise du diplôme et cohésion sociale*, Paris: Seuil.

Durkheim, E. (1934) *L'Education morale*, Paris: Alcan.

Duru-Bellat, M. (2006) *L'inflation scolaire: Les désillusions de la méritocratie*, Paris: Seuil/ République des idées.

Garnier, B. (coord.) (2007) Politiques et rhétoriques de 'l'école juste' avant la Cinquième République, *Revue Française de Pédagogie*, 159: 5–12.

Geay, B. (1997) *Le syndicalisme enseignant*, Paris: La Découverte.

Gewirtz, S. (2002) *The Managerial School: Post-welfarism and social justice in education*, Buckingham: Open University Press.

Goodson, I. and Hargreaves, A. (1996) *Teachers' Professional Lives*, Oxford: RoutledgeFalmer.

Greek, S. (2010) Governing by numbers: the PISA effect in Europe, *Journal of Education Policy*, 24(1): 23–37.

Kherroubi, M. and Rochex, J.-Y. (coord.) (2002) Les ZEP: vingt ans de politiques et de recherches, *Revue Française de Pédagogie*, 140: 5–7.

Laval, C. (2003) *L'école n'est pas une entreprise: Le néo-libéralisme à l'assaut de l'enseignement public*, Paris: La Découverte.

Lawn, M. and Novoa, A. (ed.) (2002) *Fabricating Europe: The formation of an education space*, London: Kluwer Academic.

Malet, R. (2008) *La formation des enseignants comparée: Identité, apprentissage et exercice professionnels en France et en Angleterre*, Berne: Peter Lang.

Malet, R. and Brisard, E. (2005) Travailler ensemble dans l'enseignement secondaire en France et en Angleterre, *Recherche et Formation*, 49: 17–33.

Meuret, D. (1994) L'efficacité de la politique des zones d'éducation prioritaires dans les collèges, *Revue Française de Pédagogie*, 109: 41–64.

Moisan, C. and Simon, J. (1997) *Les déterminants de la réussite scolaire en zone d'éducation prioritaire*, IGAEN & IGEN report, Paris: French Ministry of Education.

Mons, N. (2008) Evaluation des politiques éducatives et comparaisons internationales, *Revue Française de Pédagogie*, 164: 5–13.

Normand, R. (2009) The scarf unveiled: proximity to the test of law in a French school, in J.F. Schostak and J. Schostak (eds) *Researching Violence, Democracy and the Rights of People*, London: Routledge.

Obin, J.-P. and van Zanten, A. (2008) *La carte scolaire*, Paris: PUF.

Ozga, J. and Jones, R. (2006) Travelling and embedded policy: the case of knowledge transfer, *Journal of Education Policy*, 21(1): 1–17.

Prost, A. (2004) *Histoire générale de l'enseignement et de l'éducation en France*, Paris: Perrin.

Rayou, P. (2000) L'enfant au centre, un lieu commun pédagogiquement correct, in J.-L. Derouet (ed.) *L'école dans plusieurs mondes*, Paris-Bruxelles: INRP-De Boeck, pp. 245–74.

Robert, A. and Tyssens, J. (2007) Comparer deux grèves prolongées d'enseignants: Belgique francophone 1996, France 2003, *Education et Sociétés*, 20(2): 61–73.

Simon, B. (1991) *Education and the Social Order, 1940–1990*, New York: St Martin's Press.

Thélot, C. (2005) *Débattre pour réformer*, Paris: Dunod.

Thrupp, M. (2005) *School Improvement: An unofficial approach*, London: Continuum.

Thrupp, M. and Willmott, R. (2003) *Education Management in Managerialist Times: Beyond the textual apologists*, Buckingham: Open University Press.

van Zanten, A. (2001) *L'école de la périphérie: scolarité et ségrégation en banlieue*, Paris: PUF.

van Zanten, A. (2009) *Choisir son école: Stratégies familiales et médiations locales*, Paris: PUF.

12 Globalization and Educational Reform

What Choices for Teachers?

Malak Zaalouk

Introduction

There is nothing new about the practices of appropriation, economic supremacy and exploitation that are emerging as features of contemporary globalization. Sociological and political theory has been making sense of unequal global relations for centuries. The discourse of the *Dependestistas*, a largely Latin American development dating back to the 1960s and 1970s, offers significant insights into the historical origins of *peripheral* dependent social formations as they articulate with the more advanced industrialized social formations at the *centre*. They argue that this particular articulation between centre and periphery is not only economic in nature but fundamentally political. Peripheral economies manifest a particular pattern of 'extraverted' economic development, in which external exchanges undercut localized industry and perpetuate unequal distributions of wealth (Amin, 1974). Unequal exchange is entrenched through *liaison groups* that interlock the periphery and metropolitan societies. These unequal relations create hybrid classes at the periphery, with dual nationalities and corporate loyalties. They are the true engines of policy and drivers of new allegiances to world capitalism and multinational corporations (Petras, 1976).

This chapter examines these unequal relations through shifting understandings of teacher professionalism in Egypt in the era of globalization. The analysis proceeds from two premises: first, that Egypt, like other nation-states, is de-autonomizing as a sovereign entity and re-territorializing in the twenty-first century; and, second, that persistent economic inequalities rest on political relationships, which are secured and sustained in part through education and the work of teachers.

I examine how liaison groups enact processes of policy lending and borrowing in ways that shift understandings of teacher professionalism as Egypt engaged with educational reform. I draw on research and my professional experience to show how importing and exporting global models of education reform led to two models of teacher professionalization and boundary setting by educators and other multilateral actors. The Jomtien frame of action mobilized an empowerment approach that gave rise to 'facilitators' in community schools through the 1990s. The Dakar framework of action set out to borrow the approach for teacher professionalization but ended up embedding that borrowing in a context that reflected global neo-liberalism and the interests of a business oligarchy. It gave rise to the Professional Academy for Teachers (PAT), while teachers increasingly embraced a worker ideology and manifested all the traits of a controlled, fragmented and deskilled professional seeking to have a voice. Now, the Arab Spring frame of action and the challenge of political instability reopen possibilities of different value alignments between teachers and civil society actors nationally and globally.

De-Autonomization of National Boundaries and Neo-Liberal Education Reform

In the late twentieth century nation-states were losing their autonomy. Freer trade relations accompanied by free capital and labour movements, plus rapid technological proliferation, fuelled the globalization of capital and polarization between rich and poor (Appadurai, 1996; *IIEP Newsletter*, 1998; MacEwan, 2001; Maguire, 2002; Torres, 2009). The transformation of capitalism from a *Fordist* workplace orientation to preoccupations with consumption through internationalized trade also diminished the autonomy of nation-states, creating a gradual loss of sovereignty as transnational corporations gained global hegemony (Sahlberg, 2004). This diminishing of sovereignty was not uniform but depended on a nation's position in the world order (Burbules and Torres, 2000) and how various actors on the national stage managed and mediated tensions between global and national dynamics in an effort to borrow, receive, accommodate, reinterpret, appropriate, contextualize and, in sum, 'reterritorialize' the various policies accompanying the change (Torres, 2002; Sultana, 2011).

The hegemony of global capital manifests itself not just in economic terms but also in cultural, political and social terms. Neo-liberalism emerged around the world as a common dominant ideology, and accompanying discourse and mode of life, which pressed education towards greater integration in economic development and the creation of global citizens (Weber, 2007). The transnational reform agenda reoriented education systems towards competitive knowledge economies, while cutting government expenditure. Human capital, outcomes-based education (OBE) and standardizing educational reforms provided the specifications for employable and flexible labour. Increased efficiency for all stakeholders justified moves towards decentralization, privatization and new government regulatory roles (Maguire, 2002; Sahlberg, 2004; Weber, 2007; Spring, 2008; Yates and Young, 2010). Schools were more and more treated as private enterprises; education management simulated big business (Giroux, 2000) and were increasingly owned and run by large businesses (Burbules and Torres, 2000; Spring, 2008). The growth of large corporate educational enterprises blurred the boundaries between profits, learning and human development.

All these globalized shifts in educational ideologies, policies and practices meant teachers confronted contradictory demands. They were torn between neo-liberal exigencies, historical traditions of teaching and local identities. They were required to overperform towards the knowledge economy, while globally salaries were cut and status dwindled (Welmond, 2002). There was reduced scope for discretionary judgements in the interest of improved student learning and transformational education (de Guzman *et al.*, 2005). These cultural, political and social trajectories created different ways of seeing and managing teachers and understanding their professionalization.

Technicians versus Political Actors

On the one hand, neo-liberal ideology regards teachers as an input and not a creative partner in educational reform and national development (*IIEP Newsletter*, 1998). Teachers are positioned as compliant technicians, as workers or government civil servants, who comply with standards and the requirements of OBE. The tensions between professional autonomy and managerial control premised on private sector management styles mean teachers are subjected to tighter controls and surveillance systems, which erode their autonomy (Buchberger *et al.*, 2000; Weber, 2007). Practitioner training emphasizes implementation requirements rather than theoretical knowledge and teachers' ability to question the underlying assumptions and values of such requirements (Maguire, 2002). This positioning limits teachers' influence on policy and educational reforms (Macrow, 2008). It emanates from mistrust and brings home the reality that teachers are not treated as professionals but as instruments for the implementation of educational reform within a neo-liberal framework (Codd, 2005; Weber, 2007).

On the other hand, development educationalists, rather than globalized policy makers, have promoted global models of teacher professional development. They present teachers as actors in democratic educational reform. They value teachers' voice and design supportive structures to accompany teacher-centred reform processes (Darling-Hammond and McLaughlin, 1995). This rights-based approach to teacher professional development sees teachers having a social function in society. They produce knowledge necessary for the practice of their profession and attach meaning to that knowledge and they enjoy a certain level of autonomy when practising their profession. They are able to govern their profession through various mechanisms of 'collective autonomy', which steers away from state regulation and control. Finally, they uphold professional values (Jackson and Leroy, 1998; Hoyle, 1995; Villegas-Reimers and Reimers, 1996).

These different ideologies of teacher development are central to contemporary global policy debates. Neo-liberal views of teachers seem more powerful than rights-based empowerment approaches to teacher development. But it is also important to remember that globalization with a neo-liberal face emerged in a particular historical context.

Historicizing Globalization

> Educational transfer from one context to another not only occurs for different reasons, but also plays out differently.
>
> (Steiner-Khamsi, 2004: 202–3)

Globalization is not a permanent social state but a transitioning social movement. It becomes apparent as liaison groups form and re-form in ways that impact education and the ideologies governing teachers and their work. They take different forms and become prominent for different reasons across historical moments because differing models of global educational ideologies coexist and because educational ideologies that travel globally come to play in different territories. So while one educational ideology may dominate, it rarely survives as a pure form of educational thinking. Moreover, the manner in which global policies superimpose their principles over entities (e.g. a country, an organization or an occupational group, such as teachers) depends on the hosting culture, its political economy and the society at large.

Examining the way educational transfers vary across history and location shows that ideologies are transient. They are endorsed or marginalized as social actors coalesce around them, and align with national values-based networks, and with wider sub- and supra-national networks. What is borrowed and lent, and the conditions of that borrowing and lending, make a difference to educational policy and practice. For example, the work of Dewey (1900, 1916, 1934) among early critical thinkers, was taken up in revolutionary thought after the Second World War, hybridizing eastern and western critical educational thinking. It travelled from China to Latin America, influencing Freire, and spread among different groups as they resisted the homogenizing impact of global industrial capitalism.

Critical educational thinking found a home in civil society and some progressive international organizations. It anchored concerns with human rights, equity and environmental sustainability and informed efforts to influence curricula, schooling, learning and teaching (Spring, 2008).

It is against this backdrop of historical events and ideologies that the Education For All (EFA) movement in Jomtien came up with a framework of action that affirmed inclusion and equity through education (UNESCO, 1990). Much of the work and advocacy at that time focused on reaching the unreached and improving inputs to education to ensure good-quality education. During the 1990s the United Nations Children's Fund (UNICEF) sought to protect children's rights through models such as that of 'child friendly schools'. These forms of globalized movements have often been viewed as globalization from below, essentially impacting on civil society and the people.

A decade later the Dakar EFA conference placed greater emphasis on outcomes of learning with more space given to life skills and lifelong learning (UNESCO, 2000). Monitoring Learning Achievements (MLA) harmonized with standardization and testing via PISA, PIRLs and TIMSS in ways that locked in concepts of efficiency and governance, which were used to certify that schools were doing well (UNESCO, 2002–11; Mourshed *et al.*, 2010). Global institutions such as the World Bank (WB) and the Organization for Economic Cooperation and Development (OECD) became increasingly concerned with measuring the outcomes of learning and the external and internal efficiency of educational systems. This trend is viewed as globalization from above because it largely favoured and affected elites.

Yet, in practice, these processes of globalization from above and below are intertwined and interdependent. Agencies carry the flags of both; paradoxically, some countries view globalization from below as a western imposition, while others accept globalization from above as a nationalist movement (Burbules and Torres, 2000). The agenda that agencies and countries adopt depends on the way they take up different ideologies, their alignments through networks, and their effects in creating winners and losers in a given political economy

The various ideologies that mark out these different processes of globalization are combined to varying degrees by international agencies and for-profit organizations. The International Monetary Fund (IMF), WB, World Trade Organization (WTO) and the OECD are accused by critics of spreading educational policies in support of the neo-liberal paradigm (Zajda, 2011). Non-governmental organizations and United Nations agencies, notably UNESCO, UNICEF and UNDP, hold more ambiguous positions. They strive for human rights, social justice, equity, inclusion and sustainable development, while upholding policy directives such as efficiency, productivity and quality assurance. Their work is partially viewed as globalization from below since they uphold people's rights to an empowering education. Yet because ideas about rights-based education do not emerge from a clear national consciousness and will, some states see them as western globalization from above.

These agencies hold different views of teacher policies, as Table 12.1 shows. Some of their expectations reflect respect for teachers' professional autonomy; others emphasize productivity in terms of students' achievements and responsiveness to the world of work.

How globalization is received and articulated with existing national education systems depends on the way countries host global educational ideologies. The pattern of hosting is determined by the prevailing vision (or lack of), political culture and educational practices that existed prior to the hegemonic penetration

Table 12.1 International agencies' views of teacher policies

OECD	World Bank	UNESCO
Teachers to attend refresher courses for science and technical topics	Effective teachers	Technology and social change means the quality of teachers is more in demand
Lifelong learning necessary	Sustainability of teacher development	Teachers as a public resource
Teachers as collaborators	Teachers as a component of quality provision of educational goods/products	Teachers as custodians of education as a public good
Teacher reform to adapt education to society	Teacher development related to student achievement	Status of teachers to reflect the important role they play
Cost of teachers underscores reform	Teaching a complex professional activity	Teachers' development crucial in quality education
	Deploying a professional teaching force	Teachers responsive to the changing world of work

Source: Macrow (2008).

of neo-liberal ideology. Egypt shows three phases of global educational borrowing and lending that shifted the way particular teachers and their work were understood and organized. They were framed by the particular mix of globalization from above and below that characterized Jomtien, Dakar and the Arab Spring.

The Jomtien Framework: Creating Facilitators of Community Schools in Egypt

Through the 1970s and 1980s, Egypt manifested all the signs of an economy going global. It produced its globalized class, while multinationals found their liaison groups. Together they were able to reshape Egypt's political economy (Zaalouk, 1989). In the new globalized configuration of Egypt's political economy, UNESCO statistics indicate increases in economic investments in education from 4.8 per cent of GDP in 1985–94, to 5.6 per cent in 1995–2003 (World Bank, 2005). Unlike other underdeveloped countries where cuts in education were the norm, enrolment rates grew through the 1990s as schools continued to expand. Despite the relatively large investments, the returns on education were deemed to be poor and the quality of education left very much to be desired (Birdsall and O'Connell, 1999).

The 1990s are of particular significance in the educational landscape of Egypt. That decade marks the largest investment of international aid and the concept of state-led educational reform for security (Sayed, 2006). It also witnessed a fierce two-pronged debate at both policy and implementation levels. On one level the debate focused on globalization and privatization versus a rights and equity agenda; on another level the debate centred on globalization versus national identity.

National identity was contentious because of raging debates about the role of Islam in national identity and the need for increased Islamic references in education (Cook, 2000). This was of course a time of rising militant fundamentalist activity and power in Egypt. The state strategy for education and security was intended to undermine the growing strength of Islamic militants and stress the need for secular education. The prominent Minister Bahaa El Din on several occasions presented literacy maps of Egypt to drive the point home that militants were strongest in the rural pockets of Upper Egypt where female illiteracy was the highest.

Yet some intellectuals continued to be of the opinion that more rather than less religious education was needed in the curricula and educational system. A growing number of Islamic foundations and other religious organizations created Islamic private schools, which constituted about 7 per cent of total private education in 1999. They took three main forms: fundamentalist, foreign language Islamic schools, and commercial schools (Sayed, 2006). Media, information technology, universities and faculties of education and other educational institutions were gradually becoming ideologically affiliated to this trend of thinking (Starrett, 1998).

A parallel secular discourse on education was as vocal as the religious discourse. It appeared as the genesis of a globalization treatise with all the familiar ingredients: the need for higher levels of productivity, competitiveness on the global market, employability and the generation of human capital. Former President Mubarak confirmed this National Project for Education:

> in considering its national policies, Egypt has identified human resource development as a priority. Linking education and development has implied that education is a significant medium for preparing an adult labour force that is literate and skilled ... the 'global village', with its single competitive market, implies that citizens in a particular country will need the necessary skills that would enable them to compete with citizens of other countries.
>
> (Cook, 2000: 482)

These debates were a sign of coexisting globalization from above and below. What seemed to determine the blend was a combination of the terms and conditions globally and locally, which shaped narratives of educational reform, and the pattern of national educational leadership, in which particular international agencies predominated in the prevailing architecture of aid.

The Jomtien Imperative: The Global and Local Context

The EFA movement during the Jomtien era addressed the concern among developing nations for a quantitative jump to universal primary education (UPE). Several countries (155 at the time) had pledged to this agenda and Egypt was no exception. The main concern and priority for government was ensuring every child had a place in school. Although other neo-liberal discourses were in the making, in Egypt the equity and democratic discourse was still quite prevalent. According to government documents prior to the Egyptian strategic plan of 2007, one of the major policy principles in Egypt was 'identifying an enlightened educational policy within a democratic framework' (Cochrane, 2008: 99).

The interpretation of EFA among the five partner agencies, UNESCO, UNICEF, UNDP, UNFPA and the WB, were not always totally harmonious (Sayed, 2006; Torres, 2009). Being personally engaged with UNICEF at the time, it is clear that it represented a rights-based lens in education and, under the leadership of Carol Belamy, then Executive Director of UNICEF, worked to harmonize between the principles of EFA, rights and equity. The concept of 'child-friendly schools' was developed during agency-wide retreats, which emphasized affinities between the global rights movement and EFA (Black, 1999).

UNICEF in Egypt introduced the notion of reaching the hard-to-reach students through a 'community school' model in 1992. The idea resonated with the Ministry of Education as it recognized that the last quintile was usually the hardest to reach and required innovative strategies. Deprived rural areas, particularly in the south, had not been adequately serviced and had large numbers of out-of-school children in hamlets where the population was sparsely distributed. Girls were hardest hit for a number of economic and cultural reasons.

An agreement between government, communities and UNICEF led to a pilot phase, establishing community-owned schools in some of the poorest rural areas: Assiut, Sohag and Qena. While the government of Egypt was largely interested in access, UNICEF held child rights at heart. A relevant and progressive pedagogy in those schools was developed to reverse growing gender disparities and inequalities, and also to provide a liberating and empowering learning experience. This pedagogy was supported by local communities through a truly successful experience of autonomous governance. The learning was powerful and the outcomes were rewarding at personal, community and national levels. This school movement continued to spread and gain in popularity until the early part of the twenty-first century (Zaalouk, 2004).

The major players in this initiative included many international donors but, in the early 1990s, UNICEF had a privileged position vis-à-vis government. UNESCO's focus was largely on science. The education programme specialist only arrived in the later 1990s. There was a power struggle between the government of Egypt, represented by the Minister of Education and the Minister of Higher Education, and the United States Agency for International Development (USAID) and the WB. In this debacle, USAID lost some of its credibility after an earthquake destroyed schools that had been constructed by American aid money. The control of staffing and funding in a large teacher training initiative was also contentious between both ministries and the WB and USAID, which led to the project being terminated and interrupted relations between USAID, the WB and the Egyptian government. Then Minister of Education, Bahaa El Din, was not sympathetic to WB loans and resisted foreign intervention in educational policy. It was no secret that he was a bastion of resistance against globalized educational policies during the early half of the 1990s. The comeback of the WB and USAID followed the intervention of the President and other members of the ruling elite. It was the prelude to the absolute hegemony of neo-liberal economic structures and ideologies; however, the consensus was that there was very little to show for their investments (Birdsall and O'Connell, 1999; Cochrane, 2008).

This context offered perfect timing for the introduction of community schools model and its empowerment pedagogy. A historical configuration of many factors allowed this empowerment framework to be tested in some of the most underprivileged rural areas in Egypt. The establishment of this initiative with all its liberation and empowering concepts was certainly no easy matter. It required dedicated and consistent effort, over 13 years or more, working in a partnership between leading policy makers on the Egyptian side and leaders of multilateral organizations, such as UNICEF. The latter was firmly supported by the Canadian International Development Agency, at a time when Canada was ruled by a regime that was more sympathetic to anti-globalization movements.

Despite the difficulties and constraints, a miraculous alliance had occurred between leadership at UNICEF, communities and civil society, and well-positioned policy makers. The initiative was mainstreamed and included in the country's strategic plan, its main educational structures and national agenda. By 2005, 100,000 marginalized children had been reached in rural areas. But it declined in 2005–6, when shifting circumstances and a changing contextual landscape shook some of its foundations and important achievements (Zaalouk, 2005; Sultana, 2008).

Developing Facilitators as Autonomous Educators

Another important achievement of the community school initiative in Egypt, noted in numerous evaluations, was the highly empowered position of the facilitators and educators. Most teachers and educators in the programme were recruited from the most underemployed segment of the Egyptian population, female graduates of intermediary education (Cochrane, 2008). These professionals were not conventional graduates from faculties of education. They were called facilitators to underline the fact that they adopted liberation pedagogy as active learning, which allowed learners to take charge of their own learning while they facilitated the process.

As respected professionals the facilitators were offered several opportunities for growth. Some travelled to visit experiments in international contexts; the majority were offered professional development informed by the latest theories of what works best in teacher development (Hargreaves, 2000; Stronach *et al.*, 2002; Romer, 2008; Craig, 2006; Purinton, 2011). The participants practised peer support and formed their own 'community of practice', meeting daily within the teaching schedule to mutually evaluate their performance and work. Each class had two facilitators, allowing them to plan and coordinate team teaching, with a feedback and evaluation session at the end of each day. When a new teacher was recruited she would have a planned induction programme, with an older teacher mentoring her in the early days of her work. Each week, clusters of school teachers met to collectively prepare lesson plans, after discussing what worked in classrooms for the different students and presenting some of the innovations they had managed to create.

The community schools were in close partnership with faculties of education, so facilitators benefited from, and were trained in, research. They practised research with their students and other members of their communities as they tried to make sense of the context within which they taught and facilitated learning. These autonomous practitioners were generating knowledge. Mentoring was provided by support staff who supervised the schools and also from faculty in the university. Faculty also trained the facilitators each year. They benefited from comprehensive modules and training packages in active learning, human rights, classroom management, authentic assessment and portfolios, arts and creative thinking, scientific methods and research, and gender and equity, in addition to subject matter training. All this was done in collaboration with faculties of education.

Facilitators enjoyed a great deal of autonomy in the way they conducted their classes. Being physically removed from the mainstream central Ministry, autonomy was easily managed and UNICEF served as a protective mediator. They managed to reconstruct government curricula in active ways and in a style that made sense to their learners. Unlike their government counterparts, they reworked curricula and textbooks based on their classroom experience; the reinvented parts were often handwritten. Facilitators were also autonomous in the way they were evaluated. They learned to establish criteria for their own evaluation and supporting staff provided counselling, advice and technical support based on mutually agreed frameworks. At the end of each visit both supervisor/mentor and facilitator came up with an assessment sheet followed by a self-improvement plan signed off by both partners in the learning journey. Each year refresher courses were offered. The urge to learn was firmly grounded and many of the facilitators pursued their studies and went on to obtain higher education and graduate degrees. Some are even enrolled in the Open University at a distance.

The facilitators' pride in their work was reflected in their eagerness to receive visits and write up their experiences in newsletters and school magazines. Some received annual recognition and prizes for outstanding performance. A more important incentive was being invited as experts by the Centre for Curriculum and Instructional Materials Development (CCIMD) at the Ministry of Education to write up guides and textbooks on active learning and multi-grade education. Their names appeared on the guides as co-authors and they became the trainers, spreading this model of learning, which was then in demand in mainstream government schools, as well as the Girls' Education Initiative and its girl-friendly schools.

The facilitators developed a voice and were consulted on policy issues with regard to the community school initiative and the design of learning and training packages. In a country where syndicates and teacher unions were very weak, strikes were unheard of. Facilitators of the community schools were the first to go on strike in the mid to late nineties when they had not received their salaries for an entire nine months. Their professional ethics were, however, so elevated that, even when on strike and not going to schools, they insisted on receiving children in their homes so they would not be deprived of learning. The gesture of absenting themselves from school was simply to protest the violation of their right to payment, even though it was very meagre. They won the battle and their salaries were regularized for many years.

Their professional ethics went beyond their style of striking and ensured that students truly learned and achieved to the highest level of education. Private tutoring was not in their dictionary despite their very meagre salaries. Moreover, they followed their alumni closely and supported them as they moved on in their learning voyage. The incentives they sought were not purely materialistic but professional in nature. They were interested in learning and in being recognized for their work in a multiplicity of ways. They shone in technical meetings and demonstrated confidence wherever they were invited to participate. They met with Ministry officials of the highest levels and a Minister, who actually made the effort to visit them in their classrooms. International experts and educators often visited them from other systems wishing to learn from them (Zaalouk, 2004).

This model of an empowered facilitator contrasts emphatically with the model of a de-autonomized teacher managed as a worker that accompanied deeper liberalization of the world's economies. The educators in the community schools fulfilled the rights-based democratic model of professional development. They were of social significance and value. They generated knowledge. They practised autonomously and manifested a high degree of professional ethics. Their schools were not public government schools but community owned; the educators were recognized and certified within the mainstream system. This model of a teacher emerged out of a globalization movement; it was largely from below with some elements from above in the form of international funds and technical guidance.

The strength of the model dwindled as classical neo-liberal ideologies became more deeply entrenched in both the Egyptian political economy and international organizations; the community school initiative became less protected. It was replaced by other priorities, more in line with the globalization from above paradigm endorsed through the Dakar EFA.

The Dakar Framework: Forming the Professional Academy for Teachers in Egypt

A new local and global configuration emerged with the Dakar EFA framework of action. It shifted away from concerns about processes of learning and, instead, stressed measurable outcomes, mostly based on global achievement testing. The Millennium Development Goals (MDGs) also emphasized the quality of services. Quality assurance and standardization became prominent, and public–private partnerships were encouraged in all global documents discussing educational reform. Three types of reforms followed: competition-based reforms, reforms based on financial imperatives, and equity-based reforms, but competition predominated globally and in Egypt (Torres, 2009; Badrawi, 2011).

The discourse on education in Egypt in the twenty-first century became more and more aligned with the neo-liberal agenda as Egypt changed into a typical globalized economy and polity. Ibrahim Issa (2010) cogently described the situation when explaining that the heir to the Egyptian throne was to be Gamal Mubarak, a businessman with a business clique that ruled the country as a private company or a department within a multinational:

> The new elite of the twenty first century have adopted capitalism from the west with all its mechanisms and structures; however they continue to adopt the tyranny and dictatorship of the east. It is a mix of a savage unrestrained police state and a capitalism that has ensured the dazzlingly rapid enrichment of the elite, and the stability of the regime. With free trade, the regime's main objective has been to join the transnational global club of corporations and has actually treated the whole country as one large commercial representative to those large companies.

With this new era an unmatched level of disparity prevailed (Denis, 2006). The gap between the 'haves' and 'have nots' was reinforced by the educational system. Government schools continued to serve the majority of the Egyptian population but rapidly declined in quality as the system went dual, and shamelessly private. Private tutoring was the third largest expenditure in family budgets, following rent and food (Cochrane, 2008). Private and for-profit international schools mushroomed; they were lavish schools that offered students international certification and a visa to employment abroad or in multinationals operating in Egypt. Private universities joined the crowd and now exceed the number of public universities.

This dual system of schooling constructs the cultural capital assets of the new class: the westernized globalized elite that is getting ready to lead the new Egypt. The lingua franca of this new class is predominantly English. Society at large now believes that without English you are illiterate. Market schooling and the old foreign language schools of the post-colonial era under state control and supervision are accessible to the remainders of the middle class, while the new brand of international schools charge large fees. They employ international educators and 'local' educators but with salary differentials that benefit the internationals (Aziz, 2011). They also have their own curriculum (Hazem, 2011).

Like the rest of the world, measurement and standard-setting became a major objective and obsession in the early years of the twenty-first century. Egyptian educational standards were produced by 2003 by downloading existing global standards and discussing them locally. They were largely developed by teams from faculties of education, with insufficient public consultation, and encompassed five domains: effective schools, teacher performance, outcomes of learning and curricula, educational management and governance, and community participation. They did not fit the local culture of standards and were not internalized by educators at the school level, even though in many schools they were stuck on the wall of the school principal's office.

The standards endorsed by the system were technical in style and did not deal with the more humane and soft aspects of rights-based teaching and learning. Their underlying values were in line with the accountabilities proclaimed by the internationalized culture of quality assurance. To complete the cycle of measurement and assessment, the National Authority for Quality Assurance and Accreditation of Education was created in 2007, paralleling the globalized model. This agency reported to the Prime Minister and accredited and ranked educational institutions, confirming the internationalized language of the new global order (Farag, 2010).

In 2007, the government also endorsed a strategic plan for education, following initial work around 2002 and several interruptions due to ministerial changes. The plan was valid from 2007 to 2012. Decentralization, private–public partnerships, and technology development and information systems were important pillars, and some older concerns with equity and access still featured. However, when the plan's achievements were assessed a year later, the Ministry had a lot to show across domains, but community education had the weakest record of achievement (Ministry of Education, 2007, 2008). Attention was clearly shifting from community education, which touched the issue of equity in the most direct way.

The earlier priority targeting the hard-to-reach was declining. It coincided with a relative withdrawal of UNICEF while other donor agencies, notably USAID and the WB, gained stronger voices at the policy table. The challenges of access and equity remain unresolved, while the gap between served and underserved is expanding. In a meeting at the Ministry of Education in March 2011, it was reported that there was an urgent need for 232,525 classes at an estimated cost of 52 billion pounds. Moreover, about 16 per cent of villages, let alone hamlets, had no schools.

The Professional Academy for Teachers

These changes in schooling also had implications for teachers. Teachers' status in Egypt, as in many parts of the world, had been on the decline for quite some time. They were the pride and backbone of Arab education during the Nasser era, but subsequently their conditions of work and socioeconomic status fell. There was an exodus of teachers during the 1980s to the neighbouring Arab countries in the wake of the Open Door economic policy. It was less a sign of Arab pride and solidarity than an indication of extremely poor teacher salaries. Teachers travelling to Arab countries could gain a tenfold increase in pay and other venues opened to teachers. Private tutoring was a grave leakage point for the educational system and also household budgets, particularly for the poor on yearly incomes of US$150 (Cochrane, 2008).

Teachers were struggling with poor salaries and a loss of trust and respect, and also were not receiving the professional development support rightfully due to them (Mina, 1981). There is poor preparation of teachers in the Arab world generally and Egypt is certainly no exception. There is no comprehensive vision for teacher preparation, so teachers suffer from poor professional development. Curricula in universities are not well conceptualized, integrated or relevant to the needs of practice. Innovation, reflection, critical thinking and problem solving do not constitute significant components of the curricula. There is little attention to creating a culture of professionalization, research, integrated subject matter, construction of knowledge and meaning or the general knowledge one would find in a liberal arts programme. As a result of poor teacher preparation over time, practical learning and practicum school-based programmes are very weak. Relationships between faculties of education and schools are also rather weak and educational research is not well developed. On the job continuous professional development opportunities are sparse and quite rare. The quality also leaves much to be desired, with limited follow-up and weak monitoring to measure the impact of training on performance. Conditions of work are not much better than during the teacher preparation phase. Teachers are burdened with complex administrative tasks and, often, their only avenue to promotion and advancement is through administrative posts. Schools are not welcoming work environments and classes are extremely overcrowded (Zaalouk, 2011a).

An Academy for Teachers: From Empowerment to Testing

Against these rather dismal conditions, in 2003 the Ministry of Education endorsed a Professional Academy for Teachers (PAT). The Ministry had tasked some educators, including the author, to find a solution for teachers. Following analyses of international systems, with particular focus on the Canadian experience and local Egyptian conditions, the PAT was designed as an empowerment model. The design aimed to create a structure that would be owned by teachers, support the professionalization of teaching, elevate the job to the respectful position it deserved, give teachers a voice in public debate and transform them from workers and/or civil servants into full-fledged professionals, with matching incomes and possibilities for developing through varying career paths.

The model of empowered educators developed through community schools informed the original design, hence an empowering structure was added to anchor the required transformation. The Academy was to be distinguished from a union or syndicate because teachers were not to be perceived as workers. They would rule themselves through a board and have a legal status, which would allow them to protect teachers and create adjudication support systems in the case of litigation. Knowledge, research, exposure, publications, peer support and professional development were the hallmark of the model. The Academy was to administer and assess teacher promotions in accordance with criteria and standards. Evaluation would be largely peer based with additional self-assessment, such as teacher portfolios. In 2005, a series of ministerial changes, plus this author's travel to Amman, suspended work on the PAT for a while.

The PAT was formally established in 2008, with presidential decree number 129, under the supervision of the Minister of Education. The Law of Education no. 155 (2007) amended the prior Law no. 139 (1981). It established the Academy and endorsed the new cadre for teachers, now ranked in five levels: assistant beginning teachers; teachers; senior teachers; high performing senior teachers; and expert teachers. Each level had specific criteria that qualified teachers to move to the next level – a promotion that was accompanied by a 150 per cent salary increase. Where teachers had received a salary of US$25–40 per month (one of the lowest salaries in the Arab region), they could now receive a salary ranging from US$100–200 per month, if they were assessed and licensed by the PAT.

Between 2005 and 2008, USAID became involved in guiding and building the capacity of the Academy. A huge number of tools and manuals were developed to describe levels, performance and professional development packages. The 're-territorialization' of the packages resulted in an obsessive focus on testing teachers. The empowerment framework flew out of the window, replaced by a frenzy to control and test teachers before they could obtain an increase in livelihood. The PAT was installed within a despotic cultural environment (Issa, 2010). Others likened it to the authoritarian, centralized and regimented culture of the army (Cochrane, 2008).

The main function of the Academy was now to accredit training programmes and structures, license teachers, and facilitate their promotion. By the end of 2010 more than a million teachers from Ministry of Education schools, and 200,000 from Al Azhar-run religious schools, were tested, but none received professional development of any consequence. Online orientation sessions did not meet teachers' expectations of promised diversity in service providers or resources, which would enable teachers to grow and learn.

Teachers were angry and insulted. During 2010 and 2011 they either threatened, or actually went on, a countrywide strike and all hell broke out in the media. They demanded the cadre law be abolished and attempted to oust the Minister, Ahmed Gamal El Din Moussa, who, in his own way, had strongly defended teachers' rights. He wanted to maintain teacher dignity but could not abolish the tests for experienced teachers. A group of teachers calling themselves

'Teachers without a Syndicate' uncompromisingly demanded the abolition of the test and a 200 per cent salary raise. They threatened to stage an all-out teachers' strike across the entire country and demanded the Prime Minister remove the Education Minister (Sadek, 2011).

General confusion prevailed. The objectives of the PAT had not been well explained publicly, so teachers only saw humiliation and control in the new arrangement. The Minister of Education was eventually removed. The new Minister, appointed in December 2011, came from the ranks of teachers – an internal appointment from the Ministry of Education who was promoted through various leadership positions. Subsequently, the Ministry announced amendments to the cadre law of 2007, following consultation with teachers, which were sent to the Ministries of Finance and Social Insurance for action. The amendments required a 300 per cent increase in wages to allow teachers to perform professionally and ethically, thus abstaining from private tutoring. The Ministry justified these steps as a way of saving educational costs, at both systemic and household levels (Adel, 2012).

The Arab Spring: Networking Professional Academies Globally

The date of 25 January 2012 was one year on from the recent revolution in Egypt, whose slogans called for equity, social justice, dignity, freedom and democracy. Egyptians in all walks of life were engaged in protest, including teachers, some of whom lost their lives (Zaalouk, 2011b). The political affiliations and ideologies of the revolutionaries were diverse; voices of liberal democracy were heard alongside the voices of leftist social justice activists and Islamic fundamentalists. The Egyptian revolution, like many of the Arab Spring movements, concentrated globalized movements from both above and below. There was protest against neo-liberal ideologies of capitalist exploitation and the absence of social justice, as well as calls for a constitutional democracy based on the western model. Meanwhile, Islamic ideology and its political constituencies are clearly the winners so far. They won a majority in parliamentary elections and were the dominant force in most syndicate elections, including the teachers' syndicate.

In recent years a regional initiative on teachers' professional development in the Arab states was launched under the auspices of the League of Arab States. The movement worked through an extensive network and partnership of global and regional experts and organizations, which was catalysed and led by the UNICEF regional office in Amman and the author of this chapter. Now in its fifth year, this network continues to thrive as more partners, such as universities, join in. This initiative produced a progressive framework to guide teachers' enhancement and professional development, which was endorsed by all Ministries of Education in the region. Using a rights-based empowerment approach, the framework elaborated policies, strategies and programmes to allow teachers to become autonomous professionals, creators of knowledge and agents of change (League of Arab States, 2010). To further support the movement for teacher empowerment and allow them the space they need to become socially engaged and politically active, the initiative is developing mechanisms to build the capacity and support two academies as centres of excellence for the region: the Professional Academy for Teachers (PAT) in Egypt, discussed above, and the Queen Rania Academy for Teachers (QRTA) in Jordan.

These two academies are to serve as regional hubs for empowering teachers and their organizations to have a voice in policy making and to become creators of knowledge. They are intended to support teacher development in ways that reverse teachers' marginalized and disempowered position and social status. The mission of the QRTA is to promote 'excellence in teacher education and policy deliberation in Jordan and throughout the region' (QRTA, 2012). It was launched in June 2009 under the patronage of Her Majesty Queen Rania Al Abdullah. It aims to improve education in Jordan and across the Middle East. It operates under the auspices of the Jordan Education Society, in partnership with Columbia University's Teachers College (TC) and the Columbia University Middle East Research Center (CUMERC) in Amman. The regional mission of the PAT is to bridge the work of faculties of education and schools through research and reflective practice.

Teacher Professionalism Moving On?

These regional initiatives indicate a growing recognition across different agencies that educational policy can no longer continue to be made by either politicians or laypersons. Rather, educational policies need to be made by reflective and practising educators and the two academies discussed above are intended to produce more autonomous teachers and leaders of social transformation. In this, they build on the model provided by the facilitators of community schools, which earlier demonstrated the way teachers contribute to citizen empowerment and local democracy.

Adel, an enlightened and eloquent teacher, was one of many teachers who actively participated in an early event as the PAT took up its role as regional hub in November 2011. He very emphatically called for more opportunities for teachers to influence reform and educational policies. He was critical of professionalizing teaching, regarding this as a western concept. But he believed that teachers were both professionals and on mission. In perfect harmony with both Islamic traditional thinking and ancient Greek philosophy, he believed teachers should hold prophet-like status in their role as reformers, who are the holders of a prophecy and are called upon to reform society at large.

Many teachers hold Adel's views. One of Adel's choices, like many other Egyptian teachers, was to spend time teaching in one of the Gulf countries, where he learned a great deal and advanced professionally. Another choice, which Adel did not go for, was to stay in Egypt and develop into a small business teacher doing private tutoring. Today, Adel and others have a third choice; it is to become engaged teachers and intellectuals helping to shape the new generation and supporting the nascent Egyptian revolution in its struggle for freedom and liberation. This is the work that goes on in schools, Tahrir Square, Parliament and policy-making institutions, and it is possible because of a model of teacher professional development that respects global frameworks for empowerment, as well as indigenous frameworks related to the historical social functions of teachers.

Whether Islamic, liberal or leftist governments emerge out of the 25 January revolution, teachers have a critical role to play as professionals with responsibilities in socialization and education. The opportunity must not be lost. Teachers will need a political and economic base from which to act. Policies are beginning to be favourable to their lot. It is time their organizations also gained in strength. Syndicates are not the only way to organize. Professional academies are also important sources of power as creators of knowledge and collective autonomy.

References

Adel, S. (2012) Teacher cadre before the Ministries of Finance and Social Insurance, *Al Masry Al Youm*, 2765: 3.

Amin, S. (1974) *Accumulation on a World Scale: A critique of underdevelopment*, New York: Monthly Review Press.

Appadurai, A. (1996) *Modernity at Large: Cultural dimensions of globalization*, Minneapolis, MN: University of Minnesota Press.

Aziz, A. (2011) *School Data Survey: The story of AASC*, paper presented to the Graduate School of Education, American University in Cairo, Fall.

Badrawi, H. (2011) *Education: The opportunity to be saved*, Cairo: Al Dar Al Masreya Al Libnanya.

Birdsall, N. and O'Connell, L. (1999) Putting education to work in Egypt, *Carnegie Paper*, 5: 1–4.

Black, M. (1999) *Basic Education: A vision for the 21st century*, Summary Report, Florence: UNICEF International Child Development Centre.

Buchberger, F., Campos, B.P., Kallos, D. and Stephenson, J. (eds) (2000) *Green Paper on Teacher Education in Europe: High quality teacher education for high quality education and training*, Umea: TNTEE.

Burbules, N. and Torres, C. (2000) Globalization and education: an introduction, in N. Burbules and C. Thomas (eds) *Globalization and Education: Critical perspectives*, New York: Routledge, pp. 1–12.

Cochrane, J. (2008) *Educational Books of Political Crises in Egypt*, Lanham, MD: Lexington Books.

Codd, J. (2005) Teachers as 'managed' professionals in the global educational industry: the New Zealand experience, *Educational Review*, 57(2): 193–205.

Cook, B.J. (2000) Egypt's national education debate, *Comparative Education*, 36(4): 477–90. Available at http://dx.doi.org/10.1080/713656657 (accessed 2 November 2011).

Craig, J. (ed.) (2006) *Production Values: Futures for professionalism*, London: Demos.

Darling-Hammond, I. and Mclaughlin, M.W. (1995) Policies that support professional development in an era of reform, *Phi Delta Kappan*, 76(8): 597–604.

de Guzman, A.B., dela Rosa, P.S.M. and Arcangel, C.N. (2005) The impact of globalization on teacher education: the Philippine perspective, *Educational Research for Policy and Practice*, 4(2–3): 65–82.

Denis, E. (2006) Cairo as neo-liberal capital? From walled city to gated communities, in D. Singerman and P. Amar (eds) *Cairo Cosmopolitan: Politics, culture and space in the New Middle East*, Cairo: The American University in Cairo Press.

Dewey, J. (1900) *The School and Society*, Chicago, IL: Chicago University Press.

Dewey, J. (1916) *Democracy and Education*, New York: Free Press.

Dewey, J. (1934) *Art as Experience*, New York: Perigee Books.

Farag, I. (2010) The politics of educational reform in Egypt, in A. Mazauhi and R. Sultana (eds) *The World Yearbook of Education 2010*, London: Routledge, pp. 285–99.

Giroux, H.A. (2000) *Stealing Innocence: Corporate culture's war on children*, New York: Palgrave.

Hargreaves, A. (2000) Four ages of professional learning, *Teachers and Teaching: History and Practice*, 6(2).

Hazem, D. (2011) *International Schools and the Egyptian Identity: How do international schools preserve the Egyptian identity?*, paper presented to the Graduate School of Education, American University in Cairo, Fall.

Hoyle, E. (1995) Teachers as professionals, in L. Anderson (ed.) *International Encyclopedia of Teaching and Teacher Education*, 2nd edn, London: Pergamon Press.

IIEP Newsletter (1998) Changing teachers for a changing world, *IIEP Newsletter*, 16(2): 3–5. Available at http://unesdoc.unesco.org/images/0019/001928/192822e.pdf (accessed 2 November 2011).

Issa, I. (2010) *The History of the Future, 31–32*, Cairo: Madbouli.

Jackson, R.K. and Leroy, C.A. (1998) Eminent teachers' views on teacher education and development, *Action in Teacher Education*, 20(3): 15–29.

League of Arab States (2010) *Guiding Framework of Performance Standards for Arab Teachers: Policies and programs*, Cairo: League of Arab States and UNICEF.

MacEwan, A. (2001) What is globalization?, *The Radical Teacher*, 61: 2–7.

Macrow, A.V. (2008) Creating (in)capacity: teachers in globalized education policies, *Bulgarian Journal of Science and Education Policy (BJSEP)*, 2(2): 171–85.

Maguire, M. (2002) Globalization, education policy and the teacher, *International Studies in Sociology of Education*, 12(3): 261–76.

Mina, F.M. (1981) Teacher training in Egypt, *Reveu ATEE Journal*, 4: 69–75.

Ministry of Education, Arab Republic of Egypt (2007) *National Strategic Plan for Pre-university Education Reform in Egypt: Towards an educational paradigm shift 2007/08–2011/12*, Cairo: Ministry of Education.

Ministry of Education, Arab Republic of Egypt (2008) *The Strategic Plan for Pre-university Reform in Egypt 2007–2012*, power point presentation, Cairo: Ministry of Education.

Mourshed, M., Chinezi, C. and Barber, M. (2010) *How the World's Most Improved Systems Keep Getting Better*, London: McKinsey.

Petras, J. (1976) 'Class and politics in the periphery and the transition to socialism, *Review of Radical Political Economics*, 8(2): 21–5.

Purinton, T. (2011) *Six Degrees of School Improvement: Empowering a new profession of teaching*, Charlotte, NC: Information Age Publishing.

Queen Rania Teacher Academy (QRTA) (2012) *About Us: Mission*. Available at www.qrta.edu.jo/node/24 (accessed 14 November 2011).

Romer, T.A. (2008) Learning process and professional content in the theory of Donald Schön, *Reflective Practice*, 4(1): 85–93.

Sadek, A. (2011) Teacher-Minister stand-off, *The Egyptian Gazette*, Cairo, August: 12.

Sahlberg, P. (2004) Teaching and globalization, *Managing Global Transitions*, Spring, 2(1): 65–83.

Sayed, F.H. (2006) *Transforming Education in Egypt: Western influence and domestic policy reform*, Cairo: The American University in Cairo Press.

Spring, J. (2008) Research on globalization and education, *Review of Educational Research*, 78: 330–52.

Starrett, G. (1998) *Putting Islam to Work: Education, politics, and religious transforma-tion in Egypt*, Comparative studies on Muslim Societies, Berkeley, CA: University of California Press.

Sterner-Khamsi, G. (2004) Blazing a trail for policy theory and practice, in G.S. Khamsi (ed.) *The Global Politics of Educational Borrowing and Lending*, New York: Teachers College Press.

Stronach, I., Corbin, B., McNamara, O., Stark, S. and Warne, T. (2002) Towards an uncertain politics of professionalism: teachers and nurse identities in flux, *Journal of Education Policy*, 17(1): 109–38.

Sultana, R. (2008) *The Girls Education Initiative in Egypt*, Amman: UNICEF.

Sultana, R. (2011) On being a boundary person: mediating between the local and the global in career guidance policy learning, *Globalizations, Societies and Education*, 9(2): 265–83. Available at www.um.edu.mt/__data/assets/pdf_file/0012/144120/on_being_a_boundary_person.pdf (accessed 2 November 2011).

Torres, C.A. (2002) Globalization, education, and citizenship: solidarity versus markets, *American Educational Research Journal*, 39(2): 363–78.

Torres, C.A. (2009) *Education and Neoliberal Globalization*, New York: Routledge.

UNESCO (1990) *Framework for Action, World Declaration on Education for All (EFA)*, World Conference on EFA, Jomtien, Thailand, 5–8 March.

UNESCO (2000) *The Dakar Framework for Action*, Paris: UNESCO.

UNESCO (2002–11) *EFA Global Monitoring Reports*, Paris: UNESCO Publishing.

Villegas-Reimers, E. and Reimers, F. (1996) Where are 60 million teachers? The missing voice in educational reforms around the world, *Prospects*, 26, 469–92.

Weber, E. (2007) Globalization, 'glocal' development and teachers' work: a research agenda, *Review of Educational Research*, 77(3): 279–309.

Welmond, M. (2002) Globalization viewed from the periphery: the dynamics of teacher identity in the Republic of Benin, *Comparative Education Review*, 46(1): 37–65.

World Bank (2005) *The Road Not Traveled: Education reform in the Middle East and North Africa*, MENA development report, Washington, DC: World Bank.

Yates, L. and Young, M. (2010) Globalization, knowledge and curriculum, *European Journal of Education*, 45(1): 1–10.

Zaalouk, M. (1989) *Power, Class and Foreign Capital in Egypt: The rise of the new bour-geoisie*, London: Zed Books.

Zaalouk, M. (2004) *The Pedagogy of Empowerment: Community schools as a social move-ment in Egypt*, Cairo: The American University in Cairo Press.

Zaalouk, M. (2005) Innovation and mediation: the case of Egypt, in N. Rao and I. Smyth (eds) *Partnerships for Girls' Education*, Oxford: Oxfam GB.

Zaalouk, M. (2011a) 25 January Revolution and the freedom and equity in education: towards a committed teacher, *Al Shorouk*, Cairo, 772: 6.

Zaalouk, M. (2011b) *A Historical Account of the Program for the Enhancement of Teachers in the Arab Region*, paper presented at the Conference on Centers of Excellence for Teacher Professional Development, The League of Arab States, Cairo, November.

Zajda, J. (2011) Globalization and schooling: equity and access issues, *Cultural Studies Science Education*, 6: 143–52.

13 Living the Tensions

Moral Dilemmas in English Language Teaching

Phan Le Ha and Le Thuy Linh

Introduction

English language teaching (ELT) is a hotspot in the contemporary global politics of education. Global English is endorsed worldwide. Yet its character as 'English' and its teaching practices are tensioned between travelling ideas about what constitutes 'good' English and English language teaching and nationally specific norms related to English and teacher professionalism. The challenges that English language teachers confront with this transition to global English are well documented but there is less attention given to the way these contradictory imperatives are experienced by teachers within specific nations.

This chapter examines shifting professional identities among Vietnamese teachers as the profession of ELT becomes a global service industry. In Vietnam, this well-established profession has its own professionalism codes and practices embedded in ideologies that relate to the status of English and also national understandings about teachers as 'moral guides'. Yet as the status of English increases as a global medium of communication and exchange, a worldwide lingua franca and a recognized international language, Vietnamese English language teachers are drawn into a globally distributed ELT profession that is framed by discourses associated with the commercialization and the cultural politics of the ELT industry.

The chapter begins by examining the trajectory of global English and the issues that confront the English language teaching profession. Next, we use the concept of teacher professional identity to consider the implications of these global trends in ELT for Vietnamese teachers, highlighting the contradictory expectations of the Vietnamese English language teaching profession and the imperatives in teaching global English. Drawing on interview-based research, we illustrate the moral dilemmas that Vietnamese English language teachers negotiate as they talk about their teaching, using three individual cases to show different ways of dealing with ambivalence and tensions in their everyday work and lives. Finally, we suggest there is a quiet revolution in Vietnamese teacher professionalism as English language teachers negotiate global and national norms that define ELT, which both control and liberate them at the same time.

The Globalization of English Language Teaching

> If in the colonial times English language teaching (ELT) was used to spread the empire's power and support the colonial governance, then ELT today is used to back up and strengthen the current global expansion of English and its underlying cultural values.
>
> (Phan, 2008: 72)

Deeply rooted in the colonial project for several hundreds of years and now serving the spread of globalization worldwide, English and ELT have been under close examination. Critiques of the cultural politics of teaching English to speakers of other languages have raised concerns about the close relationship between English, ELT and the discourses of colonialism (Pennycook, 1994, 1998), racism and discrimination (Kubota and Lin, 2009), unethical missionary work (Edge, 2003; Pennycook and Coutand-Marin, 2004), and marketization and commercialization (Pennycook, 1994; Anderson, 2005; Chowdhury and Phan, 2008). The discourses that affirm the 'native speaker' are also premised on a fallacy that promotes British, North American and Australian English as 'standard' English, which positions the English native speaker as the superior and the ideal (and therefore desirable) target professional (Phillipson, 1992; Canagarajah, 1999; Holiday, 2005). As a result, ideal ELT professionals are 'White' 'native' speakers of English. Non-native English language teachers are judged against this native speaker model in terms of their teaching performance, expertise and professional merit. The native speakers are considered to be 'the experts' in the field and sought after for expert advice even in areas where they have little knowledge, such as teaching classes of over 40 students and classrooms with almost no teaching aids. Their advice in many ways has undermined the value of locally appropriate teaching approaches. It provokes anxiety among local teachers about their teaching ability and also creates an uncritical 'worshipping' attitude towards Western ways of teaching among both native and non-native teachers of English (Phillipson, 1992; Brown, 2000; Bax, 2003; Bright and Phan, 2011).

The belief that 'the West is better', often held by both Westerners and non-Western people, has also facilitated the spread of English and ELT, and teaching approaches promoted by 'the West' (Pennycook, 1994, 1998). Likewise, certain Western-oriented values associated with the ELT profession have been mistakenly regarded as superior and desirable. These include assumptions about 'democracy', 'freedom', 'open-mindedness', 'service orientation' and 'student–teacher equality', which are at the same time promoted as part of the 'universalized' professionalism that every ELT professional should aspire to acquire and demonstrate. This normative frame has implications for the way ELT professionals negotiate their teacher identities.

Despite these critiques, many Asian countries have introduced English language policies and programmes that favour native speakers and endorse Western theoretic-practical frameworks for English language education. Communicative language teaching (CLT) is one example, which is often presented and claimed to be 'best practice', despite ignoring students' levels of proficiencies and learning environments (Bax, 2003; Chowdhury and Phan, 2008; Phan, 2008). Teachers of English throughout Asia have been encouraged, even required, to adopt CLT, regardless of the difficulties, problems, frustration, dissatisfaction, tensions and confusion it causes many English language learners and teachers in the region (Li, 1998; Liu, 1998; Le, 2001; Rao, 2002; McKay, 2003; Gupta, 2004; Hu, 2005). Many of the embedded principles of CLT contradict and challenge what is valued as teacher professionalism throughout Asia.

CLT has been identified in most parts of the world as 'the way to go', 'the way to teach' and 'the remedy' to improve English language education. One of its key principles is *'teacher as facilitator'*, which contradicts, even threatens, student–teacher relationships where teachers are expected to provide serious teaching; giving detailed lectures and written exercises and, at the same time, keeping a certain distance from students to reflect locally appropriate norms of respect, authority, religious practice and seniority. Yet CLT and its model of 'teacher as facilitator' is endorsed by authorities at every level in a country and by institutions that are inclined to follow the recommendation of 'international experts'.

Professionals working and studying in 'the co-called West' confront CLT directly but it spreads through multiple channels. These include ELT expert consultancy to 'non-West' and/or 'non-English-speaking' countries, supervision of research students from these countries, teaching materials in postgraduate courses, and support as Western-trained ELT professionals return home. While CLT is projected through in-country ELT education reforms and national foreign language policies, the trajectory of reform is confirmed as ELT professionals take up opportunities to enhance their skills, careers and status. Such professional development builds confidence in the profession, but also individual professionals with value crises.

The authorization and endorsement of CLT by national governments and international agencies presents local teachers of English with dilemmas. The tensions between embedded national teaching values, beliefs and practices, and parallel Western practices that travel, challenge teachers' professional identities. They can put their established understandings of teaching in doubt and at risk. Nevertheless, many English language teachers also acknowledge that CLT liberates them from certain locally expected roles that they believe are ineffective in language teaching and are controlling their 'personal freedom' (Phan, 2008; Le and Phan, 2012). In Vietnam, these dilemmas become intense in relation to the idea of the teacher as 'moral guide', which is considered to be the most important feature of the teaching profession and a core value shaping local professionalism (Phan, 2008).

Contradictory ELT Professional Identities

With the global spread of English, increased demand for the language, and educational reform 'fever' everywhere in the world, the role of English language teachers is both significant and challenging. They are judged against multiple layers of professionalism, with codes defined at universal, national and local levels where professionals work in specific fields. There are conflicting viewpoints, values and expectations embedded in such frameworks. What makes it all the more complicated are the directional impacts these layers of discourse have upon one another, which challenges English language teachers to constantly negotiate professionalism constraints.

The development of ELT as a career and service, with ELT professionals as service providers, shapes a 'universalized' ELT professionalism globally. At this generalized level, ELT is a career in a field of educational specialization. It requires a specialized knowledge base obtained through both academic study and practical experience, and is a field of work where membership is based on entry requirements and standards (Barduh and Johnson, 2009, cited in Burns and Richards, 2009). ELT is a service industry, accountable for assuring that the service given is what the clients need (Farmer, 2006a, 2006b). As Clayton (1990) argues, the focus of professionalism in ELT is on responding to clients' needs. Teachers' responsibilities are to provide services to their clients, using their knowledge and skills (Goodwyn, 2005). If the goal of teaching is 'making student learning possible' (Ramsden, 1992, cited in Farmer, 2006b: 45), English language teachers should be competent to deliver all of these services.

This abstracted way of understanding reinforces a view of ELT as a profession with a universalized professionalism, but it overlooks the work of ELT, which means different things in different places. As rightly advocated by Burns and Richards (2009):

> Becoming English language teachers means becoming part of the worldwide community of professionals with shared goals, values, discourse, and practices but one with a self-critical view of its own practices and a commitment to a transformative approach to its own role.
>
> (p. 3)

However, ELT professionals develop their roles and professionalism from different collective and individual perspectives. Teachers in some places are required to have qualifications recognized by local educational authorities or by international professional organizations and to attain standards mandated by such bodies. Their practices must conform to the rules and norms that prevail in their context of work.

Leung (2009) links developing ELT professionalism with the changing status of English in the world. Like all other teachers, English language teachers have to meet common-sense obligations of the teaching profession, which are framed by the development of teaching within national traditions and expectations. Yet ELT professionals work everywhere in the world, which requires them to modify their competences, practice and roles to correspond to the different educational levels and situations. This sense of professionalism acknowledges the shift away from primary concerns in ELT, searching for the 'best way to teach to that of ideology, the values and beliefs in relation to politics and power relations' (Johnston, 2003: 51). It changes views of ELT classroom teachers' roles. ELT is not only about teachers and professional bodies that are accountable to clients in terms of service but are also charged with moral responsibility (Farmer, 2006a, 2006b). To put it differently, ELT professionalism is now centrally concerned with values and the moral roles of English language teachers.

The moral and ethical dimensions of work are central to professionalism and ELT professionalism is no exception. Morality is a complicated concept, and is extensively discussed with disagreements and confusion from diverse perspectives. Regardless of this diversity, the shared meanings suggest that 'morality includes such virtues as responsibility, respect, trustworthiness, fairness, caring and civic virtue' (Sergiovannie, 1996, cited in Campbell, 1997: 255). We see morality as '*socially acceptable and proper behaviour and manners, and in other cases, as dominant ethical values that are generally shared by the society*' (Phan and Phan, 2006: 3). Teacher morality includes personal, professional and cultural values as well as shared global ethics that inform the profession (Phan, 2008; Phan *et al.*, 2011). Extending the meaning of teacher morality in this broader sense acknowledges the social and cultural boundaries that frame the social values and contexts that account for individuals' sense of what morality means to them.

Like any other forms of teaching, ELT is a profoundly moral undertaking. It involves human relationships: 'who we are, how others see us and how we treat others and are treated by those others is above all the question of human values' (Johnston, 2003: 18). Recent studies of the moral and ethical dimension of teaching have emphasized the role of the teacher as pedagogical expert (Beijaard *et al.*, 2000), moral agent/exemplar (Festermatcher, 1990; Strike and Ternasky, 1993; Beyer, 1997; Campbell, 1997; Maslovaty, 2000; Joseph, 2003) and as role model or moral guide (Festermatcher, 1990; Phan, 2008). Because educators regard their professional responsibilities as basic moral imperatives, English language teacher identity is centred by their struggle both to teach the language and to create morally good students. The language teachers embody morality as they portray themselves as the role models for the students (Carr, 2000; Campbell, 2008a, 2008b). However, this is a morality that is embedded in the historical and sociocultural context of Vietnam.

Teacher Professional Identity in Vietnam

The philosophy of Vietnamese teaching is imbued with moral codes that developed over nearly three thousand years. At the Temple of Literature in Ha Noi there is a dedication, which captures the moral significance of knowledge and learning. It states:

> Talented and virtuous people are a nation's vitality. When this vitality flourishes, the country grows strong; when it deteriorates, the country will weaken and decline. Therefore, all clear-sighted kings seek to nurture talent, training scholars and cultivating the nation's vitality as their principal task.
>
> (Than, 1484)

Historically, culturally, philosophically and empirically, moral education and morality have been emphasized, endorsed and celebrated in pre-Vietnam and Vietnam over the past few thousand years (Duong, 2002; Phan, 2008). Teachers and teaching have always been given the highest status in society, largely because of the social and cultural appreciation of the moral responsibility embedded in teaching and the 'teacher as moral guide' role of teachers. Active religions and philosophies throughout Vietnam's history, such as Buddhism, Taoism, Confucianism, Christianity, Cao Dai and Mother-God worshipping, have, over time, all positioned moral education at the heart of their teaching and principles. Alongside religious teaching, the different ruling authorities have also consistently promoted the importance of moral education through social, cultural, educational and ideological channels. The aim of education in modern Vietnam continues to expect teachers to demonstrate morality by both behaving morally as individuals and giving students moral education. They are automatically assumed to be moral guides or role models and teachers tend to develop themselves in both knowledge and morality to meet these social, cultural and educational expectations. They find it both necessary and important to educate students morally, no matter what subject they teach, and to care for students' personal development, as well as knowledge achievement (Phan and Phan, 2006). (For a more detailed discussion of morality and education in Vietnam, see Phan (2008).)

The teacher's role in moral education is encoded in rules and regulations. For example, the Constitution of Vietnam clearly states that: 'The aim of education is to form and nurture the personality, moral qualities ... to imbue [people] with ... good morality' (Article 35). The Education Law affirms the role, tasks and rights of the teacher. Article 14 states that the teacher must constantly learn and train in order to set a good example for the learners; Article 61 states that the teacher must 'discharge their task, preserve and develop the tradition of respecting the teacher and glorifying the teaching job' and 'must have good moral qualities, ethics and ideology'; and Article 63 states that the teacher is:

> 1. to educate and teach according to the objective, principles and programs of education; 2. to be exemplary in fulfilling the citizen's duties, and observing the regulations of law and the statute of the school; 3. to preserve the quality, prestige and honour of the teacher, respect the dignity of the learners, to behave justly with learners, and protect their legitimate rights and interests; 4. to constantly study and train in order to raise their quality, ethics, professional and specialty standard and set good examples to the learners.
>
> (cited in Phan and Phan, 2006: 139)

In Vietnamese society, teaching is considered to be a noble, if not the noblest, profession. Teachers are given the highest status because they are expected to be role models and knowledge guides. They are considered responsible for the character education of their students, sharing this responsibility with the community and the family in particular. This moral role of teachers is arguably even more crucial in contemporary Vietnam, where family and community education are becoming looser due to time pressures and economic pursuits; accordingly, children's character development is completely abrogated to teachers. Teachers' manners and moral responsibility are, in consequence, more strictly judged than those of other professions (Le, 2001; Doan, 2005; Phan, 2008). Therefore, teachers in contemporary

Vietnam must constantly improve their specific expertise and continuously refine and demonstrate their moral character and manners as role models.

Unsurprisingly, teaching is identified as one of the most stressful contemporary professions. Teachers in Vietnam are not only in charge of teaching, but must also make teaching aids and attend to numerous side activities, including school cleaning and collecting tuition fees, along with a heavy curriculum load (Le, 2009a, 2009b). At the same time, teachers are still very poorly paid, even though the economy of the country has been driven by commercialization discourses associated with the market. These tensions between devotion to teaching, struggling with low salaries and being tempted to commercialize threaten the profession. These conditions make it challenging for teachers in present-day Vietnam to retain professional ethics and live up to social expectations of being the upholders of morality.

Since the Open Door policy in 1986, Vietnam has undergone dramatic sociocultural changes, partly in response to globalization. Increased social tensions have unsettled seemingly shared and stable moral perceptions of society, especially among young people (Doan, 2005; An, 2009; Le, 2009a, 2009b; Thao, 2009; Hoang, 2010). Coupled with the Open Door policy, English became the first foreign language to be taught in schools (Le, 2001; Khoa, 2008; Phan, 2008; Le and Roger, 2009). English language education is now seen as the essential element driving Vietnam's education and future development. English language teacher training and retraining have therefore become more and more important (MOET, 2009).

In Vietnam, learning English is part of the modernizing process (Phan *et al.*, 2011) and teaching English is largely about preparing the country for its integration into the global world (Le, 2004). Professionals debate the way English is becoming an international language that serves its users effectively and morally, while teachers continue to be affirmed as moral agents, who are vital to the 'negotiations, mediations, appropriation, resistance and reconstitutions of values and identities' among learners (Phan *et al.*, 2011: 150). In this sense, the role of English language teachers in educating students morally is reinforced. However, meanings associated with 'teachers as moral guides' become more complicated as English language teachers are exposed to mixed global as well as national values and ideologies. In these circumstances, teachers themselves play a major role in reconstructing teacher professionalism and identity.

Navigating Moral Dilemmas in ELT

English language teachers are confronting moral dilemmas and renegotiating their professional identities in ways that are creating a 'quiet revolution' in Vietnamese ELT. We show how several individual Vietnamese ELT professionals address and respond to the tensions in their everyday work and lives, which have been the result of conflicting ideologies and layers at all levels of their professional operation. Three sets of data were collected between 2000 and 2011. First, over 40 in-depth interviews with Vietnamese Western-trained teachers of English in both Australia and Vietnam between 2000 and 2006 investigated the teachers' professional identity formation in the context of mobility, transnationality and the globalization of English (Phan, 2008). Second, over 40 interviews were conducted with Vietnamese pre-service teachers of English, and Vietnamese teacher educators from several teacher training institutions in Vietnam from 2009 to 2011, to examine their views on the 'teacher as moral guide' in ELT in the changing context of Vietnam. Finally, a young Vietnamese English language teacher engaged in self-reflections on her own experiences in Vietnam in the course of her Master's thesis (Pham, 2012).

All these Vietnamese teachers of English have experienced the process of negotiating tensions caused by the globalization of English and ELT. However, they show different degrees of resistance to this 'professional value crisis' in this transitional period in Vietnam, since the Open Door policy in 1986. For example, these teachers, in their negotiations of conflicting identities, roles and selves, showed a tendency to self-position and other-position in relation to dichotomies, including Western-trained and/or non-Western-trained teachers of English, 'Western' versus 'Vietnamese/Asian' values, teachers of English versus teachers of other subjects, traditional versus modern, and global versus local. From this larger range of conversations with Vietnamese English language teachers, we have selected three examples to show the ways in which they worked on their professional identity.

Feeling Colonized by Universalized Professionalism

I had worked as a teacher of English at a university in Vietnam for two and a half years before pursuing my master's degree [in Australia]. Being a teacher of English, two reasons made me feel that I was not a qualified and legitimate teacher. First, like many Vietnamese teachers of English, I also worked for an English language center in which I cooperated with some native English speaking teachers (NESTs). Vietnamese teachers were normally responsible for teaching reading and grammar while their counterparts – NESTs – dealt with speaking and listening. I never felt comfortable to talk to these NESTs because I thought I was inferior to them regarding both language competency and teaching method. Second, I was unable to apply CLT thoroughly and effectively though I was taught at university that CLT was the icon of a successful and perfect ELT approach. Moreover, colleagues at my university and elsewhere in my country tried to justify a teacher's capability through how much she or he used CLT. This made me sometimes feel guilty but I could not find an adequate explanation for my failure.

(Pham, 2012: 2)

In her Master's thesis, Xuan, a young teacher in her twenties, reflected on how much she had been 'colonized' by the CLT principles during her teaching in Vietnam (Pham, 2012). She felt handicapped and incompetent, believing she would never become a good teacher with the ability to apply CLT in her teaching. This CLT model of English teaching was demanded by her university, by the ELT reforms that had been taking place in and outside Vietnam, and by all the training sessions she had been through. She thought then that she would forever look up to the native-English-speaking teachers as the ultimate model. Her training to become an English language teacher, and what was demanded by her own university as 'good ELT', mistakenly affirms native-English-speaking teachers. Endorsing them suggests that these native speakers own CLT because of their ability to perform the 'teacher as facilitator' role, while she and many other Vietnamese teachers cannot. A Vietnamese teacher needs to play many roles, and 'teacher as facilitator' appears to be the most difficult role for them, and for this reason. Xuan found it impossible to think highly of her teaching, regardless of how much she tried CLT in her classrooms, because CLT and its 'teacher as facilitator' principle have a powerful colonizing effect.

Xuan's experience indicates the nature of CLT as an assumed 'standard practice' (Chowdhury and Phan, 2008). Administrators and teachers judge other English language teachers' teaching ability on the basis of how much and how effectively they can apply CLT in their teaching. The 'CLT attitude' (Bax, 2003) and the normative 'CLT scale' exercises power in classifying ELT professionals and in creating professional norms that appear to work against the majority of English language teachers, who are non-native English speakers and work in conditions that CLT does not favour. In the late 1990s and 2000s, Phan Le Ha (2004) found that Vietnamese teachers were able to negotiate the performance of 'teacher as facilitator' in a way that seemed smoother. However, what Xuan experienced recently in Vietnam seems to be more intense and personally painful. The promotion of a teaching methodology as universally desirable and appropriate from one part of the world to another shifts over time as well as space (see Sobe, this volume). As it is internalized among English language teachers themselves, it helps standardize professionalism in that new context.

Negotiating Professional Practice

Kien is a Western-trained Vietnamese teacher of English (Phan, 2008). He presented himself as a teacher of sharp value contrasts. He was someone who would scold students in the class, believing that it was fine for a teacher to do so as long as scolding was meant to help students perform better. Equally, Kien was someone who would never go to a nightclub, believing such a place was not for a proper teacher. Studying in Australia, Kien was exposed to Western values and practices, many of which were totally different from what he had experienced in Vietnam. As he talked he seemed fascinated but also negotiating with himself about these new things.

In one conversation while he was studying in Australia, Kien talked about nightclubs and pubs in Australia and what those places had to do with teacher morality. He showed his curiosity about pubs and bars, since he had only vague ideas what they were like, but, at the same time, he made up his mind not to have those experiences:

> Sometimes I also wanted to go to a nightclub to see what it is like, but then I
> decided not to do so. We are teachers. If students in Vietnam know that I go

to such places, they would treat me differently. If other Vietnamese teachers who study in Australia go to a nightclub, I wouldn't judge them as bad, but I myself can't do it.

Kien's desire or curiosity was controlled by his professional values. He was a teacher and a Vietnamese and a Vietnamese teacher should not go to those places, which were perceived in Vietnam to be places of unhealthy and ill-cultured behaviours and activities. Although he realized that nightclubs and pubs in Australia may be different, he still did not find the courage to explore that experience. He explained that, as a teacher, he felt uneasy to be in such places. He was afraid of being caught and judged by others as a bad teacher. In his thinking, it seemed that everybody knew he was a teacher. In particular, he thought his students were watching over his shoulder.

Kien cared what other people thought, particularly when they judged his teaching profession and values badly. In other words, his professional identity set rules and limits for his personal acts. He took on what others thought about him because his teacher identity was partly formed by social expectations, and they won over his personal desire. So, even though he was in Australia, away from home and social norms, he still chose to perform his Vietnamese 'teacher' self (Phan, 2008: 172).

Being trained in the West did not seem to take away Kien's loyalty to his beliefs as a teacher. It did not seem to self-liberate him either, even when his day-to-day sense of exposure to 'Western values' appeared to be more intense than that of many other Western-trained teachers, according to his observation.

Yet in dialogue with two other teachers, Linh and Vy, Kien negotiated his 'moral guide role'. The three knew each other well and Linh worked in the same place with Kien in Vietnam. In this conversation among friends, Linh and Vy talked about their perceptions of teacher values and questioned Kien's 'noto-rious' image among his colleagues and students, which related to his habit of scolding students with his sharp tongue. After having listened to Linh, Kien said he tended to absorb teacher values embedded in social norms and made them his own. He tried to perform as a teacher in light of these norms, as he saw their necessity and positiveness. He showed his willingness to be tied to these social norms and develop himself accordingly. As Linh and Vy extended their discussion, Kien concluded that:

> It's good to follow these socially constructed norms. But the problem is that to what extent we can follow them. It doesn't mean that we can perfectly follow all the norms. If so we were gods, not human. For example, *although it is expected that teachers mustn't scold students harshly but I still do it [laughing]. But I do it just for students' sake. I want to make them study. If I am irresponsible, then I won't care, but I'm not.*

Linh and Vy did not agree with Kien's example. Linh challenged Kien, saying 'What kind of teacher are you, you always scold students?' Kien replied to Linh as someone who knew him well: 'So what? I scold them because I want them to be better.' Linh and Vy said there were other and proper ways to do it, and scolding was not at all acceptable.

Only at that moment did Kien himself 'offer' his 'hidden' identities. He could not just talk ideologically any more because he was being watched and judged by Linh; he could not afford to present himself otherwise. Rather than waiting for Linh to unveil his teacher identity because she knew that he scolded his students, he said it first, both boldly and humorously. It looked as if he shifted his identity suddenly, but this shift appeared very smooth and natural because he took a proactive role in doing it. It was clear he took on the identity others constructed for him, that of 'scolding students', and he claimed it as part of his teacher identity (Phan, 2008: 173–6).

Kien probably knew that scolding students was not acceptable anywhere in the world; it was not included in any professionalism, universal or local, social or cultural, institutional or professional. However, he created his own way of being a 'good' and 'kind' teacher who cared for his students' learning outcomes. His principle corresponds well with a Vietnamese moral saying '*Thuong cho roi cho vot, ghet cho ngot cho bui*' (If you really care for someone, be strict/demanding to the person; if you don't, then be sweet/easy to him/her). This saying presents a paradox but also reflects shared Vietnamese beliefs about nurturing good values and virtues. Its principle can be applied in all contexts and settings with different degrees of fluidity in terms of being strict and being easy. For Kien, what he was doing to students was not 'immoral', but 'caring' and 'responsible', although the way he acted could be interpreted as 'improper' and even running against the teacher's role as 'a fond mother'. According to Linh and Kien, Kien had been able to sustain and even 'sharpen' his habit by utilizing humour. It somehow blended his sharp tongue with laughter, so students tended to take his scolding and criticisms more easily. Kien also saw himself in a battlefield of conflicting moral values and beliefs, in which he declared 'war' and crowned himself for the victory, for in the end what mattered to him was students' better performance, regardless of the manner in which he pushed them to study more effectively.

While Kien appeared to be very 'strict' with his own image by not going to any nightclubs and proactively preserving this image, he dared to take criticisms from others for what he believed was good for his teaching and for his students' learning. He showed his loyalty to what is expected of a good teacher in Vietnam.

Using Professionalism

The final case is based on a 2011 discussion among a group of pre-service English language teachers in Vietnam about a teacher, Ngoc, who was pregnant without being married. In Vietnam, a teacher who has a baby without marriage was traditionally, and is still, considered immoral. She would be socially criticized and discarded from the teaching profession. This teacher, Ngoc, after becoming pregnant, still went to work and faced her colleagues and her students every day. She did not appear to avoid people's gossip about her, and many described her 'growing tummy' as a 'thorn' or 'fist to the face of teacher morality'. As the group of pre-service teachers discussed this incident, they seemed to get confused by what was or wasn't considered immoral and unethical behaviour in the profession. The group showed conflicting viewpoints about this incident; that Ngoc was not given any penalty by the teacher training institution and continued to challenge society's norms and professional ethics seemed to disappoint some of them and, simultaneously, excite others in the group.

Their disappointment resulted from the group's concern about decreasing morality, in society and in the teaching profession. They associated these weaker moral norms with the negative consequences arising from pragmatic ELT-as-a-service professionalism. Their excitement seemed to be a sign of their own 'relief' and 'empowerment' as they observed that Ngoc would not be the last one who did what she had done. Ngoc did not face 'the end of the world' because she had become pregnant. She could have had an abortion to save her face and to save the profession's face, but she decided to have a baby without getting married. As the group discussed, being a single mother is not new in the West and, as Vietnam is joining the world, tolerance with this phenomenon would be expected. Having a baby is a woman's right and being a single mother is a woman's right too, so what Ngoc did was to claim her right as a woman. That there were no obvious consequences suggested that the claim was acknowledged, at least on the surface, by both the profession and society.

The reasons for ambivalent 'disappointment' and 'excitement' among this group of teachers in training adhered to 'the West' and 'Western values' that accompanied globalization and Vietnam's economic reforms. At the same time, 'Western values' were viewed by them as liberating teachers' acts and ways of thinking and extending teachers' horizons, particularly when 'doing things that are considered notorious or improper' by the locals. Values underlying 'the West', such as 'freedom', 'open-mindedness' and 'democracy', were both appropriated and resisted by teachers and, in this incident with Ngoc, such values run in all different directions.

For Ngoc, she appeared to take advantage of the 'open-mindedness' that was believed to be a trademark of the ELT profession. As the group of pre-service teachers noted, ELT exposed teachers to English and its associated 'Western', mostly 'American Western', values, and this trademark could be manipulated. Ngoc's case was a good example. Yet, Ngoc provoked the society and her profession by violating the most 'sacred' rule: teachers are moral guides and virtue carriers. And she was able to get away with what she did and faced no formal penalties or punishments. This suggested that the profession and the institution where she worked also participated in the 'open-mindedness' and 'individual freedom' discourse.

Another way to look at it could be that teacher morality is no longer taken as seriously as it has been by Vietnamese society. The universal discourse of professionalism associated with ELT as a service provider may have taken root and established its own rules in the local context. The biggest challenge for Ngoc appeared to be with her own colleagues and students. They, like the discussion group of pre-service English language teachers, were torn between demonstrating their 'open-mindedness' as part of an appropriated universalized ELT professionalism, and preserving values that had been core and fundamental to their teacher identity and belief.

Although none of these pre-service teachers had been outside Vietnam, their perceptions of 'the West' and 'Western values' appeared to be simultaneously a fantasy and a taboo. It was this ambivalence that created mixed feelings and attitudes towards Ngoc's case. They proclaimed that their ways of thinking and their living styles had more or less changed as a result of their constant contacts with the English language and its underlying 'Western' cultures. Whether they were disappointed or excited about Ngoc's circumstances, they did show empathy and tolerance towards her rather than attitudinal judgement and criticism. In their responses, they saw themselves connecting the universal values that they acquired in their teacher training with local Vietnamese values that they too respected.

A Quiet Revolution in Vietnamese Teacher Professionalism?

These three cases indicate the existence of a values crisis in the practices of Vietnamese teacher professionalism. ELT is a particular hotspot as Vietnam transitions through its Open Door policy. This field of teacher professionalism confronts 'Western' values through ELT, with the concept of 'teacher as facilitator' as a particular and tangible expression of Western discourses of 'democracy', 'freedom' and 'student–teacher equality'. Yet these discourses are appropriated and resisted in creative ways by English language teachers worldwide.

The concept of 'teacher as facilitator' has empowered English language teachers as much as colonized them (Phan, 2004, 2008). On the one hand, adopting the 'teacher as facilitator' role can be used to get away from playing the 'teacher as moral guide' role with peers and with students, as the case of Ngoc suggested. As long as teachers facilitate students' learning for the sake of skill building and knowledge generation, the teacher has done his or her duty. The 'moral guide' role, in light of this principle, is no longer the primary concern. Hence, teachers' personal lives need not have anything to do with how they teach students language skills in the classroom. They are liberated from these moral responsibilities. However, they can also choose how to act as facilitators. As Kien's case shows, it is possible to facilitate students' learning through 'scolding' them. By mobilizing traditional understandings of teacher professionalism, he could avoid threatening his own teacher image and strengthened his position on what a teacher should be responsible for. In this way, Kien performed as expected by the profession as a whole, by universalized ELT professionals and by Vietnamese teacher professionalism embedded in the social and cultural norms that surrounded him.

Adopting the professional identity of 'teacher as facilitator' is a way of claiming membership of a profession that is believed to enjoy universal values. Yet, as Xuan's experience suggested, this can have negative effects. In her desperation to claim this membership, she had to force herself into this practice of professionalism and ended up constantly judging herself against its norms. Equally, this 'teacher as facilitator' position can be manipulated, as occurred with Ngoc, in her workplace and by those who felt 'liberated' and 'unchained' by the 'moral guide' role.

These varied ways in which teachers of English in Vietnam engage with universalized discourses of teacher professionalism play out in the everyday politics of professionalization. As individuals and groups take up the opportunities that are made available through ELT and navigate the ambivalences associated with the identity of 'teacher as facilitator', they remake their profession. These teachers, boldly as well as painfully, move forward in a process we would call *a quiet revolution* in Vietnamese ELT professionalism.

References

An, K. (2009) Đạo đức nhà giáo (Teachers' morality), *Radio Free Asia*, 11 October. Available at www.rfa.org/vietnamese/in_depth/Teachers-ethics-issue-kan-10112009104855.html (accessed 2 November 2009).

Anderson, C. (2005) *The Commodification of Education: The case of TESOL*, paper presented at the British Association for Applied Linguistics Annual Conference, Bristol University.

Bax, S. (2003) The end of CLT: a context approach to language teaching, *ELT Journal*, 57: 278–87.

Beijaard, D., Verloop, N. and Vermunt, J.D. (2000) Teachers' perceptions of professional identity: an exploratory study from a personal knowledge perspective, *Teaching and Teacher Education*, 16: 749–64.

Beyer, L.E. (1997) The moral contours of teacher education, *Journal of Teacher Education*, 48(4): 245–54.

Bright, D. and Phan, L.H. (2011) 'White' native-English-speaking teachers of English in Vietnam: negotiations of identity and the politics of English language teaching, in L. Zhang, R. Rubdy and L. Alsagoff (eds) *Asian Englishes: Changing perspectives in a globalised world*, Singapore: Pearson Education.

Brown, R. (2000) Cultural continuity and ELT teacher training, *ELT Journal*, 54: 227–33.

Burns, A. and Richards, J.C. (eds) (2009) *The Cambridge Guide to Second Language Teacher Education*, New York: Cambridge University Press.

Campbell, E. (1997) Connecting the ethics of teaching and moral education, *Journal of Teacher Education*, 48(4): 255–63.

Campbell, E. (2008a) Teaching ethically as a moral condition of professionalism, in D. Narváez and L. Nucci (eds) *The International Handbook of Moral and Character Education*, New York: Routledge.

Campbell, E. (2008b) The ethics of teaching as a moral profession, *Curriculum Inquiry*, 38: 357.

Canagarajah, A.S. (1999) *Resiting Linguistic Imperialism in English Teaching*, Oxford: Oxford University Press.

Carr, D. (2000) *Professionalism and Ethics in Teaching*, London: Routledge.

Chowdhury, R. and Phan, L.H. (2008) Reflecting on Western TESOL training and communicative language teaching: Bangladeshi perspectives, *Asia Pacific Journal of Education*, 28: 305–16.

Clayton, T. (1990) Professionalism in international English language teaching, *Cross Currents*, 17: 65.

Doan, D.H. (2005) Moral education or political education in the Vietnamese educational system, *Journal of Moral Education*, 34: 451–63.

Duong, T.T. (2002) *Suy Nghi Ve Van Hoa Giao Duc Viet Nam* (About the culture of Vietnamese education), Ho Chi Minh City: Tre Publications.

Edge, J. (2003) Imperial troopers and servants of the Lord: a vision of TESOL for the 21st century, *TESOL Quarterly*, 37(4): 701–9.

Farmer, F. (2006a) *Professionalism in ELT*, México, DF: Plaza y Valdés/Universidad de Quintana Roo.

Farmer, F. (2006b) Accountable professional practice in ELT, *ELT Journal*, 60(2): 160–70.

Festermatcher, G.D. (ed.) (1990) *Some Moral Considerations on Teaching as a Profession*, San Francisco, CA: Oxford.

Goodwyn, A. (2005) Professionalism and accountability, in A. Goodwyn and J. Branson (eds) *Teaching English: A handbook for primary and secondary school teachers*, Abingdon and New York: RoutledgeFalmer.

Gupta, D. (2004) CLT in India: context and methodology come together, *ELT Journal*, 58: 266–9.

Hoang, H. (2010) Giá trị sống đang bị chao đảo (The value of life is being shaken), *Tuoi tre online*. Available at http://tuoitre.vn/Ban-doc-viet/371214/Gia-tri-song-dang-bi-chao-dao.html (accessed 1 April 2010).

Holiday, A. (2005) *The Struggle to Teach English as an International Language*, Cambridge: Cambridge University Press.

Hu, G. (2005) 'CLT is best for China' – an untestable absolutist claim, *ELT Journal*, 59: 65–8.

Johnston, B. (2003) *Values in English Language Teaching*, Mahwah, NJ and London: Lawrence Erlbaum.

Joseph, P.B. (2003) Teaching about the moral classroom: infusing the moral imagination into teacher education, *Asia-Pacific Journal of Teacher Education*, 31: 7–20.

Khoa, A.V. (2008) Imperialism of communicative language teaching and possible resistance against it from teachers in Vietnam as an English foreign language context, *VNU Journal of Science, Foreign Languages*, 24: 167–74.

Kubota, R. and Lin, A.M.Y. (2009) *Race, Culture, and Identities in Second Language Education: Exploring critically engaged practice*, Hoboken, NJ: Taylor and Francis.

Le, M.T. (2009a) Năm 2010, giao vien song duoc bang luong? (By 2010, can teachers live on their salaries?), *Tuoi tre online*, December 12.

Le, M.T. (2009b) Nghề giáo hiện nay: nghề 'oan trái' (Teaching professions in the modern time: a 'dilemma' career), *Tuoi tre online*. Available at http://tuoitre.vn/Tuoi-tre-cuoi-tuan/355261/Nghe-giao-hien-nay-nghe-%E2%80%9Coan-trai%E2%80%9D.html (accessed 13 January 2010).

Le, T.T.H. and Phan, L.H. (2012) Problematising the culture of learning English in Vietnam: revisiting teacher identity, in L.C. Jin and M. Cortazzi (eds) *Researching Cultures of Learning*, Basingstoke and New York: Palgrave.

Le, V.C. (2001) Language and Vietnamese pedagogical contexts, *Teacher's Edition*, 7: 34–9.

Le, V.C. (2004) From ideology to inquiry: mediating Asian and Western Values in ELT, *Teacher's Edition*, 15: 28–34.

Le, V.C. and Roger, B. (2009) Curriculum innovation behind closed classroom doors: a Vietnamese case study, *Prospect*, 24: 20–33.

Leung, C. (2009) Second language teacher professionalism, in A. Burns and J.C. Richards (eds) *The Cambridge Guide to Second Language Teacher Education*, New York: Cambridge University Press.

Li, D. (1998) It's always more difficult than you plan and imagine: teachers' perceived difficulties in introducing the communicative approach in South Korea, *TESOL Quarterly*, 32: 677–703.

Liu, D. (1998) Ethnocentrisim in TESOL: teacher education and the neglected needs of international TESOL, *ELT Journal*, 52: 3–9.

McKay, S. (2003) Teaching English as an international language: the Chilean context, *ELT Journal*, 57(2): 139–48.

Maslovaty, N. (2000) Teachers' choice of teaching strategies for dealing with socio-moral dilemmas in the elementary school, *Journal of Moral Education*, 29(4): 429–44.

Ministry of Education and Training (MOET) (2009) *Strategies for the Development of Vietnam Education 2009–2020*, Hanoi: MOET.

Pennycook, A. (1994) *The Cultural Politics of English as an International Language*, London and New York: Longman.

Pennycook, A. (1998) *English and the Discourse of Colonialism*, London: Routledge.

Pennycook, A. and Coutand-Marin, S. (2004) Teaching English as a missionary language, *Discourse: Studies in the Cultural Politics of Education*, 24: 337–53.

Pham, T.T.X. (2012) *Speaking Out or Keeping Silent: International students, identity as legitimate speakers and teachers of English*, Melbourne: Monash University.

Phan, L.H. (2004) University classrooms in Vietnam: contesting the stereotypes, *ELT Journal*, 58(1): 50–7.

Phan, L.H. (2008) *Teaching English as an International Language: Identity, resistance and negotiation*, Clevedon: Multilingual Matters.

Phan, L.H. and Phan, V.Q. (2006) Vietnamese educational morality and the discursive construction of English language teacher Identity, *Journal of Multicultural Discourses*, 1: 136–50.

Phan, L.H, Phan, V.Q. and McPherron, P. (2011) English language teachers as moral guides in Vietnam and China: maintaining and retraditionalizing morality, in J. Ryan (ed.) *Understanding China's Education Reform: Creating cross cultural knowledge, pedagogies and dialogue*, London: Routledge.

Phillipson, R. (1992) *Linguistic Imperialism*, Oxford and New York: Oxford University Press.

Rao, Z. (2002) Chinese students' perceptions of communicative and non-communicative activities in EFL classrooms. *System*, 30: 85–105.

Strike, K.A. and Ternasky, P.L. (1993) *Ethics for Professionals in Education: Perspectives for preparation and practice*, New York: Teachers College Press.

Thao, K. (2009) Học lễ từ trong gia đình (Learning ethics and morality from family), *Tuoi tre online*. Available at www.tuoitre.com.vn/Tianyon/Index.aspx?ArticleID=353435&ChannelID=118 (accessed 13 January 2010).

14 Globalization and Transnational Academic Mobility

A Case Study of Chinese Academic Returnees

Qiongqiong Chen and Mei Li

Introduction

Cross-border academic mobility is not a new phenomenon in the history of higher education. What appears new, however, is that the "previously sporadic, exceptional and limited international academic links have become increasingly systematic, dense, multiple and transnational" (Kim, 2010: 400). This is not only driven by the rapid global flows of goods, people, images, technologies, and monies (Appadurai, 1996), but also shaped by both national and super-national policy discourses and practices. Moreover, the interactions of open global dealings (e.g. WTO) on higher education and the increasingly interconnected institutional networks of universities and knowledge have contributed to create the new patterns of academic mobility. This is not only changing the way in which academics mobilize and operate but is also transforming the landscapes of higher education on a global scale.

Universities around the world are becoming increasingly internationalized in their linkages, personnel, curriculum content, and activities, with an emphasis on world university rankings (Marginson and van der Wende, 2007). In order to achieve an advanced academic status worldwide, they are engaged in planning mobility schemes via such practices as encouraging study abroad, global learning and research collaborations, as well as international recruitment of students and scholars (Fahey and Kenway, 2010). Furthermore, driven by the notion of the global knowledge economy, both governments and regional bodies are promoting global flows of highly skilled professionals, including university academics, to enhance their economic productivity and positioning in relation to competitors (Rizvi, 2007). Against this backdrop, transnational academic mobility, as an emerging field of study, has received heightened attention from both researchers and policy makers.

Research into and policies concerned with the movement of highly skilled workers and university academics adopt, largely, economic and political perspectives, mainly focusing on the relations between human capital, national economic growth, and global competitiveness. An initial argument was that an unequal world economic system drives people from peripheral, or developing, countries to seek study/work in core, or developed, countries, thus resulting in unidirectional brain drain (Altbach, 2004). This view is challenged by recent research on diaspora and knowledge networks that considers the potential benefits that highly skilled people might bring back to their countries of origin, thus contributing to brain gain (Brown, 2002; Meyer and Wattiaux, 2006; Solimano, 2008). Moreover, there is growing recognition that current patterns of academic mobility have become more complex, dispersed, and multi-directional, which cannot be reduced solely to economic discourse. As Appadurai (1996) points out, there are disjunctures between transformations in the economy, culture, and politics that have barely been theorized. He further argues for the need for alternative ways of understanding the cultural dynamics of global flows.

In response, this chapter uses postcolonial theory and cultural studies as conceptual frameworks to open up a cultural analysis of academic mobility. By using China as a case in point, we concentrate on a narrow component of mobility, namely on those who have studied or worked abroad and are currently employed in Chinese universities. Our interest in this group stems from the growing trend of reverse academic mobility in China. However, the daily experiences of academic returnees and the consequence of their movement in higher education in China have yet to be examined adequately. Thus, this chapter aims to explore how returned scholars negotiate their academic identities through the processes of movement, displacement, and resettlement, and how their practices affect university culture and higher education policies in China.

Drawing upon qualitative research data, we argue that the mobility of returned academics does not simply follow a linear process of "going abroad" and "coming back" (Matus, 2009). Instead, the movement creates a new space for identity formation (Chen and Koyama, 2012) and augments the possibilities of change in higher education practices. Before developing this argument further, we first discuss the research context and introduce a conceptual framework for understanding transnational academic mobility, especially returnees' mobility. Then, we provide empirical data to present how returned scholars narrate their experiences of navigating and reconstructing the conventions, rules, and practices within Chinese institutions. The chapter concludes by considering the theoretical and policy implications of returnees' academic mobility.

China's Efforts to Encourage Return Migration

China is an important example of a nation that has sought to entice highly skilled nationals to bring back their skills to contribute to domestic development. Of the 1,211,700 students and scholars who went abroad for study over the period 1978–2007, only 319,700 or 26.38 percent returned (MOE, 2008). Those who do not return contribute to what has been identified as China's massive brain drain (Hayhoe and Zhong, 1995). Recently, there has been a shift in this overall trend, and a significant "reverse brain drain" has resulted. The return rate rose from 26 percent in 2006 to 30 percent in 2009 (Pan, 2011). In 2009, 229,300 persons moved abroad and 108,300 moved back to China (China National Department of Statistics, 2010). In order to lure more talent back "home," the Chinese government has adopted various policies to transform "brain drain" into "brain gain" or "brain circulation," such as the "Hundred Talents Program"(*bairen jihua*),[1] the "Cheung Kong Scholars Programs"(*changjiang xuezhe jiangli jihua*),[2] and the "Thousand Talents Program"(*qianren jihua*).[3]

In response to the rise of the global knowledge economy, the Chinese government set up the development strategy of "*kejiao xingguo*"(strengthening the nation through science, technology, and education) and "*rencai qiangguo*"(empowering the nation through talent) in the early 1990s to enhance its global competitiveness. In higher education, Project 211 and Project 985 are the two major projects to stimulate excellence in China's top universities, which provided significant additional funding to help them reach world-class standing (Zha, 2011). For example, for Project 985, the total financial support from the central government was 14 billion yuan (about $2.07 billion) and 18.9 billion yuan (about $2.79 billion), during the two phases of 1999–2001 and 2004–7 respectively (Wang *et al.*, 2011). These large investments, along with empowerment reforms, give 985 member universities opportunities to develop their own visions and plans to achieve excellence in curriculum reform, teaching, research, and faculty upgrading (Zha, 2011), including the recruitment of overseas Chinese academics.

Moreover, in addition to the central government, local governments and individual institutions have also shown considerable interest in attracting global talent. Many local governments set up their own talent schemes that are independent from, and in some cases ahead of, central initiatives. Shanghai is one of the most successful cities in encouraging the return of overseas Chinese. It is also one of the first cities to issue permanent residence visas for returnees with foreign passports (Zweig, 2006). From 2008 onwards the Shanghai government issued and implemented its "Eastern Scholars Program." Each year the Shanghai government sponsors universities and research institutions to attract 50 overseas scholars to work in Shanghai.[4] At the institutional level, some universities supported by Project 985 have adopted new policies and measures in favor of academic returnees for faculty recruitment and promotion, especially those with publications in top international journals, such as in SCI (Science Citation Index), SSCI (Social Science Citation Index), and EI (Engineering Index) journals.

In contextualizing the returned academics in this historical moment, we seek to understand how these scholars account for their experiences of re-entering Chinese universities and how they perceive their role in higher education development in China. To answer these questions, we use the concepts of traveling culture, in-between space, and hybridity (Bhabha, 1994; Hall, 1996a; Clifford, 1997), to inform our investigation.

Conceptualizing Traveling Culture

Theories of cultural globalization have emerged in the fields of anthropology, sociology, and cultural studies. These include the constructs of global scapes (Appadurai, 1990, 1996), third space and hybridity (Bhabha, 1994; Hall, 1996a), dwelling-in-travel (Clifford, 1997), the diasporic intellectual (Said, 1994; Hall, 1996a; Bauman, 1997), and global assemblages and imagination (Collier and Ong, 2005; Sassen, 2006; Kenway and Fahey, 2009). Here, we draw upon hybrid theoretical positionings on traveling culture to inform our research. This literature challenges the fixed notion of place, space, and time. It opens a new discourse capable of framing the relations between travel, self-reflectivity, and global research imagination. It therefore provides a nuanced perspective for critically considering the experiences of mobile scholars and the consequences of their academic travels.

The notion of diasporic intellectuals is a useful starting point for analyzing the biographies of intellectuals who "travel between edge and empires" (Fahey and Kenway, 2010: 630). Scholars such as Said (1994), Hall (1996a), and Bauman (1997) share similar experiences of dislocation and migration, and strive to theorize the meaning of travel on their intellectual sensibility. For example, Said (1994) develops his notion of the critical intellectual in exile. To him, the sense of exile is a sense of being an insider and outsider, of indifference and involvement, and of inclusion and exclusion. As Fahey and Kenway (2010) observe, "Said's exilic intellectual is a critical intellectual" (p. 631), and his way of exilic thinking represents criticality itself. Similarly, Hall (1996b) acknowledges the benefits of travel and displacement. He points out that it is the diasporic experience, "far away enough to experience the sense of exile and loss, close enough to understand the enigma of an always-postponed 'arrival'" (p. 492), that nourishes his critical intellectual work.

In a related but different vein, Clifford (1997) is interested in diasporic subjectivities in and through travel formed by the "discrepant detours and returns" (p. 30). He uses "travel" as a term of cultural comparison to theorize the diverse practices of border crossing, tactics of translation, and experiences of multiple belongings. Drawing from the notions of traveling culture, dwelling-in-travel, and contact zones, he argues that "cultural action, the making and remaking of identities, takes place in the contact zones, along the policed and transgressed intercultural frontiers of nations, people, locales" (p. 7). In this sense, a location is not a bounded site but an itinerary that encounters exchange, interpretation, and negotiations between different space and times. Clifford's traveling culture reflects his desire to invoke political significance and a cosmopolitan intellectual commitment in reconstructing the new global cultural politics (Ong, 1999).

Other cultural theorists conceptualize traveling culture from the aspects of cultural hybridity and identity (Appadurai, 1990; Bhabha, 1994; Hall, 1996a). They are concerned with how people negotiate multiple spaces and movements by forming complex identities. According to them, the meaning of culture and identity is not fixed or tied permanently, but bears the traces of other meanings or discourses. Hall (1996a) insists that the negotiation of identity is a discursive positioning, which is never complete, or stable, and is always in the process of changing and becoming. Similarly, as Bhabha (1994) argues, "it is the 'inter'—the cutting edge of translation and negotiation, the in-between space—that carriers the burden of the meaning of culture" (p. 38). This in-between space gives rise to a new area of representation, as well as new subjectivities. The implication for understanding the identities of mobile scholars is that, rather than identity being singular and fixed, one is constantly attaching oneself to different articulations between discourse and practices, which in turn leads to multiple identifications in different conditions.

Of course, the literature on traveling culture is by no means undisputed. As Kenway and Fahey (2009) remind us, we should not romanticize the traveling subject. Travel may provoke fresh thoughts or intellectual sensibility, but does not necessarily do so. Nevertheless, the intellectuals whom Kenway and Fahey (2009) interviewed on their project, "globalizing research imagination," reinforce the impact of travel on their critical intellectual inquiry. These intellectuals speak of how, through travel, they question received notions and consider a fresh perspective of the world. In line with this literature, we understand transnational movement as a way in which university travelers renegotiate academic identities.

Research Methods

To examine the everyday experiences of academic returnees, we utilized in-depth interviews (Seidman, 2006) in two major research universities in Shanghai, from September 2011 to January 2012. As noted, the city of Shanghai was selected because of its success in recruiting overseas talent. To access potential participants, we reviewed faculty profiles available publicly on the universities' websites and selected professors who received their doctoral degrees in the US. We then emailed an invitation to them to participate in the study. Once interviews began, a snowball sampling technique emerged as interviewees suggested colleagues who might be interested in participating in the research.

Based on several variables including disciplines, professional ranks, gender, and age groups, 12 academics were selected for interviews. Among them, eight were from the fields of natural sciences and engineering, including biology, physics, chemistry, genomics, information systems, computer sciences and engineering; and four were from humanities and social sciences, including English literature, education, and anthropology. In terms of gender, although we attempted to recruit more female participants, we were able to include only three women alongside nine males. Both face-to-face interviews and Skype interviews were used. Each interview lasted from one to two hours. All interviews were conducted in Mandarin and were tape-recorded with the permission of the participants, then transcribed into texts. All data were de-identified and pseudonyms are used throughout this chapter.

In analyzing the interview data, we developed four major themes: the reasons for return, the effects of mobility on family and personal life, the effects on one's professional work, and the challenges of (re)integration. Due to limited space, this chapter focuses on the last two themes.

The Effects of Overseas Experiences

The academics we interviewed acknowledge the significant effects of mobility on their personal and professional life. For their academic work, they indicated that their overseas experiences have brought added value to their work. Included here are skills, information, technology, and networks, which Zweig (2006) calls "transnational capital" (p. 78). Although our research does not provide quantitative evidence of these gains, Zweig's large-scale survey shows that returnees possess skills, information, and research methodologies that are generally unavailable to many stay-at-home faculty.

Self-Perceived Gains

While all participates emphasize the importance of acquiring specific knowledge and skills through education abroad, they give more credit to non-explicit types of knowledge. For example, both Dr Jin (a research fellow in biology) and Dr Zhang (an associate professor in education) stress that most of their gains from overseas training are evident in their ways of thinking and overall orientation of conducting research:

> In the US, everyone is encouraged and stimulated to think. No matter whether your answer is right or wrong, you are encouraged to think in your own way. No one will tell you what is the only and standard answer ... This has great impact on me and now I always tell my students that there is more than one possible answer.
>
> (Interview with Dr Jin, October 3, 2011)

> Now, whenever I encounter a problem, I do not simply think about what is the problem or what the literature says, but considering from another aspect, that is how to solve the problem, and how to find the logics, I mean, scientific logics, behind the way that I solve the problem ... I think this is my primary strength of doing educational research.
>
> (Interview with Dr Zhang, January 2, 2012)

Rather than simply being different, both of them admit that certain "tactic knowledge" (Kim, 2010) gained from transnational experiences would add distinction to their scholarship. This echoes Kim's argument that "the types of knowledge carried by mobile academics are not just *Wissenschaft* but also a way of thinking and the *overall orientation toward life and epistemic paradigms*" (p. 584). Drawing from Simmel's (1971, as cited in Kim, 2010) sociology of space, Kim employs the concept "stranger" to discuss the potential contribution of the traveling academic as both insider and outsider, "to a 'creative destruction' and reconstruction of the paradigms of academic work" (p. 584). Coincidentally, the metaphor of stranger is well embodied in Dr Wang's case.

Dr Wang is a full professor in literacy who had lived in the US for almost 20 years before returning to China. Although she shifted her base to a Chinese university, she still keeps her connections in the US and frequently travels back and forth between the two countries. Dr Wang reflects on the role of traveling on her intellectual work:

> I feel I am 'marginalized' through travelling ... No matter here or there, I always feel myself acting as a stranger ... I think it is the constant state of

jet-lag by flying back and forth, not only physical, but also emotional and intellectual, that gives me a sense of post-modern, I mean, a third eye to see the world ... I always feel myself kind of aloof from the social circuit of my colleagues, no matter in China or in the US. It doesn't mean I refuse to integrate; actually, I think I am integrating quite well, just like fish in the water ... I just don't see the world from the same angles as my colleagues. I think this is an advantage and I enjoy this state of flowing because I know that I am not bounded to any fixed place.

(Interview with Dr Wang, January 16, 2012)

Dr Wang's narratives of both distance and nearness reflect the postcolonial sense of ambiguity and hybridity, and support the emphasis on the relations of traveling and new subjectivities evident in the literature of cultural studies. According to cultural theorists (Bhabha, 1994; Hall, 1996a; Clifford, 1997), it is this interaction of back-and-forth, give-and-take, in the "in-between" space that engenders new subjectivities and creates the possibilities of change. This process is also evident in other participants' narratives, although not manifested as explicitly as Dr Wang's.

Publications and Transnational Networks

In addition to self-perceived gains, participants also highlight the influence of international experiences on their professional practices in terms of publications, transnational networks, and ways of teaching and supervising students. When asked what the major advantages are as being an overseas-educated scholar compared to those who received PhDs locally, many regarded the abilities of publishing in English journals and networking with the international academic community as the most obvious advantages. Dr Wu, a junior professor in engineering, illustrates that what makes him distinguished from his local colleagues is the amount and quality of his English publications:

I have far more publications than them. I think this is due to my strong capacity of doing research, better English academic writing skills, and good social networks in the academic circle abroad. All these together make a total difference. I have published around five or six SCI papers during the past two years, but many people don't have even one paper. The difference is quite obvious.

(Interview with Dr Wu, November 25, 2011)

To Dr Wu, publishing success is partially due to his rigid doctoral training in the US, but is also connected to his acquisition of English language skills and international resources, which are regarded as by-products of mobility experiences (Delicado, 2011). Similarly, Dr Zhou, an assistant professor in computer science, admits that her English proficiency makes it easier to read literature and to write papers, especially for publishing in international journals. As a recent academic returnee, Dr Zhou is actively involved in several joint research programs with her former host institutions and colleagues in the US:

So far, most of my work has been doing with my former advisor and colleagues in the US. I think it's easier to obtain achievements through such kind of collaborations, since we had been working together for a long time and know each other quite well … Actually, I didn't really start to collaborate with my colleagues here. I'm not ready to do that yet. It seems to me that the collaborative relationship here is quite complicated, say, the amount of work, the allocation of fund, and other personnel issues. I think I still need more time to get familiar with the rules here.

(Interview with Dr Zhou, December 15, 2011)

However, not everyone maintains the formal transnational ties of conducting joint research or co-authoring papers. In many cases, informal contacts are more common than actual partnerships. Dr Chen, a research fellow in genomics, remarks, "one good thing I keep from the US were the good friends there. Although we don't have substantial collaborations, we exchange ideas and information constantly. This helps to keep and sharp my academic sensibility."

Transnational connections, in the forms of co-authorship, conducting joint research, organizing conferences, promoting student exchanges and staff visits, and also maintaining informal contacts, are regarded as particular means for knowledge distribution and transformation (Ackers, 2005; Gill, 2005). This suggests that the ongoing transnational activities via academic mobility have changed the role of academics and their engagement with knowledge in the era of globalization (Ackers and Gill, 2008), promoting the process of higher education internationalization.

The Ways of Teaching

In the areas of teaching, both senior and young returnees state that they have actively participated in developing new courses, especially using English as a medium of instruction. This is a response to China's efforts in building world-class universities and internationalizing its higher education. Since the rise of English as the global academic lingua franca, English proficiency has become more practical for academic returnees rather than merely symbolic. Many young returnees are taking on the responsibilities of designing and teaching courses in the English language. Dr Li, a recent PhD graduate in information science, notes that he was assigned to teach one of the most important courses in his department because of his English competence: "It's a challenge but also an opportunities because I am working with the best students."

Similarly, Dr Mao, an assistant professor in anthropology, is also using English to lecture a social science class. However, he emphasizes that what he brings into the traditional classroom is not just English reading materials and English lecturing, but also a different style of teaching and working with students:

I prefer the American way of teacher–student relationship, that is professors are acting as equal friends with their students rather than acting as parents … I am trying very hard to change the stereotypical professor–student relationship in Chinese universities because I believe no one would like to see a professor with a straight face ... I use a seminar-like style of teaching and work hard to create a climate of friendship, equality, and lively inside the classroom ... I find that students actually appreciate this kind of classroom climate where they feel more comfortable, relax, and more willing to express their ideas.

(Interview with Dr Mao, December 5, 2011)

Dr Shen, a senior professor in physics, is also a strong advocate of an equal relationship with students: "I treat my graduate students as a colleague, an independent researcher, rather than an immature scholar." In spite of his busy research schedule, he is generous with his time in mentoring his students. When asked how he has such an enthusiasm for working with students, he answered, "I just followed the same way of what my advisor did on me when I was a doctoral student [in the US]." Dr Shen attributes a great part of his achievements to the mentoring he received in the US and is devoted to mentoring his Chinese students.

The narratives of Dr Li and Dr Shen provide salient examples of how returned academics encounter and take up a different orientations and ways of working with students. They not only bring back their expertise but also the commitment to cultivate the next generation and provide enthusiasm for scientific and academic excellence. However, their re-entering into the academic system in China is not always linear, nor does it lead to favorable outcomes (Delicado, 2011). Returned scholars can also face difficulties and constraints as they negotiate with the established rules and practices in Chinese universities.

The Challenges of (Re)integration and Possibilities of Change

The Challenges of Reintegration

While transnational experience, often regarded as an "added value," brings considerable opportunities and benefits for returnees as flexible social actors, their very flexibilities are simultaneously constrained by the existing power relations and institutional structures. Many participants admit in interviews that the journey home is harder than they anticipate. As Dr Zhang comments, "even though I have prepared for the worst, when it really comes I feel like I'm on the brink of having an emotional breakdown." Dr Zhang had been living in the US for almost ten years and worked as an assistant professor in education before he left the US. Even though he had a successful career in the US, he returned to devote his time to China's educational reform and at the same time to meet family obligations. Dr Zhang went back to China in 2008, but he admits that the transition lasted for almost two years:

It is until this year that I began to feel kind of productive of my work. It seems that I was busy with so many things everyday within the past two years, but very few were really related to my research ... I feel that I am gradually marginalized from the core of my scholarly field.

(Interview with Dr Zhang, January 2, 2012)

The feeling of being marginalized is not uncommon among participants. Dr Zhu, a junior professor in a foreign language department, states that it took her an entire year to reintegrate into the academic community in China: "I lost the network of friends and contacts at home since I have been abroad for so many years … I don't know very well how things work here, so initially, I could not get along well with my colleagues." To Dr Zhu, dealing with *guanxi* (interpersonal relationships) is the most frustrating part about returning:

> I know some of my friends who spent the first few years to build up networks and may not be able to concentrate on their research. It's fearful … I'm not a social person and I really don't like playing with relations. It really distracts attention from work.
> (Interview with Dr Zhu, January 6, 2012)

The theme of *guanxi* appears again and again during the interviews. Many participants acknowledge that the complicated relations within China's academic circle slow its effort to promote institutional and technological innovation. In their article published in *Science*, Shi and Rao (2010), two prominent returnees at China's top universities, claim that the current distribution of funding is determined more by personalized networks than academic ability. They divulge that, "to obtain major grants in China, it is an open secret that doing good research is not as important as schmoozing with powerful bureaucrats and their favorite experts" (p. 1128). Their comments are echoed by many participants who believe that the current funding system not only wastes resources but also rots the spirit of academic freedom.

In addition to the unequal distribution of funding, the gap in academic standards between home and abroad is another problem that frustrates many returnees. After several years working in China, Dr Zhou, a full professor in computer science, points out that the existing academic culture in China is fickle and superficial:

> Different layers of the academic bureaucracy have unrealistic expectations on returnees and want to see accomplishments as soon as possible, as many as possible. They assess scholars based on the numbers of SCI papers they publish and the amount of funds they receive. What's worse, they only account first-author publications, which seriously discourage collaborations.
> (Interview with Dr Zhou, December 30, 2011)

To Dr Zhou, this unhealthy academic culture will eventually pollute its academics and universities will stray from their original goal of academic excellence. When asked if he would consider moving back to the US, he confessed frankly that he is intending to return:

> Sure, I will do it. Actually, I am in the process of going back to [the US]. I have had some experience working in China's academy and I don't think I can integrate into it very well. I know there are lots of benefits within the

system and maybe more opportunity than that in the US. But I can't enter into the core of the circle and also I don't want to involve too much of the politics.

(Interview with Dr Zhou, December 30, 2011)

Dr Zhou regards himself as an outsider who is doing insider business. He devotes most of his time to conducting research and mentoring students. Although he enjoys working with his Chinese students, whom he compliments as self-motivated and hard working, he has decided to resume his earlier life in the US. As a US permanent resident, Dr Zhou has the flexibility of moving freely across borders between the two countries and enjoys the opportunities that come with being a scholar in a globalized world.

However, most returnees are bound to China since they do not have a green card (resident status) to guarantee the flexibility available to Dr Zhou. In order to integrate into China's academic circle, they not only have to adjust quickly to complex networks, but also have to deal with criticism from colleagues who have spent their entire lives in China. According to Wang (2010), the competition between returnees and domestics is intense, with disparities in salary and other benefits. This is true in Dr Shen's case. Dr Shen is an established returnee in physics who returned in 2005 as part of the Thousand Talents Program, which was launched in 2008 as a way to attract experts, academics, and entrepreneurs back to China by providing generous financial subsidies and other material incentives and support. He confesses that what bothers him most is the lack of support from his local colleagues:

> When I first returned from the US, I was quite frustrated because I couldn't understand well why my colleagues were so mean to me … Later, I began to understand them when I put myself in their shoes. If I were them, I might also feel angry that a newcomer is granted more research funding, better housing, faster promotion, or even higher status over me who grew up within the system. I might feel even worse that some returnees might not be as good as I am.
>
> (Interview with Dr Shen, November 11, 2011)

Dr Shen's comment is consistent with what Zweig *et al.* (2004) found in their research on returning Chinese academics. Drawing from their interview data with domestic PhDs, they pointed out that the locals considered it unfair that the government favored "outsiders" through "preferential policies" that undervalue and disadvantage their degrees. These mixed emotions of competition, envy, jealousy, and inferiority/superiority from the local PhDs have hampered the integration of returnees into the academic community, and have also limited the contributions and career opportunities of returnees.

Even though the arrival of returnees causes tensions with domestic intellectuals, Dr Shen is optimistic about China's academic future. He believes that the influx of overseas talent will bring fundamental changes to the nation's academic scene: "I am convinced that Chinese universities can do fantastically well through our collective efforts."

Possibilities of Change

As for the possibilities of change, we find examples of team mobility, whereby the majority of the research team, including the primary investigators, are returnees. This is more common in the natural sciences and applied sciences than in humanities and social sciences. It is often the case that returnees transfer back home to the original host institution's academic culture, such as the PI (principal investigator) system and tenure system in some departments. Dr Hu, a research fellow in brain science, tells us that 80 percent of his colleagues are educated abroad or at least have one-year overseas experiences:

> The level of internationalization of staff in our center is highest among the whole university. We interact and form our own academic circle, which is quite different from other departments … Our center employs PI system, that is every primary investigator, no matter junior or senior researcher, leads his/her team to do research based on one's own research interests. Although we conduct research individually, we share facilities and resources between labs. And also, the facilities here are as good as, some are even better than, my previous lab in the US.
>
> (Interview with Dr Hu, October 17, 2011).

This is an emerging phenomenon, as more and more overseas scholars re-enter China's academia. Their participation and engagement are gradually transforming the cultural landscapes of the research environment in China. Using the metaphor of a third space, we argue that they are creating a new space that enables them to pursue their academic interests at home institutions, while at the same time escaping from certain constraints caused by the conventional rules and cultures embedded in the national structures of higher education in China.

Conclusions

The above narratives illustrate how academic returnees negotiate their trajectories within the structure of Chinese academia and how they reach out to global networks and resources to remake educational spaces and workplaces associated with their profession. Such professionalizing processes have taken particular forms in China due to its current investment in, and global strategies on, knowledge building through the expansion and enhancement of higher education and research.

The findings from this study have highlighted two significant ways in which transnational academic mobility is enacted in the space of higher education in China in terms of returnees' adaption to and potential contributions to the universities and broader academic communities they occupy. Based on the interview data, there is some evidence that these returnees play an important role in their workplace by leading research teams, introducing new ideas, building international networks, overseeing reforms, teaching, research and management. They have helped China gain greater representation in the international academic community and have exerted subtle changes in China's academic culture. However, their integration into Chinese universities is not always linear and beneficial (Delicado, 2011). Their practices can also be constrained by existing power relations and circumstances, which include the bloated bureaucracies of university administration; the non-transparency of China's funding system; complicated interpersonal relationships; resentment among locals against returnees; and the lack of an effective academic culture that consistently supports high-quality teaching and research.

As for the consequences of their mobility, based on the interview data and related literature (Zweig *et al.*, 2004; Zweig, 2006; Pan, 2011), there is some evidence that the returned scholars have exerted significant influences on the internationalization of higher education in China, as well as triggering institution-level changes in the established national patterns of doing research. For example, some international norms and practices have been recognized and partially adopted by Chinese academic communities, such as peer reviews, student evaluation of teaching quality, primary investigators, open recruitment of faculty members at home and abroad, and merit-based promotion and rewards (Mohrman, 2008; Yang and Welch, 2011). There is increasing recognition that China's academics, universities, and knowledge- and technology-producing institutions are gradually integrating into and making contributions to international communities in a more harmonious and substantial way.

There are two major implications of this study. First, theoretically, our views challenge the conventional account of academic mobility based on the notions of brain drain, brain gain, and brain circulation, which is largely informed by the political economy framework on globalization and mobility. Although this framework is useful in explaining the effects of global economic structure in regulating academic exchanges and talent flows, it fails to capture fully the cultural aspects of mobility in which travel subjects are active social agents who negotiate, interpret, and contest their own social worlds (Robertson, 2010). In this regard, we suggest that a postcolonial understanding of the notions of fluidity, hybridity, and connectivity would be helpful to understand international academic mobility and its associated politics. Such a perspective has the potential to explain the "contemporary spaces of movement, connection and disconnection, the complex construction of identities and identifications, unequal geographies of knowledge and power, and the geo-politics of mobility and indeed immobility" (Kenway and Fahey, 2006: 271).

Second, the policy implication of this study is that, although academic mobility should continue to be encouraged by policy, it is also important to pay attention to the outcomes of mobility (Zweig, 2006; Zweig *et al.*, 2008; Robertson, 2010; Delicado, 2011; Pan, 2011). The case of China highlights that it is relatively easy for a government to publicize a policy for attracting overseas talents, but far more difficult to alter the institutional culture to make it not only welcoming to returnees, but also conducive to their growth. While current preferential policies have targeted primarily high-profile, high-position and high-achievement scientists and academics, both the government and universities should pay more attention to young scholars since they will become the backbone of the next generation of academics. Preferential policies should balance the distribution of resources between scholars educated at home and abroad, and also between well-established returnees and new overseas graduates.

Moreover, current policies and investments have placed too much emphasis upon research productivity, short-term effects, and external quantitative evaluation, rather than on the quality of teaching and research (Mohrman, 2008; Li and Chen, 2011). This point is emphasized by most of the interviewees who stress that a free, fair, and transparent academic climate is more important than the actual level of financial support. Finally, an additional aspect of interest for further studies would be an investigation of the situations and perceptions from host communities. To what extent are host institutions interested in and prepared for the increasing trend of returning academic migration? What are the intellectual and emotional attitudes local academics have toward their overseas-educated colleagues? What policies and mechanisms need to be in place in order to improve both the reintegration of returned scholars and their conditions for the benefits of mobility?

Notes

1 The "Hundred Talents Program" (*bairen jihua*), launched in 1994 by the Chinese Academy of Sciences, targets outstanding overseas scholars and researchers for return to work at the Academy. Each returnee is awarded 2 million RMB in research grants, a bonus for housing, and a salary supplement. During 1994 and 2009, 1,846 scholars were identified as "hundred talents." Available online at http://tech.sina.com.cn/d/2010–05–25/08064227561.shtml (accessed January 17, 2012).
2 The "Cheung Kong Scholars Program" (*changjiang xuezhe jiangli jihua*), funded by the Hong Kong tycoon Li Ka-shing, brought 537 scholars from overseas who became leaders in key research fields in the period between 1998 and 2004 (Zweig, 2006). Altogether, between 1998 and 2007, 1,308 scholars were imported to 115 universities as "Cheung Kong Scholars." Available online at www.chisa.edu.cn/zt/yczt/cjxzljh/kx/200812/t20081211_80749.html (accessed January 17, 2012).
3 The "Thousand Talents Program" (*qianren jihua*), launched by the Department of Personnel and Organization in 2008, aims to recruit overseas Chinese intellectuals to prestigious mainland universities and other fields. In the first six rounds of the program 1,510 talents were imported from all over the world, including Hong Kong and Macao, 1,161 as academic research talents and 349 who returned to open businesses in China. Available online at www.1000plan.org/qrjh/article/16778 (accessed January 17, 2012).
4 For details, see www.shanghai.gov.cn/shanghai/node2314/node2319/node12344/userobject26ai18845.html.

References

Ackers, L. (2005) Moving people and knowledge: scientific mobility in the European Union, *International Migration*, 43: 99–131.
Ackers, L. and Gill, B. (2008) *Moving People and Knowledge: Scientific mobility in an enlarging European Union*, Cheltenham: Edward Elgar.
Altbach, P.G. (2004) Higher education crosses borders, *Change*, 36(2): 18–24.
Appadurai, A. (1990) Disjuncture and difference in the global cultural economy, *Theory, Culture & Society*, 7: 295–310.

Appadurai, A. (1996) *Modernity at Large: Cultural dimensions of globalization*, Minneapolis, MN: University of Minnesota Press.

Bauman, Z. (1997) The making and unmaking of strangers, in P. Werbner and T. Modood (eds) *Debating Cultural Hybridity: Multi-cultural identities and the politics of anti-racism*, London: Zed Books, pp. 46–57.

Bhabha, H. (1994) *The Location of Culture*, London and New York: Routledge.

Brown, M. (2002) Intellectual diaspora networks: their viability as a response to highly skilled emigration, *Autrepart*, 22: 167–78.

Chen, Q. and Koyama, J. (in press) Reconceptualising diasporic intellectual networks: mobile scholars in transnational space, *Globalisation, Education and Society*, 10(4).

China National Department of Statistics (2010) *China Statistical Yearbook 2010*, Beijing: China Statistics Press.

Clifford, J. (1997) *Routes: Travel and translation in the late twentieth century*, Cambridge, MA: Harvard University Press.

Collier, S.J. and Ong, A. (2005) *Global Assemblages: Technology, politics and ethics as anthropological problems*, Malden, MA: Blackwell.

Delicado, A. (2011) The consequences of mobility: careers and work practices of Portuguese researchers with a foreign PhD degree, in F. Dervin (ed.) *Analysing the Consequences of International Academic Mobility*, Newcastle: Cambridge Scholars Publishing, pp. 163–80.

Fahey, J. and Kenway, J. (2010) Thinking in a "worldly" way: mobility, knowledge, power and geography, *Discourse: Studies in the Cultural Politics of Education*, 31(5): 627–40.

Gill, B. (2005) Homeward bound? The experience of return mobility for Italian scientists, *Innovation*, 18 (3): 319–37.

Hall, S. (1996a) Introduction: Who needs "identity," in S. Hall and P.D. Gay (eds) *Questions of Cultural Identity*, London: Sage, pp. 1–17.

Hall, S. (1996b) The formation of a diasporic intellectual: interview with Kuan-Hsing Chen, in D. Morley and K.-H. Chen (eds) *Stuart Hall: Critical dialogues in cultural studies*, London: Routledge, pp. 486–505.

Hayhoe, R. and Zhong, W. (1995) Universities and science in China: new visibility in the world community, in A.H. Yee (ed.) *East Asian Higher Education: Traditions and transformations*, Oxford: Pergamon, pp. 122–34.

Kenway, J. and Fahey, J. (2006) The research imagination in a world on the move, *Globalisation, Societies & Education*, 4(2): 261–74.

Kenway, J. and Fahey, J. (2009) *Globalizing the Research Imagination*, London: Routledge.

Kim, T. (2010) Transnational academic mobility, knowledge, and identity capital, *Discourse: Studies in the Cultural Politics of Education*, 31(5): 577–91.

Li, M. and Chen, Q. (2011) Globalization, internationalization and the world-class university movement: the China experience, in R. King, S. Marginson, and R. Naidoo (eds) *Handbook on Globalization and Higher Education*, London: Edward Elgar, pp. 241–55.

Marginson, S. and van der Wende, M. (2007) *Globalisation and Higher Education*, OECD Education Working Paper No. 8, Paris: OECD. Available at http://dx.doi.org/10.1787/173831738240.

Matus, C. (2009) Time as becoming: women and travel, *Journal of Curriculum Theorizing*, 25(3): 7–21.

Meyer, J.B. and Wattiaux, J.P. (2006) Diaspora knowledge networks: vanishing doubts and increasing evidence, *International Journal on Multicultural Societies*, 8(1): 4–24.

Ministry of Education (MOE) of People's Republic of China (2008) *Zhongguo jiaoyu nianjian 2007* (China education yearbook 2007), Beijing: Renmin Jiaoyu Chuban She (People's Education Press).

Mohrman, K. (2008) The emerging global model with Chinese characteristics, *Higher Education Policy*, 21: 29–48.

Ong, A. (1999) *Flexible Citizenship: The cultural logics of transnationality*, Durham, NC: Duke University Press.

Pan, S.Y. (2011) Education abroad, human capital development, and national competitiveness: China's brain gain strategies, *Frontiers of Education in China*, 6(1): 106–38.

Rizvi, F. (2007) Transnational academic flows, in D. Epstein and S. Wright (eds) *Geographies of Knowledge, Geometries of Power: Framing the future*, New York: Routledge, pp. 299–304.

Robertson, S.L. (2010) Critical response to special section: international academic mobility, *Discourse: Studies in the Cultural Politics of Education*, 31(5): 641–47.

Said, E.W. (1994) Intellectual exile: expatriates and marginals, in E.W. Said (ed.) *Representations of the Intellectual: The 1993 Reith Lectures*, London: Vintage, pp. 33–47.

Sassen, S. (2006) *Territory, Authority, Rights: From medieval to global assemblage*, Princeton, NJ: Princeton University Press.

Seidman, I. (2006) *Interviewing as Qualitative Research: A guide for researchers in education and the social sciences*, New York: Teachers College Press.

Shi, Y. and Rao, Y. (2010) China's research culture, *Science*, 329: 1128 (DOI:10.1126/science.1196916).

Solimano, A. (2008) The international mobility of talent and economic development: an overview of selected issues, in A. Solimano (ed.) *The International Mobility of Talent: Types, causes, and development impact*, New York: Oxford University Press, pp. 21–43.

Wang, S. (2010) Talents heed the call of home, *China Daily*, May 18. Available at www.chinadaily.com.cn/china/2010–05/18/content_9860895.htm (accessed December 1, 2011).

Wang, Q.H., Wang, Q. and Liu, N.C. (2011) Building world-class universities in China: Shanghai Jiao Tong University, in P. Altbach and J. Salmi (eds) *The Road to Academic Excellence*, Washington, DC: World Bank, pp. 33–62.

Yang, R. and Welch, A. (2011) A world-class university in China? The case study of Tsinghua, *Higher Education*, July 22, 2011 (DOI 10.1007/s10734–011–9465–4).

Zha, Q. (2011) Understanding China's move to mass higher education: from a policy perspective, in R. Hayhoe, J. Li, J. Lin, and Q. Zha (eds) *Portraits of 21st Century Chinese Universities: In the move to mass higher education*, Hong Kong: Comparative Education Research Centre, University of Hong Kong, and Springer, pp. 20–57.

Zweig, D. (2006) Learning to compete: China's efforts to encourage a reverse brain drain, *International Labour Review*, 145(1–2): 65–89.

Zweig, D., Rosen, S. and Chen, C. (2004) Globalization and transnational human capital: overseas and returnee scholars to China, *The China Quarterly*, 179: 735–57.

Zweig, D., Fung, C.S. and Han, D. (2008) Redefining the brain drain: China's "Diaspora Option," *Science, Technology & Science*, 13(1): 1–33.

Part III

Re-Engaging Professionalism

15 The Politics of Privatization

Insights from the Central Asian University

Sarah Amsler

Introduction

These are turbulent times for higher educators everywhere. They are marked, on the one hand, by a new era of capitalist initiative characterized across the world by the rapid defunding of formerly public education systems, ascendance of academic capitalist knowledge regimes, and transformation of professional identities.[1] On the other hand, there has been a considerable expansion and intensification of political resistance to these processes, with struggles against the privatization and corporatization of education at all levels becoming key elements of social movements contesting the dominance of neoliberal rationalities in labour, health care, social welfare and party politics. It therefore seems that 'the university is in crisis, almost everywhere' (Burawoy, 2011a: 1; see also Calhoun, 2006). And, when we look to the 'growing waves of struggle against these incursions as students, staff and faculty in Europe, Latin America and across the Middle East organize, occupy and resist the transformation' of educational institutions and social life, these appear to be revolutionary times indeed.[2]

It is thus possible to speak in common-sense discourses about the globalization of education (Lauder *et al.*, 2006); to identify the supranational forces of political, economic and cultural change that are redefining the meaning and purpose of higher education; and to point to intricate international networks of resistance to these changes. Despite this framing, however, the lived 'crises of the university' are not homogeneous phenomena. They can thus neither be explained with reference to a uniform assemblage of theoretical tools, nor acted upon using a singular single approach to educational, social or political action. The limits of overextending the 'neoliberalization of education' thesis – which are in fact the often-overlooked *almost* everywheres' in Burawoy's statement above – are particularly visible in the everyday lives of students and educators who are excluded from the global imaginaries that prioritize Northern and Western experiences of academic capitalism, and of those who do not contribute directly to or participate in the new networks of critical educational theory and practice that have emerged within these spaces. For, while these networks are transnational and bring together academics and students from the Middle East and North Africa, Northern and Southern Europe, the United Kingdom, and North and South America, there are still significant absences.

Notably quiet in this movement to resist the subsuming of universities into the capitalist economy and the transformation of educational work into economic labour are voices from post-Soviet and particularly Central Asian societies – which, for the purposes of this chapter, include Kazakhstan, Kyrgyzstan, Mongolia, Tajikistan, Turkmenistan and Uzbekistan. In one sense this is a remarkable exclusion, as the organization, meaning and social purpose of higher learning and research in these relatively young states have been sites of both educational crisis and some of the most ambitious projects to reform universities in the twenty-first century.[3] At the same time, while these reforms have often been connected with the expansion of neoliberal policies, practices and rationalities within the region, they are not reducible to them. Competing political projects such as the state capture of institutions and everyday life, grassroots nation building, and patriarchal and class restoration also play a role.

Across the Central Asian region, therefore, there are some trends that reflect more general tendencies in the neoliberalization of higher education: the formal and informal marketization and privatization of universities; the dominance of policy steering by national governments, international financial institutions and non-governmental organizations; the commodification of knowledge; and the reshaping of professional subjectivities and academic identities by forces external to the local spaces and professions themselves. However, there are also marked differences in what these processes mean and how they articulate with local social, professional and pedagogical practices in post-Soviet universities. There are also differences in how they are normatively evaluated, and in the historical and political traditions that can inform contemporary struggle or reform.[4]

This chapter explores some of the analytical lacunae and political disarticulations that are created when the 'crisis of the university' is theorized through generalized critiques of neoliberalism that do not account for its multiple modalities.[5] I begin by discussing current work on the international 'crisis of the university' and the emergence of globally networked fields of resistance responding to it. I then consider how the experiences of social scientists and humanities scholars in Central Asia and the Caucasus de-centre some of principal criticisms of privatized education within Anglo-European intellectual space – namely, that liberal, state-funded universities are necessarily progressive alternatives to privatized universities – and challenge the transnational alter-education movement to stretch its imagination of the conditions for higher education reform. I then consider how the post-Soviet modalities of neoliberal restructuring in Central Asia, which are dominated by international financial institutions, non-governmental organizations and local power elites, have shaped the transformations of higher education in recent decades. I argue that this has contradictory effects, at once deepening crises in the funding, politics and culture of higher education; providing new opportunities for intellectual and professional development; and contributing to the production of 'justificatory regimes' for commodifying higher education.[6] The chapter concludes on a hopeful note by pointing to cracks in the hegemonic discourses on higher education reform in Central Asia and considers how these might be expanded so that student and scholar activists and critical educators in post-socialist countries are better enabled to participate in 'global communities of concerned academics' (Burawoy, 2011b), a 'global autonomous university' (EduFactory, 2009: 168), or, most importantly, to improve the quality of higher learning in their own universities and places of everyday life.

The (Almost) Global Crisis in Higher Education

There are many ways to name the processes of change that are redefining the character of higher education today. The structural transformation of the public university has been described variously as the ascendance of a new form of 'academic capitalism' (Slaughter and Rhoades, 2004), an intensification in the privatization, marketization, financialization and commodification of knowledge (Canaan and Shumar, 2008; Brown, 2011), and an expansion of capitalist relations into the institution of education itself (Caffentzis and Federici, 2007). While these processes are regarded in some quarters as progressive, they have also been widely criticized as constituting an 'assault on universities' (Bailey and Freedman, 2011), a 'war against democracy and education' (Stevenson, 2011), and the 'unmaking' or 'death' of public higher education as both an idea and institution (Newfield, 2008; Couldry and McRobbie, 2010). And while neoliberal reforms come in 'an almost bewildering array of local trajectories, contingent forms, and hybrid assemblages' of capitalist logic (Peck *et al.*, 2009: 96), it is clear that cumulative processes of neoliberal restructuring around the world have fundamentally redefined the social meaning of higher education, higher knowledge and the academic professions themselves (Olssen and Peters, 2005; Calhoun, 2006; Fischman *et al.*, 2007; Amsler, 2011a, 2011b; Burawoy, 2011a, 2011b).

Higher education reform has been a central element of transnational political agendas to advance the geographical and institutional reach of capitalist relations and values since the 1970s. Following the early debt crises in the United Kingdom and Mexico at this time, the world's major international financial institutions developed a 'package of putatively all-purpose responses to the crisis of international Keynesianism', including a radical defunding of public education at all levels and an imposition of 'efficiencies' in schools, universities and other social institutions (Brenner *et al.*, 2009: 214; see also Henales and Edwards, 2002). Policies and mechanisms of educational privatization were further developed in the punitive 'structural adjustment' programmes subsequently imposed on Latin American and African countries by the World Bank and International Monetary Fund (IMF) during the 1970s and 1980s, which George Caffentzis argues 'tore apart every aspect of their economic and cultural life, leading to an epochal restructuring of the universities' (2011: 27; see also Levidow, 2002; Federici, 2012).[7]

At the same time, the Organisation for Economic Co-operation and Development (OECD) embarked on an ambitious project to transform mass higher education in European societies, transforming it into a system that promoted the social supremacy of vocational knowledge, efficiency and institutional accountability over more critical forms of education (Peters, 2007: 3; Taylor, 1987). By the late 1990s, the principles and practices of neoliberalizing higher education had become reified into a powerful 'gospel' of 'travelling policies' that were implemented almost unilaterally by international and non-governmental organizations in state and economic restructuring at the global level, including in post-Soviet societies. A new 'worldwide reform agenda for the finance and management of universities' was an integral component of the post-Soviet development agenda (Amsler, 2008: 110; see also Johnstone, 1998; Grubb and Lazerson, 2006).

The particular forms, lived experiences and social consequences of this process cannot be generalized. However, it is possible to identify an underlying set of ideal-type principles and practices that broadly parameterize education and the academic professions in this context (Olssen and Peters, 2005; Seddon, 2005; Harvey, 2007; Spring, 2008; Amsler, 2009, 2011a; Shore, 2010). These include:

- the undoing of welfare states and social-democratic projects in which public higher education served a particular purpose and where its existence was protected through public funds (particularly through 'shock therapy', loan conditionality, structural adjustment and programmes of fiscal austerity);
- the rapid expansion of fee-paying students, tuition-dependent universities, profit-producing educational practices, and corporate sponsorship within this broader context of defunding and privatization;
- the standardization and coordination of degrees across 'European' and 'global' space to increase levels of competition in the 'knowledge economy';
- the propagation of new values of economism and efficiency, institutional auditing, short-term and 'shock-style' educational reform, and the casualization of academic and student labour;
- the pursuit of elite 'world-class' status through the international measurement, ranking and marketing of universities;
- the commodification of knowledge, decreasing public interest in the intellectual content of curricula, and decline of commitments to social justice in education and education for social justice; and
- the cultivation of new, 'entrepreneurial' educational subjects who are prepared for precarious work in the 'new capitalism', and of consumer-subjects who regard learning, knowledge and skills primarily as tradable market commodities.

The *result* of all this, according to Craig Calhoun (2006: 8), is that 'the costs of higher education have shot up, teaching has been marginalized in many institutions' priorities (if not their rhetoric), and universities appear less as producers of public goods and more as distributors of private ones'. Consequently, spaces for the critical intellectual and professional development of higher educators are being foreclosed as teachers become more like contractual workers, are required to constantly adapt their skills and identities to the vicissitudes of market demands in universities, and begin to conceptualize the value of knowledge through abstract standardized criteria of intellectual capital and 'value added' labour (Clegg, 2010; Davies and Bansel, 2010). Perhaps most significantly for the purposes of this chapter, neoliberal forms of governance in universities tend to engender the de-professionalization and loss of autonomy of academics and higher educators (Olssen and Peters, 2005; Silova, 2009).

From the late 1990s, and particularly in response to the first (signings of the) Bologna Accords, which signalled an institutional locking-in of transnational power, localized movements of critique and opposition to these processes began to intensify in small pockets of resistance around the world. By the middle of the first decade of the twenty-first century, some of the most substantial and transnational movements for public education in recent history began to articulate. From the heavily policed street demonstrations in Greece in 2010 and 2011 to the beleaguered occupations of campus and public spaces in Europe, Latin America, the US and the UK in 2011 and 2012, and from direct action to the politicization of university life and the development of radical higher education outside formal institutions, there is a palpable feeling that 'there is a new mood in the air' (Solomon and Palmieri, 2011: 6; see also Amsler, 2011a). Calhoun (2006: 8) has argued that 'versions of the same issues are reshaping education around the world'. If so, what versions are now shaping the work and professional identities of educators in Central Asian universities?

University Crises, Decentred

In the summer of 2011, these questions travelled with me as I left to teach at a summer school in Turkey for scholars from Central Asia and the Caucasus, organized by the Central Asia and Caucasus Research and Training Initiative (an Open Society Institute programme). The school coincided with a particularly intensive wave of student-led struggles to challenge advances in the privatization, marketization and commodification of higher education in the UK, US and across Europe (Amsler, 2011b). As I was involved in the British actions and studying developments in the European struggles, I was eager to discuss both this movement and the alternative education projects with young social scientists and humanities scholars working in post-socialist space. What were their positions on the privatization of universities? How far did critiques of neoliberalization, ascendant in the global North, travel to post-Soviet contexts? Could alliances, affinities and critical professional relations be developed between and among us? I went seeking fresh readings of the global crisis of the university, wanting to hear other experiences of working through a period of major economic political restructuring within academic institutions, and hoping to discover novel strategies of analysis, critique and resistance from the quieter spaces of the globalized commons. What emerged instead were the limits of the 'radical' critiques of neoliberalization that seem so compelling in my own conditions of work and everyday life, and the poverty of understanding within these critiques of the particularities of struggles in and for higher education outside the geopolitical centres of the alter-education movement.

Most of my colleagues in the seminar were unfazed to hear that American, British and European universities were being transformed from institutions of learning, research and civic life into institutions of economic production and human capital. It was not that discourse on the global 'crisis of the university' was old news. Rather, it seemed surprising that the privatization, marketization and commodification of universities could be legitimate sources of such levels of anger and anxiety, rather than being regarded as business-as-usual or, indeed, indicators of national progress and accomplishment. In the first instance, the impoverished material conditions of many universities in the region pale in comparison with even the most underfunded public universities in the global North, with students wanting for computer technology, books and journals, appropriate buildings and, in some cases, even heat, with teachers' salaries that are described as merely 'symbolic' (Dzhaparova, 2005; DeYoung, 2007; Amsler, 2009; Silova, 2009). Second, in environments where public dissent on the scale of the recent university struggles in Euro- and Latin American spaces is not only unimaginable but often regarded conservatively, some scholars were incredulous that students – much less professional academics – were protesting at all. Perhaps most significantly, however, the radical critiques of neoliberal politics were entirely out of joint with the argument, promulgated by international institutions, non-governmental organizations and local elites, that the marketization of universities is the only viable means for improving the quality of higher education within Central Asian societies (Amsler, 2008, 2009). For today, more than two decades after the 'immediate post-collapse excitement', the liberal education reform discourse in which privatization is packaged is still often regarded as a 'contemporary, relevant, positive globalising force' (Baker, 2011: 1053).

In this context, and in the absence of alternative narratives, blunt critiques of the privatization and marketization of the university can seem like outbursts of entitlement or cruel attacks on hope. This is particularly so when, as Artemy Magun describes in the Russian context, 'the opposition perceives [a state] regime as corrupt and authoritarian and the liberal-democratic opposition often combines the language of neoliberalism (denouncing economic "inefficiency" or the lack of transparency) with slogans of "liberal" democracy' (2010: 3). In our seminar, some seminar participants agreed that it made sense for students to occupy buildings in Athens, California, London and Madrid. Here, they said, existing forms of knowledge, educational policies, academic freedoms and progressive teaching practices seem to stand a chance of being preserved either within formal universities or in autonomous educational spaces. But in Almaty, Bishkek, Dushanbe and Tblisi, academics are more directly engaged in other struggles against different techniques of power and structures of inequality, such as the personal profiteering of academic elites, the imposition of unrelenting and unaccountable state control over curricula and assessment, the routine sale of grades and degrees on informal credential markets, wage poverty and work exhaustion among professional educators, isolation of academics from supranational professional communities, an evacuation of interest in intellectual and pedagogical work among many students and teachers, the severance of links between higher learning and social mobility and, in some places, the dilapidation of physical structures in the wake of conflict and economic collapse. Our conversation also confirmed what has already been demonstrated in the studies of Iveta Silova (2009), Alan DeYoung (2011) and others: that there is both a crisis of de-professionalization in Central Asian education, and a deep desire on the part of higher educators to assume control of the meaning and purpose of universities.

It would be possible to explain each of these problems in relation to wider neoliberalizing processes; to demonstrate, for example, that global reform agendas have often led to the emergence of extreme forms of educational inequality, privatization and commodification that are unconstrained by alternative moral economies, democratic principles or social regulation (Buzgalin, 2006; Upchurch *et al.*, 2011). But neoliberalizing processes have contradictory effects that also include the fulfilment of long-standing needs and desires for geopolitical recognition, 'technological innovation, expanded global networks for human rights and social activism, and ... alternative forms of communication and information' (Fischman and Haas, 2009: 567). For higher educators, such reforms may also bring new individualized opportunities to study at prestigious universities, participate in exclusive professional development projects, and join intellectual conversations from all over the world. From the vantage of everyday life in Central Asian universities, the neoliberal discourses that have taken root in the region – those that promise bureaucratic transparency (often through the intensification of regulated governance), formal individual equality of opportunity, rapid economic prosperity, and the opportunity to access the material and political privileges of membership in global society – are therefore often interpreted as not only legitimate but desirable alternatives to the material desolation, intellectual marginalization, geopolitical isolation and abuses of political power that are common features of the academic profession in the region today.

In other words, problems of higher education in Central Asia emerge within a specific social and historical context. Generalized discourses on the 'crisis of the university' that appear to explain such problems in the contexts in which they are produced therefore do not automatically offer the same analytical insights elsewhere. My discussions with colleagues from the region thus usefully amplified a dilemma that tends to be muted in work focusing on the Euro-American university: how can we liberate education not only from the dehumanizing vicissitudes of capitalist markets, but also from dependencies on corrupt, managerialist and authoritarian states, and from uncritical discourses of the 'new capitalism' that promise to dissolve the repressions of both?[8] From where I sat then on the coast of the Aegean Sea – distant from campus occupations, demonstrations and picket lines; outside an ordinarily comfortable consensus on the evils of the marketization of education; and funded by one of the world's most notorious capitalist speculators and celebrated liberal philanthropists – I began to see that even the most exciting forms of alternative higher education could be regarded as curious forms of voluntary exclusion from the most visible promise of inclusivity on offer – the neoliberal utopia of 'world space'.

A Very Post-Soviet Neoliberalization

UNESCO has recently claimed that market reforms have had a positive impact on universities in Central Asia; that universities were made 'free to set up their own governing structures ... hire their own staff' [and] transform curricula to 'suit new social realities' (Varghese, 2009: 11–12). But how do these dominant processes of educational reform shape the possibilities for critical forms of education to flourish, for students and teachers to form meaningful educational relationships with one another, or for the creation and defence of spaces for critical academic work within the region?

The term 'neoliberalism' now signifies a complex constellation of ideas, discourses, policies and practices that, while appearing to press in a common direction, are also endlessly assembling and disarticulating in concrete, situated spaces (Larner, 2000; Bohle and Gerskovitz, 2006; Ong, 2007; Brenner *et al.*, 2009; Peck *et al.*, 2009). Ethnographers working in Central Asian education have thus argued that 'although the discourses [of educational reform] may be at least aspirationally "global", the contexts in which they are encountered and adopted are profoundly varied' (Reeves, 2005: 7; see also Verdery, 1996; Humphrey, 2002; Liu, 2003; Silova, 2005; DeYoung, 2011). However, there is a curious contradiction between this recognition of contingency, on the one hand, and the dominance of neoliberal discourses on education reform, which some critics suggest have 'become practically identical to that of African countries', on the other (Silova, 2005: 51; see also Asanova, 2006). Accounting for the persistence of this 'grand narrative of the "transition" to free markets or representative democracy' (Liu, 2003) in Central Asian higher education is thus an important part of making visible spaces for resistance and alterity.

It is often felt that the collapse of the Soviet Union simultaneously left a vacuum of institutional and cultural substance – thus creating an open field of play for a 'no-holds-barred, fang-and-claw capitalism' (Solomon and Palmieri, 2011: 2) – and opened space for the resurgence of pre-modern forms of political power. To be sure, it was the 'perceived vulnerability, exhaustion and crisis of an inherited institutional order ... that opened up a space for neoliberalized forms of regulatory experimentation' in Central Asia as it had done previously in post-colonial societies (Peck *et al.*, 2009: 114). However, in addition to the social problems wrought by systemic crisis in post-Soviet society, national independence also produced new collective desires for both autonomy and recognition. Once society was apparently liberated from authoritarian forms of political, social and cultural power, alternative social futures seemed possible: for individual and family prosperity, the expansion of civil liberties, increased international communication, and the freedom to explore different ideas and ways of life.

Many of these hopes and desires, however, were rapidly appropriated into neoliberal projects, ideologies and imaginaries that promised to fulfil them, thus giving rise to intoxicating justifications for even the most extreme initiatives of neoliberal reform (Magun, 2010). International financial institutions such as the World Bank, Asian Development Bank, IMF and OECD; international organizations such as the United Nations and European Union; and non-governmental organizations such as the Open Society Institute saw in Central Asia a new field of opportunities for the expansion of conditions for market relations in formally liberal-democratic states.[9] The political and economic spaces into which the former Soviet Socialist Republics emerged as sovereign states were therefore not just neutrally 'global,' but were in fact fields upon which increasingly expansionist and divisive capitalist initiatives had begun to struggle for influence and control. What parameters does this create for the development of the academic professions in Central Asian societies and, in turn, for the future of higher education itself?

The Case of Kyrgyzstan

Considering approaches to university reform in the Kyrgyz Republic offers one way of exploring this question. The privatization of state universities and the creation of new private ones are issues of considerable debate within Kyrgyzstani cultural politics. While they were once framed as parts of a bigger picture in which state enterprises and assets from land and natural resources to health, housing and education were privatized through various means during the 1990s, most conversations now revolve around the imperatives of 'modernizing' and 'internationalizing' higher education (Musabaeva, 2008). This debate is often couched in narrow terms: not *whether* to privatize and marketize higher education, but *how* best to do so.

In the wake of defunding from the former Soviet centre, the imposition of strict 'efficiency' regulations from international lenders, and the emergence of new opportunities for creating personal wealth through individual 'entrepreneurship' and corruption, political elites have had little sympathy for appeals to develop any new form of public higher education here. As early as 1999, one Education Minister declared that the country's universities should 'stop crying' for public funding and 'turn their eyes to the world' (Amsler, 2008: 105); a decade later, the Minister of Economy asserted that 'it is necessary to let universities go on a free voyage, in order to allow market selection to choose the strongest universities' (Musabaeva, 2008: 1). The privatization of higher education – here, in Darwinian-inflected metaphors – is pitched as an already-accomplished strategy for national survival.

But this is not privatization in any clear-cut sense of the term. While the number of universities in Kyrgyzstan has quadrupled since independence, most state-funded universities have not officially been privatized. An agenda to incorporate them was legislated in 2003, but has lain dormant in parliamentary politics since (Musabaeva, 2006, 2008; Kargaev, 2008). However, most state universities began charging formal tuition fees after the cessation of Soviet funding. The balance of 'contract' (fee-paying) students at the Kyrgyz National University, for example, tipped from approximately 30 per cent in 1995 to 87 per cent in 2009 (Varghese, 2009: 21), and by some accounts nearly 90 per cent of all students are now paying for tuition nationwide (Musabaeva, 2006). International financial organizations regarded this organic shock therapy as a success: educators' salaries fell (in some cases to poverty levels), students' tuition payments increased, the number of higher education institutions and courses expanded, and government ministries looked suitably distanced from the emerging educational markets that they were being encouraged or coerced to create.

A closer look at everyday life within the universities, however, suggests that, rather than being a market*ized* institution of learning that is more closely aligned with economic production, the university has been transformed into both a commodity and a market *in its own right*. Privatization processes take a variety of forms in universities here, including the reorganization of universities into personal business enterprises for politically powerful rectors and academics. Cashing in on the public belief that higher education remains a force for development, and unconstrained by either financial regulations or political forces within civil society to defend alternative principles of educational and social justice, they are able to extract increasing amounts of money and favours from students and their families for increasingly poor education (DeYoung, 2011: 11; see also Musabaeva, 2006, 2008; Osipian, 2009). Academics teaching in these institutions are now often paid so little that many are forced to work in two, three or four precarious posts simply in order to survive; some take up additional work outside the university in international organizations and businesses, or more incongruously in the bazaar (Niyozov, 2006). It is difficult to maintain a coherent professional identity in such conditions. Amid such hyper-precariousness, privatizing processes have created what Madeleine Reeves has called a 'new regime of value' in education – one that intensifies the commodification of knowledge from something with intrinsic use-value into a commodity that becomes valuable only upon its exchange for goods, services or financial returns. Or, as one Kyrgyz lecturer put it:

> in Soviet times it was enough when you were toasting someone on their birthday to wish for them that their children study well at school, because if that were the case then their future was taken care of, now when you say a toast, you wish them first of all money – money to pay for the school, to pay for the university, to pay so that they can get a nice job [literally, a 'warm place,' *teploe mestechko*]. It's not education you need to get a job now; it's money to get an education!
>
> (Reeves, 2005: 12)

These are not purely neoliberal problems; research into the 'spirit of capitalism' in late-Soviet economics assures us of the hybrid nature of political economy here (Paretskaya, 2010). Emerging tendencies of corruption within universities during the late Soviet period, for example – what one Kyrgyz professor of sociology has called erosions of *intellektual'niy bezsovestniy* (intellectual honesty) and professional ethics – are sometimes regarded as effects of earlier incursions of market principles into socialized space. 'From the 1970s', she says:

> they began to develop a shadow economics, shadow health service, shadowy education. And they said that now education was free of charge, but nevertheless it became not free of charge. It was [paid for] by some private persons who could manage … entering into the universities.
>
> (Asanova, 2003)

As Bikbov argues in the Russian context, 'the commercial turn that followed the political liberalization of the late 1980s brought an end to high hopes for an intellectually valid and socially just educational system' (2010: 5).

However, while there were criticisms of such tendencies during the early stages of market initiatives in republics such as Kyrgyzstan (Mitrofanskaya, 1999; DeYoung, 2007), the histories, imaginaries and systems of value that were once considered alternatives, such as including collective development, orthodox historical materialism, *vospitaniye* (moral education) and education for social cohesion – were delegitimized in development discourses and by nationalizing power elites soon after the Soviet collapse, and replaced by ideals of individualized academic 'entrepreneurship' (Silova, 2009). Even the most rhetorical promises of the 'basic contract' of socialism, like those made in the post-war 'edu-deal' of Western European welfare states, were broken (Liu, 2003; Reeves, 2005: 11).

Perhaps the most pressing problem in higher education in Kyrgyzstan is thus not that universities are marginalized in global trends of neoliberal restructuring. Rather, the particular constellation of unregulated marketization, empowerment of informal cronyism within state bureaucracies, and development of quasi-colonial dependencies on neoliberal agencies of foreign intervention have enabled – or rather, have not constrained – the emergence of some particularly 'ugly' forms of privatization (Musabaeva, 2008). As in other post-Soviet societies, it is not the case that capitalist commercialization and state regulation are competing against forces of autonomy and critical knowledge production. Rather, there seems to be a power struggle between 'two rival models of commercialization of the educational sector, namely a "black" and private model versus a centralized and seemingly more transparent manner' (Bikbov, 2010: 3). In other words, Bikbov is arguing that, although buying a university degree on the informal market and paying tuition to attend university in almost guaranteed exchange for one at the end of term are not equivalent practices, they are nevertheless grounded in a similar logic of commodity exchange. Both are expressions and effects of market relations in education, both reduce knowledge to its commodity form, and neither is conducive to the development of critical intellectual work or educational professionalism (Bikbov, 2010: 3).

In Kyrgyzstan, as across much of the region, international lenders, aid organizations and foreign academic partners have responded to this situation by urging universities to 'privatize better'. The theory is that, by wresting control of institutional resources and educational programmes from corrupt individuals and governments, more 'democratic' experts, organizations and businesses will be able to ensure that the 'correct' forms of privatization are put in place. This presents itself as a simple solution to profiteering in universities because it promises to replace informal authority with individual autonomy, bureaucratic standardization with forms of governance encouraging a limited tolerance of difference, coerced conformity with the encouragement of independent and creative thought, opaque favouritism with systems of standardized assessment, didactic pedagogies with the facilitation of active participation, and geopolitical marginalization with inclusion in local and global economies.

Yet the neoliberal paradigms of educational reform that promise all this are precisely those that academics and students have been challenging across the world. The reclamation and re-imagining of higher learning in Central Asia today clearly cannot be advanced simply by embracing the same agendas of privatization, marketization and commercialization that are contributing to the deprofessionalization of the academic professions and corroding conditions for critical, democratic education elsewhere. Nor can alternative approaches to reform be invented by simply applying knowledge that has already been produced to theorize these processes, which are rooted in historically specific intellectual traditions and struggles against particular developments in capitalist relations, and which do not necessarily account for alternative modalities of neoliberalization.

Cracks in the Crisis of the Central Asian University

Many academics now seem resigned to the privatization, marketization and commodification of higher education in Central Asia. But there are also localized, interstitial, micro-political refusals to conform to the dominant logics of practice – what John Holloway (2010) calls 'cracks'. These not only have the potential to disrupt the dominant justificatory regimes, but map on to more generalized tactics for challenging neoliberal agendas in higher education and other social institutions. Les Levidow suggests that there are four such counter-strategies that may travel and take different forms across contexts: demonstrating links among neoliberal reforms, linking resistances across constituencies and places, de-reifying information and communication technologies, and developing alternatives (2002: 12–13). The remainder of this chapter will explore where such counter-strategies are at work in Kyrgyzstan, and consider the implications this may have for the future of the university professions.

There are some excellent examples of work analysing the linkages between micro-reforms, incremental changes and practices of everyday power. 'Critics need to demonstrate,' Levidow argues, 'how all these aspects are linked, how they change the content of academic work and learning, and how they arise from efforts to discipline labour for capital, as part of a global agenda' (2002: 12). We may look to new narratives of critique and resistance of marketization that are buried in the rejected archives of Soviet social research and early post-Soviet media, as well as to more recent critical theorizations of educational privatization, aid and reform in the region (Reeves, 2005; Musabaeva, 2006, 2008; Zholdoshalieva and Shamatov, 2008; Baker, 2011; DeYoung, 2011). Such work becomes particularly illustrative when engaged through Levidow's third counter-strategy, which is to 'de-reify' learning resources by familiarizing ourselves with the histories, politics and possible uses of materials (and, in this case, imaginaries) that are presented as ideologically neutral (2002: 13). This is particularly vital where nuanced distinctions between liberal democratic and neoliberal education reform are collapsing in such ways that the relationships between pedagogy, education and institutional financing are obscured (see, for example, Amsler (2009) on the symbolic politics of 'student-centred' teaching methods, or Reeves (2005) on the implementation of credit-hour programmes in Kyrgyzstan).

A second strategy for developing professional identities beyond the neoliberal frame is 'linking resistances across constituencies and places' and building relationships of communication and solidarity between professional groups that are presently fragmented and divided. Here, the goal is to 'turn ourselves into collective subjects of resistance and learning for different futures' (Levidow, 2002: 12). Although there have been a number of serious university struggles in other areas of the former Soviet Union (Magun, 2010), there have been few in Central Asia. One example of an act that could provide opportunities for such linkages to be made in university space is the recent work by a small group of students to challenge the imposition of a major increase in tuition fees at American University.[10] The university administration argued that the increase was necessary to 'increase AUCA's prestige and attract international students, as well as to stop relying on donations' from the Open Society Institute and USAID (Mambetshaeva, 2011). While many students receive some type of US-style financial aid, the group was nevertheless 'afraid that most students of AUCA can't afford such rapid tuition changes [and] will leave this wonderful university' (We Are Against, 2011). One member drafted an open letter to the administration, suggesting that, while the group did not categorically condemn the rise, the university had failed both to acknowledge the difficulties that the increased fees would place on poor students from rural villages, and to publicize compelling reasons for its decision. 'Open up your books,' it urged, 'open up your intentions. Let us see for [ourselves] what picture you see, and let us share the same opinion as you do' (We Are Against, 2011).

While this protest appears to have been ephemeral, the group is still open and the online dialogue that it created indicates possible points of critical articulation with wider analyses and experiences of the crisis of the university. 'Thumbs up for the AUCA students finally standing up against commodification and commercialization of the education that was promised to be emancipating and community-oriented,' wrote one member. 'We should definitely challenge these neoliberal values and attitudes to education as a product and students as consumers' (We Are Against, 2011). These are spaces for mutual learning with those confronting similar processes elsewhere in the world, in which university students and academics might begin to engage critically beyond the existing parameters of their institutional professional identities. The question is, how can they be opened up and transformed into alternative radical 'pedagogies which enhance critical citizenship, cultural enrichment and social enjoyment through learning', ultimately linking them to the needs of localized struggles (Levidow, 2002: 13)?

There are also deeper tensions in the politics of Kyrgyzstani higher education that offer spaces for critique and re-imagination. In his ethnographic study of life in Kyrgyzstani universities, DeYoung (2011) highlights a perplexing problem. Despite 'catastrophic' failures in secondary education, a severance of the relationship between higher learning and labour, continual increases in private tuition fees, and widespread corruption among educators and administrators, there seems to be an *increasing* demand for higher education among Kyrgyzstani youth and their families. Much of this is driven by economic necessity. However, despite public knowledge that at present the primary value of a university degree is its exchange value in an unstable marketplace of social capital, many people still attend university in the hope of becoming 'educated'. To some extent, therefore, it is the *desire* for non-instrumentalized knowledge and principles of non-market-based intellectual integrity that makes them marketable commodities.

There is a further irony. Because non-instrumentalized knowledge is regarded as luxurious here in this environment where so much is commodified, intellectual freedom, educational access and critical thought have become 'niche markets' – and these have developed primarily in the most systematically privatized and transnationally networked universities in the region. These institutions are valued more highly than others by students, their families and many academics, not only because they offer adequate material conditions for academic work. It is also because they sell the opportunity for individuals to study, teach and conduct research in less obviously marketized and commodified ways, and frame this opportunity as part of wider projects to advance individual freedom, social progress and globalization. It is, even more ironically, from within these institutions that some of the strongest critiques of privatized higher education are now emerging, and here where there may be possibilities for rearticulating educational privilege as an educational right and social necessity.

But the difficulty of articulating such a critique from within is intensifying. In a recent turn of events, for example, the government of Kazakhstan moderated its dual agenda of privatization and state control to build a new, internationally networked, state-financed and institutionally autonomous university. Nazarbaev University (named after the country's president-for-life) is broadly exempted from governmental control over curriculum and administration, offers full test-based student scholarships, offers first-year foundation courses designed and taught by University College London and is formally affiliated to dozens of elite universities in other countries. It is a nationalist internationalizing project designed to break into the more exclusive world of academic capitalism. The creation of the university represents a shift away from the earlier, more localized and developmentalist logics of neoliberal restructuring in Central Asia towards a newer agenda that reflects the power of global ranking and marketization that is being inculcated around the world through a dense network of multinational financial institutions, non-governmental organizations, universities and media (Amsler and Bolsmann, 2012). It also indicates a shift in the priorities of foreign universities, from either exercising neo-colonial 'soft power' or salvaging a 'generation at risk' during the 1990s, towards strengthening mutual interests in the development of global academic capitalism through the creation of hyper-elite, competitive and globally networked super-universities (Silova, 2005). Joshua Kucera (2011) has argued that some US-based academics who are associated with the university hope 'to establish relationships with a country that, thanks to its booming oil- and gas-fuelled economy, is poised to be an important business center of the future'. For Kazakhstani students and academics, there are promises that this could be the next big step towards full integration into 'world space'. Kucera (2011) points out that there is evidence of a political slippage, though. For while the internationalization of higher education was once justified through imperfect discourses of liberal democracy, the new rhetoric aligns nationalist with capitalist interest without apology – and, as a result, 'notions like "democracy and civic education" went unmentioned' in academics' own explanations of what they do.

In contexts such as this, sweeping critiques of the privatization of higher education, which have the potential to be productively disruptive and prefiguratively transformative in the historically and socially specific contexts from which they often emerge, may be less useful for making sense of the impacts of neoliberalization on higher education in Central Asia. With some exceptions, neoliberalizing processes are here welcomed as alternatives to some of the very educational and social crises that, elsewhere, are understood as consequences of neoliberalist theories, practices and policies themselves. But it is at this point of tension that we may find the greatest possibilities for producing critical, comparative analyses of the structural transformation of higher education in post-socialist and late-capitalist societies; here where the experiences of Central Asian educators and students become vital for advancing understandings of the politics of privatization more generally. These experiences make visible the lacunae of Eurocentric narratives of the 'global' crisis of the university. They illustrate that the transformative potential of university struggles and autonomous alternatives (such as free universities) weakens in places where even the most basic social institutions are already interstitial, autonomous and precarious. Much of the power of contemporary critiques of the 'crisis of the university' is rooted either in collective demands for post-welfare states to recognize their previous commitments to socialized higher education and autonomous forms of educational professionalism, or in self-organized projects in autonomous education which challenge beliefs that universities must be subordinated to either state or market principles. In Central Asian societies, the framing of all socialism as Soviet socialism and the concentration of elite power within the state means that there is little basis for the first demand. As for the second, the extreme precariousness of educational professionals and students means that the economic, professional and political risks of attempting critical or autonomous action are particularly acute.

For their part, the experiences of students and educators in Central Asia demonstrate the limits of romanticized imaginaries of neoliberal capitalism as a model of progressive development. They offer practical illustrations of how repressing knowledge of the complexity of these neoliberal rationalities can undermine institutional democracy and professional development rather than strengthening them. The narrowing of discourses on the 'transition to the market economy' in turn occludes critical awareness of the slide towards authoritarian forms of governance in universities in the capitalist global North. The extant bodies of academic work on the transformations of the university as an institution are not replete with records of accomplishment in the advance of socially useful knowledge, rigorous intellectual development or professional life. They are rather dominated by the valorization of efficient management and control of corporate universities on the one hand, and on the other with critiques of the managerial takeover of higher education, the transformation of places of creative exploration and knowledge production into institutions of economic production, the impoverishment and standardization of curricula, the ascendance of instrumentally consumerist orientations towards learning, the obsessions with measuring the quality of knowledge work through alienating metrics, the erosion of free speech and tolerance for dissent within universities, the loss of professional

autonomy to audit and accountabilities, and the weakening of the social democratic mission of teaching and research on the whole.

This is not the 'world space' that most academics in Central Asia aspire to
inhabit, and it is not one that any national or international system of higher
education needs. But it is the underside, or rather the risk, of the form of global
education that is presently imagined. My conversations with colleagues working
in the region suggest that, while the necessity of alternatives is clear, we do not
necessarily have sufficient collective knowledge or vocabularies to begin developing them together. Drawing attention to a recent essay by William Brehm and
Iveta Silova (2010) may clarify this point. In it, they draw on Jacques Rancière's
radically democratic conception of the 'ignorant schoolmaster' to make an
extremely convincing case for dismantling the colonializing frames of 'rescue',
'expertise' and 'development' that continue to dominate much international
support for educational reform, and for replacing them with frames of intellectual, professional and social equality. What type of collaborations do we need to
make these conversations and practices possible? If we are to globalize communities of concerned academics and build the autonomous university – one in which
educators can re-imagine non-capitalist forms and purposes of higher education,
criticalize learning and assume control of their own professional development –
we must learn not only how to actually learn from one another, but how to find
ways of doing this together. This learning and doing will need to take new forms
of collaboration that transgress the limits of both developmentalist and neoliberal approaches to professional partnership or educational 'borrowing', and that
make it possible for educators to theorize and respond to the multiple crises of
the university in autonomous, collective and socially meaningful ways.

Notes

1   The theory of academic capitalism, which is outlined by Slaughter and Rhoades
    (2004), accounts for the gradual integration of higher educational institutions into
    the capitalist economy. The concept of capitalist initiative, which must always be
    understood in relationship with the struggles made to resist it, is from Tronti (1965).
2   For articulations between the education struggles, the 'Arab Spring' uprisings and
    Occupy movements, see EduFactory Collective (2011), Curcio and Roggero (2011)
    and Kumar (2011: 132).
3   For a brief discussion of what the Kyrgyz Ministry of Education and Science has
    referred to as the 'crisis of the pedagogical cadre' in Kyrgyzstan, see Silova (2009).
    Other forces of transformation and crisis that have affected educational work in
    these regions, including war, civil conflict and political revolution, are unfortunately
    beyond the scope of this chapter. For an example of work that addresses this dimen-
    sion, see Freedman (2007).
4   For further analysis of the structural transformation of the university since the 1970s,
    see Olssen and Peters (2005), Calhoun (2006), Fischman *et al.* (2007) and Amsler (2011a).
5   This chapter is informed by a theory of the 'variegated' modalities of neoliberalizing
    processes, developed by Brenner *et al.* (2009) as an alternative to the 'varieties of capi-
    talism' approach.
6   Luc Boltanski and Eve Chiapello (2007) define the concept of 'justificatory regimes'
    as coherent assemblages of principles, standards, values and 'tests' that are used to
    evaluate the fairness of a particular set of systemic relationships, in particular, capi-
    talist relations.

7 For a discussion of the World Bank and education, see Torres (2002: 374–5).
8 See Norman Fairclough's work (Chiapello and Fairclough, 2002) for a definition of 'new capitalism'.
9 Carlos Alberto Torres makes a useful distinction between 'liberal' and 'neoliberal' states; see Torres on 'The state, privatization and educational policy' (2002).
10 To view some of the online discussion within the group, see its Facebook page at www.facebook.com/#!/groups/122839607785321/.

References

Amsler, S. (2008) Higher education reform in post-Soviet Kyrgyzstan, in J. Canaan and W. Shumar (eds) *Structure and Agency in the Neoliberal University*, London: Routledge, pp. 101–28.

Amsler, S. (2009) Promising futures? Education as a symbolic resource of hope in Kyrgyzstan, *Europe-Asia Studies*, 61(7): 1189–206.

Amsler, S. (2011a) Beyond all reason: spaces of hope in the struggle for England's universities, *Representations*, 116: 62–87.

Amsler, S. (2011b) Strivings towards a politics of possibility, *Graduate Journal of Social Sciences*, 8(1): 67–87.

Amsler, S. and Bolsmann, C. (2012) University ranking as social exclusion, *British Journal of Sociology of Education*, 33(2): 283–301.

Asanova, J. (2006) Emerging regions, persisting rhetoric of educational aid: the impact of the Asian Development Bank on educational policy making in Kazakhstan, *International Journal of Educational Development*, 26: 6.

Asanova, U. (2003) Unpublished interview with the author, 4 June, Bishkek, Kyrgyzstan.

Bailey, M. and Freedman, D. (eds) (2011) *The Assault on Universities: A manifesto for resistance*, London: Pluto Press.

Baker, N.J. (2011) Post-Soviet universities as development in practice: local experience and global lessons, *Development in Practice*, 21(8): 1050–61.

Bikbov, A. (2010) How Russian universities became the future of world education, *Universities in Crisis: Blog of the International Sociological Association (ISA)*, 3 May. Available at www.isa-sociology.org/universities-in-crisis/?p=441 (accessed 9 January 2011).

Bohle, D. and Gerskovitz, B. (2006) Neoliberalism, embedded neoliberalism, and neocorporatism: paths towards transnational capitalism in Central-Eastern Europe, *West European Politics*, 30(3): 443–66.

Boltanski, L. and Chiapello, E. (2007) *The New Spirit of Capitalism*, London: Verso.

Brehm, W. and Silova, I. (2010) The ignorant donor: a radical reimagination of international aid, development and education, *Current Issues in Comparative Education*, 13(1): 29–36.

Brenner, N., Peck, J. and Theodore, N. (2009) Variegated neoliberalization: geographies, modalities, pathways, *Global Networks*, 10(2): 182–222.

Brown, W. (2011) The end of educated democracy, *Representations*, 116: 19–41.

Burawoy, M. (2011a) Redefining the public university: developing an analytical framework, Public Sphere Forum, *Universities in Crisis: Blog of the International Sociological Association (ISA)*, 5 May. Available at http://publicsphere.ssrc.org/burawoy-redefining-the-public-university/ (accessed 20 September 2012).

Burawoy, M. (2011b) About, *Universities in Crisis: Blog of the International Sociological Association (ISA)*. Available at www.isa-sociology.org/universities-in-crisis/?page_id=2 (accessed 9 September 2011).

Buzgalin, A. (2006) Fighting 'Jurassic Park' capitalism: Russian Social Forum success, *International Viewpoint Magazine*, 380 (July–August). Available at www.internationalviewpoint.org/spip.php?article1100 (accessed 10 June 2010).

Caffentzis, G. (2011) Hoisting the 'knowledge bank' on its own petard: the World Bank and the double crisis of African universities, *EduFactory Journal*, zero issue, January. Available at www.edu-factory.org/edu15/webjournal/n0/Caffentzis.pdf (accessed 9 January 2012).

Caffentzis, G. and Federici, S. (2007) Notes on the edu-factory and cognitive capitalism, *Transversal*, May. Available at http://eipcp.net/transversal/0809/caffentzisfederici/en (accessed 8 January 2012).

Calhoun, C. (2006) Is the university in crisis?, *Society*, May/June: 8–18.

Canaan, J. and Shumar, W. (eds) (2008) *Structure and Agency in the Neoliberal University*, London and New York: Routledge.

Chiapello, E. and Fairclough, N. (2002) Understanding the new management ideology: a transdisciplinary contribution from critical discourse analysis and new sociology of capitalism, *Discourse & Society*, 13(2): 185–208.

Clegg, S. (2010) The possibilities of sustaining critical intellectual work under regimes of evidence, audit and ethical governance, *Journal of Curriculum Theorizing*, 26(3): 21–5.

Couldry, N. and McRobbie, A. (2010) The death of the university, English style, *Culture Machine*, November. Available at www.culturemachine.net/index.php/cm/article/view/417/430 (accessed 10 January 2012).

Curcio, A. and Roggero, G. (2011) Tunisia is our university: notes and reflections from the Liberation without Borders tour (J.F. McGimsey, trans), *EduFactory*, 30 May. Available at www.edu-factory.org/wp/tunisia-is-our-university (accessed 9 January 2012).

Davies, B. and Bansel, P. (2010) Governmentality and academic work: shaping the hearts and minds of academic workers, *Journal of Curriculum Theorizing*, 26(3): 5–20.

DeYoung, A. (2007) The erosion of *vospitaniye* (social upbringing) in post-Soviet Kyrgyzstan: voices from the schools, *Communist and Post-Communist Studies*, 40: 239–56.

DeYoung, A. (2011) *Lost in Transition: Redefining students and universities in the contemporary Kyrgyz Republic*, Charlotte, NC: Information Age Publishing.

Dzhaparova, R. (2005) Modernization problems of higher education in Kyrgyzstan, *Russian Education and Society*, 47(8): 80–9.

EduFactory Collective (2009) *Towards a Global Autonomous University*, New York: Autonomedia.

EduFactory Collective (2011) The university is ours! (A call for papers on) A conference on struggles within and beyond the neoliberal university, April 27–29, 2012, *EduFactory*, Available at www.edu-factory.org/wp/the-university-is-ours (accessed 12 January 2012).

Federici, S. (2012) African roots of US university struggles: from the Occupy Movement to the anti-student-debt campaign, *Transversal*, January. Available at http://eipcp.net/transversal/0112/federici/en (accessed 19 March 2012).

Fischman, G. and Haas, E. (2009) Critical pedagogy and hope in the context of neo-liberal globalization, in W. Ayers, T. Quinn and D. Stovall (eds) *Handbook of Social Justice in Education*, New York: Routledge, pp. 565–75.

Fischman, G., Igo, S. and Rhoten, D. (2007) Are public research universities in crisis?, *Reencuentro*, 50: 117–30.

Freedman, E. (2007) After the Tulip Revolution: journalism education in Kyrgyzstan, *Asia Pacific Media Educator*, 18, 171–84.

Grubb, W. and Lazerson, M. (2006) The globalization of rhetoric and practice: the education gospel and vocationalism, in H. Lauder, P. Brown, J. Dillabough and D. Harvey (eds) *A Short History of Neo-Liberalism*, Oxford: Oxford University Press.

Henales, L. and Edwards, B. (2002) Neo-liberalism and educational reform in Latin America, *Current Issues in Comparative Education*, 2(2): 120–9.

Holloway, J. (2010) *Crack Capitalism*, London: Pluto.

Humphrey, C. (2002) Rethinking bribery in contemporary Russia, in C. Humphrey, *The Unmaking of Soviet Life: Everyday economies after socialism*, New York: Cornell University Press, pp. 127–46.

Johnstone, B. (1998) *The Financing and Management of Higher Education: A status report on worldwide reforms*, World Bank Working Paper no. 19129. Available at www-wds.worldbank.org/external/default/WDSContentServer/WDSP/IB/2000/07/19/0000949 46_99040905052384/Rendered/PDF/multi_page.pdf (accessed 10 January 2012).

Kargaev, A. (2008) Cooperation among educational institutions and industry: supply chain perspective, *Journal of International Business Research*, 7(2): 111–19.

Kucera, J. (2011) Kazakhstan rising, *Slate*, 3 August. Available at www.slate.com/articles/news_and_politics/dispatches/features/2011/kazakhstan_rising/nazarbayev_u.html (accessed 10 January 2012).

Kumar, A. (2011) Achievements and limitations of the UK student movement, in M. Bailey and D. Freedman (eds) *The Assault on Universities: A manifesto for resistance*, London: Pluto Press, pp. 132–43.

Larner, W. (2000) Neoliberalism: policy, ideology, governmentality, *Studies in Political Economy*, 63: 5–25.

Lauder, H., Brown, P., Dillabough, J. and Halsey, A.H. (eds) (2006) *Education, Globalization and Social Change*, Oxford: Oxford University Press.

Levidow, L. (2002) Marketizing higher education: neoliberal strategies and counter-strategies, in K. Robins and F. Webster (eds) *The Virtual University? Knowledge, markets and management*, Oxford: Oxford University Press, pp. 227–48.

Liu, M. (2003) Detours from utopia on the Silk Road: ethical dilemmas of neoliberal triumphalism, *Central Eurasian Studies Review*, 2(2). Available at www.cesr-cess.org/html/CESR_02_2.html#Liu (accessed 10 January 2012).

Magun, A. (2010) Higher education in post-Soviet Russia and the global crisis of the university, *Universities in Crisis: Blog of the International Sociological Association* (ISA), 4 June. Available at www.isa-sociology.org/universities-in-crisis/?p=508 (accessed 11 January 2012).

Mambetshaeva, B. (2011) AUCA tuition to rise, *New Eurasia*, 24 January. Available at www.neweurasia.net/politics-and-society/auca-tuition-to-rise (accessed 10 January 2012).

Mitrofanskaya, Y. (1999) Privatization as an international phenomenon: Kazakhstan, *American University International Law Review*, 14(5): 1399–438.

Musabaeva, A. (2006) Corporatization of higher educational institutions in Kyrgyzstan: what does the future hold?, *Institute for Public Policy*. Available at www.ipp.kg/en/print/272 (accessed 11 January 2012).

Musabaeva, A. (2008) Higher education in Kyrgyzstan: is it a public good or a private good?, *Institute for Public Policy*, 2(1): 77–83.

Newfield, C. (2008) *The Unmaking of the Public University: The forty-year assault on the middle class*, Cambridge, MA: Harvard University Press.

Niyozov, S. (2006) Trading or teaching: dilemmas of everyday life economy in Central Asia, *Inner Asia*, 8(2): 229–62.

Olssen, M. and Peters, M. (2005) Neoliberalism, higher education and the knowledge economy: from the free market to knowledge capitalism, *Journal of Educational Policy*, 3(20): 314–45.

Ong, A. (2007) Neoliberalism as a mobile technology, *Transactions of the Institute of British Geographers*, NS32: 3–8.

Osipian, A. (2009) Corruption hierarchies in higher education in the former Soviet Bloc, *International Journal of Educational Development*, 29(3): 321–30.

Paretskaya, A. (2010) The Soviet Communist Party and the other spirit of capitalism, *Sociological Theory*, 28(4): 377–401.

Peck, J., Theodore, N. and Brenner, N. (2009) Postneoliberalism and its malcontents, *Antipode*, 41(S1): 94–116.

Peters, M. (2007) Higher education, globalisation and the knowledge economy: reclaiming the cultural mission, *Ubiquity*, 8(18): 3–27.

Reeves, M. (2005) Of credits, *kontrakty* and critical thinking: encountering 'market reforms' in Kyrgyzstani higher education, *European Educational Research Journal*, 4(1): 5–21.

Seddon, T. (2005) Travelling policy in post-socialist education, *European Educational Research Journal*, 4(1): 1–3.

Shore, C. (2010) Beyond the multiversity: neoliberalism and the rise of the schizophrenic university, *Social Anthropology*, 18(1): 15–29.

Silova, I. (2005) Traveling policies: hijacked in Central Asia, *European Educational Research Journal*, 4(1): 50–9.

Silova, I. (2009) The crisis of the post-Soviet teaching profession in the Caucasus and Central Asia, *Research in Comparative and International Education*, 4(4): 366–83.

Slaughter, G. and Rhoades, S. (2004) *Academic Capitalism and the New Economy: Markets, state, and higher education*, Baltimore, MD: Johns Hopkins University Press.

Solomon, C. and Palmieri, T. (eds) (2011) *Springtime: The new student rebellions*, London: Verso.

Spring, J. (2008) Research on globalization and education, *Review of Educational Research*, 78(2): 330–63.

Stevenson, N. (2011) The war against democracy and education, in M. Bailey and D. Freedman (eds) *The Assault on Universities: A manifesto for resistance*, London: Pluto Press, pp. 71–80.

Taylor, W. (1987) *Universities under Scrutiny*, OECD report, Paris: UNESCO.

Torres, C.A. (2002) The state, privatisation and educational policy: a critique of neo-liberalism in Latin America and some political and ethical implications, *Comparative Education*, 38(4): 365–85.

Tronti, M. (1965) The strategy of the refusal, *Workers and Capital*. Available at https://webspace.utexas.edu/hcleaver/www/TrontiRefusal.html (accessed 15 March 2012).

Upchurch, M., Marinković, D. and Zivković, A. (2011) Wild capitalism, privatisation and employment relations in Serbia, *Employee Relations*, 33(4): 316–33.

Varghese, N.V. (2009) *Institutional Restructuring in Higher Education within the Commonwealth of Independent States*, IIEP Research Paper, Paris: UNESCO. Available at http://unesdoc.unesco.org/images/0018/001824/182450e.pdf (accessed 10 January 2012).

Verdery, K. (1996) *What Was Socialism, and What Comes Next?*, Princeton, NJ: Princeton University Press.

We Are Against Tuition Raise at AUCA (2011) Facebook page. Available at www.facebook.com/#!/groups/122839607785321 (accessed 11 January 2012).

Zholdoshalieva, R. and Shamatov, D. (2008) Children's voices from the 'island of democracy' in Central Asia, unpublished paper. Available at www.citized.info/pdf/commarticles (accessed 10 January 2012).

16 The Once and Future Academic

David Watson

Introduction

This chapter represents a philosophical and normative rather than an economic and sociological account of what it is like to be a higher education worker in the early twenty-first century. This is not because the latter kind of account does not exist. On the contrary, there are several ongoing surveys of what it is to be a member of the contemporary 'academic profession' (see, for example, Locke and Teichler, 2007). Sadly, many of these have been victims of poor conceptualization, of essentially backward-looking empirical categories, and hence of ideological capture.

The same can be true of more thickly descriptive, anthropological accounts of the contemporary profession (for example, Fanghanel, 2012; Macfarlane, 2012). These are also dominated by a mood of complaint. It is paradoxical that an institution with such a strong record of resilience and productivity should – at the level of the front-line worker – be relatively unaware of (and mostly negatively responsive to) the forces changing the professional environment. That is one of the main dilemmas I try to explore in *The Question of Morale* (Watson, 2009), some aspects of which are updated here.

The upshot is that in the main branches of our self-reflective, professional literature the world we have lost (and who has taken it away from us) is a recurrent motif. As Merlin says in T.H. White's *Once and Future King*, we cannot build the future by avenging the past.

I would like to present an alternative, impressionistic and descriptive perspective. Only in this way do I think it is possible to do justice to a very peculiar location and mode of knowledge production. Consequently, this chapter is about academic work: where it is done, why it is done, how it is done, and above all with what effects on the people who do it. Insofar as it is based on felt experience, it is about the United Kingdom (especially England as it moves apart from its devolved administrations) and North America; it does, however, draw on observation of similar work in many parts of the world. In broad historical sweep I suggest that it is possible to be more positive than many of the currently fashionable dystopias would suggest.

The analysis proceeds by looking first at the higher education enterprise from the 'outside-in' and then the 'inside-out'. It proceeds to consider structural and strategic questions about the organization and objectives of the sector before concluding with some comments about the 'once and future academic' – in other words, the issues of continuity and change within our trade. The objective is to probe the quality and accuracy of self-analysis by institutional leaders and members, as well as the views of those who feel that they have a 'stake' in the enterprise. The assumption is that improving this capacity for self-knowledge inside the academy is essential for establishing what it can and should be in the modern world, as well as restoring (where necessary) professional pride, effectiveness and reputation.

Expectations

During the latter half of the twentieth century higher education became more and more salient in terms of public investment, political attention and cultural impact, all around the world. This was partly the result of growth in participation, creating the goal (and in some cases the achievement) of what Martin Trow called 'mass higher education' (between 15 per cent and 40 per cent of each age cohort taking part – many countries now exceed his final frontier of 'universal' participation at 50 per cent plus), and partly the result of a move towards 'knowledge-led' industrial and commercial enterprises (Scott, 1995: 2). One result is that there is apparently now no public policy (or codified 'strategy') at any significant level (local, regional, national) or in any key sector (health, economic, growth, social cohesion, artistic and cultural life, as well as education) that lacks a role for higher education and its contributing institutions. Higher education can no longer stand apart – upstream or downstream – from these developments.

At the same time, universities and university-like institutions are subject to profoundly ambiguous if not directly contradictory expectations (Watson, 2007: 1–2). What follows is a growing list of contemporary 'outside-in' assumptions, all in pairs, about what societies think universities should be like:

1   conservative and radical;
2   critical and supportive;
3   competitive and collegial;
4   charitable and commercial;
5   autonomous and accountable;
6   excellent and equal;
7   compliant and creative;
8   entrepreneurial and caring;
9   certain and provisional;
10 ethical and technical;
11 traditional and innovative;
12 ceremonial and iconoclastic;
13 local and international;
14 private and public.

Some of these are about perceptions of universities as large, influential fixtures in civil society (1, 11, 12). Others are about how their members are expected to behave, including in advising and influencing those outside (2, 3, 7, 8). Yet a third set is about the consequences of accepting public support, including funding (4 and 6). Item 13 is even wider: universities relate intimately to their neighbour-hoods and their immediate sub-region (it may be a city), less intimately but in a highly programmatic way to their economic and political regions, perhaps also to an international region (such as the European Union) and, in a final act of moral self-identification, to the global enterprise of higher education. The final item (14) is emphasized because of its even more complex implications. In the early twenty-first century there are several influential, international enterprises that can no longer be regarded as purely public or purely private. Hybridity rules (as is also discussed below).

Meanwhile, the business of universities is to create, test, evaluate and apply knowledge. They do this in a variety of contexts, and as a consequence will some-times lead and sometimes follow the creators and users of knowledge elsewhere. Donald Kennedy, former President of Stanford, puts the point brilliantly: univer-sities will sometimes 'lead' and sometimes 'follow' or 'lag':

> Universities are in a dynamic equilibrium with society. On the one hand, they appear to lag behind it, acting as conservators of its history and archivists of its highest cultural attainments. On the other hand, they are seen as leaders, adventuring into new knowledge domains, developing transforming technol-ogies, and serving as the seedbed for novel and often disturbing ideas.
>
> Both of these roles are part of the university's academic duty.
>
> (1997: 265)

The trick is, of course, choosing when each applies. The university is prob-ably the most significant institution in both the historical and contemporary processes of creating, testing, applying and evaluating all aspects of knowledge. As Louis Menand of Harvard elaborates in his *The Marketplace of Ideas*:

> Knowledge is our most important business. The success of almost all our other business depends on it, but its value is not only economic. The pursuit, production, dissemination, application, and preservation of knowledge are the central activities of a civilization. Knowledge is social memory, a connec-tion to the past; and it is social hope, an investment in the future. The ability to create knowledge and put it to use is *the* adaptive characteristic of humans.
>
> (2010: 13)

Universities are distinctive in that they deal in a non-dogmatic, open and experimental way with both 'social memory' and 'social hope'.

The HE Mode of Production

Needless to say, these forces have had an impact in terms of changing the academic mode of production as it has been traditionally understood. In terms of re-casting professional understanding a number of simultaneous challenges have to be faced: epistemological, sociological and practical. Below is another list, of the major disruptive influences with which today's academics have to deal:

- political interference;
- the Information Age;
- generational fracture;
- new professional boundaries.

Political Interference

To demonstrate the regularity of government intervention in the system as a whole, the main landmarks of reform in the UK (and especially England) from 1963 to 2012 are set out below. To put the point crudely, for every third entry of a cohort into the system since then the system has been thrown up into the air by a government claiming that it is fixing the sins of the previous administration (including sometimes its own party). In international terms this degree of legislative hyperactivity is extraordinary:

- The Robbins Report (1963): creation of 'new' universities, plus the 'ability to benefit' criterion.
- The 'Woolwich speech' and the creation of the polytechnics (1965).
- The James Report (1972): reorganization of teacher education and 'diversification'.
- Withdrawal of the overseas student subsidy (1980), public expenditure cuts (1981) and the White Paper proposing a smaller and rationalized system (1985).
- Creation of the National Advisory Body for Public Sector HE (NAB), centralizing the former local authority responsibility for higher education outside the universities (1985).
- White Paper endorsing expansion and incorporation of the polytechnics, central institutions and large colleges (1987) achieved in the Education Reform Act (1988).
- White Paper on the ending of the binary line (1991), achieved in the Further and Higher Education Act (1992), along with Funding Councils for the devolved administrations of Scotland and Wales; creation of the 'new new' universities.
- The Dearing Report (1997), opening the way for undergraduate fees legislated for in the Teaching and Higher Education Act (1998).
- White Paper (2003), leading to 'variable' fees, establishment of the 'new new new' universities (without research degree-awarding powers), and potential foundation degree-awarding powers for further education institutions in the Higher Education Act (2004).
- White Paper, *Higher Ambitions: The future of universities in a knowledge economy* (2009).
- The Browne Review (2010), leading to proposals for higher undergraduate fees, and a revised graduate contribution scheme.

- White Paper, *Putting Students at the Heart of the System* (2011), replacing Funding Council grants to institutions in England with a higher level of fees (up to £9,000) to be advanced by the Student Loans Company and recovered through fees.

(Based on Watson, 2011)

This might not matter so much if there were a well-understood direction of travel, or a consistently articulated final goal. Instead we have had violent 'mood swings' on issues such as the size of and provision for the sector, both within and across governments of differing stripes.

The Information Age

Some of the changes are reflected in major theoretical formulations about the sociology of knowledge: for example, a new place for higher education is central to the influential formulation of the shift from 'Mode 1' to 'Mode 2' knowledge formulation and exchange (Gibbons *et al.*, 1994). Others are simply about dealing with what Jason Frand (2000) memorably called 'the Information Age'.

Generational Fracture

One of Frand's key concerns is the developing relationship between students of various types and those who are responsible for designing their academic and professional experience. Alongside the horizontal, or synchronic, tensions and dilemmas raised by external and internal pressures, universities also face a vertical, or diachronic, challenge arising from the relations between the generations. This is also the theme of Heller and D'Ambrosio's *Generational Shockwaves* (2008).

At the moment most of the dilemmas are being played out in the arena of information and communication technologies (ICT). Here on one level 'the faculty sometimes lag behind their students in technological prowess' (Heller and D'Ambrosio, 2008: 64); on another, technologically adept faculty can be frustrated by how superficial and easily satisfied their charges can be (a particularly valuable chapter explores these issues in terms of post-graduate study; it's no longer just about 18-year-old university entrants). It is surprising how rare an exercise this juxtaposition of the 'lived worlds' of the teachers and the taught is in the conventional HE literature.

Indeed, demography is one of the most influential moulders of a higher education system, with stark differences between the adjustment pressures felt by those nations and regions with rising and those with declining proportions of young people.

But what will happen, when the 'Millenials' (or 'screen-agers') get to design and manage the system, and to teach? The changes are likely not to be just about pedagogy, or about the preparation for the labour market, but also about priorities for the twenty-first century world and the place within it of higher education at its best and worst.

New Professional Boundaries

Other pressures are caught by descriptions of the greater interpenetration of what used to be called 'academic' and 'administrative' or 'support' work, notably Celia Whitchurch's discovery of the 'third space professional'. What were previously separate career streams, power bases and employment cultures are now increasingly merged into 'project work', for example on learning environments, on external relations or on the 'student experience' (Whitchurch, 2008). 'Sharing', boundary changes and fluid patterns of responsibility are increasingly common features of professional work in higher education.

New Institutional Dynamics and 'Category Mistakes'

Putting the internal and the external drivers together, we may be facing a period of very significant system-level adjustment. The future of post-compulsory education in general is likely to be messier and less predictable. In these circumstances, intelligent self-study – including a willingness to accept the death of some sacred cows – is essential.

The Oxford philosopher Gilbert Ryle coined the term 'category mistake' in his *The Concept of Mind* (1949). He talks about a 'foreigner visiting Oxford or Cambridge for the first time':

> [He is] shown a number of colleges, libraries, playing fields, museums, scientific departments and administrative offices. He then asks 'But where is the University? I have seen where the members of the Colleges live, where the Registrar works, where the scientists experiment and the rest. But I have not yet seen the University in which reside and work the members of your University.' It then has to be explained to him that the University is not another collateral institution, some visible counterpart to the colleges, laboratories and offices which he has seen. The University is just the way in which what he has already seen is organized. When they are seen and when their coordination is understood, the University has been seen.
>
> (pp. 17–18)

This passage is interesting on a number of levels, especially historical (the priority of the Colleges, the salience of the Registrar, the absence of explicit reference to students, the apparent lack of lecture halls, the scientists 'experimenting', and so on), but it is Ryle's first and strongest example of the 'category mistake'. The visitor mistakes the buildings for the concept: the infrastructure for the institution (Ryle, 1949: 17–18).

A classic dictionary defines the category mistake as follows: 'a sentence that says one thing in one category that can only intelligibly be said of something of another, as when speaking of the mind located in space' (one of Ryle's targets was Cartesian dualism of the mind and the body). Another gives the example 'what does blue smell like?'

At least eight such category mistakes are discernible in today's discourse about higher education, its problems and its prospects (see Watson, 2012a):

1   'University' performance
2   'Access'
3   The higher education 'sector'
4   Research 'selectivity'
5   'World-classness'
6   The 'public/private' divide
7   'Informed' choice
8   'Reputation' and 'quality'.

'University' Performance

The first is about *to what extent the individual university is the most sensible unit of analysis*. Here we talk about the 'university' when what is actually in question is the subject, professional area or the system in which the institution sits. Courses, subjects and evolving inter- and multidisciplinary academic and professional fields should count more than whole institutions (indeed, a rather brittle, un-self-aware species of institutional pride can be a real problem). Think about the so-called difference between 'recruiting' and 'selecting' universities. This makes sense in terms of courses, but only rarely for whole institutions. Examples are health and medicine, art and design, and engineering and technology, which often share developmental problems across the sector more than they do with other disciplines in the same institution. The UK National Student Survey has shown, for example, that differences in response between subjects – across all institutions – are much more marked (and statistically reliable) than differences between institutional aggregates (Ramsden *et al.*, 2010: para. 16.3).

'Access'

The second is about the admissions dilemma: *is it about the pursuit of 'excellence', or more about 'social mobility', or even 'social justice'?* Here we talk about 'widening participation' as if it is the same as so-called 'fair access' and vice versa. The two are logically separable phenomena. The first – getting more students qualified and to the starting-gate – is a big problem. The second – where they choose to apply and are admitted – is a comparatively tiny problem. Merging the two can also lead to empirically weak and socially patronizing conclusions. For example, there is the related category mistake of the Sutton Trust in stating that well-qualified students choosing courses (and institutions) outside the golden circle of the 'Sutton 13' top universities (all from the Russell and 94 groups) are 'wasted talent' (Sutton Trust, 2008). Many of the alternative choices made by well-qualified non-standard students are profoundly life-enhancing.

The Higher Education 'Sector'

The third is about the scope of the 'sector' from the points of view of policy, of practice and, critically, of self-image. This concerns *talking about 'higher' when we should be talking about 'tertiary' education*. In gross terms – and not withstanding the wobbles we have seen recently in terms of so-called 'dual sector' provision (when what is called in the UK 'further' education, or in Australia Technical and Further Education (TAFE) takes place in the same institution as HE) – it is 'tertiary' (including higher education) rather than exclusively 'higher' education that matters to society at large. The emerging question internationally is how both higher and further education sit within frameworks of lifelong learning (Schuller and Watson, 2009; see also http://ems.gtc.ox.ac.uk/). As an extreme example of new formations, the University of Peshawar in northern Pakistan sustains all levels of learning from nursery school to Ph.D. (see www.upesh.edu.pk/about_uop.html). Charles Darwin University in Australia's Northern Territory holds wonderful open-air awards ceremonies recognizing everything from certificates in adult literacy to doctorates (Watson *et al.*, 2011: 46).

Research 'Selectivity'

Next there is the myth of research concentration. This is not just about the stark conclusion that in the UK we have concentrated public funding of research to the point where it has become dysfunctional, but also *talking about institutional research intensity when we should be talking about inter-institutional collaboration*. As university leaders, policy makers and funders focus on league tables and so-called competitive advantage they are actually being undermined by the scientific community's ever-increasing tendency to cross boundaries. This is how the Royal Society summarizes the position:

> The scientific world is becoming increasingly interconnected, with international collaboration on the rise. Today over 35% of articles published in international journals are internationally collaborative, up from 25% 15 years ago.
>
> The primary driver of most collaboration is the scientists themselves. In developing their research and finding answers, scientists are seeking to work with the best people, institutions and equipment which complement their research, wherever they may be.
>
> The connections of people, through formal and informal channels, diaspora communities, virtual global networks and professional communities of shared interests are important drivers of international collaboration. These networks span the globe. Motivated by the bottom-up exchange of scientific insight, knowledge and skills, they are changing the focus of science from the national to the global level. Yet little is understood about the dynamics of networking and the mobility of scientists, how these affect global science and how best to harness these networks to catalyse international collaboration.
>
> (RS, 2011: 6)

Locally (in the UK) this should cause us to think long and hard about the upcoming Research Evaluation Framework (REF). Two outcomes are certain. Hyperconcentration of funding in the hands of a few 'QR (quality-related)-winners' will continue: four HEIs will continue to scoop about 30 per cent of the spoils, and up to 23 about 75 per cent. As a result we shall have to learn to live with a two-tier system. This division will not, incidentally, simply recreate the binary line: 'old universities' without medical schools will mostly be outside the charmed circle; 'new universities' will be well placed to prosper in the second tier.

Two tiers will represent a policy trap for various reasons. Entry to the top tier will become virtually impossible. New combinations of subjects (and institutional partnerships) – the very stuff of 'foresight' at its best – will wither in this part of the sector. Above all, a radically divided system represents a counsel of despair: the best of what we have now is the best we can ever hope for.

Life among the QR winners will not, however, be a bed of roses. The real value of 'dual support' has been in steady decline since 1992, and genuine FEC (full economic costing) remains out of reach (Adams and Smith, 2007). Missions here will become narrower as internal concentration of resources mirrors external funding. They will also be increasingly dominated by medicine and science; not least because funding required to 'match' investments in science and technology will progressively bleed the arts and humanities.

The favoured institutions will find themselves more and more operating against the grain of a 'Mode 2' world of knowledge creation and exchange. There will be disincentives to participate in academic partnerships that dilute the citation denominator (exacerbated, for example, by the treatment of group authorship as a single unit for the purpose of excluding self-citation). It is also likely that the QR-winners' relative decline in the ability to 'gear' or 'leverage' public money into private support will continue.

As for the rest of the institutions, life outside an inflexible and backward-looking QR-winners' circle will have its compensations, as well as some ongoing challenges. A concerted effort must be made to demonstrate that institutional reputations (including for research) can be made away from Research Assessment Exercises, which will cease to be 'the only game in town'. Such reputations will depend upon catching a number of waves: the increasing importance of the creative and service economies; a renewed interest in 'liberal' values in undergraduate education that fuses the research and teaching agenda; and a similar demand for 'translational' research, or what the surgeon Atul Gawande calls in his *Better,* the 'science of performance' (Gawande, 2007).

Together these developments will offer an alternative, forward-looking definition of 'research intensity'. Above all, they will mean adapting to a world of wider and deeper collaboration, in which at many of its scholarly frontiers the isolated institution is no longer the power it once was.

World-Classness

Fifth, this links directly with the madness of supposedly 'world-class' provision, especially as identified by international whole-institution league tables. At present both *politicians and institutional leaders (the latter should know better) are obsessed with a poorly designed concept of comparative 'world-classness' when they ought to be talking about geographically specific 'engagement'.* What governments say they want from higher education systems represents almost the opposite of what the international league tables they also exhort us to climb actually measure (see Salmi and Altbach, 2011).

Below are two starkly different lists: of what governments at a variety of different levels say they want higher education to do and what the 'world-class' tables rely on:

What doesn't count:

- teaching quality
- social mobility
- services to business and the community
- rural interests
- other public services
- collaboration
- the public interest.

What counts:

- research
- media interest
- graduate destinations
- infrastructure
- international 'executive' recruitment.

Despite Herculean efforts everything reduces to peer-reviewed research and, as suggested above, even that is problematic because of the inexorable rise of collaborative outcomes at the very highest levels of achievement. An example is the recently remodelled *Times Higher Education World Rankings, 2011–2012.* Sixty per cent of the inputs are claimed to be generated by research 'volume, income, reputation and influence' and 30 per cent for 'teaching'. When you drill down, however, you discover that 70.5 per cent of the whole data set is driven by research-based activity (*THE*, 2010: 28–9).

The 'Public/Private' Divide

Next, there is no clear blue water now (if there ever was) between the 'public' and the 'private' sectors; what often makes the difference is *how the private sector can be used for public purposes.* Meanwhile we have the ironic phenomenon that, as universities are urged to be more 'business-like' (admittedly on a rather outmoded version of what complex 'business' actually consists of), many successful businesses are becoming more 'university-like'. The whole domain of open-source software illustrates this. while other specific examples of companies include Whole Foods, W.L. Gore, Google and Linux (Hamel, 2007: 72, 95, 107, 111, 207–9).

'Informed' Choice

Penultimately, we have to ask the hard question about *who is really running the show?* What students want and need can confound the most sophisticated policy frameworks, where spokespersons react to what they regard as irrational choices by prescribing more and decreasingly plausible 'information'. Look at the ways in which student demand led the systems of the 'developed' world towards meeting the needs of the cultural, creative and service economies. Their ICT requirements (where they are normally ahead of their teachers) compound this. The UK system provides ample evidence of how (despite political voices to the contrary) a market does exist. Indeed student choices – of subjects, of institutions and of mode of study – could be said very substantially to have moulded the system as we have it today. That is why so many supply-side STEM (science, technology, engineering, and mathematics) initiatives have failed (the same is not true in the developing world (Nuffield Foundation, 2008)). That is why there is a slow but inexorable move towards studying closer to the family home. And that is why institutions (such as the UK Open University), which hold out the prospect of earning while learning, are increasingly popular.

'Reputation' and 'Quality'

Choice of institution is also a contested element, and leads to a final category mistake: *the confusion of reputation and quality.* In the United States, Andrew Delbanco (2007) concludes that 'the "quality gap" between private and public universities is much smaller than the gap in reputation'. Evidence is growing in developed systems that students are choosing 'reputation' over 'quality' in selecting universities, and that as long as employers screen for the same thing they are acting rationally in doing so.

These data and these conclusions are mirrored in the UK. The Higher Education Policy Institute's surveys of student classroom experience in 2006, 2007 and 2009 observed 'the new universities if anything making more provision and in smaller classes than the old, and less likely to use graduate students as teachers' (HEPI, 2009: para. 10). While critics have raced to comment that the older universities are more likely to have graduate students available, the impact is confirmed by other reports. The ESRC's Teaching and Learning Programme's project SOMUL (the Social and Organisational Mediation of University Learning) concluded that 'you won't necessarily learn more if you go to a posh place' (SOMUL, 2005), while similar results have been reported more recently by Paul Ashwin (Ashwin *et al.*, 2011).

The public discourse is heavily dominated at present by a perception (whether welcomed or deprecated) of student instrumentalism. What counts is 'employability' (even more than 'employment') and whether or not students are prepared for it. Meanwhile students themselves confound expectation further: not just in choice of subject of study (as above), but by delaying their entry into the job market (when they can), by being much less spooked about debt than their parents (Surowieki, 2011), by returning to volunteering (even while they simultaneously have to work much more frequently for money than their predecessors) and by reviving student-led political activism (all around the world).

The combined effect of these category mistakes is to suggest that HE research needs to put its own house together. Not all of these eight failures of analysis (and of imagination) originate from outside the academy. In addition to telling truth to power (or at least the policy makers temporarily in charge) we need also to focus on telling the truth to ourselves.

The Once and Future Academic: Work–Life Balance and Self-Care

To revert to my main topic: academic practice, attitudes and self-image are all undergoing change; sometimes explicitly, some tacitly. I have also tried to demonstrate that we are in a very peculiar business. One of our key dilemmas is about when and how we should adapt to new circumstances and when we should stand firm.

A special peculiarity is the way in which we are required to switch in and out of 'management' roles. In a university almost everybody manages something, and in turn is managed by somebody else (Watson, 2009: 118–34). In these circumstances what resonates much more than the notoriously brittle analysis of 'work–life balance' is the richer concept of 'self-care'. The former is based upon 'three flawed assumptions: life is good, work is bad, and they are divisible' (Reeves and Knell, 2009: 81). For most academics, like artists, life is work and in healthy circumstances their hinterlands of family, recreation and relaxation in some ways join in. You cannot shut the office door and stop thinking about what it is you do. As Adrian Furnham wisely observes: 'The work–life lobby all concentrate on negative spillover. They stress how work makes family life difficult, problematic and unsatisfactory. But it can also do the opposite. It can support, enhance and facilitate life outside the workplace' (2004: 160). However, in these circumstances, staying healthy is vital, and the precepts of self-care (most fully explored by the counselling profession) are helpful (Wilke, 2000; see also Watson, 2009: 130–2).

Continuity and change, leadership and lag, confidence and provisionality are all part of the attributes of the once and future academic. The bottom line is that universities are quintessentially membership organizations. Participation is voluntary – by students, staff and other 'partners'. These are the 'risk-sharers' who constitute genuine stakeholders. With the exception of the relatively new (in the UK) breed of 'for-profit' universities (designed, in the words of Harold Hotson, primarily to 'get the funding moving from federal [government] coffers to the student's debt ledger, through the university, and into the pockets of shareholders and chief executives'), the analogy with shareholding organizations just does not hold up (Hotson, 2011). However, they also have to live in a number of intersecting and overlapping worlds, which provide locations, contracts and trade, and a wider community of knowledge exchange and use. Each of these worlds can impose its own (sometimes conflicting) demands; and their representatives can also occasionally overstep the mark. In this context it is the duty of university governance, leadership and management to analyse, adjudicate and steer through choppy waters.

So where does this leave the 'once and future academic' as he or she contemplates the past, present and future of our trade? I would like to conclude on a subversive thought (see Watson, 2012b). In comparative terms, and much as it may make us feel better to argue the opposite, especially in difficult times, in the UK nationally we are a 'lucky' system. Despite the pressures of a hyperactive political context, we have maintained a 'buffer' between ourselves and the government of the day. The provision of the 1988 Education Reform Act that the Secretary of State cannot make a grant in respect of an individual institution remains in force (ERA, 134: 7). We have broadly been well funded at times, and less well funded at others (HEPI, 2006). Public funding has not kept pace with expansion but it has increased in absolute terms decade after decade since the 1960s. Even the latest major disruption is likely to have a greater impact on students than on gross levels of institutional funding (Watson, 2011). Our levels of student satisfaction are relatively high compared to those in similar national sectors, although they may be slipping – for predictable reasons. The bar remains high on degree-awarding powers and university title, while – although they creak from time to time – the processes of mutual assurance of quality and standards remain intact.

However, we are now entering another one of those periods (the late 1970s and early 1980s were the last) when we need to be a smarter system. We are facing another potential perfect storm: of national policy confusion (exacerbated by devolution), of funding uncertainty and of diminished public confidence. Survival and prosperity will once again only securely be achieved – as it has been in the past – by understanding and adapting in a framework of enduring principles.

Other systems have been and are less fortunate, but have proved equally if not more adaptable. The international study of 20 institutions in *The Engaged University* showed academics in the global South and East not only doing more with less, but being far less hung up about tactical partnerships, about the role of religion in social cohesion, about the tactical use of international partnerships (especially when allied to funding), about the call of human capital, about the strategic use of the private sector, and especially about institutional preciousness than those of us in the North and West (Watson *et al.*, 2011: 241–9). There is significant professional learning to be had in the global village of higher education.

References

Adams, J. and Smith, D. (2007) Higher education, research and the knowledge economy: from Robbins to the 'Gathering Storm', in D. Watson and M. Amoah (2007) *The Dearing Report: Ten years on*, London: Institute of Education, pp. 81–108.

Ashwin, P., Abbas, A. and McLean, M. (2001) A bad deal for 'consumers', *Times Higher Education*, 17 November.

Delbanco, A. (2007) Scandals of higher education, *New York Review of Books*, 29 March: 42–7.

Education Reform Act (ERA) (1988). Available at www.legislation.gov.uk/ukpga/1988/40/resources (accessed 20 September 2012).

Fanghanel, J. (2102) *Being An Academic*, Abingdon and New York: Routledge.

Frand, J. (2000) The Information Age mindset, *Educause Review*, 35(5): 14–24.

Furnham, A. (2004) *Management and Myths: Challenging business fads, fallacies and fashions*, Basingstoke: Palgrave Macmillan.

Gawande, A. (2007) *Better: A surgeon's notes on performance*, New York: Picador.

Gibbons, M., Limoges, C., Nowotny, H., Schwarzman, S., Scott, P. and Trow, M. (1994) *The New Production of Knowledge: The dynamics of science and research in contemporary societies*, London: Sage.

Hamel, G. (2007) *The Future of Management*, Boston, MA: Harvard Business School Press.

Heller, D. and d'Ambrosio, M. (2008) *Generational Shockwaves and the Implications for Higher Education*, Cheltenham and Northampton, MA: Edward Elgar.

Higher Education Policy Institute (HEPI) (2006) *The Prosperity of English Universities: Income growth and the prospects for new investment*, Oxford: HEPI. Available at www.hepi.ac.uk/466-1270/The-prosperity-of-English-universities--income-growth-and-the-prospects-for-new-investment--.html (accessed 19 September 2012).

Higher Education Policy Institute (HEPI) (2009) *The Academic Experience of Students in English Universities: 2009 report*, Report Summary 40 (May), Oxford: HEPI.

Hotson, H. (2011) Short cuts, *London Review of Books*, 2 June.

Kennedy, D. (1997) *Academic Duty*, Cambridge, MA: Harvard University Press.

Locke, W. and Teichler, U. (eds.) (2007) *The Changing Conditions for Academic Work and Careers in Select Countries*, Kassel: International Centre for Higher Education Research (ICHER).

Macfarlane, B. (2012) *Intellectual Leadership in Higher Education: Renewing the role of the university professor*, Abingdon: Routledge.

Menand, L. (2010) *The Marketplace of Ideas: Reform and resistance in the American University*, New York and London: W.W. Norton.

Nuffield Foundation (2008) *Science Education in Europe: Critical reflections*, London: Nuffield Foundation.

Ramsden, P., Batchelor, D., Peacock, A., Temple, P. and Watson, D. (2010) *Enhancing and Developing the National Student Survey: Report to HEFCE by the Centre for Higher Education Studies at the Institute of Education*, Bristol: Higher Education Funding Council for England (HEFCE).

Reeves, R. and Knell, J. (2009) *The 80 Minute MBA: Everything you'll never learn at business school*, London: Headline.

Royal Society (RS) (2011) *Knowledge, Networks and Nations: Global scientific collaboration in the 21st century*, Policy Document 03/11, DES2096, London: The Royal Society.

Ryle, G. (1949) *The Concept of Mind*, London: Hutchinson's University Library.

Salmi, J. and Altbach, P. (2011) New 'world-class' universities: cutting through the hype, *Chronicle of Higher Education*, 20 October.

Scott, P. (1995) *The Meanings of Mass Higher Education*, Buckingham: SRHE and Open University Press.

Schuller, T. and Watson, D. (2009) *Learning Through Life: Report of the Inquiry into the Future of Lifelong Learning*, Leicester: NIACE.

Social and Organisational Mediation of University Learning (SOMUL) (2005) *Working Paper 2*, December, York: SOMUL.

Surowiecki, J. (2011) Debt by degrees, *The New Yorker*, 21 November: 50.

Sutton Trust (2008) Wasted Talent? Attrition rates of high-achieving pupils between school and university, London: Sutton Trust.

Times Higher Education (THE) (2011) *Times Higher Education World University Rankings 2011–12.* Available at www.timeshighereducation.co.uk/world-university-rankings (accessed 29 August 2012).

Watson, D. (2007) *Managing Civic and Community Engagement*, Maidenhead: Open University Press.

Watson, D. (2009) *The Question of Morale: Managing happiness and unhappiness in university life*, Maidenhead: Open University Press.

Watson, D. (2011) Cassandra and the politicians: higher education and policy memory, *Educational Review*, 63(4) (November): 409–19.

Watson. D. (2012a) *Misunderstanding Modern Higher Education: Eight 'category mistakes'*, Occasional Report 4, Oxford: Higher Education Policy Institute (HEP1).

Watson, D. (2012b) Who runs our universities?, *Perspectives: Policy and Practice in Higher Education*, 16(2): 42–5.

Watson, D., Hollister, R., Stroud, S. and Babcock, E. (2011) *The Engaged University: International perspectives on civic engagement*, London and New York: Routledge.

Whitchurch, C. (2008) *Professional Managers in UK Higher Education: Preparing for complex futures*, Research and Development Series (November), London: Leadership Foundation for Higher Education (LFHE).

Wilke, G. (2000) Holding and fragmentation in the organisational mirror, *AUCC Newsletter and Journal*, 1: 2–8.

17 Professional Capital and the Future of Teaching

Andy Hargreaves

Capital (adj): *relating to or being assets that add to long-term net worth.*
(*Merriam-Webster's Dictionary*)

Introduction

Teaching is at a crossroads: a crossroads at the top of the world. Never before have teachers, teaching and the future of teaching had such elevated importance. There is widespread agreement that of all the factors inside the school that affect children's learning and achievement, the most important is the quality of the teacher. And there is a sense of real urgency now in politics, in the teaching profession, and also among the public about the need to train more high-quality teachers. This is putting teachers and teaching at the forefront of change.

But alongside the urgency, or perhaps even because of it, there is considerable debate and disagreement about what high-quality teaching looks like, and about the best way to get it and keep it. The crossroads are shrouded in misunderstandings about teachers and teaching, and if we take the wrong road forward, precipices are looming on many sides.

One road is just a flat-out assault on teachers' pensions and security. It comes out of the global financial collapse and expects the public sector and its large teaching force to pay the price. In England, one government minister has proclaimed that excellence will only occur in the public sector when there is "some real discipline and some fear" of job losses (Letwin, 2011). In the US, where teachers comprise 25 percent of all organized labor, other commentators have come out against teacher compensation being "heavily weighted towards retirement benefits"[1] arguing (without any real data) that younger teachers want more money sooner at the expense of security later on (Tucker, 2011: 15). There is no evidence that less security will increase teacher quality, though, or that, after a global economic meltdown, young people even want it.

A second (and related) false road is a monetary one. In the US, economists are coming up with formulae to pay teachers according to their individual performance—especially in relation to their students' test scores. They have to do this to comply with the Race To The Top grants that the Federal Government has given them. The idea is not restricted to the US, but is advancing in places like

Sweden as well. This strategy has no historical precedent of success; it flies in the face of psychological research indicating that financial reward only improves performance in areas of low-level skill, not in complex jobs such as teaching, and it creates perverse incentives for expert teachers to avoid difficult students or challenging classes that might depress their test scores (Bird *et al.*, 2005). At best, performance-related pay will motivate a few teachers while alienating others and neglecting the majority. And in New York City, high-performance/high-reward teachers are already denouncing as bogus the measures from which they benefit.

A third (and also related) false road is just to make teaching simpler: to diminish teachers' judgment and professionalism so that less-qualified people can do the job. Narrow the curriculum, turn to technology, prescribe and pace the instruction, teach to the test, reduce literacy to short comprehension passages rather than rich engagements with absorbing texts, and you start to standardize instruction, ignore cultural and linguistic diversity, treat teachers as mere delivery agents for government policies, and constrain teachers' capacity to respond to their students' varying needs. If this is the kind of teaching you want, it needn't take so long to prepare people to do it—so out go long periods of preparation and Master's degrees, and in come (cheaper) alternate routes to certification and compressed training schemes. These "alternate" approaches, such as Teach for America in the US and Teach First in the UK are not used by any of the highest-performing economies, though. Dumb down teaching, and you will dumb down learning and fall further behind the most competitive educational systems and economies. This cannot be the right response either.

This chapter argues that a better road ahead is defined by what Michael Fullan and I call "professional capital"—the development of the collective human, social, and also decisional capital of the teaching profession in order to increase the human and social capital of students in the generations to come.

Our work on professional capital emerged, like many new ideas, almost by accident, in the midst of a thinking and writing project. We had been behind in a writing commitment to produce a second edition of a book we first wrote in 1991, called *What's Worth Fighting For in Your School?* (Fullan and Hargreaves, 1991). Delayed by other projects, we were drawn back to this one by what we felt was a moral and political crisis, globally, about the future of the teaching profession, and we redirected our efforts to respond to this crisis.

Our book began with a critique of the mounting attack on teaching, teachers' performance, and teachers' pensions and security. These contained what we thought were simplified views of human capital that proposed that teaching could be improved by rewarding individuals according to performance and concentrating on the extremes of excellence and incompetence. At this point, I accidentally came into contact on an Advisory Board with business professor Carrie Leana and became acquainted with her impressive new work on the greater impact of social capital compared to individual human capital (Leana, 2011). We were now able to articulate a relationship between two kinds of capital: human and social.

Much of the attack on teaching, we felt, was grounded in stereotypes of teaching that effectively de-professionalized it, so we returned to classic texts on the nature of teachers' work to unpack those stereotypes, especially Willard Waller's *Sociology of Teaching* (1932). We were now engaged in trying to articulate the professional nature of teachers' work—something we had each been engaged with, off and on, for over two decades. We looked at recent research, in particular on how teachers' capital, human or social, changed over time during the course of their careers; and we looked especially closely at the key study by Chris Day and colleagues (2006) on the lives of teachers, which effectively looked at what happened to teachers' capabilities and commitments, or to their capital as we saw it, over time.

This work, and other studies we had come across, pointed to the importance of the often neglected mid-stage of teachers' careers when many teachers seemed to reach the peak of their performance. Clearly, something was at work with the accumulating nature of experience and judgment here, which took us back to classic texts on reflective practice on the one hand, and, because we were essentially looking at the developing of capacities for judgment on the other, into the field of judging in law, where we came across something called decisional law or case law. This gave rise to what we believed was a third kind of capital—decisional capital.

Now we had recognized and started to understand three kinds of capital. We went to bed with this on our minds one night, and next morning awoke with the idea of professional capital as a way to draw these together. We assumed a lot must have been written about this and checked various search engines, but apart from about three articles in social science, and a couple of paragraphs in a small article by Tom Sergiovanni many years ago, the idea had been subjected to little development or analysis up to this point.

We began to refine the concept and considered adding other kinds of capital—cultural capital and symbolic capital etc.—but while these had something to offer, they introduced complexities that were too large to handle in the scope of our work and that would have been a distraction from its core argument.

Our work is not an empirical research study as such, but Michael Fullan drew on many examples from his advisory work in Ontario and across the world, and I drew on instances of realizations of what we now call professional capital from three projects, in particular involving nine schools and local authorities performing beyond expectations that were investigated with my co-Director Alma Harris; an investigation of the special education reform strategy in Ontario among one seventh of its school districts—co-directed with Henry Braun; and an evaluation of the Alberta Initiative for School Improvement, co-directed with Dennis Shirley. These empirical reference points provided a check for our own ideas and a means of contesting their development between ourselves as authors as we struggled to forge a common position on which we genuinely agreed and that was consistent with the evidence we had to hand.

Given this lineage, professional capital is an emergent and provisional construct that will benefit from considerable further research of a qualitative and quantitative kind, especially in terms of its contribution to change over time, and its nature, presence, or absence within high-performing and low-performing educational systems.

Two Kinds of Capital

Capital relates to one's own or a group's worth, particularly concerning assets that can be leveraged to accomplish desired goals. We already know about business and financial capital. You have to make an investment if you want a return. If you want growth, you can't just squirrel your assets away but need to put them to work. Capital has to circulate if assets are going to grow. And governments are crucial in creating the conditions and the levels of confidence that can stimulate or discourage capital investment. Of course, this doesn't only apply to economic capital. It concerns how we invest in people and get returns from those investments too.

People have written about and argued for developing many different kinds of capital. Economic capital is the obvious one. But cultural capital, "natural" capital, and even "erotic" capital all have their proponents too. Professional capital takes the basic idea of capital and articulates its importance for professional work, professional capability, and professional effectiveness—particularly in the teaching profession.

Although there is little disagreement about the importance of good teachers and good teaching, two schools of thought about different kinds of capital are driving entire nations in diametrically opposite directions on this front.

Business Capital

In the first view, what kinds of teachers we need and how best to get them are driven by ideas about *business capital.* Here, following the collapse of worldwide property and financial markets, the primary purpose of education is to serve as a big new market for investment in technology, curriculum and testing materials, and in schools themselves as for-profit enterprises. In the estimates of some multinational moguls, this is a massive $500 billion market.[2]

When education is organized to get quick returns on business investment, and to increase immediate returns by lowering that investment, it favors a teaching force that is young, flexible, temporary, inexpensive to train at the beginning, un-pensioned at the end (except by teachers' own self-investment), and replaceable wherever possible by technology. Finding and keeping good teachers then becomes about seeking out and deploying (but not really developing or investing in) *existing human capital*—hunting for talented individuals, working them hard, and moving them on when they get restless or become spent.

The business capital view of teaching assumes that:

- Good teaching may be emotionally demanding, but it is technically simple.
- Good teaching is a quick study requiring only moderate intellectual ability.
- Good teaching is hard at first, but with dedication can be mastered readily.
- Good teaching should be driven by hard performance data about what works and where best to target one's efforts.
- Good teaching comes down to enthusiasm, hard work, raw talent, and measurable results.
- Good teaching is often replaceable by online instruction.

The business capital strategy toward teaching is advocated aggressively in the US and is gaining ground in places like the UK and several other countries in Europe. Yet, none of the world's most successful school systems adopt this approach in building their most valuable societal assets. In Finland and Singapore, for example, teachers are regarded as indispensable national assets in the building of their nations.

Professional Capital

Against the business capital view is what Michael Fullan and I call *professional capital*. This strategy has already been adopted by the highest-performing economies and educational systems in the world. Countries and communities that invest in professional capital recognize that educational spending is a long-term investment in developing human capital from early childhood to adult life, to reap rewards of economic productivity and social cohesion in the next generation. A significant part of this investment is in high-quality teachers and teaching. In this view, getting good teaching for all learners requires teachers to be highly committed, thoroughly prepared, continuously developed, properly paid, well networked with each other to maximize their own improvement, and able to make effective judgments using all their capabilities and experience.

The professional capital view of teaching assumes that:

- Good teaching is technically sophisticated and difficult.
- Good teaching requires high levels of education and long periods of training.
- Good teaching is perfected through continuous and continued improvement.
- Good teaching involves wise judgment informed by evidence and experience.
- Good teaching is a collective accomplishment and responsibility.
- Good teaching mediates and moderates online instruction.

Professional capital is itself made up of three other kinds of capital—human, social, and decisional. These are now examined in turn.

Human Capital

For a long time, capital was regarded as a financial phenomenon that came out of economic production. But in the 1960s, a group of economists pointed to the importance of another kind of capital: *human capital*.[3] This referred to the economically valuable knowledge and skills that could be developed in people—especially through education and training. In the human capital view of education and economies, investing in people's education and development brings economic returns later on. The sooner people start their education in early childhood, at home or at school, and the longer their period of schooling, then the more economic returns a nation will get on this investment in its people. Education is a capital investment—and so too is teaching.

Human capital in teaching is about having and developing the requisite knowledge and skills. It is about knowing your subject and knowing how to teach it, knowing children and understanding how they learn, understanding the diverse cultural and family circumstances that your students come from, being familiar with and able to sift and sort the science of successful and innovative practice, and having the emotional capabilities to empathize with diverse groups of children and indeed adults in and around a school.

Human capital is about individual talent, commitment, and capability. Alan Odden's (2011) book on *The Strategic Management of Human Capital in Education* defines human capital as "talent" and describes how to get more of it, develop it, and sustain it.

The human capital argument has been bolstered by one of today's arguably most abused educational research findings: that *"the quality of the teacher is the single most important determinant in the learning of the student."* This finding was first presented by an agricultural economist, William Sanders, who made some remarkable claims about the impact of individual teacher quality on student achievement[4] (Sanders and Rivers, 1996; Sanders, 1998). Using value-added evidence that took two hypothetical students starting equally at the 50th percentile of performance, Sanders and Rivers demonstrated what happens when Student A receives three years of learning from a high-quality teacher (top 20 percent), while Student B experiences three years of a low-performing teacher (bottom 20 percent). At the end of the three years, Student A performs at the 90th percentile, while student B is at the 37th percentile. One has gained ground substantially; the other has actually gone backwards—a difference of 53 percentile points.

If this evidence seems outdated, in 2010 the *Los Angeles Times* shook the US teacher-quality debate with another explosive set of findings. Reporters gained access to seven years of value-added test performance data of 6,000 3rd through 5th grade teachers in English and mathematics in the LA Unified Public School District—one of the poorest performing districts in the US. They passed the data to expert economists who came up with an even more remarkable finding. There were differences of up to 41 percent in value-added performance between teachers of the same kinds of children *in the very same school!* Reporters even identified the poorest-performing culprits by name, heaping shame and scorn upon them (Felch, 2010).

With such shocking and seemingly self-evident findings, judgments about variations in individual human capital have not been slow to follow—especially in terms of devising systems of individual reward and punishment for high-performing and low-performing teachers respectively. There is little sympathy for the bottom 20 percent of teachers who are so clearly letting their students down, and strong advocacy that the top 20 percent should be awarded extra pay because of their determination to succeed against the odds. Get tough at the bottom and reward those at the top!—these are the results of individual human capital theory when it is applied to individualistic systems of performance-based reward.

Interestingly, merit pay in teaching has a century-old track record of failure. Time and again, attempts to pay teachers based on their students' test scores as a way to improve practice just have not worked.[5] More than this, as business psychology expert Daniel Pink points out, merit pay does not even work in the corporate world except for the simplest and most standardized of jobs (Pink, 2009). With work that requires sophisticated levels of judgment and skill, merit pay has *no* positive effect on performance. Indeed, it actually makes performance *worse* by distracting people from their core purpose with short-term rewards. So either merit pay will make the best teachers worse, or teaching will have to be turned into standardized, simplified, and scripted operations so the reward system can have a positive effect. This second option is what many US systems have actually been doing—reducing teaching to basic skills where what teachers have to do is set out in step-by-step, rigidly paced manuals under tight regimes of strict compliance.

The issue of individual human capital in teaching is important, but outside the low-performing nations of the UK and US, high-performing countries participating in PISA adopt a different approach altogether. Their approach is based on developing all individual teachers to a high professional standard, not on discriminating between the best and worst among them in relation to educational test scores.

High-performing countries such as Finland, Singapore, and Canada—which make up the leading nations on the OECD's international PISA tests of student achievement—draw their teachers from the top 30 percent of the university graduating class, while the US and other lower-performing countries like England (both positioned way down in the low teens to twenties percent on the PISA rankings) at best recruit mostly from the bottom 40 percent (Auguste *et al.*, 2010). Just as crucially, the top nations invest in better working conditions on the job—a clear and commonly held sense of purpose and direction, the opportunity to work with good colleagues, professional development to increase skills, new leadership roles, access to technology and good data, and so on. In short, both initial attraction to the profession and continued learning on the job with others combine to systematically foster, strengthen, and maintain professional capital.

Teaching is an attractive profession in all high-performing countries. Teachers are praised and prized for what they do. They are seen as the builders of their nations. Starting salaries for teachers in Singapore, for example, compare favorably with engineers and other professionals so that teaching can attract the best of the best—even, and especially, in mathematics and science. Finnish teachers have such high status that teaching is one of the top two preferred occupations for a future spouse—right up with medicine and higher than business or law (Kangasniemi, 2008)! In stark contrast, in the US especially, teachers and teacher unions are constantly vilified by politicians and in the media. There, teachers are the new bankers—soft targets for all of society's complaints.

Then there's the matter of working conditions. In Canada, with the exception of a few schools in remote aboriginal communities, the most isolated rural backwaters or the toughest urban neighborhoods have well-resourced schools staffed by knowledgeable, competent, and highly qualified teachers (Levin and Naylor, 2007). In Finland, whatever the socioeconomic status of a school's students, all schools are good to the extent that this nation has the narrowest achievement gaps in the world. In Singapore, where no schools are run-down or shabby, teachers regard it as an honor to be asked to move to a school or a track that serves a challenging cohort of students. The reassignment is seen as recognition of their professional quality and a test of their commitment and their skills.

There's something else about these three high-performing nations. Their private school systems are either very tiny or virtually non-existent. Almost all the public is invested in their nation's public schools and in the quality of teachers who work there. By comparison, many US urban schools are disgracefully dilapidated, woefully lacking in technology and other resources, and little more than sinkholes for poor minorities. Affluent and even not-so-affluent white families have long since abandoned these for schools in the plusher suburbs or the privileged independent sector. England's schools and also Australia's are also typically divided by private options, residence, and individual choice. Individual human capital cannot be separated from the quality of the school context and working environment.

Successful countries do not only prize academic qualities or individual human capital in their teachers; they also focus on "suitability to teach" in initial selection, on rigorous pre-service development, and on support on the job. These high-performing systems deliberately develop professional capital in their teaching force. And in every case, almost all the public is invested in having high-quality teachers serving practically all the children who are their nations' future.

An example of how all this comes together is Finland. Finland does not only get some of the best achievement results in the world, but also has the smallest differences between children from better-off and poorer families. In 2007, on behalf of the Organisation for Economic Co-operation and Development (OECD) I took a team, including Beatriz Pont and Gabor Halasz, to undertake the first external international review of Finland's modern educational system and the reasons for its high performance. This is what we found out about the country's teachers:

> Other nations are experimenting with ways of rewarding differential performance within the established teaching profession. Teaching is already an attractive and desired profession in Finland. It has high status in a learner-centered society where it contributes to the wider social mission of economic prosperity, cultural creativity and social justice. In a society with high taxation and relatively modest income differentials, teaching is paid quite satisfactorily. Working conditions and resources are supportive, schools are well equipped, and like other professionals, teachers enjoy considerable trust and autonomy. Teaching is highly competitive and attracts high performing secondary school graduates. Professional entry also requires Masters' degrees. Teacher training blends theoretical and practical components, and continuing professional development is becoming more integrated into the collective life and needs of the school.
>
> (Hargreaves *et al.*, 2008: 81)

Pasi Sahlberg, former educational reform specialist for the World Bank, and now Director of the Centre for International Mobility in Finland, has written the most comprehensive and insightful account that only an insider could assemble, of the reasons for his nation's success. In *Finnish Lessons*, he compares Finland's improvement path to what he calls the "Global Educational Reform Movement" (or GERM) and its preoccupations with standardization, external accountability, high-stakes testing, and market-driven competition, which are supposed to drive up the performance of schools and teachers (Sahlberg, 2011). GERM, he points out, characterizes low-performing systems as in the US and in the UK under its previous governments. It restricts teachers' autonomy, subjects teachers to endless intervention, drives them to compete instead of collaborate, and makes the work of teaching so unappealing that it cannot attract the best-qualified university graduates. In Finland, however:

> Teachers at all levels of schooling expect that they are given the full range of professional autonomy to practice what they have been educated to do: to plan, teach, diagnose, execute, and evaluate. They also expect to be provided time to accomplish all of these goals in and out of normal classroom duties. Indeed, in Finland, teachers spend relatively less time teaching than their peers in many other countries. For example, in North American schools, teachers are engaged in teaching during the vast majority of their daily working time in school, which leaves little space for any other professional activities.
>
> Interestingly [in Sahlberg's interviews with primary school teachers about what would make them leave the profession], practically nobody cites their salary as a reason to quit teaching. Instead, many point out that if they were to lose their professional autonomy in schools and their classrooms, their career choice would be called into question. For example, if an external inspection to judge the quality of their work or a merit-based compensation policy influenced by external measures was introduced, many would change their jobs. Many Finnish teachers report that if they encountered similar external pressure through external standardized measuring and test-based accountability, as do their peers in the UK or North America, they would seek other professional challenges. It is, first and foremost, the working conditions and moral professional environment that count as young Finns decide whether they will pursue a teaching career or seek work in another field.
>
> (Sahlberg, 2011: 76)

In contrast to such high performers, many of the lower-performing Anglo-American nations have been experimenting with other ways of recruiting and selecting teachers. Schemes such as *Teach for America* (TfA) or *Teach First* in the UK, which are now extending into Australia, New Zealand, and China, are designed in part to give future corporate and political leaders a taste of teaching for two or three years at the start of their careers—so that they might become informed influential advocates for public education a generation from now. Yet even if they do become influential eventually, what kinds of reforms will they advocate, given that their experiences have likely been to prop up what they see as low-performing schools with teachers inferior to themselves? To be fair, in some US inner cities, conditions and support for teachers are so poor that many schools could not even operate without TfA. But even if you triple or quadruple the number of teachers trained this way, through TfA or Teach First, it is but a pinprick on the teacher supply problem—especially when only 60 percent of these teachers remain after two years, and only 15 percent remain in low-income schools after four years (Donaldson and Johnson, 2011).[6] Alternate routes of certification that concentrate on bright and enthusiastic graduates or career changers contradict the rigorous academic and experiential preparation processes of high-performing nations and, in any case, address only a portion of the teaching force and its human capital, rather than all or most of it.

Beyond the many critiques and all the quibbles about the accuracy and validity of value-added assessments, and beyond the unsettling findings that perceived quality in teacher performance varies wildly according to what measure is chosen, or even, for the same teacher, from one class to another and one year to the next, judging teachers according to their individual performance has one more fatal flaw—the neglect of social capital (McCaffrey *et al.*, 2009; Braun *et al.*, 2010).

Social Capital

Teaching, like any other profession, does not come down only to individual skill or will, or to capability and commitment alone. It is also profoundly affected by the environment—by the culture of the workplace where the job is carried out. If the teaching in a school is all over the place, we shouldn't so much be asking questions about the abilities or commitments of individual teachers. We should be wondering what is wrong with the school. Just because there is one outstanding pioneer in a school, this does not mean that, by will and effort alone, all or most of the teachers in that school can be pioneers as well—not unless we do something about the school as a whole.

This is true in just about any line of work. You don't expect an airline crew to be courteous or cranky depending on which particular flight attendant you get. If one hairdresser in a salon makes you look like a fashion model, while next time their colleague turns you into a scary clown, there is something wrong with the salon. In any good airline, salon, or school, you should expect quality and consistency that is personalized for you. If you have no way of predicting how different people in an organization will deal with you, something is profoundly amiss with that organization. And rewarding the good people, while removing or intervening with the poor ones, will not give you greater consistency or turn the whole organization around.

The answer is not to be found in the addition of individual capabilities or human capital, but in the collective product or function of how the community works together as a whole. This is called "culture" (Deal and Kennedy, 1982). Culture shapes the experience you are likely to get when you fly with a high- or low-performing airline just as much as when you enter a school! At its best, culture doesn't give you a good teacher here and a weaker teacher there, but many strong and capable teachers, working passionately together, under visionary leadership, so all their students succeed—and not just in a few schools, but in all schools across the system.

You do not accumulate much human capital by just focusing on the capital of individuals. Capital has to be circulated and shared in order to reap a return on investment. Groups, teams, and communities are far more powerful than individuals when it comes to developing human capital.

Human capital therefore has to be complemented by, and even organized in terms of, what is called *social capital*. Economist Glenn Loury first brought social capital into the modern limelight in the 1970s (Loury, 1977, 1987). In the late 1980s, sociologist James Coleman put it front and center of his influential analysis of the reasons for high-school drop-out and why educational outcomes varied between Catholic schools and regular public schools (Coleman, 1986, 1988). Social capital, Coleman said, exists in the relations among people. It's a resource for them. And like economic and human capital, it contributes to productive activity. "For example, a group within which there is extensive trustworthiness and extensive trust is able to accomplish much more than a comparable group without that trustworthiness and trust" (Coleman, 1988: S101). Groups with purpose that are based on trust also learn more. They get better at their work.

Social capital refers to how the quantity and quality of interactions and social relationships among people affects their access to knowledge and information; their senses of expectation, obligation, and trust; and how far they are likely to adhere to the same norms or codes of behavior. In families, social capital "depends both on the physical presence of adults in the family and on the attention given by the adults to the child" (Coleman, 1988: S111).

Social capital increases your knowledge—it gives you access to other people's *human capital*. It expands your networks of influence and opportunity. And it develops resilience when you know there are people to go to who can give you advice and be your advocates. In *Bowling Alone*, Robert Putnam (2011) famously bemoaned the decline of social capital and community life in modern American society. The decline of public schools in the US has also weakened social capital in urban communities, as connecting with others in those communities through one's children is a prime way to build relationships with neighbors.

More recently, Pickett and Wilkinson, in *The Spirit Level* (2011), show that societies with low levels of trust have higher levels of income inequality. People who are insulated from each other by income in different neighborhoods, or even gated communities, don't trust people they don't know. The same patterns hold between different states in the US—high-trust states have smaller income disparities than low-trust states.

Social capital is significant in education too. For example, in their modern classic, *Trust in Schools*, Tony Bryk and Beverly Schneider (2002) demonstrate that among public schools in Chicago that deal with similar kinds of students, the ones that reach greater achievement levels have higher levels of trust between teachers and students, parents, administrators, and colleagues—levels that precede the gains in achievement.

Of particular interest for the argument here is the role of social capital among teachers and in teaching, and the relative impact of social capital on teachers' effectiveness and results, compared to individual human capital. In a landmark study, Carrie Leana (2011) points out that social capital in terms of patterns of interaction among teachers and between teachers and administrators that are focused on student learning makes a large measurable difference to student achievement and sustained improvement.

Leana examined the relationship between human and social capital. She and her team followed over 1,000 4th and 5th grade teachers in a representative sample of 130 elementary schools across New York City. The human capital measures included individual teacher qualifications, experience, and ability to teach. Social capital was measured in terms of the frequency and focus of conversations and interactions with peers that centered on instruction, and was based on feelings of trust and closeness between teachers.

Leana also obtained the mathematics scores of the students at the beginning of the year compared to the gains by year-end. She found that teachers with high social capital increased their mathematics scores by 5.7 percent more than teachers with lower social capital scores. Teachers who were both more able (high human capital) and had stronger ties with their peers (high social capital) had the biggest gains in mathematics achievement. She also found that low-ability teachers perform as well as teachers of average ability "*if* they have strong social capital in their school" (Leana, 2011: 34).

In short, high social capital and high human capital are both valuable assets. However, not only did the students of teachers who reported higher social capital have a higher increase in mathematics scores than those whose teachers who scored well on individual human capital alone, but even teachers with lower human capital did better if they were in a school with greater social capital. Social capital can lift the performance of those who are weak in human capital, but the converse is not true. Strong human capital does not compensate for weak social capital. Overall, though, the most important thing to stress is that the best results are obtained from teachers who are high in human and also social capital—well-qualified and knowledgeable teachers who work in supportive and collaborative cultures of teaching.

Decisional Capital

But even human capital and social capital are not enough. There is still something missing. We call it *decisional capital*. The essence of professionalism is the ability to make discretionary judgments. When you put a difficult question to an employee and they ask you to wait until they consult their supervisor, you know they are not professional because they cannot exercise any discretion. If a teacher always has to consult a teachers' manual, or follow the lesson line-by-line, in a script, you know they are not a professional either, because they do not know how to judge or they aren't being allowed to.

Judges have to judge even when the evidence is not conclusive. In fact, if the evidence *were* conclusive, there would be no need for judges at all. Doctors have to judge when they examine a set of symptoms or interpret a brain scan. Teachers have to judge when they treat acting out by one child differently from that by another, because they know different things about those children: how they learn, what frustrates them if they have a disability, and so on. You can't be a judge if you can't judge, and neither can you be a doctor or a teacher (or at least an effective one). The capacity to judge and judge well depends on the ability to make decisions in situations of unavoidable uncertainty when the evidence or the rules are not usually categorically clear.

The idea of decisional capital is taken from *case law*, although it could come just as easily from any other profession. Decisional law is "the law as determined by reference to the reported decisions of the courts."[7] In Anglo-American legal systems, this is known simply as *common law*. Becoming a lawyer in these systems involves remembering reams of factual information but also understanding how this mass of information relates to and can be interpreted through particular cases. Case law is always developing as cases refer to and move on from each other over time. This kind of law sets out the facts of the case but also describes how judges came to their decision, including the judges who held minority dissenting views.

If you know how to examine a case and have practiced this with hundreds or even thousands of cases, alongside partners, associates, and other counsel, then eventually you know how to judge. Decisional capital here is the capital that professionals acquire and accumulate through structured and unstructured experience, practice, and reflection, that enables them to make wise judgments in circumstances where there is no fixed rule or piece of incontrovertible evidence to guide them. Decisional capital is enhanced by drawing on the insights and experiences of colleagues in forming judgments over many occasions. In other words, in teaching and other professions, social capital is actually an integral part of decisional capital as well as an addition to it.

Practice, deliberately pursued, really does make perfect. In his best-selling book, *Outliers*, Canadian writer Malcolm Gladwell (2008) brought this simple principle to widespread popular attention. In a chapter on exceptionally high performance, he discussed a classic study that compared amateur and professional pianists:

> The amateurs never practiced more than about three hours a week over the course of their childhood, and by the age of twenty they had totaled two thousand hours of practice. The professionals, on the other hand, steadily increased their practice time every year, until by the age of twenty, they had reached ten thousand hours.[8]

Ten thousand hours, Gladwell says, is the figure that comes up time and again as the number of hours it seems to take the brain "to assimilate all that it needs to know to achieve true mastery" (Gladwell, 2008: 40). This is true in music, professional sports, or any other especially accomplished area in life. It is what separates professionals from the rest.

In any profession, it is important to practice, to keep practicing, and to get the opportunity to practice. Gladwell points out that "even Mozart—the greatest musical prodigy of all time—couldn't hit his stride until he had invested his ten thousand hours" (Gladwell, 2008: 42).

In a classic study of teachers' commitment and capability among 300 teachers in 100 schools over two years, Chris Day and his team (2006) in the UK highlighted the career stages when teachers were, on average, at their peak of commitment and capability. This occurred about eight or ten years into the job, which is, depending on the system the teacher is in, about 10,000 hours! Of course, this does not mean that every teacher who has clocked up these hours is necessarily a maestro by this point. It depends on what the hours are like. And it doesn't rule out the prior learning or previous hours that incoming teachers might already have accumulated in sports coaching, youth work, or leadership of young people in general, that might shorten the hours needed to become truly expert when they start teaching for real. But on average, with these hours behind them, the evidence is clear that teachers have attained higher proficiency than their colleagues who have put in less time, and who may be high on enthusiasm but not yet on capability (though school principals too often mistake the second for the first).

So it is practice and a great deal of it that develops decisional capital—that makes teachers skilled professionals and not just keen amateurs. Leave teaching before eight years and it is likely you will never develop decisional capital and therefore professional capital to a high level. If recruitment and reward systems in teaching are based on acceptance and even advancement of the idea that many teachers will or should move on after three to five years, before their wages rise or their resistance kicks in, then the development of professional capital in individual teachers is prevented, and professional capital is depleted from the system—all for a quick gain in business capital that sees public education as a cost instead of an investment.

Decisional capital is also sharpened when it is mediated through interaction with colleagues (social capital). High-yield strategies become more precise and more embedded when they are developed and deployed in teams that are constantly refining and interpreting them. At the same time, poor judgments and ineffective practices get discarded along the way. And when clear evidence is lacking or conflicting, accumulated collective experience carries much more weight than idiosyncratic experience or little experience at all. As in medicine, a second opinion often matters—the opportunity to reflect on intuition and to compare it with the experiences and perceptions of colleagues. In other words, it's more likely that practice will make perfect when it is shared and also when it is thoughtful and reflective.

In the 1980s, Boston-born philosopher and erstwhile jazz pianist Donald Schön (1983; 1987), who helped found the study of organizational learning, wrote a remarkable series of books about reflective practice and reflective practitioners. Schön was critical of what he called *technical rationality*—the belief that science and objective evidence would provide all the answers in professional practice. He wouldn't be impressed with data warehouses or with the way some administrators worship evidence-based practices today. Instead, the defining core of what it meant to be professional for Schön was to be able to engage in what he called *reflective practice*.

Reflective practice, he said, has two aspects: reflecting in action and reflecting on action. *Reflecting in action* is the capacity to walk around a problem while you are right in the middle of it, to think about what you are doing even as you are improvising it. When you have considered whether to speed up or slow down a presentation, to stop and ask a question or tell a joke, to move to the back of the classroom or stay at the front, or to explain an idea another way with another example, you are reflecting in action. *Reflection on action* is reflection after the fact, once the practice has finished: "I wonder why the boys don't like writing as much as the girls?" "Am I drawing answers to questions only from the front three rows and not from the back?" "Why are some of the children never choosing art as an activity?" These are the kinds of questions that you pose when you are reflecting on what you have done.

Both these kinds of reflection are central to professional practice, and both of them benefit from practice. But in the main, they benefit from having a mentor or coach who can pull you back, slow you down, give you feedback, and cause you to reflect on what you have been doing, why you have done it that way, and how you might do it differently. Get the reflection *on* action right and it enables you to start reflecting *in* action more effectively too. So it is not so much practice that makes perfect then, as practice that is reflective.

Liz MacDonald and Dennis Shirley (2009) draw attention to this in their study of mindfulness with a group of urban Boston public school teachers. One of the seven principles of mindful teaching these teachers developed was simply "stopping"—"reflecting on the rush of events and attending to forms of learning … that find scant realization" in a test-driven curriculum. What prevents mindfulness and reflection, MacDonald and Shirley say, is not lack of willingness by teachers, but a school environment that is overloaded with tests and targets, awash with data and spreadsheets, and overcome by a frenetic rush of endless interventions.

So it is important that teachers and leaders also engage in a third kind of reflection—*reflection about action*—about the things in their environment that distract them from what is important, that get them so immersed in busy activity there is no time left to think, and that are an endless set of responses and reactions to other people's agendas instead of actions driven by purposes that are teachers' own. Reflection about action drives you to change the context and conditions of what you practice, so that your practice can improve a lot more.

Reflective practice isn't just an act of will or the result of encouragement. You have to build it into people's practice—make it part of their day. When reflection becomes more structured and systematic, it turns into what German émigré and psychological warfare expert Kurt Lewin (1946) first termed *action research* in 1946. Action research, said Lewin, was research designed to solve social problems. It was "comparative research on the conditions and effects of various forms of social action, and research leading to social action." "Research that produces nothing but books," he continued, "will not suffice" (p. 35).

Today, this work in education is known more as *inquiry* or *teacher inquiry*, which encourages teachers inquiring into their own practice to follow similar processes. Teacher inquiry does not mean being driven by data or becoming a slave to external evidence. Teachers as action researchers or inquirers use external and internally collected evidence to inquire into their practices, assess their effectiveness, identify the reasons for difficulties and also successes, and plan how to improve and make interventions as a result. Here, action research and inquiry are not activities undertaken in teacher preparation programs that are never used again in "real" teaching; nor are they isolated projects or procedures that educators use when developing an improvement plan for the district, for example. Instead, action research and inquiry are part of the job, integral to teaching, a stance that teachers take, and a key part of what it means to be professional and to improve practice on a continuing basis (Cochran-Smith and Lytle, 2009).

In most schools and school systems, this ethic of inquiry as something that is integral to teaching is a distant dream—an unrealistic ideal in a world where teachers are always in their classrooms and never able to stand aside and inquire into what they are doing together. But teacher inquiry *is* a priority in high-performing Alberta, for example, where over 90 percent of the province's schools are continuously engaged in school-designed innovations that involve inquiry as part of their development and evaluation. In Finland too, teachers are able to engage in inquiry because they spend less of their school day in classroom teaching than most other nations, while the US has one of the highest figures of all for how much in-class time its teachers spend. If you spend all your day teaching, you are not going to have much opportunity to inquire into, reflect on, and adjust it over time. You turn teaching into the Legal Aid of educational change.

Practice, especially collective reflective practice, then, is integral to decisional capital and, by that token, to professional capital as a whole. In sum, when we add reflective capacity and action research to stocks of human and social capital, we hone our decisional capacity to take informed decisions. Like medicine, teaching is an imperfect science and we need qualified and thinking professionals working together to maximize its effectiveness.

Conclusion

Professional capital is essential for effective teaching, and it is most essential in the most challenging educational circumstances. We can now express it in a formula. Where PC is professional capital, HC is human capital, SC is social capital, and DC is decisional capital, it can be summed up in the following equation:

PC = f (HC, SC, DC).

If any one of the elements on the right-hand side of the equation is missing, then professional capital will be depleted and the standard of teaching will fall short. Teachers will be short on professional capital if they are under-qualified, if they come from the lower end of the graduation range, and if they have not been screened for their emotional capability and for their previous experiences of working with young people. Teachers will be short on professional capital if they spend most of their professional time alone, if they do not get feedback and support from colleagues, and if they are not connected to teachers in other schools. And teachers will be short on professional capital if they do not put in the years required to perfect their practice, and if they are not provided with the coaching, mentoring, and time that help them reflect on that practice.

The globalization of educational change is being contested by two visions of capital in education. Short-term business capital is advancing the immediate interests of technology conglomerates by increasing the attention to personalized learning as customized instruction in ways that increasingly replace the teacher with the mouse. It is placing national governments in hock to large testing corporations, which link processes of standardization and testing to nationally designed and imposed curricula that are indifferent to the diversity of students that those national standards are supposed to address. And it is eroding and eliminating the power of local authorities, districts, and municipalities by creating an educational order of national governments on the one hand and of fragmented, individualized, and increasingly privately run schools on the other that are easy prey to the tests and technologies of corporate giants without resistance from the democratic local authorities that have always been the cornerstone of public education. The business capital view of education prefers and promotes a teaching force that is largely young, inexperienced, un-unionized, temporary, and flexible, even though the teachers in high-performing countries do not conform to these criteria at all. The business capital vision of teaching is one that sacrifices evidence and effectiveness to ideology and economic self-interest.

Against this ideology stands the position of professional capital that coheres with best practice in the highest-performing countries where education serves long-term economic (and social) interests and development, not the interests of immediate profit for rapid financial gain. It is a position that has been adopted by high-performing nations of different political ideologies but common and transcendent commitments to public education and public good. The power of professional capital is that it draws in the best and most qualified people in society into a highly valued and high-status lifetime career that offers security and flexibility, rewarding collaboration, and supportive working conditions, and a commitment to a common good that is greater than oneself, one's class or one's school but that encompasses the development of the society as a whole.

Nelson Mandela (1995) once tellingly observed: "There can be no keener revelation of a society's soul, than the way in which it treats its children." It is clear and proven that the Number One factor that makes the greatest difference to children's lives and children's futures within our schools is these children's teachers. So we should also say that:

> There can be no keener revelation of a society's soul than the way in which it treats its children and their teachers.

We can treat teaching as just a short-term investment of business capital, and finance the present by mortgaging our children's future. Or we can make teaching a sustainable investment for professional capital, and give birth to a world of many happy returns to come. The choice is ours. The consequences will be profound. The responsibility belongs to all of us.

Notes

1   In *Aftershock*, former US Secretary of Labor, Robert Reich, has undertaken an extensive analysis of US responses to the global economic collapse. This response, he argues, protects very high income inequalities and prevents wealth, consumption, and economic growth circulating throughout the society; and instead reduces any squeeze on existing profits by attacking pensions, social security, and other public sector services. See Reich (2010).

2   The "$500 billion market" comment was made by News Corporation Chairman and CEO, Rupert Murdoch, in a press release after his company acquired Wireless Generation, an education technology company. Retrieved from www.newscorp.com/news/news_464.html.

3   The concept of "human capital" was perhaps first used by Adam Smith (1776) who referred to it as:

> the acquired and useful abilities of all the inhabitants or members of the society. The acquisition of such talents, by the maintenance of the acquirer during his education, study, or apprenticeship, always costs a real expense, which is a capital fixed and realized, as it were, in his person. Those talents, as they make a part of his fortune, so do they likewise that of the society to which he belongs. The improved dexterity of a workman may be considered in the same light as a machine or instrument of trade which facilitates and abridges labor, and which, though it costs a certain expense, repays that expense with a profit.
>
> (Smith, 1776/2009: 202)

A discussion of Adam Smith's conception of "human capital" is found in Spengler (1977).

4   Classic references in the wider debate on measuring teacher effects include Hanushek (1992) and Rivkin *et al.* (1998). More recent work includes Carey (2004), Braun (2005), Walsh (2007), and Koretz (2008). More recently, John Hattie examined more than 800 meta-analyses in this area over a 15-year period. In one of six key points, he notes that "Teachers are among the most powerful influences in learning" (2009: 238).

5   For literature on merit pay, see Gatz (2011). Jesse Rothstein (2008) has written about the issues with value-added measures. See also Viadero (2009). Other seminal pieces on merit pay date as far back as the 1980s, for example Murnane and Cohen (1986). For background and proposals for teacher compensation, see Johnson and Liu (2004) and Johnson and Papay (2009).

6   For additional references on the attrition rates for TfA teachers, see Darling-Hammond *et al.* (2005). The attrition rates of alternatively certified teachers are also reported in Kane *et al.* (2008) and Heilig and Jez (2010).

7   A search on "decisional law" in Westlaw, a search engine frequently used by lawyers, indicates that decisional law is like case law. Westlaw defines "case law" as legal principles enunciated and embodied in judicial decisions or cases. In the US and Canada, this is also similar to common law or laws set on court decisions. Here is an example using Florida's rules of criminal procedure: "New decisional law which announces new procedural principles applicable to the trial or appeal of criminal cases and which is not 'prospective only' will also generally not apply in criminal cases that are already final when the new decision is handed down" [22 Fla. Prac., Criminal Procedure § 1:13 (2011)]. Our use of decisional capital diverges slightly from the juridical definition of decisional law in that we define decisional capital as an informal as well as a formal process of developing the capacity for expert judgment over time.

8   The studies in the 1990s by K. Anders Ericsson and his colleagues mentioned in Gladwell's book can be found in Ericsson *et al.* (1993).

References

Auguste, B., Kihn, P. and Miller, M. (2010) *Closing the Talent Gap: Attracting and retaining top third graduates to a career in teaching*, London: McKinsey & Company. Available at http://mckinseyonsociety.com/downloads/reports/Education/Closing_the_talent_gap.pdf (accessed August 4, 2012).

Bird, S.M., Cox, D., Farewell, V.T., Goldstein, H., Holt, T. and Smith, P.C. (2005) Performance indicators: good, bad, and ugly, *Journal of the Royal Statistical Society*, Series A (Statistics in Society), 1–27.

Braun, H.I. (2005) *Using Student Progress to Evaluate Teachers: A primer on value-added models*, Princeton, NJ: Education Testing Service.

Braun, H.I., Chudowsky, N., and Koenig, J. (eds) (2010) *Getting Value out of Value-added*, Washington, DC: National Academies Press.

Bryk, A. and Schneider, B. (2002) *Trust in Schools*, New York: Russell Sage.

Carey, K. (2004) The real value of teachers: Using new information about teacher effectiveness to close the achievement gap. *Thinking K–16*, 8(1): 3–42.

Cochran-Smith, M. and Lytle, S.L. (2009) *Inquiry as Stance: Practitioner research in the next generation*, New York: Teachers College Press.

Coleman, J.S. (1986) Social theory, social research and a theory of action, *American Journal of Sociology*, 91(6): 1309–35.

Coleman, J.S. (1988) Social capital in the creation of human capital, *American Journal of Sociology*, 94, supplement: *Organizations and Institutions: Sociological and economic approaches to the analysis of social structure*, S95–S120. Available at http://onemvweb.com/sources/sources/social_capital.pdf (accessed September 10, 2012).

Darling-Hammond, L., Holtzman, D.J., Gatlin, S.J. and Heilig, J.V. (2005) Does teacher preparation matter? Evidence about teacher certification, Teach for America, and teacher effectiveness, *Educational Policy Analysis Archives*, 13(42): 1–48. Available at http://epaa.asu.edu/ojs/article/view/147/273 (accessed July 14, 2012).

Day, C., Stobart, G., Sammons, P., Kington, A., Gu, Q., Smees, R. and Mujtaba, T. (2006) *Variations in Teachers' Work, Lives and Effectiveness*, Research Report 743, London: DfES.

Deal, T. and Kennedy, A.A. (1982) *Corporate Cultures: The rite and rituals of corporate life*, New York: Basic Books.

Donaldson, D.L. and Johnson, S.M. (2011) TFA teachers: How long do they teach? Why do they leave? *Phi Delta Kappa International*. Available at www.edweek.org/ew/articles/2011/10/04/kappan_donaldson.html (accessed August 21, 2012).

Ericsson, K.A., Krampe, R.T. and Tesch-Römer, C. (1993) The role of deliberate practice in the acquisition of expert performance, *Psychological Review*, 100(3): 363–406.

Felch, J. (2010) How good is your child's teacher? *The Times* crunches the numbers, *L.A. Times*, August 14. Available at http://latimesblogs.latimes.com/lanow/2010/08/times-evaluates-teachers.html (accessed August 21, 2010).

Fullan, M. and Hargreaves, A. (1996) *What's Worth Fighting for in Your School?* New York: Teachers College Press.

Gatz, D.B. (2011) Performance pay: path to improvement, *Kappa Delta Pi*, Summer: 156–61.

Gladwell, M. (2008) *Outliers: The story of success*, New York: Little, Brown.

Hanushek, E.A. (1992) The trade-off between child quantity and quality, *Journal of Political Economy*, 100(1): 84–117.

Hargreaves, A., Halász, G. and Pont, B. (2008) The Finnish approach to system leadership, in B. Pont, D. Nusche and D. Hopkins (eds) *Improving School Leadership, vol 2: Case studies on system leadership*, Paris: OECD, pp. 69–109.

Hattie, J. (2009) *Visible Learning: A synthesis of over 800 meta-analyses relating to student achievement*, London: Routledge.

Heilig, J.V. and Jez, S.J. (2010) *Teach for America: A review of the evidence*, East Lansing, MI: The Great Lakes Center for Education Research & Practice. Available at www.greatlakescenter.org/docs/Policy_Briefs/Heilig_TeachForAmerica.pdf (accessed November 12, 2010).

Johnson, S.M. and Liu, E. (2004) What teaching pays, what teaching costs, in S.M. Johnson and The Project on the Next Generation of Teachers, *Finders and Keepers: Helping new teachers survive and thrive in our schools*, San Francisco, CA: Jossey-Bass, pp. 49–68.

Johnson, S.M. and Papay, J.P. (2009) *Redesigning Teacher Pay: A system for the next generation of educators*, Washington, DC: Economic Policy Institute.

Kane, T.J., Rockoff, J.E. and Staiger, D.O. (2008) What does certification tell us about teacher effectiveness: evidence from New York City, *Economics of Education Review*, 27(6): 615–31.

Kangasniemi, S. (2008) Millä ammatilla pääsee naimisiin? (With which profession to get married?), *Helsingin Sanomat—Koulutusliite*, 27 February: 4–6.

Koretz, D. (2008) A measured approach: value-added measures are a promising improvement, but no one measure can evaluate teacher performance, *The American Educator*, Fall: 18–39.

Leana, C. (2011) The missing link in school reform, *Stanford Social Innovation Review*, 9: 34. Available at www.ssireview.org/articles/entry/the_missing_link_in_school_reform (accessed June 24, 2012).

Letwin, O. (2011) Public sector workers need "discipline and fear", says Oliver Letwin, quoted in *The Guardian*, July 30, 2011. Available at www.guardian.co.uk/politics/2011/jul/30/public-sector-jobs-oliver-letwin (accessed July 31, 2011).

Levin, B. and Naylor, N. (2007) Using resources effectively in education, in J. Burger, C.F. Webber, and P. Klinck (eds) *Intelligent Leadership: Constructs for thinking education leaders*, Dordrecht: Springer, pp. 143–58.

Lewin, K. (1946) Action research and minority problems, *Journal of Social Issues*, 2(4): 34–46.

Loury, G.C. (1977) A dynamic theory of racial income differences, in P.A. Wallace and A. LeMund (eds) *Women, Minorities, and Employment Discrimination*, Lexington, MA: Lexington Books, pp. 153–88.

Loury, G.C. (1987) Why should we care about group inequality? *Social Philosophy and Policy*, 5(1): 249–71.

McCaffrey, D.F., Sass, T.R., Lockwood, J.R. and Mhaly, K. (2009) *The Inter-temporal Variability of Teacher Effect Estimates*, Working Paper 2009-03, Nashville, TN: National Center on Performance Incentives. Available at www.performanceincentives.org/data/files/news/PapersNews/200903_McCaffrey_etAl_TeacherEffectEstimate1.pdf (accessed January 4, 2010).

MacDonald, E. and Shirley, D. (2009) *The Mindful Teacher*, New York: Teachers College Press.

Mandela, N. (1995) Speech by President Nelson Mandela at the launch of the Nelson Mandela Children's Fund, Mahlamba'ndlopfu, Pretoria, May 8.

Murnane, R.J. and Cohen, D.K. (1986) Merit pay and the evaluation problem: why most merit pay plans fail and a few survive, *Harvard Educational Review*, 56(1): 1–17.

Odden, A.R. (2011) *The Strategic Management of Human Capital in Education: Improving instructional practice and student learning in schools*, New York: Routledge.

Pickett, K. and Wilkinson, R. (2011) *The Spirit Level: Why greater equality makes societies stronger*, New York: Bloomsbury Press.

Pink, D.H. (2009) *Drive: The Surprising Truth about What Motivates Us*, New York: Riverhead Books.

Putnam, R.D. (2001) *Bowling Alone: The collapse and revival of American community*, New York: Simon & Schuster.

Reich, R.B. (2010) *Aftershock: The next economy and America's future*, New York: Alfred A. Knopf.

Rivkin, S.G., Hanushek, E.A. and Kain, J.F. (1998) *Teachers, Schools, and Academic Achievement*, Working Paper 6691, Cambridge, MA: National Bureau of Economic Research.

Rothstein, J. (2008) *Teacher Quality in Educational Production: Tracking, decay, and student achievement*, Cambridge, MA: Princeton University and NBER. Available at www.irs.princeton.edu/pubs/pdfs/25ers.pdf (accessed June 29, 2009).

Sahlberg, P. (2011) *Finnish Lessons: What can the world learn from educational change in Finland?*, New York: Teachers College Press.

Sanders, W.L. (1998) Value-added assessment, *The School Administrator*, 55(11): 24–32.

Sanders, W.L. and Rivers, J.C. (1996) *Cumulative and Residual Effects of Teachers on Future Student Academic Achievement*, Knoxville, TN: University of Tennessee Value-Added Research and Assessment Center.

Schön, D.A. (1983) *The Reflective Practitioner: How professionals think in action*, New York: Basic Books.

Schön, D.A. (1987) *Educating the Reflective Practitioner: Toward a new design for teaching and learning in the professions*, San Francisco, CA: Jossey-Bass.

Smith, A. (1776/2009) *The Wealth of Nations: Books I–III*, New York: Classic House Books.

Spengler, J.J. (1977) The invisible hand and other matters: Adam Smith on human capital, *The American Economic Review*, 67(1): 32–6.

Tucker, M.S. (2011) *Standing on the Shoulders of Giants: An American agenda for education reform*, National Center on Education and the Economy, May 24. Available at www.ncee.org/wp-content/uploads/2011/05/Standing-on-the-Shoulders-of-Giants-An-American-Agenda-for-Education-Reform.pdf (accessed August 12, 2012).

Viadero, V. (2009) Value-added gauge of teaching probed, *Education Week*, 28(36): 1–13.

Waller, W.W. (1932) *The Sociology of Teaching*, New York: John Wiley.

Walsh, K. (2007) *If Wishes Were Horses: The reality behind teacher quality findings*, Washington, DC: National Council for Teacher Quality.

Index

Kent, R. 154
Kenway, J. 239, 240
Kim, T. 241
Knorr Cetina, Karen 48, 49, 51
knowledge building 19, 29
knowledge economy: barriers 124; and
  citizenship 6; competitive 83, 92; global 238;
  LCE 174; and 'learning society' 5; South
  Africa 141; TALIS 100; and teachers 202
knowledge transfer 189
knowledge-based economy 78, 87, 98
knowledge-based regulation tools *see* KBRTs
Kucera, J. 268
Kyrgyzstan 263–6, 267

Lamont, M. 11
Lancastrianism 47
Landman, M. 89
Larson, M.S. 104
Lascoumes, P. 99
Latour, Bruno 47
Lawn, Martin 49, 98
LCE (learner-centred education) 172–81;
  and cultural appropriateness 177;
  implementation 176–7; inspection 175; as
  travelling policy 173–4
Le Galès, P. 99
League of Arab States 215
league tables 10
Leana, Carrie 291, 301
learner-centred education *see* LCE
'learnerships' 139
'learning environment' 10
Leung, C. 223
Levidow, Les 266
Levy, D. 120
Lewin, Kurt 304
lifelong learning 190
*Lifelong Learning for the Global Knowledge
  Economy (LLGKE)* (World Bank 2003) 87
Lindblad, S. 61
Lipman, Pauline 44
'liquid learning' 12
'liquid modernity' 5
Lisbon agenda 101, 184
literacy 81, 206
Los Angeles Times 295
Loury, Glenn 300
low-income countries 78

MacDonald, Liz 304
Maclure, William 45
Macrow, A.V. 205t
Maguire, M. 10
Magun, Artemy 260
Making Schools Work (Bruns et al) 88
Malawi 178
Malaysia 118t, 122, 126
managerialism 197
Mandela, Nelson 306
Marais, Hein 134

The Marketplace of Ideas (Menand) 277
Marx, Karl 5
'mass higher education' 276
massification 118–20
Matric 137
McGrath, Simon 134
McMurry, Charles 45
McMurry, Frank 45
MDGs (Millennium Development Goals) 59
Mecca 125
Meirieu, Philipe 189
Men and Their Work (Hughes) 11
MENA (Middle East and North Africa) 37, 126
Menand, Louis 277
methodologies 10–12
Mexico 153–69; academic achievement
  types 165; accountability 164; debt crisis
  257; decentralization 155; elitist nature
  of university 154; faculty salaries 159;
  goal of university 154; infrastructure
  160; institutional standards 161–3; low
  qualifications of faculty 155; methodology
  158–9; productivity 163–5; professional
  identity 160; programs for restructuring
  156–7; re-boundarying 154–7; regulation
  155; research facilities 160; types of higher
  education 158; unregulated expansion,
  universities 154, 155
Middle East and North Africa *see* MENA
Millennium Development Goals *see* MDGs
minority populations 12
MLA (Monitoring Learning Achievements) 204
Molnar, V. 11
Montessori, Maria 50
Moore Johnson, Susan 89
motivation, teacher 178
Mubarak, President 207
Mundy, K. 80

NAPTOSA (National Professional Teachers'
  Organization of South Africa 145
National Council for Science and Technology
  see CONACYT
National Qualifications Framework *see* NQF
National System of Researchers *see* SNI
National University, Mexico 154
National Vocational Qualifications *see* NVQs
nation-building project C20 5, 6, 13, 80, 128
neo-liberal reforms: and change 6, 7–8; demand
  for 59–62; effect of dominance on education
  16, 78, 133; and former communist states 55
networks 47–8
New York City 301
Niukko, S. 108
Nóvoa, A. 99
NQF (National Qualifications Framework) 135
NVQs (National Vocational Qualifications) 135

OBE (outcome-based education) 179, 180, 202,
  203
Ochs, K. 173